# The impact of high-stakes examinations on classroom teaching

*A case study using insights from testing and innovation theory*

G000065298

# The impact of high-stakes examinations on classroom teaching

## A case study using insights from testing and innovation theory

Dianne Wall

CAMBRIDGE
UNIVERSITY PRESS

CAMBRIDGE UNIVERSITY PRESS
Cambridge, New York, Melbourne, Madrid, Cape Town, Singapore, São Paulo, Delhi

Cambridge University Press
The Edinburgh Building, Cambridge CB2 8RU, UK

Published in the United States of America by Cambridge University Press, New York

www.cambridge.org
Information on this title: www.cambridge.org/9780521542494

© UCLES 2005

This publication is in copyright. Subject to statutory exception
and to the provisions of relevant collective licensing agreements,
no reproduction of any part may take place without the written
permission of Cambridge University Press.

First published 2005

A catalogue record for this publication is available from the British Library

ISBN 978-0-521-54249-4 paperback

Transferred to digital printing 2008

Cambridge University Press has no responsibility for the persistence or
accuracy of URLs for external or third-party Internet websites referred to in
this publication, and does not guarantee that any content on such websites is,
or will remain, accurate or appropriate.

The author is grateful to the copyright holders for permission to use the copyright
material reproduced in this publication. Every effort has been made to trace the copyright
holders. Cambridge University Press apologizes for any unintentional omissions
and would be pleased, in such cases, to add an acknowledgement in further
editions.

For Charles

# Contents

*Contents*

**Chapter 9**
Implementation factors: characteristics of the
  innovation: the new examination

**Chapter 10**
Implementation factors: characteristics of the
  user system

**Chapter 11**
Implementation factors: characteristics of the users

**Chapter 12**
Discussion and future directions

# List of figures

# List of tables

# Acknowledgements

I wish to express my gratitude to all of the following colleagues:

The Sri Lankan Impact Study Team – Charmaine Bandara, Nalinie de Silva, Sunil de Silva, M S Jowzakiyun, Prabha Karunaratna, Shirani Perera, Sumitra Panagoda, N G Thilakajeewa, Lakshmi Weerasekera and Kalyani Wijetunga – for their hard work and commitment throughout the O level Evaluation Project.

Ethel Nanayakkara, for sharing so many insights into the teaching and testing situation in Sri Lanka.

Ian Pearson, for the first invitation to Sri Lanka and all the discussions afterwards, both there and in St Petersburg.

Richard Webber, for making the Impact Study visits possible.

The Lancaster Language Testing Research Group, for valuable feedback and for being there every Tuesday.

Mick Short, for helping me to see what had to be done.

John McGovern, for teaching me about managing change.

Caroline Clapham, for understanding and promising me music when it was all over.

My PhD supervisor, Keith Johnson, for many useful suggestions and for his patience.

Cyril Weir and Mike Milanovic for editorial guidance, and Sally Downes and Lucy Bater for taking charge and being so positive during the shaping of this final version.

I consider myself fortunate to have some very good friends, and I thank them with all my heart for being there when I needed them.

Lastly, I thank Charles Alderson, for inspiring me always and for years of encouragement, collaboration and support.

The author and publishers are grateful to the copyright holders for permission to use the copyright materials identified in the text. Every effort has been made to trace copyright owners of all the materials used. In the case of unintentional omissions, the publishers would welcome information from copyright owners.

*Examinations: Comparative and International Studies* by M A Eckstein and H J Noah (eds). Stephen P Heyneman and Angela W Ransom, Using Examinations and Testing to Improve Educational Quality, pages 105 & 108, Copyright © 1992, with permission from Elsevier.

Paul Woods, Pulling out of a project: twelve tips for project planners, *ELT Journal* 1998, 42 (3) page 200, by permission of Oxford University Press.

J Charles Alderson & Dianne Wall, Does Washback Exist? *Applied Linguistics* 1993, 14 (2) pages 120–121 &127, by permission of Oxford University Press.

Edmond Holmes (1911) *What is and What Might Be*, pages 107–108. Reproduced with permission of the publisher, Constable & Robinson Ltd.

*International Journal of Educational Development*, volume 10 (1), Thomas Owen Eisemon, Examination Policies to Strengthen Primary Schooling in African Countries, page 78, Copyright © 1990, with permission from Elsevier.

*Examinations: Comparative and International Studies* by M A Eckstein and H J Noah (eds). Angela Little, Decontextualizing Assessment Policy: Does It Make Economic Sense? pages 130 & 131, Copyright © 1992, with permission from Elsevier.

Chris Kennedy, Evaluation of the Management of Change in ELT Projects, *Applied Linguistics* 1988, 9 (4) pages 332 & 336, by permission of Oxford University Press.

Alan Beretta, Implementation of the Bangalore Project, *Applied Linguistics* 1990, 11 (4) page 324, by permission of Oxford University Press.

DIFFUSION OF INNOVATIONS, 4th Edition by Everett M. Rogers. Copyright © 1995 by Everett M. Rogers. Reprinted with the permission of The Free Press, a Division of Simon & Schuster Adult Publishing Group, Copyright © 1962, 1971, 1983 by The Free Press. All rights reserved.

*Diffusion of Innovations in English Language Teaching: The ELEC Effort in Japan, 1956–1968* by L E Henrichsen. Copyright © 1989 by L E Henrichsen. Reproduced with permission of Greenwood Publishing Group, Inc., Westport, CT.

Richard E Snow, Theory Construction for Research on Teaching, in *Second Handbook of Research on Teaching: A Project of the American Educational Reseach Association, 78*. Copyright © 1973 by the American Educational Research Association. Reproduced with permission of the publisher.

Udo Keller (ed.) *Computer-aided Qualitative Data Analysis: Theory, Methods and Practice*, Copyright © Udo Keller 1995. John Siedel and Udo Kelle, Different functions of coding in the analysis of textual data, page 52. Reprinted by permission of Sage Publications Ltd.

# Series Editors' note

There is a growing consensus that validity is a unified concept with theory-based, content- and criterion-related validation processes all having a part to play in contributing evidence in respect of the interpretation of test scores. High-stakes test providers such as Cambridge ESOL are also concerned with consequential validity (i.e. the impact of a test on individuals and society) and place equal emphasis on social values and social consequences in any consideration of the validity of test scores.

This volume, together with those of companion volumes in the SILT series by Liying Cheng and Tony Green, is concerned with the influence of tests on general educational processes and on the individuals who are affected by the test results. The concern is whether examination boards have a major impact on educational processes and on society in general. Wall is concerned with washback as an important element of test impact in language education. While impact may occur at a 'macro' or social and institutional level, washback is more a phenomenon at the 'micro' level of the individual participant (primarily teachers and students).

Given that language teachers have to equip students with the skills that tests are intended to provide information about, it would seem likely the closer the relationship between the test and the teaching that precedes it, the more the test is likely to have washback on both staff and students. Wall was concerned with the extent to which exams can promote such change. She takes as a case study the Sri Lankan O level Evaluation Project where the purpose was to evaluate whether a new national examination in English had created positive impact in the classroom. The project was based on extensive observational data and distinguished between impact on content in teaching for the new examination and impact on methodology. It also investigated the effect of the examination on teacher-designed assessments and on teachers' attitudes.

Wall's study is an extension of the original project employing data collected in the final stages and re-analysing it using a framework based not only on the literature in language testing and language education but also the field of educational innovation. She aims to shed light on how examinations have the impact they do by drawing on theories of innovation and change in educational settings. A survey of key ideas in educational innovation is provided and due importance is given to the social context in which change is taking place. The importance of antecedent conditions and implementation factors operating in the context of the innovation is investigated. A unique feature of this study is that it attempts to explicate the causes that lead to both intended and negative or unintended consequences and offers advice on how the latter can be avoided, ameliorated or monitored.

Wall points out the importance of carrying out detailed a priori studies in advance of any major examination reform programme to establish how much change the institutions and individuals will tolerate. Such studies need to be iterative during the first years of implementation, to establish whether the examination is having the intended impact or whether adjustments are necessary.

The study provides useful guidelines to assist educators in other settings in determining whether innovation through test reform is realistic i.e. whether compatibility exists with the users, and additionally between the resource system and the user system.

Wall's study demonstrates that, as a result of the interactions among these environmental considerations, impact is a complex phenomenon, and intended positive impact is by no means a natural or inevitable consequence of introducing a new well designed examination into an educational setting. Good examinations are not guaranteed to produce positive results and bad examinations do not necessarily produce bad ones.

In the wider context of washback studies Wall concludes that change in examinations might be a necessary condition for change in the curriculum, but argues that her study shows that in itself it is not a sufficient one.

Despite widespread lip service to the notion of 'washback' in the international testing community, until recently only a limited number of research studies have been undertaken to study the effects of high stakes language tests on teaching and learning. This volume, together with the two other volumes to date in this series on washback by Liying Cheng on the HKEA English examination and Tony Green on IELTS, serves to enrich our understanding of this under-researched but critical aspect of validity and further grounds the methodology for investigating it. A further volume reviewing the work of Cambridge ESOL on the study of test impact is being compiled by Roger Hawkey.

Michael Milanovic<br>
Cyril Weir<br>
Cambridge<br>
September 2004

# 1 Introduction

It is widely held that examinations, particularly public examinations used for selection and accreditation purposes, have a powerful effect on what happens in education.

Some educators emphasize the positive effects, both on practice and policy:

> A well-designed examination system can monitor and measure achievement and occasionally aptitude, provide performance feedback to individual districts, schools and students, inform education officials about the overall strengths and weaknesses of their education systems, and suggest directions for change and improvement. (Heyneman and Ransom 1990:180)

Indeed, examinations are often used as a key component in plans to introduce educational change, both in countries with well-resourced education systems (see Lam 1993 and Cheng 1997 on Hong Kong; and Shohamy, Donitsa-Schmidt and Ferman 1996 on Israel) and others whose systems are less well-funded (see Kellaghan and Greaney 1992 on the impact of examinations in developing countries). It is argued that using examinations to promote change is particularly effective in countries where there is 'less money to invest in items that boost learning such as textbooks, instructional materials, good teachers and teacher training' (Heyneman and Ransom 1990: 177). In these situations examinations '... can be a powerful, low cost means of influencing the quality of what teachers teach and what students learn in school' (Heyneman and Ransom 1990:178).

Many educators believe that it is futile to attempt to change the curriculum without making changes in the way it is assessed:

> The most innovative and up-to-date curriculum packages will not succeed unless assessment and examination procedures and formats are correspondingly revised. (Woods 1988:200)

Others, however, take a more cynical view. Madaus, for example, predicts only negative consequences if examinations are used as the 'primary motivating power of the educational process'.

> Measurement-driven instruction invariably leads to cramming; narrows the curriculum; concentrates attention on those skills most amenable to testing ...'; constrains the creativity and spontaneity of teachers and students; and finally demeans the professional judgment of teachers. (1988:85)

Little attention was given to examination impact in language education until the early 1990s. Before then there were only a few references to the power of tests in different educational settings (e.g. Malaysia (Davies 1985), Turkey (Hughes 1988a), and China (Li 1990)), with little empirical study. Several test-development projects had been set up with the intention of creating positive impact on some aspects of teaching and learning (e.g. Swain 1985 and Pearson 1988), yet there was little analysis of the results of such endeavours, and would-be innovators had little evidence to refer to when making decisions about the role of examinations in their own reform programmes.

An exception to this general pattern was the Sri Lankan O level Evaluation Project. The purpose of this project was to evaluate whether a new national examination in English had created positive impact in the classroom. When the project began it was difficult to find accounts of research into impact in either ELT or education more generally. Most of the work that had been carried out was based on questionnaires or interviews, or on analyses of test results, rather than on analyses of what happened in the classroom. The Sri Lankan Project was novel in that it included a large-scale and fairly long-term observation programme. It distinguished between impact on content and impact on methodology, and investigated the effect of the examination on teacher-designed assessments. It also questioned how examinations fit in with other components of the educational system, and signalled the need for better coordination and communication between the various bodies responsible for improving the curriculum. All of this was documented in a series of reports for the Overseas Development Administration, who funded the project (Alderson and Wall 1989, 1990, 1991, 1992), and in several articles published soon after (Alderson and Wall 1993, Wall and Alderson 1993, and Wall 1994).

This book reports on an extension of the original Evaluation Project. It is based on data collected in the final stages and re-analysed using a framework incorporating ideas not only from language testing and language education, but from the field of educational innovation as well. It thus represents an attempt to understand *how* examinations have the impact they do by drawing on theories of innovation, as called for in Alderson and Wall (1993):

> it will be important to take account of findings in the research literature in at least two areas: that of motivation and performance, and that of innovation and change in educational settings. (1993:127)

As we will see in Chapter 3, early studies of examination impact concentrated on describing the effects of exams. However, attention in language education has now shifted towards not only documenting the effects but seeking to understand them and trying to unravel the causes that lead to examinations having both intended and unintended consequences. It is this exploration of causes, the attempt to understand the myriad factors underlying the complexity of innovation and resistance to innovation that is, I believe, the contribution of this book to theories of examination impact and '*washback*'.

## How this book is organized

In Chapter 2, I present an overview of the work that I was involved in in Sri Lanka. This includes a description of the educational setting, a description of the new examination, and a description of the evaluation project which investigated whether the examination was having the effects that were intended. I describe the methods that were used to determine whether the examination was producing the desired impact, and I summarize the findings as of 1992, the official end of the project. The chapter concludes with questions that were still unanswered at that time, and an explanation of why I decided to continue the investigation using concepts from general education and educational innovation.

In Chapters 3 and 4, I present a review of the literature on examination impact and a summary of relevant ideas from the field of educational innovation. I distinguish between what is generally believed about the influence of examinations on teaching, and what has been shown to be true in empirical studies. Much of this work focuses on the qualities of the examination itself. The work in Sri Lanka suggested that there were factors beyond the examination which determined whether the innovation would not only 'take' but whether it would also prove stable and sustainable. I explore these other factors, and explain how unlikely it is that innovations will survive if there has not been a careful analysis of the environment into which they are being introduced and a careful monitoring as time goes by.

In Chapter 5, I describe the approach I followed when planning the original data collection and the decisions that I took at each stage in the process of analysis and interpretation. I present the findings in Chapters 6–11.

In Chapter 6, I discuss whether the new examination affected the process of teaching in the ways that it was originally meant to do. I first present an analysis of the goals of the curriculum and predictions about the type of impact that was most likely to occur, given the format of the examination when it was first administered in early 1989. I then review the findings of a baseline study carried out in 1988 and an observation programme carried out in 1990–91, and use these as points of comparison for the findings from group interviews with teachers. This analysis indicates that there was a strong impact on the content of teaching and on the way teachers carried out their classroom assessment, but little to no impact on their methodology.

In Chapters 7–11, I apply a framework derived from Henrichsen (1989) to investigate why the impact on content and assessment took the form it did and why there was so little impact on methodology. In Chapter 7, I discuss the 'antecedent situation' in Sri Lankan classrooms (what teaching practices looked like before there was any change in textbooks or examinations). In Chapters 8–11, I discuss the characteristics of the innovation (the textbooks and the examination), the user system (classrooms, schools, the educational administration, and the broader political and economic situation); and the users (the teachers and students). I then explain how these characteristics either facilitated or worked against the intentions of the educational policy-makers.

In Chapter 12, I review these findings and draw conclusions about examination impact in this particular context, and the implications of this study for other educational settings. What becomes clear throughout the analysis is the importance of carrying out detailed investigations before initiating any major examination reform programme, in order to determine how much change the educational setting will welcome or support. It is important to continue these investigations during at least the first few years of implementation, in order to discover whether the examination is having the impact that it is supposed to have, or whether there is a need for adjustments, either in the examination or in the setting itself. I conclude with a discussion of the implications of this investigation for future research into examination impact, and I make a series of recommendations that will hopefully lead to an enhanced understanding of why examinations have the impact they do and of how negative or unintended consequences can be avoided, ameliorated or monitored.

1 June 2003

# 2 The origins of the present investigation: the Sri Lankan O level Examination Project

## Background

The analysis which forms the focus of this study was carried out on data collected in 1991, during the final phase of the Sri Lankan O level Evaluation Project. This was a four-year project which set out to evaluate a new national examination of English and to determine whether it was having the effect on classroom teaching that its designers intended.

The present investigation is an extension of the original evaluation project: a re-analysis of data using a conceptual framework and analytical tools that were not available at the time the data was collected. This investigation was motivated by questions emerging from the original project, and it requires knowledge not only of the findings of the project but also of the context in which it took place. This chapter provides an overview of the original project and its findings. The aims are presented, together with the stages which were most relevant to this investigation: identifying the main features of the materials on which the new examination was based, identifying the type of impact the new examination was meant to have, and carrying out a baseline study and a two-year observation programme. The results of the observation programme are presented in some detail, in order to give a clear picture of the type of English teaching that was most prevalent at the time and a wider understanding of the kinds of questions that remained outstanding. The chapter concludes with an explanation of my decision to exploit the data further, utilizing a framework for analysis derived from language testing, assessment in general education, and educational innovation. The theoretical background to this framework is presented in Chapters 3 and 4, my methodology is described in Chapter 5, and the findings of the analysis are presented in Chapters 6–11.

## Political and educational setting

Sri Lanka gained its independence in 1948, after 150 years of British rule. English had played an important role during the colonial period, in both the administrative and social structure of the country and its educational system. It was the medium of instruction for the privileged classes from the mid-19th century onwards, and it retained this status even after independence in private denominational schools and in government-run 'central schools' set up for scholarship students from rural areas (Punchihetti 1994:21). However, political changes in 1956 led to a new language policy and by the end of the decade almost all schools in the country had adopted either Sinhala or Tamil, the two indigenous languages, as their medium of education. English was an ordinary subject on the timetable for the next 20 years, no more important than any other. The teaching was similar to that in many other countries in the 1960s and 70s, with a great deal of emphasis on language form, some attention to reading comprehension, and a neglect of listening, speaking and writing. The Ministry of Education introduced new textbooks in the mid-1970s which reinforced this approach. Every unit followed the same pattern: the presentation of a new language structure through model sentences, two reading passages followed by comprehension questions, and further language practice 'exercises' which were in fact tests of vocabulary and grammar.

There were further political changes in the late 1970s, which led to the opening up of the country to foreign investment and trade (Mosback 1990:53). Tourism became an important industry at home, and at the same time more Sri Lankans were able to travel and work abroad. There were clear incentives for those who were able to communicate in English. The language was also important academically: it had served as the medium of instruction for many university courses (Wijemanne and de Silva 1994:32), but it would now be useful for those who wished to study in other countries. There was a growing need for English to serve as a 'link language' between the majority Sinhala-speaking population and the Tamil-speaking minority.

Policy-makers realized that the country was not equipped to cope with the new demands for the language, and that action was needed to prepare future generations for these opportunities. The Ministry of Education embarked on a large-scale English language teaching reform programme in the early 1980s. The reform was to create change in three areas: materials, teacher training, and testing.

On the materials front, work began on two new textbook series: the *English for Me* series for primary schools (developed from 1980–1985, by a Sri Lankan team with Norwegian financial assistance), and the *English Every Day* series for secondary schools (developed from 1981–1989, by a Sri Lankan team working with British consultants, with financial assistance from the then Overseas Development Administration, now known as the Department for International Development – DFID). Both series stressed the need to communicate in English rather than to just master the grammar. The emphasis was on practical language and there were exercises to develop listening and speaking, two of the skills which had been neglected in the past.

There were attempts to develop both pre-service and in-service training (see Woolger 1994 for details). Much of the in-service work was carried out by members of the textbook design team, with the aim of showing teacher advisers and teachers how to use the new teaching materials (Mosback 1994:55).

The keystone of the reform was to be a new examination. It was recognized from quite early on that it would be difficult to persuade teachers and students to use the new materials and methods if there was not also a change in assessment.

## The O level English examination

Students who stayed in school until the end of Year 11 took a series of examinations called 'the O level'. O level results determined whether they would be allowed to continue on to the 'collegiate' level of schooling (the equivalent of the 'Sixth Form' and 'A level' in England and Wales), or whether they had to leave school and find employment. Competition was intense for the few places available at the collegiate level and for the limited number of good jobs that school-leavers could aspire to. Students' O level grades, including English, were amongst the most important in their academic career.

The 'Old Syllabus' English examination, like the teaching materials, focused on language structure and reading comprehension, and it followed the same pattern year after year. Of the 105 'objective' questions, 90 tested some aspect of language form: spelling, vocabulary, prepositions, word order, verb forms, pronouns, etc. There were two reading passages with a total of 15 comprehension questions, many of which tested reading at sentence level only. Candidates could choose to respond to one out of four writing tasks, but it was well known that they could gain good marks without attempting to write at all. Listening and speaking were not tested. (See Appendix 1 for a copy of the 'Old Syllabus' examination, 1987.)

Very few students managed to pass this examination: the pass mark of 35% was usually met by only 20% of the population. There were claims that the examination had 'doubtful validity' (Wijemanne and de Silva 1994:33), but an inspection of both the examination and the textbooks suggests that face and content validity were quite high (see Alderson, Clapham and Wall 1995 for a definition of these terms). However, it was now considered important to produce an examination which matched the new teaching materials. Furthermore, it was argued by several policy-makers, including the Secretary of State for Education, that:

> reformed examinations should and could be used to encourage and engender changes in the attitudes and practices of students and teachers in the English classroom ... a new examination should be developed and used 'as a lever for change', to encourage teachers and students to make a serious and committed response to the evolutionary (and sometimes revolutionary) changes that were already under way through teacher, curriculum, and course development. (Pearson 1994:85)

Development work on the 'New Syllabus' examination began in early 1986, with the first drafting of test specifications (Pearson 1994:91). The examination was meant to test all four skills, and it would build upon work that had been carried out earlier to find practical ways of testing speaking and listening. (Pearson 1994, and Alderson, Wall and Clapham 1987.) It was necessary to change plans within a year though, following a Ministry announcement that the O level examinations for all subjects should contain an element of continuous (i.e. classroom-based) assessment. The English O level would now consist of two parts: a centrally designed and marked examination paper testing reading and writing, and a series of teacher-designed and assessed classroom activities which would focus on listening and speaking.

Everything about the continuous assessment idea was alien to the Sri Lankan context – from the notion that teachers' judgements about their own pupils could be relied upon (the country had a long tradition of external examining), to the mechanics of conducting in-class assessment and recording the results for the examination authorities. The examination design team now had to devote time to preparing teacher support material for continuous assessment – on top of their work to produce a valid and reliable written paper. Ironically, the continuous assessment programme was withdrawn just after the first administration of the new examination, and none of the marks that teachers had collected were calculated into students' final O level grades. No official reason was given for this decision, but many believed that it had been introduced too hastily, had been too unwieldy, and was too sensitive an issue at a time when there was a great deal of political turmoil in the country. (Some opponents of the government felt that this form of assessment favoured pupils from urban areas and privileged families, who had more exposure to English and more resources and support than pupils from rural areas.) With the withdrawal of continuous assessment the written paper became the sole means of assessing students' English.

The new examination would now only focus on reading and writing. There would be several low-level tasks which any Year 11 student might be expected to complete, several intermediate-level tasks, and several difficult ones. Different text types and tasks would be included each year, and over a number of years the whole syllabus would be covered. This would oblige teachers to cover the whole textbook series rather than focus on content they predicted would appear on the examination. (See Appendix 2 for a copy of the new examination, 1988.)

Teachers received an official orientation to the examination in May 1988, approximately six months before it was due to be administered for the first time. The orientation booklet included the types of texts that students would be expected to cope with, the reading skills they were expected to master, and the types of writing they would be expected to produce. One copy of the booklet was sent to each school, to be shared amongst the members of the teaching staff. Further publications were distributed to schools and to students in 1989 and 1990.

# The O level Evaluation Project

## Aims of the project

An important feature of the new examination effort was that evaluation was built into the plans from the beginning. The organization which funded much of the development work – the British Overseas Development Administration – also commissioned an evaluation of the examination and its impact on teaching. The project documentation stated that there was a need:

> to establish not only the validity, reliability and practicality of the new examination and associated procedures, but also to assess the extent to which these innovations help to bring about changes in the day-to-day teaching of English, and consequent pupil attainment and ability. (Institute for English Language Education 1988:1)

The project had three aims:

1. to assess the reliability and feasibility of the new O level examination in English, including the arrangements for its administration, the training and monitoring of examiners and the validity of the results,
2. to evaluate and advise on the monitoring, moderation and implementation of continuous assessment in English, and
3. to evaluate the effect on the classroom teaching of English of innovations at O level. (op. cit:2)

The evaluation project was to run from mid-1988 to the end of 1991.

There were two teams involved in the evaluation: a team from Lancaster University, which consisted of a Project Director (Charles Alderson) and a Research Associate (Dianne Wall), and a Sri Lankan team, which consisted of the O level designers, a group of secondary school teachers who would carry out classroom observations, and the British Council Consultant for Testing and Evaluation.

The project was a collaborative effort from the start. The Lancaster team was to design and co-ordinate the evaluation in consultation with the Sri Lankan team, and major decisions were to be taken jointly. A Lancaster team member would visit Sri Lanka twice a year, to investigate the feasibility of various proposals, consult with stakeholders, carry out data collection, and give advice on technical matters. The Sri Lankan team would share their insights into the desirability and practicality of proposed plans, collect data and react to suggestions made after the analysis and interpretation of data. The project had a summative function – to evaluate whether the examination influenced teaching over a given period of time – but it was also meant to provide formative feedback. Findings and recommendations were to be sent to Sri Lanka regularly so that colleagues could make changes in their programme if they agreed that these were necessary.

In the first year the project focused on the first aim – evaluating the examination and associated procedures. I observed the administration of the examination and the training and monitoring of examiners, and carried out a detailed analysis of test results and examiner reliability (see Alderson and Wall 1989 for details). The examination reflected the nature and the spirit of the textbook quite well (content validity) and proved a fairly reliable means of assessing what students were supposed to have learned during their years of English study. There were a number of 'teething troubles', but the design team was able to address problems in content and procedures before the second administration. The team took over some of the evaluation work during the second year and by the third year had sole responsibility for carrying out observations of administration and marking, conducting qualitative and statistical analyses of results, and making recommendations for further improvements of the examination.

The second aim of the project – examining continuous assessment – was dropped when the continuous assessment programme itself was abandoned.

The third aim – measuring the influence of the examination on teaching – was to have become the project's focus during its second year. The design team had carried out a set of observations in mid-1988, before most teachers knew what the new examination would look like or could be affected by its characteristics. Further observations were to be carried out in 1989, to see whether there had been any changes in the way teachers conducted their classes and if this could be traced in any way to the influence of the exam. Unfortunately serious political conflicts forced schools to close for much of that year. It was not until early 1990, when teaching was back to normal and it was safe to travel in most areas of the country, that further observations could be undertaken. This marked the beginning of the 'Impact Study', the two-year observation programme which formed the core of the evaluation project.

Although there was a delay in starting the observation, it had been necessary to begin thinking about how the examination might influence teaching from the earliest days of the project. This meant analysing all of the official statements about the goals of the examination and, because the exam was meant to reinforce the new textbook series, of the textbook as well. These goals are discussed in detail in Chapter 8: Characteristics of the Textbook Series. Only a brief description of the textbook series will be provided at this point to give an idea of what the Impact Study was meant to ascertain.

## *English Every Day*

*English Every Day* (*EED*) was a five-book series designed by a team of Sri Lankan teachers working with two British Council consultants. The series introduced a number of new ideas into Sri Lankan ELT, both in terms of content and methodology. It presented texts and topics that were meant to be relevant to Sri Lankan students, tasks that resembled the types of activities they might have to carry out in their second-language environment, and exercises which attempted to develop language skills rather than just grammar. The texts ranged from short messages to informative academic texts in the case of reading, and application forms to quite lengthy reports in the case of writing. The reading skills included skimming and scanning, deducing the meaning of unknown words, picking out the main idea from supporting detail, understanding the communicative function or value of sentences, etc. The writing skills included planning and organizing information, giving information explicitly, transferring information from pictures to reports, and so on. Grammar was also taught but it was meant to play a supporting role rather than lead the students' learning: its importance was acknowledged but it was not presented in a regular or systematic way.

Finally, there were many exercises to develop listening and speaking: role plays, dialogues, picture descriptions, and discussion tasks. It was this attention to oral skills that most distinguished *English Every Day* from earlier materials.

The textbook writers also hoped to encourage innovation in methodology. One of their aims was to persuade teachers to take a less dominant role in the classroom. Another was to give the students opportunities to practise the language in pairs or groups:

> As a general rule, the course writer would make sure that wherever possible, a teaching point would be presented and practised in a pupil-centred communicative activity. (Mosback 1994:57)

The Teacher's Guide which accompanied the first textbook (Year 7) set out the essentials of the new approach and gave suggestions about how to handle the new material. It was hoped that these suggestions, along with the in-service training that was carried out before and at the time the series reached the schools, would change traditional classrooms into a more active places for learning.

As stated earlier, the examination was meant to reinforce the textbooks, both in terms of content and methodology. The evaluation project was to investigate whether this was really happening. Were teachers teaching the way the textbook and examination teams wanted them to? If so, was the examination exerting any influence on their teaching? If not, could the exam be held responsible?

## Defining *washback*

The phenomenon which the evaluation project was meant to study was known as *washback*. At the time the project began, very little had been written about washback in the field of language education. Several testing handbooks offered definitions of washback, but these were very general. A few articles claimed that washback had occurred or would occur, but there was little evidence to support these claims. There was some discussion of the phenomenon in the general education literature, but this literature was not well known to language educators. There is now a greater awareness of the work that has been carried out in other fields and a number of studies have been carried out in language education, but very little of this work was available at the end of the 1980s. (See Chapter 3 for a review of the literature on examination impact.)

The view that I started out with, which was a common view in language education at that time, was that washback was inevitable. It was the 'effect' in a simple cause-and-effect relationship, where an important ('high-stakes') examination was the 'cause'. Washback could either be positive or negative. It was more likely to be positive if the aims and content of the examination matched those of the syllabus (or of the textbook if no syllabus existed). The assumption here was that the syllabus/textbook was always 'good'.

If the washback were positive teachers would be guided by both the textbook and the examination. The following outcomes could be expected:

**Table 2.1 Forms that positive washback might take**

| Type of washback | What would this look like in the classroom? |
| --- | --- |
| Content of teaching | Teachers would pay attention to all parts of the textbook, because they would realize that any of the text types or tasks appearing in the textbook might appear on the examination as well. |
| | They would not give more emphasis to any one skill than the textbook gave, because the weighting in the examination would reflect the weighting in the textbook. |
| Method of teaching | Teachers would use the general approach and the methods suggested by the Teacher's Guides, as they would recognize these to be effective means of developing the skills that would be assessed on the exam. |
| Assessing students | Teachers would write tests that would mirror the content of the textbook, because this would also be the content that would appear on the exam. |
| | They would mark their students' work using the criteria laid down in the textbook guidelines, which would also be the criteria used by examiners when marking the examination. |

Washback could also be negative. If the examination and the textbook had different aims or content they might pull in different directions. Teachers would be driven by the examination rather than by the textbook. The outcomes would then be as follows:

**Table 2.2. Forms that negative washback might take**

| Type of washback | What would this look like in the classroom? |
|---|---|
| Content of teaching | Teachers would not pay attention to all parts of the textbook because they would realise that some skills were not assessed and that it was more useful to concentrate on the ones that were. |
| | Even when teaching these skills teachers might neglect some text types or activities, feeling that these never appeared on the examination and were not worth spending time on. |
| | Teachers might stop working from the textbook, and begin to use materials which were more related to the examination. These might include teacher-designed materials, past examination papers, or publications designed to help students to prepare for the examination. |
| Method of teaching | Teachers would use whatever methodology they felt was most expedient to help them to prepare their students for the exam. Some methods might be sacrificed if the teachers felt that they did not achieve results efficiently. |
| Assessing students | Teachers would write tests which would mirror the content of past examination papers rather than the content of the textbook. They would adapt questions, or would simply 'lift' them, either from past papers or from publications designed to prepare students for the exam. |
| | Teachers would adopt the marking criteria used by the exam and would ignore advice in the textbook which went against this way of marking. |

It was difficult to predict what the outcomes would be in the case of the new O level examination. The reading and writing tasks resembled the tasks in *English Every Day*, but the lack of oral skills might lead to negative consequences.

The evaluation project used several methods to investigate whether the exam was having the effect that was intended, but the method that distinguished it from the few empirical studies available was classroom observation. Observation took place at two different stages in the project: during the 'Baseline Study', to investigate what teaching looked like before the introduction of the examination, and during the 'Impact Study', to see whether the examination was having any influence on teaching during the first two years of its existence.

## The Baseline Study

In order to determine whether the new O level examination was having any impact on teaching, it was first necessary to describe teaching before the examination was introduced. This meant carrying out a *baseline study* – an investigation which looks at certain conditions before the implementation of an education innovation, to 'help us to monitor any effects that occur during or after "treatment" ' (Weir and Roberts 1994:46). The examination design team managed to visit a number of schools just before the official orientation booklet was distributed. Their intention was to see how teachers were coping with the new textbook and to inform their own process of examination development, but the data they collected also provided a good picture of the type of teaching being carried out before the teachers heard about the new examination. This could serve as a point of comparison for data-gathering exercises in the future.

The design team interviewed teachers at 18 schools and observed classes at 14. This was only a small sample of the schools on the island, but the team was satisfied that it was a representative one. The investigation provided valuable information about how teachers viewed their own teaching and the influences on it. The most important finding was that there was a difference between the claims teachers made about their teaching and the way that they handled their classrooms. They claimed that they had changed their way of teaching once they began using the new textbooks, and that they were now using a 'communicative approach', but their classrooms were very formal and students spent much of their time listening to the teacher or practising language form rather than developing the skills that the textbook promoted. The team felt that many of the teachers had not understood what they were supposed to be teaching, and that more than half had not achieved the objectives of the material they were working with. The teachers' methods were not noticeably different from the teacher-centred methods which the textbook designers had originally tried to discourage.

In addition to investigating what typical lessons looked like, the team tried to find out how much teachers knew about the examination. Half the teachers felt that the official circulars from the Ministry were confusing. A quarter of them had just received the official introduction to the examination but they did not have a clear idea of what the new exam would look like. Only one teacher out of 18 understood correctly what would be tested and how, but she knew this because she had previously worked with the design team. About three quarters of the teachers expected to receive more guidance in future, and half expected to receive 'model papers' that would give them a clear idea of the text types and item types that would be tested. (This finding was significant because the design team had already decided that they would not provide a 'model paper', since this might give teachers the idea that specific text types and item types would appear on the examination and might itself create exam-oriented teaching.)

The observations showed that teachers had begun to teach the content of the new textbooks but that the new ideas about methodology had not yet taken hold. The teachers knew almost nothing about the new examination, which would be given for the first time in six months' time. The observations provided a reasonable baseline from which to measure whether the textbook or, more importantly for the evaluation project, the examination, would have any influence on teaching in the years to come. (Details of this study can be found in Alderson and Wall 1989.)

# The Impact Study: 1990–1991

The aim of the Impact Study was to find out whether the examination was having any impact on teaching during the first two years of its existence.

At the core of this study were seven Sri Lankan teachers who had agreed to be part of the research team. Six of them had attended a training course in Lancaster, where they had learned about classroom observation, and several had contributed to the design of the observation/interview schedule which would be used in the early part of the study. The seventh member of the team was a field supervisor for a teacher training college who was familiar with both the new teaching materials and the examination. The teachers were based in five different parts of the country: Colombo and the surrounding area, Wennapuwa, Ratnapura, Tangalle and Bandarawela. I visited each of them in their home areas in early 1990, to discuss their role in the Impact Study and to explain the importance of their participation to the principals of the schools they taught in. Getting the principals' support was an important step because the teachers would need to leave their own classes in order to visit other, sometimes quite distant, schools. They would need to be absent from their own classes for up to 25 days a year.

Each of the observers agreed to monitor seven schools. This gave a total of 49 schools across the country. The observers were in charge of selecting their own sample, but it was understood that this had to be representative of the schools in their area. Each sample was to include urban and rural schools, Sinhala- and Tamil-medium, and schools with different levels of achievement. The observers were to observe each school six times, once every term for two academic years. They were to observe one Year 11 class (the final year before the O level exam) during every visit, and were to continue to observe the same teacher, if possible, throughout the length of the study.

The observers were to interview the target teachers before they taught their lessons, in order to establish what materials they were intending to use and how they intended to use them. They would then observe the lessons and record what they saw and their impressions of whether the teaching was influenced by the new materials or by the examination. They would interview the teachers again after the lessons, to ask for their impressions of the lessons and to find out why they had decided to teach in the way they had. They would also ask teachers for their opinions of the textbook and the examination, and try to find out whether they felt that the exam was influencing particular aspects of their teaching: the way they chose the content of their lessons, the methodology they adopted, the way they designed classroom tests and the way they marked their students.

Note: Throughout this study the term *content* will refer to the type of knowledge that teachers were trying to transmit to their students (e.g. the form of a specific grammar structure, or facts relating to a particular topic), or to the general skill they were focusing on (e.g. reading, listening). *Methodology* will refer to either the general approach the teachers adopted (e.g. grammar-translation or 'communicative') or the specific techniques they used. Did they, for example, ask students to translate reading passages from English into their mother tongue? Did they ask them to read them aloud? Or did they encourage them to look for certain types of information in certain places, to cut down the time they needed to read a text for a particular purpose?

The observers would record all of this information on an observation/interview schedule which had been specially designed for the study. They would send their completed schedules to Lancaster, where I would analyse their responses and attempt to draw conclusions about the relationship between the teaching that was taking place and the examination. I would record my impressions of the data-gathering process and send my reactions back to Sri Lanka, along with instructions for the next round of observations.

The first round of observations took place in May/June 1990. This was practically equivalent to another baseline measure since very little normal teaching had taken place since the first administration of the exam 14 months before. The comments made by the observers and teachers gave useful insights into the kinds of teaching and learning that were taking place and into the teachers' views of materials and the exam. They also provided a clear idea of the conditions that many teachers were working in which might prevent washback from occurring in the near future. Amongst these conditions were the shortage of Teacher's Guides for the new textbook series, inadequate understanding of what the series was trying to achieve, a lack of familiarity with the examination due to problems in the distribution of exam support materials, crowded teaching halls often shared by as many as seven or eight different classes, and lack of teaching resources such as books, duplicating facilities etc.

Feedback from the observers led to several modifications in the observation/interview schedule: more questions were added about the school, teaching conditions, and the impact of the textbook, and more attention was given to the teacher's point of view rather than to just the observer's. A revised version of the schedule was used in Rounds 2 and 3 (July and November 1990). In December my UK colleague and I visited all the observers, to ask for their impressions of the revised schedule and their opinions of how to improve the data-gathering process for the remainder of the study. The product of these consultations was a third version of the schedule, which asked for the same sorts of data but made the collection procedure more systematic and the analysis more straightforward than in earlier rounds. The major changes were a reduction in the number of open-ended questions and the addition of checklists which listed the kinds of text types and activities that would appear in the classroom if the examination were having an effect on the teaching. (A copy of the revised observation/interview schedule can be found in Appendix 3.)

Rounds 4, 5 and 6 took place in 1991, the first 'normal' academic year that much of Sri Lanka had experienced since before the introduction of the exam. (The school closures in 1988 and 1989 had had a 'knock-on' effect into 1990, but many areas of the country were able to enjoy a full three terms of teaching in 1991.) The size of the observation sample fluctuated during this year, due to the resignation of one of the original observation team members, the arrival of several new members, and the difficulties that all observers had getting leave to carry out the research. At its largest the sample contained 64 schools; at its smallest it contained 36.

A full analysis of the observations is available elsewhere (Alderson and Wall 1992) and a table comparing the rounds is presented in Appendix 4. What follows is a brief description of two of the rounds – a round of 'ordinary teaching' and a round of 'examination preparation' – to provide readers with the background necessary to follow the discussion in Chapters 6–11.

## Round 5 – 'Ordinary teaching'

Round 5 took place in June and July 1991, five months before the examination. The observers visited Year 11 classrooms in 64 schools. They observed classes which were using the textbook and classes which were using other material.

### *Lessons where teachers were using the textbook: content*

Approximately 75% of the teachers were using the textbook on the day of the observation. About 70% of these were working on material which resembled the exam, but almost half of them were taking their content (texts and exercises) straight from the textbook. They added nothing of their own to the lessons. Almost all of the teachers stated that they had chosen their content because it was 'next in line' in the textbook.

The other half were using texts from the textbook but were adding their own questions or activities. The questions were the sort that might appear on the exam, but this did not mean that the exam was influencing them. The teachers' desire to check their students' comprehension was understandable, and the fact that they used certain question types more than others (mainly short-answer questions) might have been because they were not familiar with any others. Only a quarter of these teachers reported that they were preparing their students for the exam on the day of the observation; almost all the others reported that they were using the material that was 'next in line'.

It was important to consider how much attention the teachers paid to each skill area. Table 2.3 shows that the percentage of teachers focusing on reading was much greater than the percentage for any other skill, especially listening. This could have been the influence of the examination since roughly half of the exam paper was devoted to reading; however, this would not explain why writing, which also accounted for half the paper, was the focus of so few classes. An analysis of the textbook units that the teachers were covering provided a possible explanation for the discrepancy. The third column of Table 2.3 presents the percentage of unit exercises devoted to each of the skills:

### Table 2.3 Round 5 – Comparison of teachers and textbook exercises by skill

| Skill | % of teachers focusing on this skill | % of unit exercises devoted to this skill |
|---|---|---|
| Reading | 52 | 40 |
| Writing | 27 | 20 |
| Listening | 5 | 10 |
| Speaking | 17 | 25 |
| Language form | 10 | 5 |

(Note: The figures in the second column add up to more than 100% because some teachers covered more than one skill in a lesson.)

The percentage of teachers focusing on each skill and the percentage of unit exercises devoted to each skill was roughly the same. Only the figure for reading seemed out of line, but this could be accounted for by the few teachers who said they were preparing their students for the exam rather than teaching what was next in line. There was little evidence from these observations that the teachers were modifying the content of the textbook because of the exam or that they were emphasizing any skills more than the textbook would have suggested, with the possible exception of reading.

## Lessons where teachers were using the textbook: methodology

The Impact Study also looked into whether the exam was having any effect on the teachers' methodology. There was no evidence in Round 5 (or any of the earlier rounds) that the exam was affecting the approach to the teaching of reading of the teachers who were using the textbook. Their methods were similar to the methods that were observed in the Baseline Study classrooms, which resembled the kind of teaching that the textbook designers had tried to discourage. The examination design team had hoped that by specifying skills like 'Skimming to obtain the gist' and 'Finding specific information' in the official exam support documents and by including fairly long passages in the exam itself they could convince teachers to give their students training in reading quickly. This could take many forms – e.g. giving students hints on how to locate important points or timing them to encourage them to read more quickly. There were no occurrences of these techniques, however, nor of others that emphasized speed. Teachers were teaching their students to understand all the words and structures in every passage.

The Teacher's Guides to the textbook series may have been responsible for this state of affairs as they did not provide clear alternatives to a word-by-word approach to reading. The Guide for Years 10/11 provided 'pre-reading' and 'scanning' questions, but it did not explain how to handle the questions in the classroom. It referred to a procedure called 'Finding Out', but this procedure, which had been explained in the Guide to Year 7, encouraged teachers to develop reading by giving background information to the topic, clarifying difficult structures or vocabulary, reading the passage aloud, having the students read it silently for five minutes, reading it aloud again, and getting the students to read it aloud – all before asking the students to answer any content questions!  This method might have been suitable for students at the start of their secondary school studies, but it did not seem appropriate for O level students, who had to read longer, more complex passages and needed to do everything more quickly.

Many teachers provided even more support than the Teacher's Guide to Year 7 recommended, up to the point of 'spoon-feeding'. Teachers were observed explaining *all* of the difficult words of the passage (see Teacher's Guide: 'The pupil's own skill of guessing intelligently from context and relating mutually explanatory parts of the passage MUST be given scope'), dissecting passages sentence by sentence ('They must learn to focus their attention on the GENERAL message in the first instance and not on minor details'), and doing considerable amounts of explaining in the first language ('Don't kill their interest by giving them everything "on a plate" in advance'). Students had to read at the pace of the group rather than at their own pace.

Nor was there evidence of washback on the methodology used for teaching writing. It had been hoped that the exam might reinforce suggestions given in the Teacher's Guides to get students to think about what should go into a piece of writing (e.g. Teacher's Guide to Years 10/11, pages 46, 52 and 59). In general, though, the teachers did not give students the chance to work things out for themselves. As with reading they tended to give more guidance than the Teacher's Guides recommended, even to the point of interference.

To summarize, there was no evidence of washback on the methodology in classes where the teachers were using the textbook. In fact, the way teachers presented content and got students to practise might have run contrary to some of the principles of the textbook series. There are several possible explanations for why this was happening, but one which emerged as early as the Baseline Study was that many teachers might not have understood the methodology of the textbook in the first place. Why else would they have claimed that they were using a 'communicative' approach when the observations were showing something quite different? (A more detailed analysis of the textbook series and Teacher's Guides will be presented in Chapter 8, and of the characteristics of the teachers in Chapter 11.)

### *Lessons where teachers were using other materials: content*

There were 17 classes (25%) where the teachers were using other materials and there seemed to be washback on the content of all of them. The first indicator of this was the teachers' own admission that they had chosen content in order to prepare their students for examinations or tests: two-thirds referred to the O level examination, and one-third referred to teacher-made tests. It is known from other studies (Wall 1994) that teacher-made tests often resembled the O level examination.

The second indicator was the emphasis that the teachers placed on written skills: 40% focused on reading, 40% on writing, and 20% on language form. There was almost no listening or speaking to be seen in these classes apart from students listening to the teacher and answering the teacher's questions.

The third indicator was the type and source of materials that were being used in the classrooms. Nearly all the reading passages and writing tasks were taken from past examination papers, official exam support material, or commercial examination preparation books. In classes concentrating on language form, the tasks were designed by teachers but the task types had all appeared on past exams.

### *Lessons where teachers were using other materials: methodology*

The methodology of these lessons was similar to the methodology followed by teachers working with the textbook. The main difference was that these teachers had to spend a lot of time copying reading passages and comprehension questions on to the board because students rarely had their own copies of test preparation material. The typical pattern for teaching reading can be seen in Figure 2.1.

### Figure 2.1 Typical pattern for teaching reading

Teacher writes passage on board.
▼
Students copy passage into copybooks.
▼
Teacher and/or student reads passage aloud.
▼
Teacher writes (occasionally dictates) questions.
▼
Students copy questions into copybooks.
▼
Teacher explains instructions, often using L1.
▼
Students take much time to answer questions on own (although occasionally they work in lockstep, question by question).
▼
Teacher asks for answers to questions and students supply them.
▼
Teacher and students discuss incorrect answers (sometimes).
▼
Teacher asks how many students have got all the answers right, all but one, all but two etc.

The teachers occasionally dissected texts before they asked their students to answer the questions – explaining or translating the difficult words, paraphrasing or translating difficult sentences. However, this process was often missing when it would have been most useful – when students gave incorrect answers and needed help to find out how they had gone wrong. Students' answers were discussed in only 60% of the lessons. In the remainder they were merely accepted or rejected before the teacher went on to the next question.

This way of teaching obviously precluded skimming and scanning. Students usually read through the passage several times (as the teacher was writing it on the board, as they were copying it into their copybooks, and as they heard it being read aloud or read it aloud themselves) before they read and copied the questions. There was no opportunity for students to practise selective reading. When they were allowed to work on their own there were no strict time limits, so they did not get used to the idea of having to read quickly. When they worked in lockstep, some did not have a chance to read at all as others who worked more quickly were often asked by the teacher to supply answers to the whole group.

The pattern for writing lessons was less rigid but still visible, as can be seen in Figure 2.2.

## Figure 2.2 Typical pattern for teaching writing

Teacher writes rubric on blackboard.
▼
Students copy rubric into copybooks.
▼
Teacher spends some time explaining instructions, often using L1.
▼
Teacher asks students questions about the task.
▼
Teacher either puts key words or full sentences on blackboard. (On one occasion teacher dictated full sentences.)
▼
Students write individually.
▼
Correction:
▼
Students read what they have written to the rest of the group. Teacher corrects the student who is reading and the other students try to correct themselves, or:
▼
Teacher walks around correcting as he/she goes, or:
▼
Students take copybooks to teacher for correction.

- In only one class were students allowed to brainstorm in small groups.
- There was no correction in several classes because the writing itself took up the whole period.
- Teachers did not discuss marking criteria in any of the classes.

Although the content of the writing lessons matched that of past examination papers, the methodology bore little resemblance to what students would have to do when sitting the exam. The biggest difference was in the amount of support that the teachers gave the students, which included writing out sentences for them to copy. The students did not get many opportunities to think independently (either alone or with their classmates) and there was no evidence that they could name, much less explain, the criteria that would be used to judge them on the O level examination.

To summarize, there was no evidence of impact on the methodology used by teachers when they used materials from sources other than the textbook. The routines they followed when getting students to practise reading and writing did not include the types of activities which the textbook series wished to encourage and which the examination was meant to be reinforcing.

## Round 6 – 'Examination preparation'

Round 6 took place in October and November 1991, approximately one month before the examination. The observers visited Year 11 classes in 41 schools. Only 12 (29%) of these teachers were using the textbook on the day of the observation; the other 29 (71%) were using different material. As was the case in Round 5, it was easier to identify examination impact in classes where the teachers were using other sorts of material.

### *Lessons where teachers were using the textbook: content*

The content of these lessons resembled the content of the examination in 11 out of the 12 classrooms. Most of the teachers made no changes to the content of the textbook: the two who did added comprehension questions, as had occurred in Round 5. These teachers were not necessarily under the influence of the examination however: if the textbooks did not contain enough exercises then it would be natural for teachers to want to add more.

Most of the teachers were working on one of the last three units of Book 11. Table 2.4 shows the percentage of teachers paying attention to each of the four skills, as well as the percentage of exercises in the last three units which were intended to develop these skills.

**Table 2.4 Round 6 – Comparison of teachers and textbook exercises by skill**

| Skill | % of teachers focusing on this skill | % of unit exercises devoted to this skill |
|---|---|---|
| Reading | 58 | 32 |
| Writing | 33 | 27 |
| Listening | 0 | 7 |
| Speaking | 8 | 27 |

The teachers were clearly paying less attention to listening and speaking than the textbook intended, and much more attention to reading. The emphasis on reading might have indicated impact from the examination, but it was difficult to prove this given that most of the teachers reported that they were teaching the lesson which came next in line rather than doing exam preparation.

As with Round 5, there was little evidence of washback on the content of lessons where the textbook was being used.

### Lessons where teachers were using the textbook: methodology

The methodology used in Round 6 was similar to that in Round 5, all of the earlier rounds and the baseline observations. The comments made in the previous section about the inappropriateness of the methodology when compared to the goals of the exam and the textbook also apply here.

### Lessons where teachers were using other materials: content

About 70% of the teachers were using other materials on the day of the observations. All of them stated that they were doing 'exam preparation', and nearly all referred to the O level exam rather than to internal year-end tests.

A quarter of these teachers were using teacher-made materials and about half were using commercial publications designed to help teachers and students to prepare for the examination. The fact that so many teachers used commercial examination preparation materials is an obvious impact of the examination. A few teachers were using past examination papers, and only one was using official exam support material. It is important to note how little use was made of the official support materials, despite the fact that they were informative and well written. This may have been due to problems in distribution (only half the teachers owned or had access to either of the two official booklets), or it may have been that the commercial materials held some attraction we could not see during these observations.

The skills that these teachers were concentrating on during Round 6 were reading (52% of the sample), writing (31%) and language form (17%). No-one was working on listening and speaking. The students listened only to their teachers reading aloud or explaining the lessons. The most common form of 'speaking' was answering questions asked by the teacher, although occasionally some students were asked to read aloud.

The text types and exercise or task types being used were clearly related to the exam. The two most commonly used text types had appeared frequently on the exam, and all of the task types had appeared on past papers. In the writing classes students were practising the filling in of application forms in all but two of the classes. This type of writing had appeared on the new exam every year. In most of the language form classes students were doing transformation exercises. Again, this type of task had appeared on the new exam every year.

It was clear that the exam was having an impact on the content of classes where the textbook was not being used, with the most obvious effect being the lack of listening and speaking, and the attention given to text and task types which had appeared frequently on past exams.

## *Lessons where teachers were using other materials: methodology*

The methodology that was being used by the teachers who were teaching reading was similar to that used in Round 5. In approximately half the reading classes the students did not have copies of the passages they were supposed to study. Large amounts of class time were spent on writing, with the teacher transferring a text and questions from a past paper or a commercial publication on to the blackboard and the students copying from the board into their copybooks. Sometimes the students spent so much time copying that there was not enough time left for answering the questions or for checking whether the answers were correct.

In the other half of the reading classes the teachers had either borrowed sets of books which came earlier in the textbook series (students had to return their books to the school at the end of each year), or had collected money from the students to pay for the duplication of past papers, or they had asked the students to buy copies of the commercial publications. Duplicating was less expensive than getting students to buy books; however, both options were beyond the means of many families. Only one teacher had found a way around the problem of providing supplementary texts in poor areas: she brought in authentic texts from newspapers and distributed different texts to different students, allowing them to read and answer questions at their own pace and then providing answers for each student individually. This is the kind of activity that the Teacher's Guides to the textbooks and the examination support materials could have been recommending, but were not. This may be because the textbook team and the examination team did not see this type of teacher support as part of their duties. It is unlikely that they were unaware of the shortage of resources, but they may have assumed that teachers were more able to come up with solutions than they really were.

The methodology for writing classes and for language form classes was again similar to that in Round 5. Some groups managed to get through several tasks in one period if the tasks required only short responses. It was difficult, however, to deal with longer tasks like those found towards the middle and the end of the exam because there would be too much input material to copy. This meant that students from poorer families and in schools with fewer resources were not always able to do certain types of exam practice, and were therefore less likely than their counterparts in better-off schools to do well on certain parts of the examination.

## Results of the observations

Rounds 5 and 6, in combination with the earlier rounds of observations, seemed to suggest the following:

Content of teaching:

- Most teachers followed the textbook during the first two terms of the year. They worked their way through the materials, unit by unit. They may have believed that a thorough approach would help their students to do well on the exam, but there was no evidence from the observations to prove this.
- The teachers paid more attention to reading and writing than to listening and speaking, even when they were covering the textbook carefully. This might have been because the textbook itself paid less attention to these skills, or they may not have wished to cover certain skills if they did not appear on the examination.
- There was little visible exam impact on the content of reading, writing or grammar lessons if teachers were using the textbook. Teachers occasionally added comprehension questions to the day's lesson, but this might have been to compensate for a lack of suitable exercises in the textbooks rather than because of the exam. It is important to note, however, that the changes that they did make were always in the direction of the exam.
- There was obvious impact from the exam when the teachers were using materials other than the textbook. They themselves said that they were doing examination practice and the materials they used were designed for this purpose.
- The third term was openly examination-oriented. Teachers finished or abandoned their textbooks and began intensive work with past papers and commercial publications to prepare their students for the exam. No attention was given to listening and speaking. Much attention was given to topics and text types that teachers believed might appear on the examination.

Methodology:
- There was no relationship between the methodology that teachers used, whatever the time of year, and the methodology which was recommended in the textbook or which might have seemed suitable for developing the

skills that were needed in the examination. It is worth noting here that when the observers were asked to judge the effectiveness of the teachers they had visited, they judged fewer than half to be effective. They were not convinced that the teachers understood the basic principles of the textbook or that they were in command of communicative teaching techniques.

The observations gave a clear picture of what was happening in the classroom but they could not cast much light on the teachers' reasons for doing what they were doing. It was therefore necessary to gather other types of data in order to understand what was happening at a deeper level.

# The need for complementary data

Although the observations revealed a great deal about the relationship between teaching and the examination, they also gave rise to questions like the following:

- Many teachers reported that they were teaching the lesson which was next in line in the textbook. Why were they doing this?
- Some teachers reported that they concentrated on certain parts of the textbook in order to prepare their students for the exam. Which parts did they think were most important?
- Were there any topics or activities that teachers consistently omitted?
- If teachers brought in supplementary material, what were they trying to achieve?
- What was the attraction of the commercial publications that so many teachers were using in Rounds 5 and 6?
- How much did the teachers really understand of the aims of the textbook series?
- How much did they really know about the exam?
- How much influence did they feel the exam had had on the way they chose their content and methodology, and the way they designed and marked their tests?
- Did they believe the exam influenced their teaching in Years 9 and 10, when the exam was still a long way off?
- What other factors influenced the way that teachers conducted their lessons?

Various methods for collecting data were used in earlier stages of the evaluation project: *document analysis*, in order to find out about the aims

27

of the ELT reform programme and the examination development activities; *materials analysis*, in order to determine whether the exam had had any influence on teacher-made tests; and *questionnaires*, in order to find out how teachers, teacher advisers and examiners were reacting to the examination. The first two methods were not suitable for delving into the 'why' of teachers' actions. Questionnaires were a possibility but they were problematic for at least two reasons. The first was that respondents sometimes did not understand the questions and/or gave answers that were not relevant. The second was that their responses were sometimes difficult to interpret and it was not possible to probe to get a better idea of what they were saying. Using *interviews* would provide a way of overcoming these problems. (Details of the research procedure are presented in Chapter 5: Methodology.)

I conducted ten group interviews in November 1991, with 64 teachers in seven different regions of the country. The results of the first analysis of the data were incorporated into the final report for the project (May 1992). Although I had confidence in the first analysis, I remained curious about whether I had taken from the data as much as the teachers had to offer. I later decided to carry out a new analysis of the same data, using ideas about examination impact that I was becoming aware of in general education, as well as ideas on educational innovation that I had learned about during my involvement in a number of ELT projects in the mid-1990s.

In Chapter 3, I will discuss the educational literature on examination impact, and in Chapter 4, I will discuss a number of important issues in the area of educational innovation. These chapters, along with the description of my methodology in Chapter 5, will provide the foundations for the new analysis of 'old data' which makes up Chapters 6–11.

# 3  The impact of high-stakes examinations on teaching

## Background

It is generally accepted that 'high-stakes' examinations (defined by Madaus 1988:7 as 'those whose results are seen – rightly or wrongly – by students, teachers, administrators, parents, or the general public, as being used to make important decisions that immediately and directly affect them') can have significant impact not only on individuals but also on practices and policies – in the classroom, the school, the education system and in society as a whole. They may influence the way that teachers and students behave as well as their perceptions of their own abilities and worth. They may influence the content and methodology of teaching programmes, attitudes towards the value of certain educational objectives and activities, the academic and employment options that are open to individuals, and, in the long term, they may even 'reduce the diversity of talent available to schools and society' (Ebel 1966, cited in Kirkland 1971:305). Given this potential power, they may 'become targets for contending parties who seek to maintain or establish a particular vision of what education and society should be' (Eckstein and Noah 1993:191).

The notion that important examinations may have important consequences has been discussed in education literature for years. It was not until the early 1990s, however, that language educators began to ask whether examinations were as powerful as they were generally believed to be, where their supposed power came from, what kinds of effects they really had on teaching and learning, and what other factors might influence what happened in the classroom.

This chapter begins with a review of some of the functions of high-stakes examinations in society, and then presents views from the literature of general education about why examination impact occurs and the forms it can take. There is a separate section on research that has been carried out in developing countries, which is particularly relevant to my work in Sri Lanka. I then review the literature in language education, distinguishing between studies which merely assert the existence of examination impact and those which are based on research findings. Finally, I present a summary of the issues which are most relevant to this investigation and indicate how they will inform the analysis presented in Chapters 6–11.

# The functions of high-stakes examinations in society

The functions of assessment can be viewed from different perspectives. It is common in language education to focus on how assessment serves individuals or the educational institutions that they are part of or wish to join: tests are used to measure aptitude, achievement or proficiency, or perhaps to diagnose special problems. These functions are important but it is also useful to consider the functions that assessment serves in society. These are what policy-makers must consider when they make decisions about assessment at regional or national levels.

There are a number of reviews of the functions of examinations in society and the impact that they have on the systems they are introduced into. One of the most comprehensive is by Eckstein and Noah (1993). They claim that the first documented use of 'written, public, competitive examination systems' occurred under the Han Dynasty in China, about 200 BC. The function of these examinations was to select candidates for entry into government service: they were used to 'break the monopoly over government jobs enjoyed by an aristocratic or feudal class' (1993:5). Their impact was substantial: 'to establish and control an education programme' in which prospective mandarins prepared themselves for a major professional hurdle (Spolsky 1995b:55). This system lasted until the beginning of the 20th century, and influenced the development of examinations for similar purposes under Frederick the Great in Prussia (the *Abitur*, 1748) and Napoleon in France (the *Baccalaureat*, 1808). The Meiji emperors in Japan also used competitive examinations to lessen the influence of the Samurai in government service, and to encourage an influx of new blood, new talents and new loyalties (Eckstein and Noah 1993:6–8).

The second function that Eckstein and Noah list was to check patronage and corruption. Britain is presented as an example of a country where people could gain entry into higher education or the professions on the strength of whom – rather than what – they knew. This situation only began to change in the middle of the 19th century, with the establishment of examinations for military commissions (1849), entry into the Indian Civil Service (1853), and entry into the military academies (1858)(op. cit:10). An important consequence was the establishment of numerous 'public schools', which specialized in preparing students for the examinations. Although this impact did not reach all segments of society (only the middle classes could afford to send their offspring to such schools), there was nonetheless some broadening of the base from which selection choices could be made (Eggleston 1984:18).

The third function of high-stakes examinations was to encourage 'higher levels of competence and knowledge' amongst those who were entering government service or the professions. The intention was to design examinations which reflected the demands of the target situation. The key examinations in France were those controlling entry to the *grandes ecoles*; in Germany it was the *Staatsexamen*. Candidates preparing for these exams would have to develop skills which were relevant to the work they hoped to do in the future. This did not apply to Britain, however, where it was a knowledge of the humanities, especially classical languages, that mattered, not a command of mathematics or the sciences or the law (Eckstein and Noah 1993:12).

The fourth function was that of allocating sparse places in higher education. A good example of this is Japan at the beginning of the 20th century, where examinations were used as a means of selecting the most able candidates for the few places available at secondary and tertiary levels. Selection by examination is still the rule in modern Japan, although the focus has changed from gaining entry into any institution to gaining entry into the most prestigious institutions at every level (Eckstein and Noah 1993:13). This competition has led to what is commonly referred to as 'examination hell' and to the proliferation of *juku* and *yobiko*, which are 'cramming schools' for the most important entrance examinations (Dore 1976 and 1997, Watanabe 1996). (For similar effects in China see Lewin 1997, and Min and Xiuwen 2001.)

The fifth function of examinations was to measure and improve the effectiveness of teachers and schools. Eckstein and Noah again use Britain as an example, describing how in 1862 the government set up a system of examinations to monitor the performance of primary schools which were receiving public funding (op. cit:14). The amount of funding that a school received depended on how its students performed. The 'Payment by Results' system had serious unintended consequences. A former Senior Inspector presented his own observations as evidence before the Consultative Committee on Examinations in Secondary Schools in 1911:

> The children ... were drilled in the contents of those books until they knew them almost by heart. In arithmetic they worked abstract sums in obedience to formal rules, day after day, month after month ... They learned a few lines of poetry by heart, and committed all the 'meanings and illusions' to memory ... In geography, history and grammar they were the victims of unintelligent oral cram, which they were compelled, under pains and penalties, to take in and retain until the examination day was over ... Not a thought was given, except in a small minority of the schools, to the real training of the child, to the fostering of his mental (and other) growth. To get him through the yearly examination by hook or by crook was the one concern of the teacher. (Holmes 1911:107–108, cited in Stobart and Gipps 1997:4)

The final function mentioned by Eckstein and Noah was limiting curriculum differentiation. In Britain in the 19th and early 20th centuries there was considerable resistance to the idea of centralized education, and all schools had the freedom to decide on their own curriculum and means of assessment. It was not until 1917, with the establishment of the School Certificate examinations, that schools had a common target they could aim for. The School Certificate examinations were replaced by the General Certificate of Education (GCE) O level and A level examinations in 1951, and these were supplemented by the Certificate of Secondary Education (CSE) examinations in 1965. These examinations exercised an 'indirect control of the curriculum' which continued until 1988, when the National Curriculum for England and Wales took on the role of setting objectives and standards for primary and secondary education (Eckstein and Noah 1993:5–17).

Eggleston (1984) introduces a number of sociological concepts which enrich the discussion of the impact of examinations on education and society. He refers to the proposal made by Bernstein, Elvin and Peters (1966) that there are two types of school rituals: *consensual rituals* and *differentiating rituals*. Examinations are a form of consensual ritual in that they reflect the values of the society that creates them, but they also serve a differentiating function as they play such an important role in determining the fate of individuals (Eggleston 1984:20). Also important are the notions of *contest mobility* and *sponsorship*, which are discussed by Turner (1961). 'Contest mobility' describes a model of open competition for educational and occupational achievement, in which examinations play an important role. 'Sponsorship' refers to a model in which certain people are 'chosen', usually as a result of their social background, to compete for educational and occupational achievement. Eggleston states that research carried out since the 1960s indicates that 'most, if not all, educational systems approximated far more closely to a sponsorship system rather than a contest system' and that 'the distribution of examination success remained persistently linked to class, sex and race' (Eggleston 1984:21). In spite of this shortcoming, however, and problems such as the tendency for examinations to respond only very slowly to educational change, they still possess 'a high degree of legitimacy in modern society' (Eckstein and Noah 1993:217). Success in examinations is:

> an essential prelude to the legitimate exercise of power, responsibility and status throughout modern societies; lack of accreditation constitutes a severe limitation ... There is abundant evidence that the examination system, despite its technical and ideological critics, enjoys widespread public acceptance. (Eggleston 1984:32)

It is important to note at this stage that some of the claims that are reviewed in this chapter are not based on evidence and that some authors make references to research but do not give specific details. This is a common phenomenon in the field of testing, especially when it comes to discussing test consequences (Kellaghan, Madaus and Airasian 1982:3). It does, however, place the reviewer of the literature in the awkward position of having to decide whether to ignore views which are not supported by evidence, or whether to include them since although they do not 'abide by the canons that normally apply in scholarly publications' (ibid.) they have stimulated discussion and inspired other investigations. I have chosen to include references to such studies in this book, because this will reflect the extent of the debate and the strength of feeling surrounding the subject of test impact. When the positions that I am reviewing are not supported by empirical findings, I will make this clear.

# The impact of high-stakes examinations: views from general education

## Early claims

The impact of examinations on teaching has been of interest to those in education for many years. Early references include Vernon (1956), Wiseman (1961) and Kirkland (1971).

Vernon (1956), one of the first British educators to write about the measurement of 'mental abilities', was critical of the use of examinations in schools. He believed that although it was rarely discussed openly, one of the major functions of examinations was to act as an incentive for stimulating students to study and for 'keeping teachers up to the mark' (1956:198). He claimed that they were:

> an essential feature of the whole education system, which relies largely upon extraneous motives, such as competition, fear of punishment and blame. (Ibid.)

Vernon wrote that the most common criticism directed at examinations was that 'they dominate and distort the whole curriculum'. He was particularly concerned about the negative effects of the 11-plus examination (a selection examination for secondary schools) on primary education. These effects included the neglect of certain subjects if they did not contribute to examination success, the streaming of children even in infant classes, and the ubiquity of out-of-school coaching. Vernon claimed that examinations encouraged cramming and rote memorization, and that 'reasoning power' could be stunted as a result of too much memorization (1956:199). It is important to note, however, that Vernon does not provide details of the sources of this criticism; nor does he mention the research it is based on.

Wiseman (1961:155) claimed that educators should investigate not only the 'technical efficiency' of examinations (their reliability and validity) but also whether they were 'educationally profitable'. This involved looking at both their 'credits' and their 'debits' – the positive and the negative results of using them. Wiseman illustrated this by reproducing an extract from 'a forgotten classic': the *1911 Report of the Consultative Committee on Examinations in Secondary Schools*. The extract listed a number of effects that an examination might have on teachers and on pupils. The possible positive effects on teachers included inducing them to cover their subjects thoroughly, making them complete their syllabuses within the prescribed time limits, compelling them to pay as much attention to weak pupils as to strong ones, and making them familiar with the standards which other teachers and other schools were able to achieve. The possible negative effects included encouraging teachers to 'watch the examiner's foibles and to note his idiosyncrasies' in order to prepare the pupils for the questions that were likely to appear, limiting their freedom to teach subjects in their own way, encouraging them to do the work that the pupils should be doing, tempting them to overvalue the type of skills that led to successful examination performance, and convincing them to pay attention to the 'purely examinable side' of their professional work and to neglect the side which would not be tested (1961:159–161).

Wiseman claimed that most of the negative effects of examinations could be avoided 'if the papers are set with the aims of the curriculum in mind' (1961:162). He offered no evidence to back up this assertion.

Kirkland (1971) concentrated on the importance of standardized testing in the United States, beginning in World War 1, when tests were used to solve 'manpower allocation problems' and continuing up to the 1960s, when it was estimated that between 150 and 250 million tests were given each year in schools alone. There were batteries of standardized tests for entry into higher education, and many other tests and measuring devices for occupational and professional purposes (1971:303-304). Kirkland reported that a great deal of criticism had been levelled at tests in the 1960s, particularly regarding their social consequences. She felt that much of this criticism was uninformed ('a battlefield for laymen and professionals' 1971:307), and she undertook a review of the empirical and theoretical research on the impact of tests on students, parents, teachers, schools and society.

The research on impact on teachers is the most relevant to this study. Kirkland concluded that tests had little influence on what teachers taught or how they taught unless they were being used for admission to higher education. Some of the tests that were used for this purpose (e.g. the Regents Examination in New York) had a 'potentially significant impact'. She cited research which found that most teachers concentrated on examination objectives rather than local curriculum objectives, abandoned their textbooks in order to use test preparation booklets and past examination papers, and began test revision weeks before the test administration (sometimes even at the beginning of the school year) (1971:331).

## More recent claims

The late 1980s saw the publication of several influential articles on test impact. Some of these advocated the use of high-stakes testing to force change on the education system (Popham 1987, Frederiksen and Collins 1989), while others either urged a cautious approach (Airasian 1988a) or totally rejected the idea that tests could improve teaching and learning (Madaus 1988).

## Positive impact

Popham (1987) was one of the educators who believed that high-stakes testing could lead to educational improvement, and he introduced the term *measurement-driven instruction* (MDI) to describe this phenomenon. He stated that there were two types of high-stakes tests: tests which have important consequences for students (for example, school-leaving examinations used to determine entry into university), and tests which have important consequences for teachers and schools (for instance, tests whose results are published in the press and thereby affect the public's view of the quality of education provided by the school). High-stakes tests serve as 'curricular magnets' in that 'teachers tend to focus a significant portion of the instructional activities on the knowledge and skills assessed by them' (1987:680). Popham argued that if such tests are 'properly conceived and implemented' focusing teaching on what they assess is sensible. He rejected the notion that MDI leads to curricular reductionism, curricular stagnation, constrained teacher creativity, and lowered student aspirations.

Popham supported his arguments by citing studies where there was 'substantial improvement' in the number of students reaching established standards on basic skills tests when 'measurement-driven instruction is properly installed'. (Ibid.)

In order for a test to be 'properly installed' it must meet five conditions:

1. It must be *criterion-referenced*, because 'the descriptive clarity of well-constructed criterion-referenced tests gives teachers a comprehensible description of what is being tested'.

2. It must contain *defensible content* – that is, important knowledge and skills rather than trivial material.

3. There must be a *manageable number of targets* rather than the 'endless litanies of minuscule instructional targets' that teachers were faced with during the 'heyday of behavioral objectives'.

4. The test must provide for *instructional illumination* – that is, it should encourage teachers to design 'effective instructional sequences'.

5. The test must be accompanied by *instructional support*, to help teachers to cope with its demands. Popham gave the example of a set of guidelines issued by a state education authority, which contained a description of each skill to be tested, a sample test item, an analysis of how the skill could be taught, and examples of useful teaching activities and exercises. (1987:680–681)

Frederiksen and Collins (1989) also believe in the positive potential of high-stakes testing. They base their arguments on two premises: that educational systems adjust their curricular and instructional practices in order to achieve their goals, and that one of these goals is maximizing results on high-stakes examinations. It is therefore important to ensure that examinations have 'systemic validity'. A test with systemic validity:

> is one that induces in the education system curricular and instructional changes that foster the development of the cognitive skills that the test is designed to measure. Evidence for systemic validity would be an improvement in those skills after the test has been in place within the educational system for a period of time. (1989:27)

A systemically valid test will have two important features: directness of cognitive assessment, and a need for a certain degree of subjectivity in the assigning of scores to test performances. Frederiksen and Collins' notion of 'directness' matches the notion which is commonly accepted in language testing: a direct test:

> measures ability directly in an authentic context and format, as opposed to an indirect test that requires performance of a contrived task from which inference is drawn about the presence of the ability concerned. (Henning 1987:191)

The term 'subjectivity', however, is used in a more positive way than is customary in language testing. Subjective tests 'require judgement, analysis and reflection on the part of the scorer' (1989:28). Scorers must understand the 'scoring categories' and be trained to use them in a reliable manner. A systemically valid testing system would include sets of tasks which represent the whole range of knowledge and skills relevant to the domain being tested, a limited number of 'primary traits' for each task, a library of exemplars representing different levels of performance for each primary trait (this would be accessible to markers, teachers and students), and a training system for marking test performances. The latter would also be available to the markers, teachers and students. They stress the importance of directness, scope, reliability and transparency of standards, and maintain that the testing system should include practice in self-assessment, repeated testing, feedback on test performance and multiple layers of success (1989:31).

It is important to note that Frederiksen and Collins present theoretical arguments rather than empirical ones. They refer to other studies to support some of their arguments, but they produce no evidence to back up the idea that good tests will lead to good teaching and learning.

## More cautious views

Other educators are more cautious in their views of how tests can influence teaching. Airasian (1988a) questions whether Measurement-Driven

Instruction and Popham's five conditions apply to all pupils and teachers in all situations. He argues that there are a number of factors which interact 'to produce varying and non-uniform instructional consequences' (1988a:8). It is important to analyse not only how high the stakes are for each test, but also how high the standards are and the type of content the test contains. He contrasts the high-stakes, high-standards external examinations in Europe with high-stakes, low-standards examinations in the United States, and concludes that 'The greatest impact on instruction will occur when high standards and high stakes are present' (1988a:7). This is also the situation in which the greatest number of failures are likely to occur.

'Type of content' refers to two things. The first is whether the test assesses learning which takes place over a number of courses and a relatively long period of time, as in the United States, or whether it is based on specific courses, as is the case with the British GCSE and A level examinations. Airasian argues that:

> The more course-specific the test content, the more easily instructional responses can be localised in the curriculum sequence and the more likely that the test will drive instruction. (1988a:8)

It is also important to consider whether the test assesses low-level cognitive skills or higher-level operations such as reasoning, problem-solving and critical thinking. The inclusion of higher-level operations will not necessarily lead to better learning, because of other factors in the educational system – namely, the quality of teaching:

> Most MDI programmes are based upon the implicit assumption that the science of instruction is sufficiently developed and articulated and that teachers can apply it to guide pupils to the attainment of any desired educational end. (Airasian 1988a:9)

Airasian claims that those who advocate MDI are 'state-level educational administrators, legislators and psychometricians', who are not aware of classroom realities. They need to explain what they mean when they use terms like 'higher-level skills' and consider carefully whether the instructional materials currently available give adequate guidance in the development of such skills (1988a:10)

Airasian paints a convincing picture of the complexity of the nature of examination impact, but he too lacks empirical support for his arguments.

## Negative impact

Perhaps the strongest critic of Measurement-Driven Instruction is Madaus (1988), who condemns it as 'nothing more than psychometric imperialism' (1988:84). He predicts only negative effects if testing is used as the 'primary motivating power of the educational process'. He claims that:

> Measurement-driven instruction invariably leads to cramming; narrows the curriculum; concentrates attention on those skills most amenable to testing...; constrains the creativity and spontaneity of teachers and students and finally demeans the professional judgement of teachers. (1988:85)

Madaus reviews a number of studies on the impact of testing on teaching and presents a set of seven 'principles' to summarize his own position:

1. The power of tests and exams to affect individuals, institutions, curriculum or instruction is a perceptual phenomenon. If students, teachers or administrators believe that the results of an examination are important, it matters very little whether this is really true. The effect is produced by what individuals perceive to be the case.

2. The more any quantitative social indicator is used for social decision making, the more likely it will be to distort and corrupt the social processes it is intended to monitor.

3. If important decisions are presumed to be related to test results, then teachers will teach to the test.

4. In every setting where a high-stakes exam operates, a tradition of past exams develops, which eventually de facto defines the curriculum.

5. Teachers pay particular attention to the form of the questions on a high-stakes test (for example, short answer essay, multiple choice) and adjust their instruction accordingly.

6. When test results are the sole, or even partial, arbiter of future educational or life choices, society tends to treat them as the major goal of schooling, rather than as a useful but fallible indicator of achievement.

7. A high-stakes test transfers control over the curriculum to the agency which sets or controls the exam. (Madaus 1988:88–97)

Behind Madaus' principles is the assumption that individuals and institutions are guided in their actions by self-interest. Madaus argues that looking at the matter any other way would require 'a staggeringly optimistic view of human nature' (1988:93).

Other educators share Madaus' concern about the negative effects of testing. Haladyna, Nolen and Haas (1991) use the term 'test score pollution' to refer to practices which 'increase or decrease test performance without connection to the construct represented by the test' (1991:4). There are three sources of test score pollution: the manner in which schools prepare students for tests, the activities that take place during the administration of the test, and factors which are beyond the control of the school (these include factors such as the students' proficiency in the language in which the examination is being given – if it is a history examination given in the medium of English a student with low proficiency in this language would not be able to display his/her true ability). Only the first two sources of pollution are relevant to this discussion.

Haladyna et al discuss nine different types of test-preparation activity, which they place on a continuum from 'ethical' to 'highly unethical' (1991:4). Ethical practices include activities such as training students in test-wiseness skills or attempting to motivate them to perform well by discussing the importance of the tests with them. Unethical practices include developing a curriculum which is based on the test, preparing teaching objectives which match the test, presenting material in class which is similar to the test and so on. They quote earlier research (Haas, Haladyna and Nolen 1989 and Nolen, Haladyna and Haas 1989), which indicated that the practices that they consider to be unethical or highly unethical are actually quite common in schools. They also discuss 'non-standard administration' practices, including deviating when reading test instructions, giving extra time, and helping students to answer test questions. (See Mehrens and Kaminsky 1989, and Hamp-Lyons 1998 for further discussion of ethical and unethical practices.)

There were few differences between schools where test scores were rising and those where they were stable or falling. Teachers in schools where scores were rising felt more pressure from parents and the community to increase scores, and teachers in schools where scores were stable or falling were more likely to feel that this was due to factors beyond their control (1993:24).

For Herman and Golan these results can be seen as either positive or negative:

> Whether this is good news or bad news depends largely on whether or not one views the standards and skills embodied in mandated tests as educationally valid and significant. (1993:24)

Frederiksen (1984) was interested in the long-term impact of test format. He was concerned that the item-type used in basic skills testing, which was mainly multiple choice, 'may influence the cognitive processes involved in dealing with test items and hence the nature of the skills taught and learned' (1984:195). He reviewed studies which claim that it is easier to produce multiple-choice items which test factual knowledge than those which test 'inference, analysis, interpretation or application of a principle' (1984:195, citing Aiken 1982), and further studies which suggest that when multiple-choice items are substituted for free response items designed to measure higher order skills, different constructs are tested (1984:197–199). Since it is easier and more economical to use multiple-choice questions in testing, teaching will eventually focus on the abilities that can be taught in this manner. The consequence over time will be a bias against the teaching of higher-level skills ('the real test bias'). Fredericksen believed that educators and psychologists must:

> develop instruments that will better reflect the whole domain of educational goals and ... find ways to use them in improving the educational process. (1984:201)

Although Frederiksen presented an interesting case, and one which led logically to the arguments on 'systemic validity' that were reviewed earlier in this section, it is important to note that his conclusions are predictions only, not backed by empirical studies. In contrast, Wesdorp (1983) found that multiple-choice examinations did not have as much impact on teaching and learning as teachers believed.

Smith (1991) reports the findings of an extensive investigation carried out in schools in Arizona (Smith, Edelsky, Draper, Rottenberg and Cherland 1989). This study used a number of data-collecting methods, for which Smith gave this rationale:

> To understand fully the consequences of high-stakes external testing on teachers, one must look beyond their verbal statements to underlying meanings within the institution. One must sit with them in the initial faculty meetings when school expectations are laid out, follow them as they collect formidable piles of textbooks, teaching manuals, and the other materials they are required to cover, observe their everyday classroom life throughout the school year, watch their sometimes frenzied preparation for the tests themselves, examine what topics and subject matter gets slighted or left by the wayside for the sake of the tests, and finally learn what reactions to these experiences are incorporated into the teachers' identities and subsequent definitions of teaching. (Smith 1991:8)

The study revealed serious effects of high-stakes tests on teaching. It took teachers the equivalent of three to four weeks to prepare their students for tests, administer them and recover from them: this was a significant amount of time given how little time was available to them for teaching to begin with and the 'packed curriculum' they were supposed to cover. The curriculum was narrowed dramatically, with a neglect of untested subjects which was seasonal in some cases but proved more long lasting in others.

It is Smith's investigation of teachers' attitudes, however, which merits most attention. Many teachers reacted to the high-stakes tests with 'feelings of dissonance and alienation', believing that the numeric test scores meant nothing because of 'the psychometric inadequacies of the tests, the mismatch between what was taught and what was tested, and the vagaries of pupil effort and emotional status at the time of the tests' (1991:9). The publication of these results, in the form of league tables, led to 'feelings of shame, embarrassment, guilt and anger ... and the determination to do what is necessary to avoid such feeling in the future' (ibid.). The teachers also felt that the scores were being used against them (principals were pressured by school districts to raise test scores, and principals shifted this pressure downwards), and that their control over the curriculum and their working lives was being threatened. Most teachers gave in to the pressure; the few who resisted were aware that there would be a price to pay for their actions:

They are likely to be subject to frequent demands to defend their programs
on other grounds, and to fears that they will suffer sanctions and loss of
autonomy because of low scores. (1991:10)

To summarize, I have reviewed a number of important studies concerning
the impact of high-stakes testing on teaching. Some of the studies have
focused on specific tests in specific situations (Vernon 1956, Wiseman 1961,
Smith 1991), but the majority have had a broader aim: to survey the literature
for evidence of general tendencies (Kirkland 1971) or to discuss issues which
are of relevance to the wider educational community (Popham 1987,
Frederiksen and Collins 1989, Airasian 1988a, Madaus 1988, Haladyna et al
1991, Herman and Golan 1993 and Frederiksen 1984). What all of the studies
have in common is a conviction that high-stakes tests will influence teaching.
Where they differ is in the form this influence will take: some authors are
optimistic that tests can have a positive effect (Popham 1987, Frederiksen and
Collins 1989), while others, principally but not only Madaus (1988), believe
that this influence is more likely to be negative. The only evidence for positive
impact on the system as a whole (rather than on individuals) is a rise in the
percentage of students gaining mastery of basic skills (Popham 1987). The
view that the right kind of testing will lead to a mastery of more complex skills
or encourage higher levels of cognitive ability is not backed up by research
findings. In contrast there is considerable support for the idea that high-stakes
testing is harmful.

(For further discussion of potential positive impact see Biggs 1995, Wolf
1997, James 2000 and Stiggins 2001. For further discussion of potential
negative impact see Crooks 1988, Newstead and Findlay 1997, Shohamy
1997, Black and William 1998, and Zeidner 1998.)

## Examination impact in developing countries

It is useful to turn to work carried out in developing countries, which may
offer insights of special relevance to Sri Lanka. The functions of examinations
in these countries are often similar to those mentioned earlier, but the fact that
there are far fewer places available in the upper levels of education makes
their stakes much higher. Mathews (1985:23) writes that 'it is in the
developing countries where the pressure of selection by examination may be
most severe'. Foster (1992:123) concurs: 'Educational credentials are much
more important in many LDCs [Less Developed Countries] than they have
perhaps ever been in the developed world'.

Heyneman and Ransom (1992) draw on their experience conducting
research for the World Bank and similar organizations in developing
countries. Their main interest is in high-stakes examinations (mainly for
selection purposes) at national level, which they believe 'can be a powerful,
low-cost means of influencing the quality of what teachers teach and what

students learn in school' (1992:105). They argue along the same lines as Frederiksen and Collins (1989), that teachers adjust their teaching to suit the requirements of examinations and that 'if examinations fail to test useful skills, teachers will have little incentive to teach them' (1992:110). They believe that examining authorities must do two things to improve the effects of tests on teaching: they must raise the quality of their examinations, and they must provide useful feedback on student performance.

Heyneman and Ransom present a list of eight recommendations to help examination bodies to achieve the right balance in their examinations. The recommendations include requiring students to restructure information rather than reproduce it; answer 'why' and 'how' questions rather than 'who', 'what' and 'where' ones; and generate answers as well as select them (ibid.). Test results and other observations about the exam should be provided to teachers and a wide range of other parties if change is to occur in the system as a whole. The feedback should include an analysis of the errors that students make and explanations of why they make them, as well as recommendations for improving teaching.

Eisemon (1990) presents a short history of the use of exams for educational improvement in English- and French-colonized Africa. He notes that the original mandate for examining authorities in these regions included not only the production and processing of examination papers but also 'strengthening the quality of instruction' (1990:71). Eisemon believes that changes in teaching and cognitive outcomes are possible if examining bodies are prepared to investigate the effects of their tests on teaching. He gives an example of research that he carried out in Kenya (1988) into the reasons teachers engaged in 'bad cramming' – that is, drilling in the classroom with little emphasis on independent study, continuous exposure to possible examination questions and correct answers without developing basic skills and knowledge, and a distortion of the teaching programme to make room for exam revision. Eisemon suggests that such practice occurs because teachers do not really understand what is being tested: they might be able to give the correct answer to specific questions but might not recognize which knowledge and skills the questions are supposed to be measuring. The investigation showed that what was happening in examination practice classes was also occurring in ordinary teaching. These practices were not useful for the students, but:

> they persist since they are rooted in a complex of factors such as insufficient teacher understanding of subject matter, insufficient assistance from principals and others (inspectors, Ministry of Education staff development personnel), lack of textbooks and other instructional material, lack of instructional time, pressures for examination success as well as the content and construction of the examinations. (1990:78)

Eisemon refers to an earlier study in Kenya (Eisemon, Patel and Abagi 1988), which showed that changes made to the types of questions asked led teachers to spend more time preparing lessons, read the relevant parts of student textbooks and teacher support materials, and explain meanings and processes in the lessons. This led to a significant improvement in teaching and in student learning. (See also Somerset 1997.)

Kellaghan and Greaney (1992) review World Bank research carried out in 14 African countries into the effects that examinations have on the curriculum and on the quality of teaching and learning. Many of their references are to the negative effects high-stakes examinations can have on the classroom (the neglect of subjects and skills which are not examined, the excessive use of past exam papers as teaching material, frequent practice in examination-taking techniques) and on individuals (the promotion of a 'passive' concept of learning, the rejection by society of individuals who do not do well in their exams). However, they stress that there is a possibility of positive effects as well, and refer to the World Bank's interest in strengthening examination systems as part of a renewed commitment to academic standards (1992:7). They are careful to point out that examinations alone cannot change education systems (examinations are just one component of an education system, and other factors such as teaching quality and availability of resources will also affect teaching outcomes); however, 'they can be made to reflect the objectives of curriculum developers and educational planners' (1992:3).

Kellaghan and Greaney offer a number of recommendations for improving assessment in public examinations. The following are the most relevant to this investigation:

- examinations should reflect the full curriculum, not merely a limited aspect of it;

- higher-order cognitive skills should be assessed to ensure they are taught;

- skills to be tested should not be limited to academic areas but should also be relevant to out-of-school tasks;

- a variety of examination formats should be used, including written, oral, aural and practical;

- in evaluating published examination results and national rankings, account should be taken of factors other than teaching effort;

- detailed, timely feedback should be provided to schools on levels of pupil performance and areas of difficulty in public examinations;

- predictive validity studies of public examinations should be conducted;

- the professional competence of examination authorities needs to be developed, especially in test construction;

- each examination board should have a research capacity;

- examination authorities should work closely with curriculum organisations and with educational administrators;

- regional professional networks should be developed to initiate exchange programmes and share common interests and concerns. (1992:3)

Little (1992) criticizes the work of Heyneman and Ransom (1992), implying that they are promoting 'a party line' (inverted commas mine) – that is, a view espoused by the World Bank and similar organizations. Little declares that Heyneman and Ransom's article is:

> an excellent example of a growing but debatable trend in some quarters of comparative and international education – the uprooting of an educational policy idea from one particular country, its elevation to a general set of principles and its translation into global policies and guidelines for lending banks. (1992:130)

She claims that their arguments are based on 'the experience of a handful of countries in the 1970s', and that they should not take this experience out of the original context and apply it to other countries in the 1990s. She argues that the context of each country should be analysed before deciding on the policy that will be right for that country. She specifies a number of factors (educational, economic and political) that need to be taken into account in order to do this correctly.

Little also criticizes the notion that changing an examination is a sufficient condition for changing the curriculum: just because examinations which are out of line with the curriculum can constrain it does not mean that examinations that are in line will ensure its implementation. She believes that these matters need to be discussed more fully, and the first question that she would ask in any such discussion is:

> Do we know enough about the relationships between assessment practice, curriculum practice, teachers, learning traditions, allocation and reward systems in every country of the world to be confident about drawing global prescriptions from empirically-grounded global propositions? (1992:131)

This question is of central importance in this study, and the analyses presented in Chapters 6–11 cover many of the areas Little believes to be significant.

Many of the issues facing developing countries are similar to those facing their wealthier neighbours. The main factor which distinguishes these countries from others is that there are very limited opportunities for upward mobility within education and the world of employment, and this makes the stakes of the examinations which control entry to these areas much higher. Other differences include a lack of resources and, often, a lack of trained personnel, both in the schools and in the examination authorities, which may limit the extent of examination reform that can be undertaken. (For further discussion see Hargreaves 1997, Lewin 1997, Chapman and Snyder 2000, Min and Xiuwen 2001.)

# Views from language education

## Early references to examination impact, or 'washback'

There were few references in language education to examination impact before the early 1990s. What discussion there was included definitions and brief explanations in language testing handbooks, claims about the importance of tests that did not include references to research, and expressions of hope or worry concerning the impact of specific examinations on the contexts they were being introduced into.

The discussions in language testing handbooks tended to focus on the effects of testing on the classroom, rather than on individuals or on society. Some writers used the term *washback* and others *backwash* to describe these effects, stating that tests can influence 'what and how the students choose to study and ... teaching procedures' (Finocchiaro and Sako 1983:311), 'teaching and learning' (Hughes 1989:1), or simply 'instruction' (Bachman 1990:283).

Some of the references to test impact were very brief. Madsen stated simply that 'an occasional focus on grammar or vocabulary or mechanics can have a good "backwash" effect on the teaching of writing' (1983:120). He offered no support for his claim.

Heaton (1990) claimed that teachers would always base their teaching on exams that were used for selection purposes, and which were designed by bodies external to the schools (1990:17). He generalized about the influence these examinations would have:

> If it is a good examination, it will have a useful effect on teaching; if bad, then it will have a damaging effect on teaching. (Ibid.)

Davies also believed that 'all language tests and examinations exert an influence on the curriculum and on the teaching', and claimed that test designers should 'at least try to ensure that the exams are good ones' (1977:42).

Davies later stated that all good educational tests should meet three demands, the third of which was that the effects of the test should be beneficial (op. cit:56). He quoted from a report he had written for the West African Examination Council on the introduction of a new oral test, which, it was hoped, would have positive effects on the educational system. In order to do this the test would have to have content and predictive validity, be based on realistic and appropriate goals, and discriminate meaningfully (op. cit:57).

Finocchiaro and Sako (1983) referred to the 'four persistent problems in testing', the last of which was the 'degree to which testing either enhanced instruction or, alternatively, distorted it through various feedback effects from the tests' (1983:11). They claimed that testing should not distort learning if the testing and the teaching 'both derive from sharply defined objectives based on sound inter-disciplinary theory'. However, they did not elaborate on what the theory should contain or how it would ensure that tests 'will be a positive motivating force for student and teacher alike' (1983:41).

Weir (1990) claimed that an evaluation of communicative tests should include the systematic gathering of data on construct, content, face and 'washback validity' ('a measure of how far the intended washback effect [is] actually being met in practice' – see Morrow 1986 for further discussion). He stated that:

> a communicative approach to language teaching is more likely to be adopted when the test at the end of a course of instruction is itself communicative. (1990:27)

Hughes (1989) presented a more complete treatment of washback, claiming that it could either be 'harmful' or 'beneficial'. He gave a hypothetical example to illustrate the former and a brief example from his own experience to illustrate the latter (1989:1-2). Hughes challenged Davies' belief that 'the good test is an obedient servant since it follows and apes the teaching' (1968:5), stating that testing should not only follow teaching but should also 'where necessary, exert a corrective influence on bad teaching' (Hughes 1989:2). He presents guidelines for achieving beneficial backwash, which included testing the abilities that need to be encouraged, sampling widely and unpredictably, using direct testing, using criterion-referenced testing, basing achievement on objectives, ensuring that the test is known and understood by teachers and students, and providing guidance for teachers who do not understand how to teach towards the test's demands (1989:44-46).

Other authors who express hope in the power of tests to cause positive changes include Swain and Alderson. Swain (1985) described a test which she and colleagues developed in Canada for use in French immersion situations. She stated that 'Work for washback' was one of the principles that guided the team's thinking. They believed that they could promote positive washback by involving teachers in all stages of the testing process and by providing detailed support materials to help them to administer and mark the tests and 'to suggest alternative teaching-learning strategies' (1985:44). Alderson (1986) argued that 'the potentially powerful influence of tests can be harnessed in the cause of independently justified, or justifiable innovation'. He cited the case of the Graded Objectives movement in England, and suggested that the success of the movement stemmed from the fact that the tests were designed by teachers and represented goals that both teachers and learners considered desirable (1986:104).

Articles which express a negative view include Forbes (1973) and Madsen (1976) on the introduction of a multiple-choice school-leaving exam in Ethiopia, Buck (1988) on the effects of testing in Japan, and Davies (1985) on the mis-match between curricula and examinations in Malaysia and in West Africa. Raimes (1990) lamented the 'proliferation of coaching and test-specific instruction materials' for the Test of Written English, and Norton Peirce (1992) was concerned that the TOEFL Reading Test might encourage an approach to reading texts which would not match what test-takers needed outside the testing situation.

Although all of these researchers offer interesting ideas about potential and perceived test impact, they do not provide details of the research which led them to their conclusions. It is therefore necessary to question whether the impact was as positive or as negative as they supposed it to be.

## Empirical studies

There were only a few empirical studies available before the early 1990s, amongst them Wesdorp (1983) on the use of multiple-choice tests in the Netherlands; Li (1990) on the effects of the Matriculation English Test (MET) in China; Hughes (1988a) on the effects of a high-stakes EAP (English for Academic Purposes) test in Turkey; and Shohamy (1993) on the effects of three different tests introduced into the Israeli school system.

Wesdorp (1983) reported on several studies carried out in the Netherlands in the late 1970s to investigate whether objections to the introduction of multiple-choice tests in the assessment of mother tongue and foreign language education had any empirical justification. There were fears that multiple-choice tests incorporated into the final examinations of some types of secondary institution would lead to an 'impoverishment of the curriculum' (skills that could not be tested through multiple-choice would not be practised and would eventually disappear), an 'impoverishment of teaching methodology' (there would be a decline in the use of certain teaching methods), and changes in the way that students prepared themselves for tests.

The investigation into a possible impoverishment of the curriculum focused on writing skills: a comparison of essays written before the introduction of multiple-choice tests and twelve years later showed that there were no differences in student ability. The investigation into methodology in schools with and without multiple-choice final tests failed to reveal any clear differences in teaching practices, and the investigation into students' preparation methods also failed to show any differences. Wesdorp concluded that although teachers continued to express grave concerns about the effects of multiple choice:

> the so-called backwash effects are a myth. If they do exist, they must be
> so weak or small that our research methods cannot detect them.
> (1983:103)

Li (1990) focused on the Matriculation English Test, a high-stakes examination taken by Chinese students at the end of secondary school. The English component, along with parallel components in other subjects of the curriculum, helped to determine which students would be allowed to continue on to higher education (600,000 out of a candidature of three million in 1990).

The examination was introduced in 1984, to replace an earlier exam with little validity or reliability. Li claimed that the MET had both extrinsic and intrinsic power: extrinsic because of its status in the educational system, and intrinsic because it was valid and reliable, had the power to 'inform significantly', and most important for this discussion, could 'influence benevolently' (1990:393).

Li supported her claim by referring to a study carried out in 1987, which analysed questionnaires from 229 teachers and local teaching-and-research officers who were responsible for about 2.4 million students. The analysis revealed changes in three different areas: teaching materials, the content of lessons, and activities outside the classroom. The most important change in teaching materials was that there was a greater use of imported and teacher-made materials, since the official textbooks did not match the requirements of the examination as much as the teachers wanted. The change in lesson content had to do with the increased attention given to 'the practice skills' (the traditional four skills) as opposed to 'the knowledge subjects' (phonetics, grammar and vocabulary), although these were still at the heart of the curriculum. Finally, there seemed to be a new enthusiasm for learning English outside the classroom, which included more after-class learning (undefined) and high sales of simplified English readers. Li claimed that teachers' and students' attitudes towards the test were positive. She wrote dramatically of the different types of power that tests could have:

> Tests that are able to subjugate the minds of millions of people to conform
> to the thraldom of forced memorisation may be said to be powerful indeed.
> But we would say it is a greater kind of power to be able to liberate
> people's mind from such thraldom. (1990:402)

Hughes (1988a) reported on a project at Bogazici University in Istanbul, where the introduction of a test in English for Academic Purposes was meant to lead not only to improved English performance in the University's English-medium undergraduate courses but also to beneficial washback in the Foreign Languages School, where most students were required to study English before they were allowed to begin their undergraduate studies. Prior to the start of the project decisions about whether students could pass from the English course into mainstream departments were based mainly on a series of progress tests, some of them teacher-constructed. The effects of this policy were disastrous: many students who gained entry were unable to cope with the demands of their courses, and at one stage the University considered switching from English to Turkish medium.

The aim of the project reported by Hughes was to devise a new proficiency test which would serve as the sole filter for students wishing to enter the undergraduate programme (1988a:137). The test was based on a needs analysis and included sections on academic listening, reading and writing. Hughes remarked that the mere threat of introducing a new test caused 'consternation' amongst the English language staff, and then a recognition that they would have to take drastic action if they wanted their students to do well:

> For the first time, at least for some years, the Foreign Languages School
> teachers were compelled, by the test, to consider seriously just how to
> provide their students with training appropriate for the tasks which would
> face them at the end of the course. (1988a:144)

Hughes reported that there were changes in the syllabus and in the materials used in the Foreign Languages School, and that the test had had 'considerable impact on teaching and learning'. He attributed this impact to the fact that the test was criterion-referenced and that it was based on the needs of the undergraduates. This meant that:

> teaching for the test (which may be regarded as inevitable) became
> teaching towards the proper objectives of the course. (1988a:145)

The main question left unanswered, however, was what was actually going on in the classrooms. Hughes assumed that teachers were 'teaching for the test'; however, he gave no details about what they were teaching and how.

Shohamy (1993) presents the findings of three studies that examined the impact of language tests on the educational systems in which they operated, and she reported on how the results of these tests were used or mis-used.

The first study was of an Arabic test which had been introduced by a Ministry of Education in order to 'raise the prestige of the Arabic language ... to motivate teachers to speed up the teaching of Arabic, and to increase the motivation of both teachers and students'. Shohamy investigated whether the test affected teaching practices or student behaviour, and whether it had long-range impact on teaching. Her methodology included a review of teaching materials, interviews with teachers, student questionnaires and lesson observations. Shohamy reported that there was a 'sharp distinction' between the preparation period for the test and the teaching that occurred after it was administered: differences in the types of material used, the activities that took place, the amount and type of homework given, the use of the mother tongue in teaching, and the atmosphere in the classroom. There were far fewer differences recorded four years later. By this time new textbooks had been introduced which matched the test material. Half the teachers admitted that they had been influenced by the test 'in terms of direction and guidance'. The other half claimed that they had not, but these were teachers who had just graduated from teacher-training institutions which had changed their curricula to match the test. Shohamy considered that the Ministry of Education had succeeded in its attempts to introduce change through testing.

The second study concerned the introduction of an EFL oral test. This test had been introduced in order to 'increase the emphasis on oral language in the EFL classroom, and to upgrade the speaking proficiency of students'. The study included observations and interviews with fifteen teachers of varying levels of experience. Experienced teachers 'turned to the test as their main source of guidance for teaching oral language' as their own training had not prepared them to emphasize oral skills. Novice teachers were much less dependent on the test, and actually claimed that it 'opened new teaching avenues to them' and allowed them to experiment with innovative activities.

The third study concerned the introduction of a test of L1 reading comprehension, which teachers had received with a great deal of hostility. The study was based on the analysis of materials that had been produced after the introduction of the test and on interviews with teachers. Shohamy found that a great deal of new material appeared after the introduction of the test, most of which was very similar to the test itself; much more time was allocated to reading comprehension across the curriculum; and teachers suffered a great deal of bitterness and stress. They resented the way the test had been introduced, and they believed that the educational system was using poor test results as an excuse to punish teachers who were not performing according to their superiors' wishes.

Synthesizing the findings from all three studies, Shohamy concluded that teaching materials and methods had become 'test-like', longer-serving teachers turned to the tests for guidance since they had not been trained to teach the new areas being tested, and the tests had become 'de facto curriculums' [*sic*]. She claimed that the tests did not provide information that was useful for future teaching, and that teachers felt degraded as a result of having tests imposed upon them and having to submit to their demands. The ministries involved may have achieved their purposes in terms of short-term 'instrumental impact', but Shohamy questioned whether their methods would bring about long-term 'conceptual impact'.

To summarize, little was written about examination impact in the field of language testing before the beginning of the 1990s. There were short definitions of 'backwash' or 'washback', some guidelines about how to achieve positive impact (e.g. Davies 1977, Hughes 1989), and a few brief references to the effects of tests on the contexts they had been introduced into (e.g. Davies 1985, Alderson 1986), but there were few detailed accounts of specific attempts to innovate through testing. Most of the research was based on questionnaires or on test results rather than on direct observations in classrooms. Shohamy (1993) used the most ambitious research design, which included a focus on three different tests and several different methods for gathering data. Her work highlighted the complexity of the impact situation, and how many factors needed to be taken into account before it was possible to say that a specific test had had a specific effect on a specific context.

## The 1990s and more recent research

### Exploring the theory

The first critical discussion of the notion of washback appeared in 1993. The authors, Alderson and Wall, reviewed the concept as it had been presented by language testers up to that time. They concluded that the concept was too vaguely defined to be useful and that much of what had been written had been based on assertion rather than empirical findings. They presented a number of 'Washback Hypotheses', which were meant to illustrate some of the effects that tests might have on teaching and learning. They argued that test developers should specify the types of impact that they wished to promote and the kinds of effects test evaluators should look for when deciding whether the desired washback has occurred.

The Washback Hypotheses are as follows:

1. A test will influence teaching.
2. A test will influence learning.
3. A test will influence what teachers teach.
4. A test will influence how teachers teach.
5. A test will influence what learners learn.
6. A test will influence how learners learn.
7. A test will influence the rate and sequence of teaching.
8. A test will influence the rate and sequence of learning.
9. A test will influence the degree and depth of teaching.
10. A test will influence the degree and depth of learning.
11. A test will influence attitudes to the content, method, etc. of teaching and learning.
12. Tests that have important consequences will have washback.
13. Tests that do not have important consequences will have no washback.
14. Tests will have washback on all learners and teachers.
15. Tests will have washback effects for some learners, but not for others.
    (1993:120-121)

Alderson and Wall also considered the methodology that should be used when investigating washback, stating that many studies which presented evidence relied on surveys of teachers' self-report data or on test results rather than on analyses of classroom behaviour.

They discussed the importance of accounting for what occurs in the classroom rather than just describing it, taking into consideration not only characteristics of the test design but variables which appear in the literature on motivation and educational innovation as well.

This theoretical article was accompanied by a research-based one (Wall and Alderson 1993), which described an investigation of the washback of a new O level examination in English in Sri Lanka. The authors made explicit statements about the type of washback that they expected to find and described a complex research programme which included a baseline study (a description of teaching before the examination was introduced) and a long-term large-scale classroom observation programme. (See Chapter 2 for details.)

These two papers provoked considerable interest in the topic of washback, which led to further investigations by others. In 1994 the Educational Testing Service commissioned a comprehensive study of washback, with the intention of incorporating new insights into its work on TOEFL 2000. The study took as its starting point the papers by Alderson and Wall (1993) and Wall and Alderson (1993), and further contributions from Hughes (1994) and Bailey (1994, revised 1996 and 1999). Hughes introduced a way of categorizing the types of effects that might occur, making a distinction between washback on the participants, the processes and the products of an educational system. Among the participants who could be affected by tests were teachers, learners, educational administrators, materials' writers and publishers. Tests could affect their thinking and the activities they engaged in (processes), and they could also affect the amount and quality of learning (products).

Hughes speculated that at least five conditions had to be in place before possible washback effects could occur:

1. Success on the test must be important to the learners.
2. Teachers must want their learners to succeed.
3. Participants must be familiar with the test 'and understand the implications of its nature and content'.
4. Participants must have the expertise which is demanded by the test (including teaching methods, syllabus design and materials writing expertise), and
5. the necessary resources for successful test preparation must be available. (1994:2-3).

Bailey's paper attempted to identify what washback was, how it worked, the ways in which positive washback could be promoted, and how it should be investigated. She combined the Washback Hypotheses from Alderson and Wall (1993) and Hughes' (1994) distinction between participants, processes and products to produce her own 'basic model of washback' (see Figure 3.1.)

Bailey suggested a distinction between 'washback to the learners', the result of supplying 'test-derived information' to the test-takers, and 'washback to the programme', the result of supplying information to all of the other participants in the education system. She suggested that five of the Alderson and Wall hypotheses (2, 5, 6, 8 and 10) corresponded to the 'washback to the learners' heading, and she provides ten examples of the processes that learners might engage in when preparing for important tests. These ranged from practising items similar in format to those in the test, to practising test-taking strategies, to enrolling in test-preparation courses, to skipping language classes to study for the test (1996:264-265). She stated that six of the hypotheses (1, 3, 4, 7, 9, and 11) fit under the 'washback to the programme' heading; however, she did not specify what kinds of processes the participants (in this case, the teachers) might participate in. She stated only that there was room here for future research.

## Figure 3.1 A basic model of washback

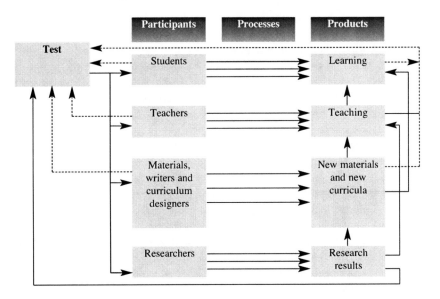

*Source*: Bailey (1996:264)

Bailey also discussed the difficulties of investigating washback, which include working in 'naturally occurring settings', using a 'non-random sample of subjects', and attempting to sort out how much of what happens in classrooms can be 'evidentially linked to the introduction and use of the test' (Messick 1996:242). She referred to Alderson and Wall's (1993) insistence on classroom observation and triangulation, and on collecting baseline data. She concluded with a set of questions which should be asked of any 'external-to-programme' examination which is intended to promote positive washback:

1. Do the participants understand the purpose(s) of the test and the intended use(s) of the results?
2. Are the results provided in a clear, informative and timely fashion?
3. Are the results perceived as believable and fair by the participants?
4. Does the test measure what the programme intends to teach?
5. Is the test based on clearly articulated goals and objectives?
6. Is the test based on sound theoretical principles which have current credibility in the field?
7. Does the test utilize authentic texts and authentic tasks?
8. Are the participants invested [sic] in the assessment processes? (1996:276–277)

# Empirical studies

A number of empirical studies have been carried out since 1993, which have led to a more detailed understanding of test impact in language education and of the factors which contribute to it.

Lam (1993) developed a series of ten hypotheses to explore the impact of the New Use of English examination in Hong Kong. He administered a questionnaire to 61 teachers and did an analysis of examination papers, examination scripts and textbooks that were in use before and after the introduction of the new examination.

He investigated whether the new exam had affected the following: the amount of time that schools dedicated to English language teaching, whether schools set aside special time to prepare for one particular section of the exam, the attitude of the teachers and their perceptions of the attitudes and abilities of the students, the quality of English language textbooks, the content of the teaching, and the students' language performance. He found positive and negative washback in most of the areas, and gave interesting explanations about how different factors in the context might be interacting with one another to produce a more complicated picture than the examination designers might have expected.

Of particular interest is Lam's reference to 'teacher culture': how different teachers reacted to the examination in different ways, depending on the amount of teaching experience they had, their own language competence, their understanding of the aims of the test, their own motivation and commitment to the profession, and their fears of an increasing workload. He found that the more experienced teachers (those who had taught before and after the introduction of the new examination) were more likely to do traditional examination practice, and that the less experienced teachers were more likely to work with authentic materials and use activities which required student participation or an integration of the skills rather than isolated skills work. Lam believed that the more experienced teachers had more confidence in their own ability to choose what was best for their students, and were more convinced about the value of 'pragmatic' teaching – i.e. using examination practice activities rather than innovatory activities, despite explicit advice to the contrary.

Cheng (1997) attempted to trace the impact of the revised Hong Kong Certificate of Education Examination in English (HKCEE) from the time of the first official announcement that the exam was to be changed. As with many Hong Kong Education Authority (HKEA) examinations, the revision of the HKCEE in English was a deliberate attempt to provoke changes in teaching and learning. The announcement concerning the changes was followed very quickly by training seminars all over the territory, given by the HKEA itself, tertiary institutions, and textbook publishers. The publishers' seminars, which included presentations of materials and demonstration of many classroom activities, attracted the largest audiences. Cheng used questionnaires, interviews and observations during the first year after the announcement, and discovered that the new examination was having considerable influence on the types of materials that teachers were using and on the activities that they were presenting in the lessons. She suggests, however, that these changes were changes of 'form' rather than of 'substance' (p.52), and that teachers were more influenced by publishers' understanding of the new HKCEE than by their own. (See also Cheng 1998; and Andrews, Fullilove and Wong 2002.)

Shohamy, Donitsa-Schmidt and Ferman (1996) report from Israel on the long-term effects of two of the three tests that Shohamy reported on in 1993 – one in Arabic as a Second Language and one in English as a Foreign Language. The authors used questionnaires and structured interviews with teachers, students and inspectors, as well as analyses of Ministry documents and teaching materials. They found that whereas both tests had had some impact on teaching when they were first introduced they had very different effects several years later. The impact of the Arabic test had almost disappeared: there was little preparation for the test, no new materials had been published for several years, there was little awareness of the test or its content, and those who were aware of the test felt that it was of poor quality. There were mixed opinions amongst teachers about whether the test promoted learning, but Ministry officials felt that unless it continued, proficiency levels in Arabic, the numbers of students taking courses and the status of the subject would drop even further.

The EFL test has continued to have an impact on the content and methodology of teaching, in spite of the fact that the Ministry has provided little in the way of training. New teaching material has appeared, there is a high degree of awareness of the exam, the test creates anxiety amongst teachers and students, and the subject enjoys high status. As with the Arabic test, teachers complain of poor test quality, but they are happy with some of the changes that have been made. They feel that the test is important, and that it has promoted learning.

Shohamy et al conclude that washback can change over time and that the form that it assumes will depend on several factors: the importance of the test (is it high-stakes or low-stakes?), the status of the language within the society, the purpose of the test, the format of the test, and the number of skills and type of skills tested.

Alderson and Hamp-Lyons (1996) present an investigation into the effects of the TOEFL examination in a language institute in the United States, analysing TOEFL preparation classes and 'normal' classes being taught by the same teachers. They conducted interviews with teachers and students and observations of two teachers teaching both TOEFL-preparation classes and 'normal' language classes. They found that there were differences between the

TOEFL and non-TOEFL classes for each teacher, but that the difference between the teachers was at least as great as the difference between types of classes. This led them to conclude that it is not the test alone which determines what will happen in the classroom, but rather a complex set of factors, including the status of the test, the extent to which the test runs 'counter to current practice', the extent to which teachers and materials designers think about appropriate ways of preparing students for the test, and the extent to which teachers and materials designers are willing and have the ability to innovate. (1996:296)

Watanabe (1996) discusses whether there is any connection between university entrance examinations in Japan and the prevalence of grammar-translation teaching in that country. He analyses the teaching which takes place at a *yobiko* (examination preparation centre) in central Tokyo, comparing the lessons given by two different teachers to prepare their students for two different university entrance exams – one which emphasizes grammar-translation and one which does not. Watanabe concludes that it is too simple to expect that an examination will affect all teachers in the same way: like Alderson and Hamp-Lyons (1996) he considers that the personal characteristic of the teachers (in this case, educational background and beliefs about teaching) and, possibly, the proximity of the exam in terms of time have an important role to play in how teachers conduct their lessons. (See also Watanabe 2003.)

Qi (2003) reports the results of her investigation of the impact of the National Matriculation English Test (NMET) in China. The main function of this examination is to select students for higher education, but it also seeks to influence classroom teaching in secondary schools in a positive way. Qi found that the NMET had considerable impact on materials and learning activities but not the kind of influence that was envisaged by its designers. Qi concluded that one of the reasons for this was that the selection function and the 'directing function' were in conflict: when stakes are very high teachers feel pressured to work for good results rather than to help their students to develop more lasting skills. She argues that neither low-stakes nor very high-stakes examinations will produce the impact originally intended.

Most of the recent studies reported here deal with the effect of examinations on classroom processes, particularly in the area of content. The examinations investigated seem to have had an effect on the types of materials that teachers use, both for teaching and for exam preparation, and on the types of skills that they focus on in the classroom. In some cases examinations have affected timetabling, with more attention being given to the subject which is being examined. The fact that class time is devoted to examination preparation is also important, although this should not necessarily be seen as the impact of a specific examination, but rather of examinations in general in the systems/organization under investigation.

About two-thirds of the recent studies deal with the methods that teachers use in the classroom. They indicate that the examinations either have no effect on the teachers' methods or that they restrict them or make them more test-like. In only two cases did the exam seem to encourage the introduction of new activities in the classroom. In one case this was facilitated by the guidance of publishers (Cheng 1997); in the other it was a phenomenon associated with younger teachers rather than more experienced, more pragmatic ones (Lam 1993).

Only two studies to date (Wesdorp 1983, Wall and Alderson 1993) have looked at the effect of exams on classroom assessment. Both looked at the impact on test questions, and came up with mixed findings. One study (Wall and Alderson 1993) also investigated the impact on teacher marking, and found that there was little effect because teachers were not familiar with the marking criteria used on the exam.

Only three studies have looked at the effect of examinations on the product of teaching, which is student learning. Here both Hughes (1988a) and Lam (1993) report improvements in student learning, which can be interpreted as positive washback. Wesdorp (1983) demonstrates that using the multiple-choice technique does not necessarily lead to a decline in abilities such as writing.

Many of the studies comment on the impact of examinations on participants. Most of these indicate that teachers suffer from negative feelings such as anxiety and self-doubt, at least when the examinations are first introduced, and sometimes after it has been in place for some time.

The studies which have appeared in the last decade have used a wider range of methods than those that were carried out earlier, including analyses of materials and documents, classroom observations, and individual and group interviews. (See Saville 2003 and Watanabe 2003 for further reflections on methodology in impact research.) Another important feature of the more recent work is that it has tended not to restrict itself to describing impact but has attempted to explain why impact has or has not appeared and why it has taken on the form it has.

An important step forward for the field of language testing would be to construct a model of washback which would take account of the many factors which may play a part in determining why teachers react to tests in the way they do. The recent research has shown that such factors are likely to include characteristics of the teachers, the status of the subject being tested, classroom conditions, management practice, etc. Writers have stressed how important it is for teachers and students to understand the tests they are preparing for and for teachers to receive help if they do not understand (Hughes 1989), for schools to receive feedback from testers (Shohamy 1992), and for teachers and principals to be involved at different phases of the assessment process since they are the ones who will have to implement change (Shohamy 1992).

What is not included in such lists, however, are references to the settings in which tests are to be introduced, the resources that are available to support their introduction, and the way that innovation should be managed. This may not be a problem for those who are concerned with testing on a relatively small scale (within a single institution or a cluster of closely linked bodies), but it should be of interest to those who have to manage developments at a regional or national level. If specialists in language testing have not paid enough attention to these factors, then it is important to examine work being produced in other disciplines – particularly work based on research findings rather than on speculation.

In 1993 Alderson and Wall wrote that in order to understand how washback works 'it will be important to take account of findings in the research literature in at least two areas: that of motivation and performance, and that of innovation and change in educational settings' (1993:127). Chapter 4 will review the literature in innovation and change for insights which may prove beneficial in the understanding of this phenomenon.

(For further discussion of impact see Wall 2000, Alderson and Banerjee 2001, Shohamy 2001, and Cheng and Watanabe 2003.)

# 4 Innovation in education

## Background

It was argued in Chapter 3 that in order to understand the impact of a new examination it is first necessary to understand the context into which it is being introduced. Many studies into examination impact focus on the examination itself rather than the characteristics of the educational system. Perhaps this is to be expected, given how little cross-over there has been between language testing and the field of educational innovation. Language testing is not alone in this regard. White (1993) claims that most applied linguistics and language teaching literature 'tends to skim over the issues of innovation' (1993:245). Beretta (1990) claims that while some attention is paid to the theory underlying innovative programmes, little is paid to questions of implementation. Bowers (1980) argues for a common descriptive framework so that the lessons learned in major educational projects can be passed on to innovators in the future.

There are a number of ideas in education innovation which can be of use to language testers. The aim of this chapter is to introduce these ideas and to identify a framework which can help examination developers to judge whether their innovations (the examinations they are designing) are likely to have the impact they intend them to.

It is not possible to cover all of innovation theory in a single chapter, so the discussion will be limited to the ideas which are most relevant to my work in Sri Lanka. These ideas are arranged by theme, in order to help readers find a way through what might otherwise seem a bewildering array of theory. I begin with a brief look at the term *innovation*: what distinguishes it from other types of change and what is the difference between an innovation and its *diffusion*? This will be followed by a discussion of the process of innovation (Fullan 1991, Rogers 1995) and of the meaning of change for the individuals who are most affected by it (Fullan 1991). I then turn to an analysis of each of the segments in the composite question 'Who adopts what, where, when, why and how?' (Cooper 1989, cited by Markee 1993, 1997). I conclude with a discussion of several models of innovation, including the Hybrid Model of the Diffusion/Implementation Process by Henrichsen (1989), which served as the starting point for my analysis of data from Sri Lanka.

## Definitions of 'innovation'

The first question that needs to be addressed is what the term 'innovation' actually refers to. For Rogers (1995) an innovation is 'an idea, practice, or object that is perceived as new by an individual or other unit of adoption' (1995:11). It does not matter whether the idea is 'objectively new' (in terms of the amount of time that has passed since its discovery or invention), but rather whether it is felt to be new by those who may be adopting or using it.

Some researchers make a distinction between innovation and other types of change. For White (1993) the difference has to do with intentionality: while 'change' is 'any difference that occurs between Time One and Time Two', an 'innovation' requires human intervention (1993:244). For Miles, innovation is:

> a deliberate, novel, specific change, which is thought to be more efficacious in accomplishing the goals of a system. (1964a, cited by White 1987:211)

Other researchers use the terms as synonyms. Though I believe the distinction is a valid one, I use them interchangeably in this study. This allows me to cite authors who used the terms in different ways, without having to resort to excessive glossing.

Levin (1976, cited by Fullan 1991:17) gives three reasons why educational systems might seek to create change: natural disasters, external forces (imported technology and values, immigration), or internal contradictions (new social patterns and needs). We saw in Chapter 2 that the second and third reasons are relevant to Sri Lanka.

Fullan claims that there will always be a demand for change in pluralistic societies (1991:17), but that many educators do not understand the cost of change or what it can mean for the individuals who experience it (1991:30). According to Adams and Chen (1981, in Markee 1993:231), as many as three-quarters of proposed innovations are likely to fail. Since the efforts required to launch an innovation are so high and the prospects for success so low, it would make sense for those who are interested in creating change to try to learn from the experiences of others.

Fullan (1991) states there are two main aspects to educational change: the 'what' and the 'how'. 'What' refers to the type of change that is intended, which is often decided by reference to theories of education. 'How' refers to the process by which change can be introduced and sustained, which requires an understanding of 'theories of change' (1991:46). Rogers (1995) also distinguishes between the innovation itself and its 'diffusion': 'the process by which the innovation is communicated through certain channels over time among the members of a social system' (1995:5). Both Fullan and Rogers explore the 'what' and the 'how' in detail – Fullan in the field of education – and Rogers in education, anthropology, sociology, marketing and a range of other social sciences (see Rogers 1995:42-43 for a comparison of the major diffusion research traditions).

It is probably Markee (1993, 1997) who has made the most use of innovation theory in the field of language education. Markee recommends that language teaching professionals should adopt a 'diffusion-of-innovations perspective' in order to understand why their attempts to innovate meet with success or failure. This means being aware of the issues and findings reported by specialists in innovation. Markee argues that this approach will not only provide language educators with 'a coherent set of guiding principles' for the development of their own innovations, but will also supply them with 'criteria for retrospective evaluations of the extent to which these innovations have actually been implemented' (1993:229).

# The process of innovation

## Fullan's view

One of the most comprehensive surveys of innovation in education is Fullan's *The New Meaning of Educational Change* (1991). A major theme emerging from this work is that innovation should be seen as a process rather than as an event – a process which is not only lengthy, but complicated and 'snarled' (1991:48). Researchers have identified three basic phases in the process (*Initiation, Implementation* and *Continuation*), but they are not able to predict how events in one phase will influence those in the others or how long it will take for one phase to change into another. Evaluators often make the mistake of claiming that innovations have failed when in fact they have not had time to assume their final form – the 'outcome' presented in Figure 4.1 below.

**Figure 4.1 A simplified overview of the change process**

*Source*: Fullan (1991:48)

*Initiation* is the process that occurs between the first appearance of an idea for change and the time when it is adopted. Fullan suggests that a number of questions should be asked during this phase, to determine whether the idea is worth investing in. These include the following:

- Where did the idea for change come from? From a teacher, or a group of teachers? From an academic? From a politician?
- What was the motivation behind the idea? Was it to solve a problem practitioners agreed needed solving? To test out a theory? Or to take advantage of opportune funding? What do these different motivations suggest about the long-term commitment of the initiator?
- What can be said about the 'quality' of the innovation? Has the idea been well thought through? Is it clearly described? Is it specific enough without being too prescriptive?
- Do teachers have access to information that will help them to understand the idea or begin to implement it? Or is this information available only to its originators (who are sometimes academics out of touch with the classroom)?
- Who in The Establishment will support the idea? Will they have enough influence to get it adopted?
- Will teachers support the idea? What conditions must be there to convince them that it is practical and helpful?
- Are external change agents involved in any way? What role should they play?

Fullan discusses each of these questions in turn and concludes that:

> the best beginnings combine the three R's of relevance, readiness, and resources. *Relevance* includes the interaction of need, clarity of the innovation (and practitioners' understandings of it), and utility, or what it really has to offer teachers and students ...
>
> *Readiness* involves the school's practical and conceptual capacity to initiate, develop, or adopt a given innovation – what Firestone (1989) calls the school's 'capacity to use reform'...
>
> *Resources* concern the accumulation and provision of support as a part of the change process. Just because it is a good and pressing idea doesn't mean that the resources are available to carry it out. (1991:63-64)

Once innovation has been adopted, it must pass through the phases of implementation and continuation.

*Implementation* is 'the process of putting into practice an idea, program, or set of activities and structures new to the people attempting or expected to change' (1991:65). The factors which are important in this phase include the characteristics of the innovation itself (need, clarity, complexity and quality/practicality), the characteristics of the local context (the district, the community, the principal and the teachers), and the characteristics of external bodies, such as government agencies (1991:82).

*Continuation* refers to whether an innovation which survives the implementation period becomes part of the educational system or whether it fades away, either because it is officially terminated or because the conditions that are needed to sustain it are no longer present in the environment (1991:88). Several new factors will also need to be considered, such as:

- The degree to which the innovation has been built into the system. Is it written into policy? Does it have a budget? Has room been made for it on the timetable?
- The number of people who are committed to and skilled in the change. Is there a 'critical mass' of supporters?
- The strength of the procedures to provide continued support, to new teachers and administrators in particular.
- The degree of staff turnover in the target situation, which has implications for provisions for training.

One factor which does not seem to influence the decision to continue is the availability of evaluation data, as it is not common (or was not in 1984) for schools to collect this type of information. (Corbett et al. 1984, referred to by Fullan 1991:89–90.)

# Rogers' view

Rogers (1995) discusses the 'innovation-decision process', which he describes from the point of view of the individual or the organization deciding whether to adopt or reject an innovation. Whereas Fullan presents three phases in the process, Rogers proposes five:

- the *knowledge stage*, in which the individual first learns of the innovation and begins to understand how it works;
- the *persuasion stage*, in which the individual forms an attitude toward the innovation;
- the *decision stage*, in which the individual tries out the innovation in some way in order to decide whether to accept it or reject it;
- the *implementation stage*, in which the innovation is 'put into use'; and
- the *confirmation stage*, in which the individual 'seeks reinforcement of the innovation-decision already made or reverses a previous decision to adopt or reject the innovation if exposed to conflicting messages about the innovation' (1995:181). (See Figure 4.2 below.)

## Figure 4.2 The innovation–decision process

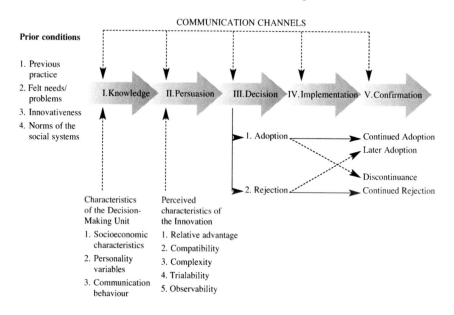

*Source*: Rogers (1995:163). Reprinted with the permission of The Free Press, a Division of Simon & Schuster Adult Publishing Group, from DIFFUSION OF INNOVATIONS, 4th Edition by Everett M. Rogers. Copyright ©1995 by Everett M. Rogers. Copyright ©1962, 1971, 1983 by The Free Press. All rights reserved.

Like Fullan, Rogers discusses factors which are at work in each of these stages. During the *knowledge stage* what matters is who gets to know about the innovation and the types of knowledge these people are exposed to. The types of knowledge include 'awareness knowledge' (knowing that an innovation exists), 'how-to knowledge' (knowing what is necessary to put it to good use) and 'principles knowledge' (understanding the principles underlying the innovation). The most common type of knowledge at this stage is awareness knowledge. How-to knowledge is sometimes not available until later stages, and principles knowledge is often not available at all.

In the *persuasion stage* it is the perceived characteristics of the innovation which play the most important role. Potential adopters will seek 'innovation–evaluation information' to inform their attitude towards the innovation. They will ask questions about the relative advantage of the innovation over previous practice, its complexity, and other features which will be discussed in the section entitled 'Why?' below. Once they have formed an opinion of the innovation they may take some time before deciding to adopt or reject it. The factors which influence them include the channel by which they have received their information (the opinion of 'near-peers' is most convincing) and the confidence they have in their own ability to cope with the innovation.

In the *decision stage* individuals may decide to adopt the innovation or reject it. The trialability of the innovation is often important at this stage: what people can learn from trying out the product on a small scale or by asking peers to try it out for them.

The *implementation stage* begins when adopters put the innovation into use and it continues until they either reject it or it 'becomes an institutionalized and regularised part of (their) ongoing operations' (1995:173). The innovation often changes during this stage, a concept which is referred to as 're-invention' (1995:174) (see also Fullan 1991:52, regarding 'local interpretation' of innovations). Adopters may simplify the innovation or modify it, either out of ignorance or in order to make it suitable to their own contexts. They may also change it in order to pass it off as their own invention. Rogers refers to a large-scale survey of innovation which found that when educational innovations are re-invented in schools, their adoption is more likely to be continued (1995:177).

In the *confirmation stage*, individuals seek information that will support their earlier decision to adopt or reject an innovation, or they reverse the decision they made in the decision stage.

There is a broad correspondence between Rogers' stages and Fullan's phases, as can be seen in Figure 4.3 below:

### Figure 4.3 The phases/stages of the process of innovation

| As viewed by Fullan (1991) | As viewed by Rogers (1995) |
| --- | --- |
| Initiation phase | Knowledge stage |
| | Persuasion stage |
| | Decision stage |
| Implementation phase | Implementation stage |
| Continuation phase | Confirmation stage |

The major difference is that Rogers divides Fullan's Initiation Phase into three separate stages (*Knowledge, Persuasion* and *Decision*). The last two stages are basically the same. The authors have different ideas about which factors are most important in each of the different stages but they both stress the importance of analysing the attributes of the innovation, the features of the local context and the characteristics of potential adopters.

## The meaning of change

A further theme emerging from the innovation literature is the difference between the *objective reality* of educational innovations and the *subjective meaning* that the innovation takes on for every individual who is affected by it. The 'objective reality' of an innovation refers to the changes which are intended in three different respects: the use of new or revised materials, the use of new teaching approaches, and the alteration of beliefs (Fullan 1991:37). Innovations differ in the amount of change they require in each area. Fullan argues that there must be change in all three 'because together they represent the means of achieving a particular educational goal or set of goals' (ibid.). However, some changes are easier to effect than others. Introducing or revising materials is 'the most visible aspect of change and the easiest to employ' (1991:42), but this on its own is superficial. It is more difficult to bring about changes in teaching approaches since these often require the learning of new skills. Changing beliefs is the hardest task, not only because it involves challenging people's 'core values' but also because:

> beliefs are often not explicit, discussed, or understood, but rather are buried at the level of unstated assumptions. (Ibid.)

Kennedy (1988:329) believes that even behavioural changes are only 'a surface phenomenon', and that significant change does not come about unless people 'change the way they think about certain issues, which is a deeper and more complex change'.

Individual teachers may change in one or two dimensions, in all or none at all. The amount and type of change they experience is determined not only by the characteristics of the innovation, but also by the conditions they find themselves working in. Fullan refers to several studies which discuss the 'daily subjective reality of teachers': isolation from other adults, the need to carry out many tasks simultaneously, the need for on-the-spot decisions, the need to deal with unpredictability, the need to focus on the short-term perspective. Teachers are pressured to accomplish a great deal but are given little time to achieve their goals and less time to reflect on better solutions (1991:33). When, on top of all their other pressures, they are expected to implement an innovation that someone else has designed and imposed on them, life can become very difficult. Fullan quotes House (1974:73):

> The personal costs of trying new innovations are often high ... and seldom is there any indication that innovations are worth the investment. Innovations are acts of faith. They require that one believe that they will ultimately bear fruit and be worth the personal investment, often without the hope of immediate return. Costs are also high. The amount of energy and time required to learn the new skills or roles associated with the new innovation is a useful index to the magnitude of resistance. (in Fullan 1991:34)

This overload often leads to what Goodlad et al (1970) call 'false clarity' or 'painful unclarity'. False clarity occurs when teachers think that they have changed but the changes are only superficial (e.g. they may use new materials but not new teaching techniques, or they change their behaviour but not their attitudes). Painful unclarity occurs when teachers are asked to implement changes that they really do not understand. This can result in 'confusion, frustration, anxiety, and abandonment of the effort' (Huberman and Miles 1984, in Fullan 1991:35).

## Who adopts what, where, when, why and how?

There have only been a few attempts in language education to summarize and show the relevance of ideas from innovation theory. One of the most accessible is by Markee (1993), who organizes his discussion by using a question originally posed by Cooper (1982a, 1989): 'Who adopts what, where, when, why and how?'. Markee discusses each component of this question in turn, referring to research he believes would-be innovators should be aware of. I employ the same organizing principle below, referring to some of the research that Markee discusses but adding other relevant sources.

## Who?

Markee uses the 'Who?' question to introduce a discussion of the participants in the innovation process. There are many ways to categorize these participants, but Markee concentrates on the social roles they play and how these affect their relationships with one another (1993:230). His categorization was originally used in urban planning by Lambright and Flynn (1980) and was introduced into language education by Kennedy (1988). It divides participants into five main categories: adopters, implementers, clients, suppliers and entrepreneurs (or 'change agents').

Kennedy sees adopters as 'those who take the initial decision to initiate some sort of change'. They usually have power within the system and some control over resources (e.g. Ministry officials). Implementers are those who have to put the innovation into practice (teachers), clients are on the receiving end of the services (students), and suppliers are responsible for providing the products that the innovation requires (materials' designers, test designers). Entrepreneurs 'act as a link between the different participants and as a catalyst for change' (1988:334). Kennedy claims that this categorization is useful for determining whether attempts at innovation have been successful, and for identifying problem areas if they have not. He stresses the importance of keeping all parties involved and properly informed of what is going on:

> the more the participants' roles are differentiated, the harder
> communication and co-ordination are going to be, and the greater the risk
> that the innovation may not be appropriate to the situation. (1988:336)

This might occur if suppliers, such as materials designers, are brought in from outside the system to provide materials for implementers (teachers) who work within the system. If there is insufficient contact between the two groups then the materials may not be suitable for the implementers' needs. It would be more useful to select the suppliers from amongst the implementers, although this approach may introduce complications of a different kind.

Another issue Kennedy discusses is the role of the entrepreneur or change agent, especially if this person comes from outside the system. The outsider may enter a project with assumptions about language and learning which are very different to those of the insiders. These must be discussed and resolved if the innovation is to have any chance of successful implementation (1987:167). Outsiders may also bring different assumptions about introducing change: these will be a product of their own particular experiences and may be inappropriate for their new surroundings. Markee (1997:12) describes a project that he worked on in Sudan, where he and his expatriate colleagues were 'linguistically, culturally, and professionally ill-equipped to devise solutions that were appropriate for ... or compatible with local conditions'. Holliday (1992) uses 'tissue rejection' as a metaphor to describe what happens to educational innovations when outsiders do not understand the 'informal orders' – the unspoken rules of behaviour that operate within a culture.

Rogers (1995) presents a different categorization of the participants in the innovation process, which is based on 'innovativeness'. He defines this as 'the degree to which an individual or other unit of adoption is relatively earlier in adopting new ideas than other members of a social system'. Rogers divides Kennedy's 'implementers' into innovators, early adopters, early majority, late majority, and laggards. He describes the 'ideal types' which fit into each category, using 'abstractions from empirical investigations' (1995:263). (See Figure 4.4.)

Innovators are 'the first 2.5 percent of the individuals in a system to adopt an innovation': they are venturesome, capable of coping with uncertainty, and they are willing to take risks and to accept the consequences if a new idea does not work. They are often part of an elite clique, however, and not part of the local peer network.

Early adopters are more integrated into the local system and generally play some leadership role. Rogers claims that change agents often seek out early adopters to serve 'as a local missionary for speeding the diffusion process' (op. cit:264).

The early majority are those who 'follow with deliberate willingness in adopting innovations, but seldom lead'.

The late majority will adopt an innovation eventually, but only if they can afford it, pressure from peers is great, and they are certain that it will work.

**Figure 4.4. Adopter categorization on the basis of innovativeness**

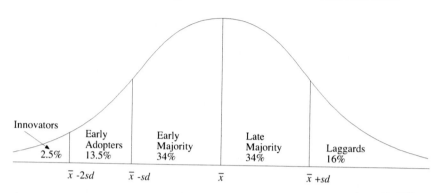

*Source*: (Rogers 1995:262). Reprinted with the permission of The Free Press, a Division of Simon & Schuster Adult Publishing Group, from DIFFUSION OF INNOVATIONS, 4th Edition by Everett M. Rogers. Copyright ©1995 by Everett M. Rogers. Copyright ©1962, 1971, 1983 by The Free Press. All rights reserved.

Laggards are the last to adopt an innovation. Rogers makes two important points about this category. The first has to do with the label 'laggard', which has a negative connotation. This is a result of a 'pro-innovation bias' in diffusion research: the assumption that all innovations should be diffused and adopted, that this should take place smoothly, and that there should not be any re-invention (op. cit:100). The second point has to do with who is at fault when an innovation that deserves to be adopted is not. 'Laggard' suggests that the blame lies with the individual; however, Rogers notes that 'System-blame may more accurately describe the reality ...' (op. cit:266).

In summary, there are different ways of categorizing the participants in the process of innovation. Kennedy (1988) describes participants at all stages in the process, each with different needs and agendas, and he stresses the need for communication and co-operation between all parties if the innovation is not to founder. Rogers offers a more detailed classification of the participants that Kennedy would label 'implementers'. Of special interest here are the 'early adopters', who seem to be key because of their ability to influence others to adopt or reject an innovation. (See the section on 'Why?' for further discussion of these categories.)

## Adopts

Under 'Adopts', Markee (1993) presents Rogers' (1983 – later Rogers 1995) five stages in the diffusion process, and Fullan's (1991) three stages in the innovation process. These were discussed in the section on 'The process of innovation' and will not be repeated here.

Markee (1993:31) also discusses the notion of 'levels of implementation', first written about by Hall and Loucks in 1977 and introduced into applied linguistics by Beretta (1990) in an evaluation of the Communicational

Teaching Project (CTP) in Bangalore. Beretta described this project as 'an attempt at methodological innovation based on unconscious learning strategies'. He was concerned that although a great deal had been written about the theory underlying the CTP, there was little evidence that teachers were implementing it in the way it was originally conceived. He designed an 'implementation measure' to investigate teachers' perceptions of the project and how they attempted to use its ideas in their own classrooms. The teachers were asked to produce a 'historical narrative' of their experience on the project and to fill in a bio-data form. Their responses were then rated according to three 'levels of implementation':

1. *Orientation* – The teacher is not fully aware of the CTP, nor how to use it, nor what its effect might be.

2. *Routine* – The teacher's awareness of the principles and methodology of the CTP is well-developed, and his/her use is relatively stable.

3. *Renewal* – The teacher is aware of the strengths and weakness of the CTP and is consciously seeking modifications that will benefit the learners. (Beretta 1990:324)

Beretta found that while 47% of the teachers fit into the Routine level and 13% into Renewal, a full 40% failed to reach an 'adequate' level of implementation. Most of the teachers in the higher levels of implementation were 'non-regular teachers', who were more highly qualified than regular classroom teachers, worked in training colleges or universities or the British Council, and felt a sense of 'ownership' towards the project as a result of having worked on it since its inception and helping to develop the approach 'rather than just carrying it out' (1990:328). Most of the teachers in the lower levels were ordinary school teachers, who were more likely to have problems with time, discipline and the language itself, and who had a tendency to revert to structural teaching. Beretta concluded that the CTP approach would not be appropriate for typical teachers in South India or in other regions where there were 'similar antecedent conditions' (1990:333. See also Chapter 7 of this volume for a discussion of 'antecedents'.). He recommended that programme planners and administrators should consider carefully the levels of English and the types of training that teachers need before they set out to promote fluency-based innovations (1990:233).

A further perspective on teacher change is presented by Freeman (1989), in the context of teacher education programmes. Freeman suggests that it is useful to think in terms of the 'evolutionary' nature of the change process rather than to expect immediate and apparent changes in those who have participated in a teacher education programme. He stresses that changes may take place on the inside even if they are not visible in a teacher's behaviour (e.g. changes in attitude); they may take a long time and they may not be quantifiable (1989:38).

These views take on particular significance for those who must evaluate whether an innovation such as a new examination has brought about desired outcomes. If the most profound changes are those of attitude (Kennedy 1988:529, and others) and if these are difficult to detect because they are not visible, there are serious implications for research design and analysis.

## What?

Under 'What?' Markee attempts to define the term 'innovation', using as a starting point a definition proposed by Nicholls:

> An innovation is an idea, object or practice perceived as new by an individual or individuals, which is intended to bring about improvement in relation to desired objectives, which is fundamental in nature and which is planned and deliberate. (1983:4, cited by Markee 1993:231)

Markee agrees that it is the perception of newness rather than objective newness which matters, citing Krashen and Terrell's 'Natural Approach' (1983) as an example of an approach regarded as innovatory despite the promoters' beliefs that it is only a reformulation and updating of traditional methods (Markee 1993:232). He feels that Nicholls' definition is inadequate as it does not deal with the following:

- the nature of the context that the innovation is being introduced into and how this can influence whether it is adopted or not,
- the question of what constitutes fundamental change. Markee believes that fundamental change occurs only when there is a change in values (see also Fullan 1991),
- the fact that some innovations are not improvements, and
- the question of whether innovations need to be planned and deliberate. (1993:233)

Markee offered his own definition of curricular innovation in 1997:

> Curricular innovation is a managed process of development whose principal products are teaching (and/or testing) materials, methodological skills, and pedagogical values that are perceived as new by potential adopters. (Markee 1997:46)

Here Markee addresses two of the issues he felt were missing from Nicholl's definition: the notion of fundamental change and the question of whether innovations need to be planned; however, he still does not deal with the issues of context and whether innovation is beneficial or not.

## Where?

Under 'Where?', Markee (1993) stresses the importance of understanding the socio-cultural context of an innovation, and refers to the way many factors (cultural, ideological, historical, political, economic, administrative, institutional and sociolinguistic) affected the innovation work he was involved in in Sudan (Markee 1986a and b). He also reproduces Kennedy's diagram of 'interrelating subsystems' (Figure 4.5, from Kennedy 1988:332), which illustrates not only how many subsystems are at play but also which ones exert the most influence on any innovation. Kennedy places what he considers to be the most powerful forces in the outer circles of his diagram, and he predicts problems if the manager of an innovation is either ignorant of these factors, does not take them into account, or tries to change them as part of the project (1988:333).

**Figure 4.5 The hierarchy of inter-relating subsystems in which an innovation has to operate (Kennedy 1988:332)**

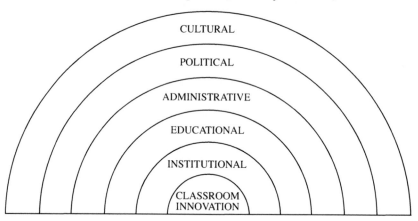

*Source*: Kennedy (1988:332)

Markee objects to Kennedy's assumption that the cultural subsystem is the most powerful one: he claims that such assumptions are based on personal beliefs, and that change agents with differing ideological views will come up with different conclusions. He believes that 'the relative importance of each factor varies from one context of implementation to another', and that language educators are really only at the 'pre-theoretical stage' of understanding which variables are most important or even what all of the variables are (ibid.).

It is interesting to note that all of the research accounts that Markee (1993) refers to have been written by 'outsiders': expatriates working in unfamiliar contexts where they had to learn about what was possible/acceptable by trial and error (Bowers 1983, Holliday and Cooke 1982, Kennedy 1982 and 1988, and Swales 1980 and 1989). This might well have had some bearing on whether the innovations they were associated with were welcomed and whether they survived after the outsiders' departure. (See also Fullan's questions about the source of ideas for change and the role of external agents of change in the earlier section on 'The process of innovation'.)

## When?

Under 'When?' Markee (1993) discusses what is known about rates of diffusion, focusing on Rogers' (1983 – later 1995) categories of adopters (innovators, early adopters, early majority, late majority and laggards – see section on 'Who?' above), and on the 'S-shaped diffusion curve', which represents the 'rate of adoption' of an innovation, or 'the relative speed with which an innovation is adopted by members of a social system' (Rogers 1995:22). Markee presents a simplified version of the S-shaped curve in his publications, but Rogers' own version is presented in Figure 4.6 on page 74.

Rogers claims that most innovations follow the same pattern: the rate of adoption is slow in the beginning, but after a certain number of people have adopted the innovation (the 'critical mass' – represented in the diagram by cross-hatching), others will join in more quickly. This is indicated by the steep climb in the curve, which eases off in later stages. According to Rogers the rate of adoption is determined by five types of variables: the perceived attributes of the innovation (see discussion under 'Why?' below), the type of innovation decision (see 'How?' below), the communication channels operating in the environment, the nature of the social system (see 'Where?' above), and the extent of the change agents' promotion efforts.

Fullan (1991) also comments on how long it takes for change to be effected and accepted. The initiation phase 'may be in the works for years', and implementation may take two years or more. Fullan claims that the total time from initiation to continuation may be three to five years for 'moderately complex changes', and that 'major restructuring efforts' can take five to ten years (1991:49). This time scale must be kept in mind when carrying out project evaluations: otherwise there is a risk of judging an innovation unsuccessful when in fact it is still being implemented.

**Figure 4.6 The rate of adoption of an innovation (the S-shaped diffusion curve)**

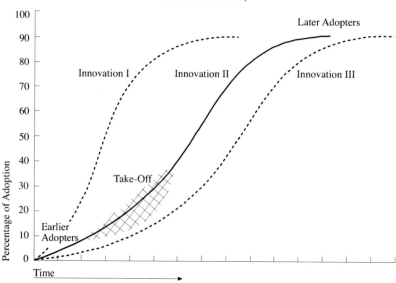

*Source*: Rogers (1995:11). Reprinted with the permission of The Free Press, a Division of Simon & Schuster Adult Publishing Group, from DIFFUSION OF INNOVATIONS, 4th Edition by Everett M. Rogers. Copyright ©1995 by Everett M. Rogers. Copyright ©1962, 1971, 1983 by The Free Press. All rights reserved.

# Why?

Under 'Why?' Markee discusses the characteristics of adopters and of successful innovations. He refers to Rogers' (1983) five categories of adopters (presented under 'Who?' above), but he emphasizes how an awareness of the characteristics of different types of adopters can help change agents to develop strategies for convincing them that the innovation is appropriate for them. Rogers uses the phrase 'audience segmentation' to refer to the use of different communication channels or messages to appeal to different categories of adopters (1983:275).

Change agents also need to keep in mind the 'characteristics of the innovation' (also called 'attributes of the innovation' – Rogers 1995:204), or those features which can either facilitate or hinder adoption. Rogers (1995) stresses that it is the potential adopters' perceptions of the characteristics rather than the real characteristics that affect whether they decide to adopt or reject an innovation (1995:209). He discusses five attributes which research has shown to be important (this list was originally proposed by Rogers and Shoemaker in 1971, after they surveyed the results of 1500 empirical and non-empirical studies) and which he believes provide for 'maximum generality and succinctness' (1995:208). These characteristics are *relative advantage, compatibility, complexity, trialability* and *observability*. Rogers gives the following definitions:

- *Relative advantage* is 'the degree to which an innovation is perceived as being better than the idea it supersedes'. The innovation may be seen to be more economical than the current practice or other available alternatives, it might confer more prestige upon the user, or it may offer other advantages. (1995:212)
- *Compatibility* is 'the degree to which an innovation is perceived as consistent with the existing values, past experiences and the needs of potential adopters'. (1995:224)
- *Complexity* is 'the degree to which an innovation is perceived as relatively difficult to understand and use'. (1995:242)
- *Trialability* is 'the degree to which an innovation may be experimented with on a limited basis'. (1995:243)
- *Observability* is 'the degree to which the results of an innovation are visible to others'. (1995:244)

Fullan (1991) also offers a list of factors which he believes affect the implementation of an innovation. These include:

- *need* (Do teachers or other potential adopters see the need for the proposed change?)
- *clarity* (Can they identify the defining features of the change?)
- *complexity* (What skills are required by the change, and what alterations in beliefs, strategies and materials? – 1991:71), and
- *quality* and *practicality* ('quality' is not defined, but 'practicality' refers to how well the innovation fits the teachers' situation, how focused it is and whether it includes 'how-to-do-it' possibilities) (Mortimore et al 1988, cited by Fullan 1991:72).

Fullan argues that many ambitious projects have their origin in political decisions, and that the implementation phase is forced on the users too quickly so that the originators can show that 'something is happening'. This often means that there are not enough good-quality materials to support the change, and inadequate practical guidance (1991:72-73).

Henrichsen (1989), in a study of an attempt to change teaching methods and materials in Japan in the 1950s and 1960s, proposed eleven attributes which he believed were crucial to the fate of an innovation. Among these were four attributes mentioned by Rogers (relative advantage, complexity, trialability and observability) and one mentioned by Fullan (practicality). The six attributes he adds to the list are:

- *originality* – this refers to whether an innovation is 'invented locally without benefit of a prior model' (origination), 'modified from external examples' (adaptation), or 'a standardized model copied with little change' (borrowing). These categories are taken from Pelz (1985).

- *explicitness* – this refers to the clarity of the description of the innovation, and 'the degree of its development or formulation' (1989:84). Henrichsen states that the originators of the term (Dow, Whitehead and Wright 1984) used it to refer to the rationale, philosophy, goals and objectives of an innovation.

- *status* – this refers to 'association with a higher social level which can import legitimacy and attract attention to an innovation'. Henrichsen claims that this can be a very influential factor in academic circles (1989:85).

- *flexibility/adaptability* – this refers to whether an innovation can be adjusted by users to fit their particular circumstances (1989:85).

- *primacy* – this refers to the timing of the innovation relative to other innovations. Innovations which appear after other innovations may have difficulty finding supporters. As Henrichsen explains:

  > Previously adopted practices form a barrier to the promotion of an innovation that is especially difficult to overcome in societies that value tradition and loyalty. (1989:85)

- *form* – this refers to whether an innovation is accompanied by concrete materials or whether it remains in the abstract as 'an instructional philosophy'. Publishers promote textbooks and send their authors on tour in order to create profits, but in so doing they also spread the ideas and the practice that are contained in the materials (Henrichsen 1989:85, referring to Richards 1984:13–4).

Markee (1997) describes six innovations in language teaching and lists the attributes which research has suggested promoted or inhibited the adoption of each of them. His list includes the five attributes proposed by Rogers, four proposed by Henrichsen (originality, explicitness, adaptability and form), and the concept of *feasibility*. Markee does not define 'feasibility', but we can infer from context that he is concerned with whether the innovation is perceived to be realistic, and whether potential adopters believe it can be achieved.

Finally, Stoller (1994) describes her study of innovation in Intensive English Programmes (IEPs) in the United States. She selected 13 variables for investigation. Most of these have been discussed above (compatibility, complexity, explicitness, feasibility, flexibility, originality, practicality, trialability and visibility (another term for 'observability') but Stoller adds dissatisfaction with past practices, improved status of IEP, improvement over past practices, and usefulness.

Stoller carried out a factor analysis which suggested that there were three 'composite' factors which determined whether proposed innovations would be seen as acceptable by potential adopters. Two of these factors – *Viability* (including practicality, feasibility and usefulness) and *Dissatisfaction* (including dissatisfaction with past practice and improvement over past practice) – were perceived to play strong facilitative roles in the implementation of innovation. A third factor – the *Balanced Divergence* factor (comprising explicitness, complexity, visibility, flexibility, and originality) – could be either facilitative or inhibitory, depending on the degree of the attribute present in a given innovation at a given time. For example, an innovation that was too original might strike potential adopters as unrealistic, and might therefore be rejected. However, another that was not original enough might also be rejected, on the grounds that it offered nothing new. A successful innovation will be one that fits into a narrow 'zone of innovation': the space between 'not too original' (or explicit, complex, visible etc.) and 'not original enough'.

Stoller also tries to determine the role these attributes play in relation to certain types of innovations, including innovations in evaluation. Here the factor that plays the most facilitative role is 'Dissatisfaction': potential adopters are more likely to accept a new form of evaluation if they are dissatisfied with the status quo or if they can see that the proposed change offers some improvement over past practice. The second most facilitative factor is 'Viability': a change in evaluation is more likely to be accepted if it seems practical, feasible and useful.

In summary, various specialists have argued that the characteristics of the innovation itself influence whether potential adopters will accept or reject it. Some, such as Markee (1997) and Stoller (1994), make explicit statements about whether certain factors are facilitative or inhibitory, and Stoller also investigates which characteristics are most important for which types of innovations. All of this information relates to the 'Why?' question in that change agents can decide which characteristics to emphasize and which to play down when they are attempting to sell their ideas to different segments of the population.

(Table 4.1 presents a comparison of the characteristics proposed by Rogers 1995, Fullan 1991, Henrichsen 1989, Markee 1997 and Stoller 1994. The characteristics are listed in the order they are discussed in the discussion of Henrichsen 1989. An asterisk signals that a particular characteristic is mentioned by the researcher in question.)

**Table 4.1 Characteristics of the innovation
(as discussed in the literature on educational innovation)**

| Characteristic | Rogers & Shoemaker 1971 (refined by Rogers 1983, 1995) | Fullan 1991 | Henrichsen 1989 | Markee 1997 | Stoller 1994 |
|---|---|---|---|---|---|
| originality | *referred to as 'compatibility' | | * | * | *referred to as 'compatibility' |
| complexity | * | * | * | * | * |
| explicitness | | *referred to as 'clarity" | * | * | * |
| relative advantage | * | *need | * | * | * improvement over past practices, usefulness |
| trialability | * | | * | * | |
| observability | * | | * | * | *referred to as 'visibility' |
| status | | | *from Havelock 1973 | | * |
| practicality | | * + 'quality' (undefined) | * | *feasibility + practicality | *feasibility + practicality |
| flexibility | | | *from Dow, Whitehead and Wright 1984 | * | * |
| primacy | | | *from Havelock 1973 | | |
| form | | | *from Richards 1984 | | |

# How?

Under 'How?' Markee (1997) describes five approaches to effecting change: four which are discussed by Havelock (1971) and one (the Centre-Periphery model) which derives from Phillipson (1992). Along with these models he discusses the strategies of change (Chin and Benne 1976) and leadership styles (Rondinelli et al 1990) which are often associated with them.

The *Social Interaction model* sees the diffusion of an innovation as a question of communication: individuals belong to one or more networks and information about an innovation spreads as colleagues interact with others in their own social groupings (Markee 1997:62–63). According to Henrichsen (1989:67) the advantage of this model is that it acknowledges that individuals are connected to one another in complex ways, and that group identity or loyalty can be an important factor in the implementation of innovations. A weakness is that it does not consider the psychology of the individual: what is going on inside the head of the user-adopter. This model is associated more with concrete innovations than with educational innovations, which are often affected by or affect the psychological processes of the potential adopters.

The *Centre-Periphery model* is more 'top-down': policy-makers decide whether an innovation will be adopted and what form it should take, and pass their decision on to subordinates (e.g. teachers) who must try to manage the implementation. Markee claims that this model is common with international aid agencies, and in countries with very centralized educational systems. The strategy for change is 'power-coercive' and the leadership style 'mechanistic'. This approach can lead to various problems, including passiveness amongst teachers, lack of ownership, and covert resistance (1997:63–64).

The *Research, Development and Diffusion (RD&D) model* assumes that research, long-term planning and specialist teams working on different aspects of development can ensure high-quality innovations. This is the most familiar model in the world of academics, and Markee states that it should be used when introducing 'complex technical innovations, such as language tests'. It can be accompanied by empirical-rational change strategies and an open-mechanistic leadership style, or, in very centralized systems, by power-coercive strategies and a mechanistic leadership style. The main problem associated with this model is that it may lead to changes which are only superficial, and not to changes in behaviour or beliefs (1997:65–66).

The *Problem-Solving model* is a 'bottom-up' approach, where it is the potential users of an innovation who decide whether there is a need for change. They identify possible solutions, trial and evaluate them (often through action research in their own classrooms), and repeat the process until they reach a satisfactory outcome. Markee states that this is the most common approach to change in education, at least in theory. The model is associated with normative-re-educative strategies, which may involve 'changes in attitudes, values, skills, and relationships'. The style of leadership is typically 'adaptive', which involves discussion and persuasion rather than power (1997:67–68).

*Linkage models* also exist, which incorporate features from the Social Interaction, RD&D and Problem-Solving models, and which acknowledge that different approaches should be used in different situations, depending on the type of problem that needs to be solved (Markee 1997:68). Henrichsen (1989) adds that linkage models highlight the connections between the outside agency responsible for introducing change and the intended user of the innovation, viewing change as the product of 'collaborative interaction'

(1989:68). These models allow for flexibility in the approach to change, but also demand considerable versatility from the change agent.

## Principles for and models of innovation

I have so far examined a number of ideas from innovation theory – ideas about the process of change, the meaning of change, participants in the process, the context, the rate of adoption, the characteristics of the innovation, and approaches to and strategies for effecting change. The challenge now is to synthesize all of these ideas, to make them accessible and coherent for future innovators. The purpose of this section is to present four attempts to bring these ideas together: a set of principles for curricular innovation by Markee (1997) and models of innovation by Rogers (1995), Smith (1991) and Henrichsen (1989). The latter two are discussed in some detail because of their relevance to language education and to ELT projects in other countries.

Markee (1997) presents a set of general principles of curricular innovation which are based on his experience as a change agent in Sudan and in the United States, and on the insights of various researchers in language education, general education, sociology and development planning. His principles are as follows:

1. Curricular innovation is a complex phenomenon.
2. The principal job of change agents is to effect desired changes.
3. Good communication among project participants is a key to successful curricular innovation.
4. The successful implementation of educational innovations is based on a strategic approach to managing change.
5. Innovation is an inherently messy, unpredictable business.
6. It always takes longer to effect change than originally anticipated.
7. There is a high likelihood that change agents' proposals will be misunderstood.
8. It is important for implementers to have a stake in the innovations they are expected to implement.
9. It is important for change agents to work through opinion leaders, who can influence their peers. (1997:172–180)

Rogers (1995) proposes a model of the Innovation-Decision Process, which takes into account the conditions which exist before the introduction of the innovation ('prior conditions'), the factors which affect activity in the Knowledge and Persuasion stages, and the communication channels which are at work throughout the process. (See Figure 4.2 above.) He presents a number of 'generalisations', based on relevant literature, which relate to stages in the Innovation-Decision Process, attributes of innovations, adopter categories, diffusion networks, the change agent, innovation in organizations, and the consequences of innovation. (See Appendix 5.) These are significant because of the influence they have had on several of the ELT specialists referred to in this chapter – most notably Henrichsen (1989), whose Hybrid Model of the Diffusion/Implementation Process will be discussed below.

Smith (1989) discusses ELT aid projects as an example of planned change. He surveys various views of what 'success' means in project terms, and then attempts to construct his own model of the variables involved in attempts to introduce change. His basic model shows five 'components of change': the Target System, the Management System, the innovation itself, the resources available, and the environment in which the change is supposed to take place. (See Figure 4.7 below.) Smith discusses each of these components in turn, explaining the kinds of questions would-be innovators need to ask and the sorts of problems evaluators need to be aware of when deciding whether an innovation has been successful.

**Figure 4.7 The components of change – static version**

*Source*: Smith (1989:11)

The '*Target System*' is composed of two main elements: the members of the system and the structures within the system. The members of the Target System can be categorized in several different ways (see the discussion of the Kennedy 1988 and Rogers 1995 categorizations under 'Who?' above), but Smith (1989) prefers to talk in terms of 'clients' (those who are seen to have the responsibility for creating change – e.g. Ministry officials), 'enablers' (those who are really responsible for organizing the change – often the funders of a change programme), 'changers' (those who are expected to change in some way – usually teachers or teacher trainers), and 'beneficiaries' (those whose lives should be better off as a result of the change – usually students, but sometimes teachers). The structures of the Target System include the hierarchies within the system, the incentive structures and the career structures. Those who wish to innovate need to be familiar with all the elements of the system and with the relationships between the various members.

They need to consider questions such as:

- Who wants the innovation to occur?
- Who needs it?
- Who will really benefit from it?
- Is there the will within the system to make an innovation work?
- Is there the skill?
- What are the chances for co-operation, or conflict?
- Is there enough stability in the system to ensure that an innovation will be implemented or that it will be sustained?

The '*Management System*' also consists of members and structures. The members of the Management System may also be members of the Target System, or they may be outsiders who have been brought in solely to organize and direct the implementation of the innovation. Their responsibilities include planning, negotiating, designing, co-ordinating, communicating, training others etc. It is crucial that this team has the characteristics and skills they need to introduce the innovation and to maintain the necessary momentum.

- Are the members of the Management System in agreement about what is needed?
- Are they able to work within the established structures?
- Do they have the necessary skills?

Smith then analyses the innovation itself. Each innovation will have its own combination of characteristics (see the discussion on 'Characteristics of the innovation' above), which makes it different from every other innovation and which make its outcomes difficult to predict with certainty. Would-be innovators need to consider whether the innovation will really solve the problem it is meant to solve, and how much time it will take before the innovation is fully adopted.

Smith also analyses the role of resources (financial, human, material and time) in innovations, and the importance of the environment. He stresses that the outcome of an innovation is 'a function of the compatibility of the environment with the innovation' (1989:13): the more alien the innovation the more difficult it will be to implement.

Smith criticizes his own visual representation of the components of change, stating how difficult it is to illustrate the effect of time on each of the components and the interaction of each of the components with all of the others. He discusses, for example, the interaction between the Target System and the Management System. The behaviour (values, goals etc.) of Target System members can influence the behaviour (values, goals) of the Management System members, and vice versa. Elements in the Target System can also affect the attributes of the innovation, the resources available, or factors in the environment, and all of these can affect the Target System. A large number of interactions can occur, each with a different effect. Smith attempts to capture these interactions in a set of fifteen 'propositions', which can be found in Appendix 6.

Henrichsen (1989) works along the same lines as Smith, preferring not to list principles or generalizations but to illustrate the many factors at work in the diffusion process and how these factors interact with one another. His 'Hybrid Model of the Diffusion/Implementation Process' is based on other models he analysed but found wanting. He claims that this model meets the criteria of coherence, abstractness, completeness, relevance to 'directed contact change' (the type of change effort which he believes was operational in the situation he describes), and cross-cultural applicability (the context of his study was Japan).

Henrichsen sees the diffusion process as having three key components: *Antecedents, Process* and *Consequences.*

The '*Antecedents*' component includes the conditions in place in the educational context or environment before an innovation is proposed. It corresponds roughly to the 'Prior Conditions' component in Rogers' model (Figure 4.2), and it contains some of the elements that Kennedy (1988) presented in his 'Interrelating Systems' diagram (Figure 4.4) and that Smith (1989) discusses in his 'Management System' and 'Target System' components (Figure 4.6). Henrichsen believes that innovators must be aware of the characteristics of the intended user system, the characteristics of the intended users, traditional pedagogical practices and the experiences of previous reformers before they decide on the type of innovation that would be most suitable for the circumstances. The characteristics of the intended user system include the structure and power relationships in schools and society. The characteristics of the intended users include their attitudes, values, norms and abilities. Traditional pedagogical practices derive from a variety of cultural and historical influences. The experiences of previous reformers will give insights into how they achieved their goals or what stood in their way if they did not. Two of the elements in the Antecedents section – the characteristics of the intended user system and the characteristics of intended users – serve not only as the foundation upon which new practices will be laid but will continue to influence the innovation in the second part of the model, the Process.

In the '*Process*' component, Henrichsen stresses the importance of analysing not only the source of an innovation (see Fullan's questions under 'The process of innovation'), the message, the plans and strategies (see section on 'How?') and the channels of communication, but also of analysing the

**Figure 4.8 The hybrid model of the diffusion/implementation process**

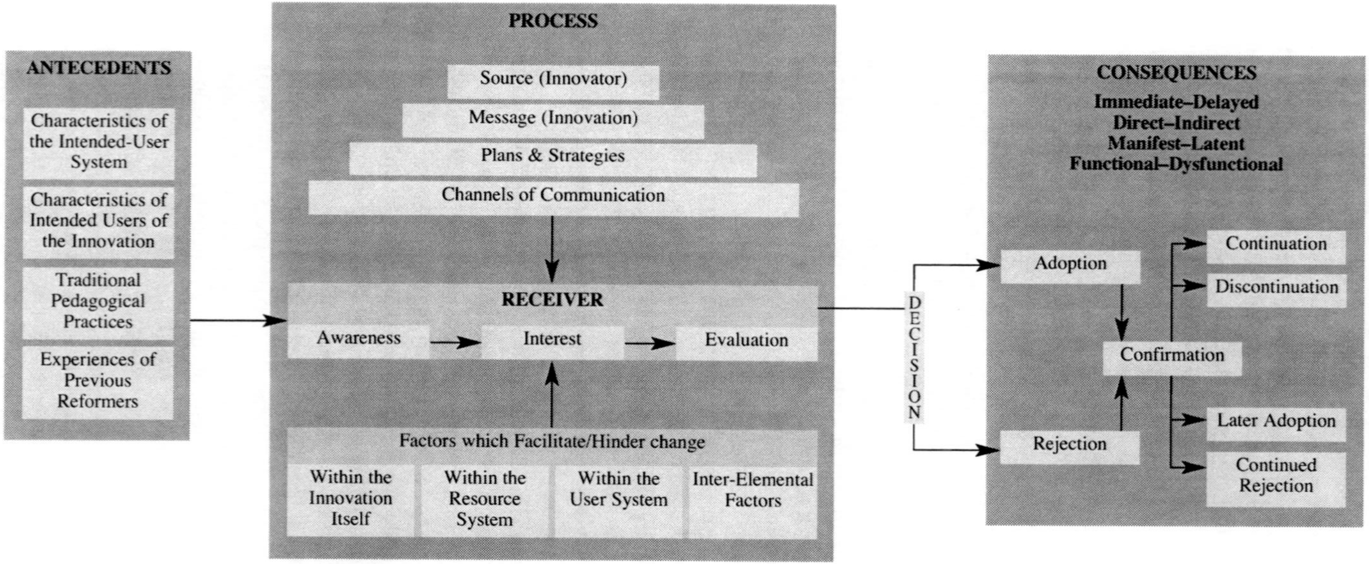

*Source:* Henrichsen (1989:80). Reprinted from *Diffusion of Innovations in English Language Teaching: The ELEC Effort in Japan, 1956–1968* by L E Henrichsen. Copyright © 1989 by L E Henrichsen. Reproduced with permission of Greenwood Publishing Group, Inc., Westport, CT.

factors which influence the change process, either facilitating or hindering change. (See the discussion of Stoller 1994.) These include factors within the innovation itself, factors within the resource system (this corresponds to Smith's 1991 Management System), factors within the intended-user system, and inter-elemental factors. Figure 4.9 presents the features that Henrichsen believes should be investigated under each heading.

The 'factors within the innovation itself' have been discussed above, but Henrichsen gives his own explanations of whether they are likely to promote or hold back change. The two factors he considered most likely to hinder change are 'originality' (because it may lessen the compatibility between an innovation and the intended users) and 'complexity' (1989:82).

### Figure 4.9 Factors that hinder/facilitate change

| Within the Innovation Itself | Within the Resource System | Within the Intended-User System | Inter-Elemental |
|---|---|---|---|
| Originality | Capacity | Geographic Location | Compatibility |
| Complexity | Structure | Centralization of Power and Administration | Linkage |
| Explicitness | Openness | | Reward |
| Relative Advantage | Harmony | Size of the Adopting Unit | Proximity |
| Trialability | | Communication Structure | Synergism |
| Observability | | | |
| Status | | Group Orientation and Tolerance of Deviancy | |
| Practicality | | Openness | |
| Flexibility/ Adaptability | | Teacher Factors | |
| Primacy | | Capacities | |
| Form | | Education Philosophy | |
| | | Examinations | |

*Source*: Henrichsen (1989:83). Reprinted from *Diffusion of Innovations in English Language Teaching: The ELEC Effort in Japan, 1956–1968* by L E Henrichsen. Copyright © 1989 by L E Henrichsen. Reproduced with permission of Greenwood Publishing Group, Inc., Westport, CT.

The 'factors within the intended-user system' are fairly easy to understand from their labels, apart from 'openness' ('the intended users' willingness to seek and receive new information from outside sources' 1989:89) and 'capacities' (the intended users' abilities 'to perform in new ways', as well as the physical capacities of the adopting unit. (See also Smith's Resources component 1989:91.)

The 'factors within the resources system' require some explanation.

Henrichsen gives these definitions:

- 'Capacity' refers to the system's ability to 'retrieve and marshal diverse resources' and to convey, store and retrieve large amounts of information. It also refers to the system's ability to influence potential adopters.
- 'Structure' refers to the division of labour and co-ordination of effort within the system, the coherence of its view of the client system, and its ability to plan and get messages across in a structured way.
- 'Openness' refers to whether the system has 'a willingness to help and a willingness to listen and to be influenced by user needs and aspirations'.
- 'Harmony' refers to the social relationship between all individuals within the resource system. (1989:87) (See also Smith's 1989 Management System and Kennedy's 1988 discussion of change agents.)

The 'inter-elemental factors' describe the interactions between the innovation, the resource system and the intended-user system. Henrichsen explains these as follows:

- 'Compatibility' refers to the degree of 'fit' between the innovation and the intended users, as well as to the fit between the resource system and the intended-user system.
- 'Linkage' refers to 'the number, variety and mutuality of contacts between the resource system and the user system'.
- 'Reward' refers to 'the frequency, immediacy, amount, mutuality of, planning, and structure of positive reinforcements' – such as economic gain, status, satisfaction, etc.
- 'Proximity' refers to 'the nearness in time, place, and context' of the resource system and the user system.
- 'Synergism' refers to 'the number, variety, frequency, and persistence of forces that can be mobilized to produce a knowledge utilization effect'. (1989:92-94) (See also Smith's 1989 discussion of interactions between components of change.)

The third component in Henrichsen's model is *'Consequences'*, which includes various elements from Rogers' (1995) discussion of the Decision and Confirmation stages, and also corresponds to the 'Outcome' mentioned by Fullan (1991). Henrichsen describes how a decision to adopt or reject an innovation can be changed at a later stage. He also labels the types of outcomes that can result: immediate or delayed, direct or indirect (when the outcome is influenced by another outcome instead of by the innovation), manifest (intended by the resource system and recognized by the users) or latent (neither recognized nor intended), and functional or dysfunctional (welcome or undesirable). (Rogers and Shoemaker 1971, cited in Henrichsen 1989:95)

Henrichsen applied this model to an investigation of an intended ELT innovation in Japan, using interviews, document analysis and reviews of the literature to reveal the antecedents and factors affecting the change process and to relate these to the eventual outcomes.

## Summary and way forward

The purpose of this chapter has been to explain a number of key ideas from the field of educational innovation, and to identify a framework for the analysis of the data from Sri Lanka. The key ideas are as follows:

- Innovation is different from other sorts of change in that it is deliberate, it is planned, and it is designed to bring about improvements in the system it is introduced into;
- The process of innovation is long and complex, consisting of many stages, and innovators should ask different sorts of questions at every stage to make sure that the innovation is going the way they want it to;
- It takes time before an innovation can bring about fundamental changes, so innovators should not be too hasty in their judgement of whether innovations have succeeded or failed;
- There are many participants involved in the process of innovation, each with their own needs and constraints. There must be good co-ordination and communication amongst all parties if the innovation is not to founder;
- The meaning of an innovation will be different for every individual involved in the process;
- A successful innovation will involve change on three levels: content, methodology and attitudes. It is easier for teachers to change the content of their teaching than to change their behaviour, and easier to change their behaviour than to change their attitudes or values;
- The users of an innovation will reach different 'levels of implementation'. Some will take full advantage of the innovation and be able to build on it, while others will never be able to respond to it in the way that was intended;
- It is difficult to measure some kinds of changes, especially changes in awareness or changes which are open-ended;
- It is necessary to analyse the context of an innovation in order to judge whether it is likely to be adopted. The context involves not only the classroom and the school, but the educational system, the political system, the cultural system etc.
- The rate of adoption of an innovation is determined by many factors, including the characteristics of the innovation, the potential user system, and the potential users;
- Every innovation has a number of characteristics, some of which may

facilitate its adoption and some of which may hinder it. Innovators may need to emphasize different characteristics when trying to promote the innovation to different potential adopters.

- There are several models for introducing change, each accompanied by specific strategies and leadership styles. Some approaches are more suitable for certain types of innovations. Linkage models incorporate features from different types of models, and acknowledge that flexibility is needed to suit different circumstances.

It is clear that different commentators see the change phenomenon in different ways: in this brief review alone we have seen two ways of describing the process of innovation, three ways of categorizing participants, five ways of describing the characteristics of an innovation, etc. We have also discussed four attempts to synthesize the lessons that have been learned about innovation (Markee 1997, Rogers 1995, Smith 1991 and Henrichsen 1989). There is overlap between some of the descriptions and categorizations, but most of them also contribute something new to this field of study.

We saw in Chapter 3 that there were many factors which might affect whether an examination had positive or negative impact. What was lacking, however, was a way of organizing these factors which would help future innovators to make predictions about the likely outcomes of their attempts to innovate through testing and to carry out effective investigations of the impact of their testing programmes.

There are advantages in using any of the syntheses that have been presented, but I chose to use the Henrichsen framework as the starting point for my analysis of the data from Sri Lanka. Rogers' 1995 model (Figure 4.2) and his 'generalizations' are useful but the distinctions that he makes are sometimes too fine for the type of data that I collected – for example, he gives detailed information about adopter categories and diffusion networks which I cannot confirm or contradict because I did not focus on these points during the group interviews. In contrast, his discussion of the characteristics of innovation is quite general: he refers to only a handful of characteristics of the innovation when I have references in my data for twice that number. Smith's 1991 framework 'propositions' are well explained, but it is difficult to work out how time enters the picture and to pinpoint exactly which characteristics to look for in each of the five major components. Henrichsen's framework incorporates many of the features that Rogers offers, but he adds ideas from other specialists, and he has arranged these visually so that it is easier to see which factors are most important at which particular stages in the process. His lists of characteristics of the innovation, the resource system and the user system are full and informative, but not so detailed that they become unmanageable. The framework seemed to offer the right amount of descriptive power while retaining a degree of flexibility: it provides a clear and user-friendly starting point for the first stages of my analysis.

# Methodology

## Background

In Chapter 2, I described an attempt to improve English language teaching in Sri Lanka by introducing a new examination, and I presented the findings of a project which investigated whether the examination had had any impact on classroom teaching. One of the questions emerging from this project was whether it was possible to identify the factors which influenced the type of impact that appeared in the system. In Chapters 3 and 4, I reviewed research into examination impact and educational innovation, attempting to identify concepts and themes which could be drawn upon in a new investigation to identify these factors.

In this chapter I describe my approach to data collection and analysis. The results of the analysis will follow in Chapters 6–11.

## A qualitative approach to the investigation

The general approach that I used during this investigation was a 'qualitative' one. Qualitative approaches are becoming more common in the area of applied linguistics (Eisner and Peshkin 1990, cited in Lazaraton 1995:456), but it is still difficult to find a simple explanation of what distinguishes them from the approaches which are referred to as 'quantitative'. Lazaraton writes that there is a lack of explanatory material written by or for applied linguists and that this 'undoubtedly accounts at least in part for the lack of consensus on, and the confusion about, what qualitative research is and what it can and cannot do' (1995:458). There is more discussion in other areas of the social sciences, but even here it is difficult to find a precise definition of 'qualitative' research or a straightforward account of how qualitative and quantitative research differ. Mason (1996:4) believes that it is a strength of qualitative research that it 'cannot be neatly pigeonholed and reduced to a simple and prescriptive set of principles'. She argues that this is because qualitative researchers come from many different philosophical traditions, including phenomenology, ethnomethodology, and symbolic interactionism (1996:3). One of the features these traditions have in common though is their 'interpretivist' orientation: their concern with 'how the social world is interpreted, understood, experienced or produced' (1996:4). For Patton (1987:20) the challenge to the researcher is to develop an empathetic understanding of the participants' way of seeing the world, rather than imposing a particular framework or set of ideas upon them.

Although Mason and Patton do not give definitions, they discuss features which they believe typify qualitative investigations. Mason mentions methods of data gathering which are 'flexible and sensitive to the social context' (not 'rigidly standardized or structured' as in some types of experimental research), and data analysis methods which are 'holistic' and which 'involve understandings of complexity, detail and context' (1996:4). Patton mentions naturalistic enquiry (recording what happens normally rather than attempting to manipulate the situation as part of the research), inductive analysis, 'going into the field', a holistic perspective (examining not only the phenomenon which is of interest but the context in which it is situated), a developmental perspective (Patton focuses on programme evaluation and assumes that programmes are always in a state of flux), and the use of case studies (1987:13).

Stake (1995) presents three major differences between qualitative and quantitative research: qualitative research stresses understanding rather than explanation, it requires a personal rather than an impersonal role for the researcher, and it views knowledge as constructed rather than discovered (1995:37). Also important are a holistic treatment of phenomena, which recognizes the importance of 'temporal, spatial, historical, political, economic, cultural, social and personal contexts' (compare with Kennedy's 1988 diagram of 'interrelating subsystems' Figure 4.5); and a 'non-interventionist' stance from the researcher (naturalistic observation). Finally, Miles and Huberman (1994) present what they consider to be recurring features of qualitative research: intense and/or prolonged contact with 'the field', a holistic view of the context, an attempt to gather the local actors' point of view, relatively little standardized instrumentation, and analyses which are based on words instead of numbers (1994:6-7).

Figure 5.1 presents a digest of the features mentioned by each of these researchers. The features mentioned most often – namely, the interpretivist perspective, naturalistic enquiry, holistic data analysis, and the importance of field work – can all be found in this investigation. I had already spent a significant amount of time in the field during the four years of the evaluation project. I used methods of enquiry which attempted to capture important aspects of the teachers' behaviour and attitudes without attempting to influence them (naturalistic enquiry). I recognized the importance of local context from the outset (holistic data analysis), and I concentrated on presenting the teachers' meanings, in their own words, rather than asking them to comment on my views or expectations (interpretivist perspective).

This approach seemed appropriate in the final stage of the examination evaluation project, when I was interested not so much in the amount of

## Figure 5.1 Features of qualitative research, by researcher

(An asterisk marks the presence of this feature in definitions and explanations given by each researcher.)

| Feature | Mason (1996) | Patton (1987) (1994) | Stake (1995) | Miles & Huberman |
|---|---|---|---|---|
| interpretivist perspective | * '...concern with how the social world is interpreted' | * '...an empathetic understanding of the participants' way of seeing the world' | * '...knowledge is constructed rather than discovered' | * '...an attempt to gather the local actors' point of view' |
| naturalistic methods of enquiry | * '...flexible and sensitive to the social context' | * '...recording what happens normally' | * '...a non-interventionist stance | * 'relatively little standardized instrumentation |
| holistic data analysis | * 'understandings of complexity, details and context' | * 'examining not only the phenomenon... but the context' | * 'recognizing the importance of context' | * 'a holistic view of the context' |
| importance of field work | | * | | * |
| inductive analysis | | * | | |
| developmental perspective | | * | | |
| use of case studies | | * | | |
| personal role for researcher | | | * | |
| analysis based on words rather than numbers | | | | * |

examination impact that was visible as in the explanations teachers could give of how the examination and other factors shaped their actions and reactions.

However, using a qualitative approach did not mean going into the research with no preconceptions or hypotheses about what might emerge. Davis (1995:436) explains that it is a misconception that qualitative researchers have no underlying notions about the area they are investigating. I did not have a theoretical framework when I planned the group interviews, but I did have views on what might be important, given my experience during the earlier years of the project. (This included carrying out my own observations during frequent visits to Sri Lanka, analysing several hundred observation schedules completed by the local researchers, and analysing nearly 650 questionnaires to teachers and teacher advisers. See Alderson and Wall 1989, 1990 and 1991 for details.) There were certain factors which would almost certainly be affecting the amount and type of impact the examination could have on teaching, including the teachers' understanding of the textbook and the examination, their access to teacher's guides and official publications about the examination, and the amount and type of teacher training they had been exposed to. I hoped to learn more about these factors and to become aware of others once it was possible to talk to teachers directly and not just observe their behaviour in the classroom or read their responses in questionnaires. I also hoped that this co-operation with many informants would provide examples of these factors and show how they interacted with one another.

I was reluctant to force my notions on to my informants during the interviews because I wished to gain an understanding of their views of the world and see if they could tell me things that I had not thought of. This attitude fits into the 'interpretive qualitative research' paradigm, where the researcher attempts to gain an 'emic' perspective – that is, 'an understanding of the actors' meanings for social actions', as opposed to an 'etic' or outsider's perspective (Davis 1995:433). (See also Norton Peirce and Stein 1995:57 on investigating 'the way individuals make sense of their own experience'.) What I was seeking was the participants' own 'meaning of change', described by Fullan (1991) and discussed in Chapter 4 of this book.

## An *ex-post facto* perspective

It is important to remember the timing of the group interviews in relation to other data-gathering exercises in the Sri Lankan O level Evaluation Project. The project included a number of separate studies: a baseline investigation, several questionnaire surveys, document and materials analyses, and a two-year observation programme. The group interviews took place near the end of the observation programme, nearly three years after the introduction of the new examination. While the observations had provided a great deal of information about the teachers' behaviour in the classroom, they had not provided much insight into the teachers' way of seeing the world. The purpose of the interviews was to get teachers to talk about their teaching, before and after the introduction of the textbooks and the examination, in the hope that they would provide information that could help to explain why the impact of the examination took the form that it did. This meant adopting an *ex-post facto* perspective, one defined by Kerlinger as a:

> systematic empirical inquiry in which the scientist does not have direct control of independent variables because their manifestations have already occurred or because they are inherently not manipulable. Inferences about relations among variables are made, without direct intervention, from concomitant variation of independent and dependent variables. (1973:379)

What this means in less technical language is that the researcher observes the current state of affairs (in this case, the way teaching was taking place in 1990 and 1991), and works back in time to establish possible causes.

This type of design is appropriate in situations where an experimental design is not possible – when the researcher cannot manipulate factors to test out cause-and-effect hypotheses, when it is not possible to control the other variables, or when attempting to control them would be 'impractical, costly or ethically undesirable' (Cohen and Manion 1994:150).

# Triangulation

Cohen and Manion (1994:238) claim that the teaching-learning process in schools is so complex that using a single method of investigation 'yields only limited and sometimes misleading data'. They seem to support Smith's (1975) belief that research methods 'act as filters through which the environment is selectively experienced', and Lin's (1976) warning that the data that is generated may only be 'artefacts' of a particular method of collection (Cohen and Manion 1994:233). They recommend that researchers gather data by several different methods, and they claim that the greater the difference is between the methods the more confidence the researchers can have in their findings.

The attempt to view a phenomenon from more than one angle is known as *'triangulation'*, a term first used by Webb, Campbell, Schwartz and Sechrest in 1965 (Miles and Huberman 1994:266-267). There are several types of triangulation. Cohen and Manion focus on 'methodological triangulation' (using different means of data collection – observation, interview, etc.), but they also refer to Denzin's (1970) categorization of triangulation by time (collecting data from the same group at different points in time), space (using different groups of people), investigator (using more than one observer or analyst), theory (comparing competing theories), and combined levels (comparing different levels of analysis – the individual, the group, the organization, society, etc.) (1994:235-238). Miles and Huberman refer to a later version of Denzin's 'classic distinctions' (1978), and add a new category of their own – triangulation by data type (text, tape recordings etc.) (1994:267).

Several types of triangulation were used in the earlier stages of the evaluation project: methodological (analysis of official documents, inspection of classroom materials, interviews with individuals, and classroom observation), time (visiting the same classrooms at different points in the year), space (visiting classrooms in different parts of the country and administering questionnaires in different venues), investigator (using a number of different classroom observers and more than one on several occasions) and data type. It was not until the end of the study that I decided to use group interviews, to explore teachers' reactions to the examination in more depth than had been possible in the questionnaires and observations.

# Interviews

Cannell and Kahn define an interview as:

> a two-person conversation initiated by the interviewer for the specific purpose of obtaining research-relevant information, and focused by him on content specified by research objectives of systematic description, prediction, or explanation. (1968, cited in Cohen and Manion 1994:271)

Patton believes that interviews 'add an inner perspective to outward behaviours' (1987:109). They provide an opportunity to explore what is going on inside respondents' heads (their memories, experience, complex thinking), while still allowing the interviewer some degree of control over what is talked about and in what depth of detail (Stake 1995:66).

Cohen and Manion summarize the relative advantages of interviews and questionnaires, indicating that interviews provide more opportunities for personalization, questioning and probing; provide a better rate of return; and put less emphasis on the writing skills of the respondents. However, it is usually more difficult to reach a large number of respondents, there is more need for data reduction, and there are more possible sources of error (the interviewer and the coding system, as well as the instrument and the sample) (1994:272).

Interviewing seemed an appropriate technique as it would allow me to probe into areas that the local researchers had not investigated, either because they saw no reason to ask for more detailed explanations of what they had observed or because they did not have the time or the confidence to go into details. An example of one such area would be the teachers' approach to teaching reading:why were so many teachers continuing to use a word-by-word approach in their classrooms when this was discouraged in the teacher's guides?

One of the challenges of interviewing would be to create enough trust so that the teachers would want to communicate and not hold back what they were thinking (Cicourel 1964). Another would be sorting out how much of what the teachers said was accurate rather than an attempt to be 'helpful' (giving answers they thought I would like to hear) or to present themselves in a good light. There was also the risk that respondents would not be able to remember what they had experienced or explain what they were feeling (Tuckman 1972, cited by Cohen and Manion 1994:282-283). I hoped that I could overcome some of these problems by using techniques such as rephrasing questions to make them more comprehensible, paraphrasing what I thought was being said and asking for reactions to my interpretation, and repeating some questions later in the interview to check the consistency of the responses.

There were extra challenges using group interviews. Patton (1987:135-136) mentions four of these. The first is a technical matter: it is not possible to ask as many questions in a group interview if the interviewer wants everyone to respond to each question. The other challenges have to do with social interaction: the interviewer must ensure that no one dominates and that everyone gets the same opportunity to speak; there may be 'unexpected diversions' if the respondents know one another (conflicts, power plays); and the notion of confidentiality loses its meaning if those who are present know one another. Watts and Ebbutt (1987) also refer to the difficulty of discussing personal matters in company, and they point out that it may also be difficult for interviewers to go into depth with any individual since group dynamics work against this (in Cohen and Manion 1994:287). One aspect that I did not anticipate was how difficult it might be to gather information from teachers with lower levels of English. They would find it difficult not only to answer my questions, but also to interact with other teachers.

However, there are also advantages in interviewing a number of teachers together. The more people there are the more varied the views are likely to be, which makes for a broader discussion (Watts and Ebbutt 1987, in Cohen and Manion 1994:287). The information which emerges may also be of a higher quality, because the participants will listen and check one another (Patton 1987:135). It was also apparent during all of the interviews that the teachers enjoyed hearing what other teachers had to say: they had few opportunities to discuss teaching even within their own schools, and there were few training events where they could present their own views or learn from listening to the views of others. (See Fullan's notion of 'the daily subjective reality of teachers', as discussed in Chapter 4 of this book.)

## The form of the interview

The type of interview that I chose to conduct is what Cohen and Manion would call 'unstructured', where the questions are determined by the purpose of the research but where the interviewer is free to vary the content, wording and sequence to suit the interview situation (Kerlinger 1973:481). Patton (1987) uses the phrase 'interview guide approach' to refer to the same sort of procedure. An interview guide lists topics that the interviewer wishes to cover, but it does not prescribe the order of the questions or their wording. The interview guide reminds the interviewer to cover the same topics with every respondent, but it allows him/her to respond to the discussion as it develops rather than have to stick to a pre-determined script. Patton claims that the interview guide is very useful in group interviews, as it 'keeps interaction focused, but allows individual perspectives to emerge' (1987:111).

Stake (1995) discusses two types of questions: 'topical information questions', which elicit information needed for describing the situation under investigation (1995:25), and 'issue questions', which 'direct attention to the major concerns and perplexities to be resolved' (1995:28). Most of the questions in my interview guide were of the topical information variety, eliciting descriptions, beliefs and opinions. (See Appendix 7.)

Examples of topical information questions include:

- How did you teach your students before *English Every Day?*
- What do you remember of the Old Syllabus examination?
- Did it influence your teaching in any way?
- Did you have any problems during this period?

I used issue questions during the analysis stage of the research, when I had a better idea of what the teachers' concerns were and of the factors which appeared most often in their responses. Examples of issue questions would be:

- Was there any difference in the amount or types of impact in schools in richer and poorer areas?
- Which factors were the most 'facilitative' in the attempt to produce positive examination impact?

Patton (1987) classifies questions according to whether they ask for information about background characteristics, knowledge, experience or behaviour, opinion or belief, feelings, or sensory perceptions (1987:115-120). My questions elicited responses in all categories apart from sensory perceptions.

The interview guide covered six general topics:

1. What and how did teachers teach before the introduction of the *English Every Day* textbooks?
2. How did they prepare their students for the Old Syllabus examination?
3. What and how had they taught since the introduction of the *English Every Day* textbooks?
4. How did they prepare their students for the new examination?
5. What were their opinions of the new examination and did they believe it affected their teaching?
6. What were their main problems in teaching, under the Old Syllabus and *English Every Day?*

The plan was to cover three or four topics with each group, as time constraints would make it difficult to cover all the topics with any one group. (I judged that two hours was the outside limit for teachers who were talking to me in their free time.) The questions in the interview guide would serve as 'starters' which might lead to further questions, to clarify points already made or to explore new issues.

## The sample

The sample consisted of 64 Sri Lankan teachers: 57 Year 11 teachers (one of whom was also an in-service adviser responsible for 83 schools), five Year 10 teachers, a teacher in a pre-service District English Language Improvement Centre (DELIC), and the Co-ordinator of a Regional English Support Centre (RESC)). All of the teachers were using the national textbook series, *English Every Day*. They were based in 11 different areas of the country (see map in Figure 5.2), and 37 (58%) of them had been observed during the two-year observation programme. The sample for the observation programme had been a 'stratified purposeful sample' (Miles and Huberman 1994:28), in which schools had been selected according to their medium of instruction, whether they were urban or rural, and whether they had a reputation for high, average, or low-achievement. All of the teachers who were observed in the later stages of the programme were invited to participate in the interviews, and 37 accepted. Most of the teachers were from Sinhala-medium schools. About 70% of these taught in urban areas, and were divided evenly between high- and average-achieving schools. About 25% of the teachers who taught in rural areas worked in average-achieving schools and 75% worked in low-achieving schools.

Of the 27 teachers who had not been observed, 13 were members of a Regional English Support Centre (RESC) in Nuwara Eliya. There had been no observations in Nuwara Eliya because none of the local researchers lived in the region, but the Co-ordinator of the RESC agreed to invite teachers to take part in the interviews. Six other teachers were from the north and east of the country and were attending a training seminar in Anuradhapura, where I was an observer. It had not been possible to observe classrooms in the north and the east because of political problems, so I asked these teachers if I could take advantage of their presence in Anuradhapura to find out more about teaching and testing activities in their parts of the country. Five other teachers were from the same school in a coastal town to the north of Colombo, and the last three were teachers who had heard that interviews were taking place in their schools and decided to attend out of interest. These 27 teachers made up an 'opportunity sample', one which allows researchers to 'follow new leads' and 'take advantage of the unexpected' (Miles and Huberman 1994:28).

The details of the full sample can be seen in Figure 5.3. About 75% of the schools were Sinhala-medium, with the other quarter divided equally between Tamil-medium and mixed-medium. About 65% were urban schools. There

**Figure 5.2 Map of Sri Lanka, showing where the interview
subjects were working**

were similar numbers of high, average, and low-achieving schools (16, 18 and
12 respectively), with an urban-rural distribution as follows:

| | | |
|---|---|---|
| Urban *high-achieving* | 16 (35%) | (n = 46) |
| Urban *average-achieving* | 14 (30%) | |
| Urban *low-achieving* | 5 (11%) | |
| | | |
| Rural *high-achieving* | 0 | |
| Rural *average-achieving* | 4 (9%) | |
| Rural *low-achieving* | 11 (24%) | |

There may have been a slight bias in the sample in that none of the teachers

### Figure 5.3 Details of the sample, group interviews, November 1991
### (n = 64 teachers)

| Interview venue | No. of teachers (n=64) | No. of years of experience | No. of Sinhala, Tamil, and mixed-medium schools (n=54) | | No. of urban and rural schools (n=54) | | No. of high, medium and low-achieving schools (n=54) | |
|---|---|---|---|---|---|---|---|---|
| Anuradhapura (teachers from North and East) | 6 (1 Yr 10) | estimated 5–20 years | Sinhala<br>Tamil<br>? | 2<br>2<br>1 | Urban<br>Rural<br>? | 1<br>1<br>3 | High<br>? | 1<br>4 |
| Asgiriya | 5 (1 Yr 10) | 1–17 years | Sinhala | 3 | Urban | 3 | Average<br>Low | 2<br>1 |
| Colombo Centre | 7 | not recorded | Sinhala | 6 | Urban<br>Rural | 4<br>2 | High<br>Average<br>Low | 2<br>3<br>1 |
| Colombo-Wellawatte | 6 | 19–27 years | Sinhala<br>Mixed | 3<br>3 | Urban<br>? | 5<br>1 | High<br>Average<br>Low<br>? | 2<br>2<br>1<br>1 |
| Nugegoda | 6 | 4–21 years | Sinhala | 6 | Urban<br>Rural | 4<br>2 | High<br>Average<br>Low | 2<br>3<br>1 |
| Nuwara Eliya | 13 (5 Yr 10, 1 DELIC, 1 RESC) | 1.5–34 years | Sinhala<br>Tamil<br>Mixed | 7<br>1<br>3 | Urban<br>Rural<br>? | 6<br>2<br>3 | High<br>Average<br>Low<br>? | 1<br>3<br>4<br>3 |
| Ratnapura | 8 | 5–20 years | Sinhala | 8 | Urban<br>Rural | 4<br>4 | High<br>Average<br>Low | 2<br>4<br>2 |
| Tangalle | 3 | not recorded | Sinhala | 3 | Urban | 3 | High | 3 |
| Welimada | 5 | 5 months–19 years | Sinhala<br>Mixed | 4<br>1 | Urban<br>Rural | 3<br>2 | High<br>Average<br>Low | 2<br>1<br>2 |
| Wennapuwa | 5 (same school) | 5–20 years | Sinhala | 1 | Urban | 1 | High | 1 |
| TOTAL | 64 | 5 months–34 years | Sinhala<br>Tamil<br>Mixed<br>? | 41<br>6<br>6<br>1 | Urban<br>Rural<br>? | 34<br>13<br>7 | High<br>Average<br>Low<br>? | 16<br>18<br>12<br>8 |

were participating in the interviews as part of their ordinary duties: they chose to accept the invitation and gave up their free time to join in the discussion. This may indicate that they were more interested in teaching matters than other teachers in the population or that they were more confident in talking about what they were doing. This cannot be known for certain though, so there is no reason to doubt that the sample was representative of most secondary schools in Sri Lanka. It included a wide range of geographical areas (nationally and in terms of the urban-rural divide), different media of instruction and levels of achievement, and teachers with varying degrees of experience.

## Procedure

All but two of the interviews were organized by members of the Impact Study observation team, who invited teachers they had observed to come to a discussion about teaching and testing in Sri Lanka, with 'a consultant to the Ministry of Education' (me). Approximately 70% of the teachers they invited accepted the invitation.

The interviews in Nuwara Eliya and Anuradhapura were organized in a different way, as explained in the previous section on 'The sample'.

The 'normal' interviews were held in schools, mainly, but not always, at the end of the school day. Present at most of them were the observer who had organized the session and the head of the O level examination design team (hereafter referred to as the 'exam developer'), who was there to learn more about how teachers were reacting to the examination. The observer and the exam developer were asked to play a low-profile role during the proceedings so that the teachers would not feel self-conscious about giving their own views. Both of them would monitor the discussion carefully and intervene if they felt it was necessary to correct misunderstandings or to explain references whose importance I might not understand. They were also ready to translate into Sinhala if any Sinhala-speaking teachers had difficulties expressing themselves in English. This was only necessary in one session, to allow a teacher with quite low proficiency to explain her views fully. The exam developer translated this teacher's contributions during the interview and provided a more complete explanation of what had been said afterwards for the interview transcript. (There were no Tamil-speaking observers at this stage of the project, so if any Tamil-speaking teacher had had problems it would have been necessary to rely on other teachers to translate.)

All of the interviews followed the same procedure, which involved asking every member of the group the same question and following up interesting leads before going on to the next question. The technique was appropriate for drawing teachers out and for checking that what they were saying was understandable. The interviews were recorded so that they would be available for detailed analysis. (See Wall 1999 for a full account of the interviewing and transcribing processes.)

# Framework for data analysis

As explained earlier, I did not have a theoretical framework when I planned the interviews, so I based my questions on insights I had gained when analysing questionnaires and observations in earlier stages of the project. My first analysis of the transcripts was also carried out without the benefit of theory, as there was little discussion of examination impact in the applied linguistics literature at the time and almost no awareness of discussions which were taking place in general education. I constructed my own framework as I proceeded through the data, noting down anything that the teachers said which related either to the examination and their teaching, or to other conditions which might have affected the teaching situation. The first analysis had to be done quickly, so that the results could be incorporated into the final report for the funding body, but it revealed many factors which could be preventing the examination from having the impact that was intended. These included an inadequate understanding of the principles underlying the teaching materials, problems with pre-service and in-service training, and poor resourcing. (See Wall 1996:349-350 for further factors.) Many of the factors related not to the examination itself but to other features in the environment. This convinced me that I needed to look beyond language testing to find explanations for why the new examination was not working the way that it was meant to. The field of educational innovation seemed the obvious place to turn to (Wall and Alderson 1993:68, Alderson and Wall 1993:127-128). What I hoped to discover was a theory that I could use as a starting point for a more thorough analysis of the same data, which I could refine during the analysis and perhaps use in other assessment settings.

According to Snow a theory is:

> a symbolic construction designed to bring generalisable facts (or laws) into systematic connections. It consists of a) a set of units (facts, concepts, variables) and b) a system of relationships among the units. These are defined and interpreted in statements that are understandable to others and that make predictions about empirical events. (1973:78)

For Kaplan the purpose of theory was to enable people to learn *from* experience, rather than *through* it (1964, cited in Snow 1973:78). This purpose matched my own but it was difficult to find a set of ideas which was formulated enough to match Snow's requirements. Fullan (1991), for example, presented Snow's 'facts, concepts and variables', but he did not show how these ideas fit together in one overall scheme. Rogers (1995) presented several useful schemes, one of which is reproduced in Figure 4.2, but it was equally difficult to see how all of his ideas related to one another.

A model is 'a well-developed descriptive analogy used to help visualize, often in a simplified or miniature way, phenomena that cannot be easily or directly observed' (Snow 1973:81). London (1949) wrote that the form of a model could range from 'the mathematical rigor of the closely articulated symbolical...to the free looseness of the suggestive metaphor and simile...' (cited in Snow 1973:82). What I was looking for was something between these two extremes, which offered coherence while still being flexible enough to accommodate the features of my particular data set. Henrichsen's Hybrid Model of the Diffusion/Implementation Process (Figure 4.8) seemed the most appropriate in the end. It incorporated many of the notions that had emerged from the first analysis of the data, including the different stages in the change process, characteristics of the innovation itself and the context, and different types of consequences, and it displayed them in a way that made the relationships between them clear. My main reservation was that it did not pay much attention to the characteristics of teachers and learners during the implementation phase of the innovation, as opposed to during the antecedent period. However, this did not prevent me from opting to try out the model since, as I have already explained, I wanted to use it as a starting point for developing a new framework rather than as a rule which had to be obeyed unquestioningly.

The first analysis of the data showed that there was not enough information to make significant comments about some sections of Henrichsen's model. This was to be expected since my focus when planning and conducting the interviews had been on whether the teachers believed that examination impact had occurred rather than on their impressions of the change process. I knew that I would find little that was relevant to the experience of previous reformers, the source of the innovation, the plans and strategies used by the innovators, the channels of communication, the characteristics of the resource system and inter-elemental factors. I believed, however, that there was useful information about the antecedent situation, the characteristics of the innovation and the user system, and about the consequences of the decision to introduce a new examination. I hoped that even though the data was not originally intended for an analysis of innovation, ideas would still emerge that could provide useful lessons for innovators in the future.

## Analysing the data

The first step in the analysis was coding the data: labelling segments that corresponded to key concepts. According to Seidel and Kelle:

> codes represent the decisive link between the original 'raw data', that is, the textual material such as interview transcripts or field notes, on the one hand, and the researcher's theoretical concepts on the other. (1995:52, cited in Coffey and Atkinson 1996:27)

The 'concepts' included many features of Henrichsen's model and ideas that emerged from my reading of the literature on examination impact. My task was to identify all of the utterances that related to a particular concept, bring them together to compare them, identify the ways in which they were similar or different, and decide whether anything new was emerging which might lead to deeper insights about the nature of the concept. This would lead to more coding and a gradual refining of the original concepts.

My initial coding system was divided into four main sections: Old Syllabus Teaching, New Syllabus Teaching (*English Every Day*), Innovation Features, and Washback. Each of these sections was further divided, in ways that related to sections in the Henrichsen model and to ideas about examination impact that had emerged from my review of the literature. The general features of each section are described in the paragraphs that follow. The initial coding scheme itself can be found in Appendix 8.

The Old Syllabus Teaching section corresponded to what Henrichsen called 'Traditional Pedagogical Practices': this can be found in the 'Antecedents' section in Figure 4.8. This section was divided into several sub-sections: Textbook, Ordinary teaching, Examination paper, Examination preparation, and Problems, and each of these sub-sections was further divided. Any comments which teachers made about teaching before the introduction of *English Every Day* received a code or codes from this section.

The New Syllabus Teaching (*English Every Day*) section corresponded to the 'Consequences' section in Figure 4.8. The idea was that the teaching that was taking place in 1991 was the result of the decisions which had been made about English teaching up to that point, including the decision to introduce a new English O level examination. This section was also sub-divided. Whenever teachers talked about the textbook they were currently using, their ordinary teaching, the new examination paper, their examination preparation practices or their problems their comments would receive codes from this section.

The Innovation Features section covered all of the 'Antecedents' sections in Figure 4.8 apart from 'Traditional pedagogical practices', and all of the 'Factors which facilitate/hinder change'. Whenever teachers made comments about themselves, their students, or the environment they were working in the comments would receive a code or codes from this section.

The Washback section contained comments that the teachers made about the impact of the new examination on their teaching. There were sub-sections on predictions that teachers made about the next examination; factors that seemed to facilitate or hinder positive examination impact; a breakdown of impact according to whether it affected the participants themselves, the process of teaching, or the products (Hughes 1994, as reported in Chapter 4 of this book); and the types of publications that were in existence to help teachers and students prepare for the examination.

Segments could receive as many codes as were relevant. If a teacher talked, for example, about how hard it was to find time to teach speaking the comment would receive codes relating to the content of ordinary teaching under the New Syllabus, the problems of teaching under the New Syllabus, characteristics of the innovation (the quantity of material in the textbook), characteristics of the user system (time pressure within the daily schedule, overcrowded classrooms, student ability etc.), and washback (speaking is not tested).

This analysis required multiple readings of each interview, coding and recoding of the transcripts, and refining and revising of the coding categories until I reached a framework that was logical and coherent. A sample of coded transcript can be found in Appendix 9, and the revised coding scheme can be found in Appendix 10. (See Wall 1999 for details of this process, including a description of how qualitative analysis software facilitated the analysis.)

## Summary

In this chapter I have explained the approach I followed when planning and analysing a series of group interviews in order to discover teachers' views on the impact of the new examination on their teaching. I hoped that my analysis would help me not only to understand how these teachers understood their particular situation, but also to identify themes and patterns which could be tested in other situations and eventually contribute to a general theory. I have explained my reasons for adopting a qualitative approach to data gathering and analysis and for using an *ex-post facto* perspective, why I decided to use group interviews, the types of questions I chose to ask, the characteristics of my sample, and the stages I went through to arrive at a framework for data analysis. The results of the data analysis will be presented in Chapters 6–11.

# 6 The impact of the new examination on teaching: the teachers' view

## Background

We saw in Chapter 2 that one of the ways in which the Sri Lankan Ministry of Education hoped to raise standards in English language education was by introducing a new O level examination. This examination was meant to reflect and reinforce the new *English Every Day* textbook series: it would not only assess whether students had learned what they were supposed to be learning, but it would also have a positive impact on teaching. I described in Chapter 2 what observers discovered about what and how teachers were teaching.

The purpose of this chapter is to explore the impact of the new O level examination more thoroughly. The first step is to identify what the goals of the textbook were, in terms of content and methodology, to see what kind of changes it was meant to have. The next step is to review what teaching was like before the new exam appeared (the 1988 Baseline Study) and what it was like at the end of the two-year observation programme. I will then discuss the results of group interviews I held with teachers across the island (late 1991), and, finally, I will summarize what was revealed about the effects of the examination on teaching.

## What kind of impact was intended?

I explained in Chapter 2 that the new O level examination was only one of several English language developments that were taking place in the 1980s. The first was the design and introduction of two new textbook series, one for primary schools and another, *English Every Day*, for secondary schools. Next came in-service training seminars to familiarize teachers with the approach to teaching that was promoted in the new textbooks. The third was the examination, which was meant to be the 'lever' to make teachers take the new materials seriously.

One of the aims of the O level Evaluation Project was to investigate whether the examination was supporting the new materials in the way it was meant to. This meant identifying the objectives of 'those involved in innovation in syllabus design, textbook development and the updating of teaching methodology' (Institute for English Language Education 1988:1) – the team of consultants and teachers who had designed the textbook series. This was more difficult than it sounds. The first problem was that the textbook team no longer existed. They had finished their work long before the start of the evaluation project and had all gone in different directions – the lead consultant to a different country, the teachers to schools or to other parts of the education system. The second problem was that there was no single document that listed all of the textbook objectives. It was necessary to track down many documents (including teacher's guides, workshop materials, working papers, and the report of a visiting consultant) in order to reconstruct what the team's objectives must have been when they were putting the materials together. This process highlighted six general objectives: three relating to the content of teaching, and three relating to methodology. These are presented below, accompanied by references to the sources where they were found and by my own commentary. (A more detailed discussion of these objectives can be found in Alderson and Wall 1989.)

# Objectives of *English Every Day (EED)*

## Content objectives

1. The English that pupils learn must meet the requirements of the country – economic, social and cultural. (Mosback 1982:1)

It was not possible to locate an official statement specifying what these requirements were, but it was logical to infer that students needed to be able to operate in trade, tourism and higher education. It was also hard to find a statement about the level of proficiency that was desired. This became clearer in 1990 when the lead consultant for the textbook project wrote about its aims retrospectively. The team had originally decided that the Council of Europe Threshold Level was an appropriate target (Mosback 1990:22). This level was for learners who wished to:

> be able to cope, linguistically speaking, in temporary contacts with foreign language speakers in everyday situations, whether as visitors to the foreign country or with visitors to their own country, and to establish and maintain social contacts. (van Ek, Alexander and Fitzpatrick 1980:1)

They later settled on a point halfway between Threshold and Waystage, the next level down, taking from each specification 'what seemed appropriate to the Sri Lankan school learner' (ibid.). (Note: The former Threshold and Waystage levels correspond to the current Council of Europe levels B1 and A2 – see Council of Europe 2001.)

2. 'In addition to facts ABOUT the language (vocabulary meanings, word order and structural changes) the pupils need constantly to be able to develop their ability to USE the language.' (Teacher's Guide for Year 7:1)

The Teacher's Guide for Year 7 explained what 'using the language' would mean for each of the four skills:

Speaking – The Teacher's Guide stated that 'traditional classroom language in the past ... gave children access only to a rather stiff and formal register of English with little scope for the expression of any emotion, friendliness or opinion'. The *EED* series would develop the students' ability to use common expressions in different contexts, 'fillers', 'signposts', first and second person verb forms, question forms, rhythms, intonation, stress and normal conversational speed (ibid.). There were several speaking sections in every unit: a 'role play dialogue' to introduce new language; a section called 'Learning Together', which contained games and other communicative activities; and an 'everyday conversation', which students could practise for immediate use in the outside world (Mosback 1990:21). (See sample unit in Appendix 11, for an illustration of how the *English Every Day* objectives were operationalized.)

Listening – The Teacher's Guide explained that in traditional classrooms students spent most of their time listening to 'teacher talk', which was full of repetition, explanation, slow speed and translation (p. 38). It was difficult for them to cope with 'real life talk': radio and television broadcasts, public speeches and announcements, and conversation with foreign visitors and Sri Lankans who spoke a different first language. The *EED* series would prepare students 'for listening first time round', by giving them pre-listening questions to activate their background knowledge, short texts, and simple tasks which they could carry out while listening and which would not tax their memory.

Reading – The Teacher's Guide tried to discourage a 'spoon-feeding' approach to the teaching of reading, especially the practice of translating passages word for word. Teachers were advised that students should 'sense the overall meaning first' and then 'split up the passage into smaller units if necessary'. The Guide did not proscribe traditional activities such as reading aloud but it stressed that teachers should not spend too much time on them. They were to concentrate on getting students to guess the meaning of new words in context, understand the relationships between different parts of a passage, and find things out for themselves (p. 15).

Writing – The Teacher's Guide explained that 'We have come a long way from the time when students were assigned an 'essay' topic such as MY FAMILY, HAPPINESS, A HOLIDAY and were expected to produce a composition of some kind without any further assistance.' (p. 50) The new series would provide writing activities of many sorts, and teachers were encouraged to explain how these related to the writing the students might need to do in 'the outside world' (p. 56). There would be an emphasis on producing whole texts rather than 'unrelated scraps', writing for a purpose, and writing with a particular reader in mind.

3. The syllabus for the new secondary school course, *English Every Day*, shall give as much weight to listening and speaking as to reading and writing.' (Teacher's Guide for Years 10/11:3)

Reading and writing had been at the centre of the English language curriculum for 30 years (Mosback 1982). Proposing oral skills was a novel and ambitious undertaking. Each unit of the series provided opportunities for pupils to speak and listen, often in pairs and small groups. They could practise dialogues, ask and answer questions about reading or listening materials, or they could simply do vocabulary and grammar work together. The aim was to give them as many opportunities as possible to practise communicating orally.

## Methodology objectives

Teacher training was an important goal of the *EED* series. The general approach to teaching was presented in the Teacher's Guide for Year 7, which gave advice in three broad areas:

- It presented many examples of the differences between 'traditional' classrooms and more 'pupil-centred' ones. The traditional classroom had a teacher at the front and the students in rows and working silently; the 'pupil-centred' classroom had the teacher moving around the room and the students working productively with one another. Teachers were encouraged to give up their traditional role (this was referred to in terms such as 'lecture', 'drills', 'demonstrate', 'discipline', 'impersonal', 'authoritative', 'drill sergeant', 'humiliate', and 'threatening'), at least some of the time, and to take on other roles such as 'supporter' or 'monitor'.
- It explained the nature of the skills the students were supposed to be acquiring, and presented a variety of techniques for developing these skills in the classroom.
- It briefly recalled some of the skills all good teachers were supposed to have, regardless of whether they were 'traditional' or 'pupil-centred' teachers. These included having clear objectives and good pacing, being well prepared with necessary materials and instructions, being visible to all the students, knowing how to use the blackboard etc. (Teacher's Guide for Year 7:5).

If this advice were rewritten in the form of objectives the results would be as follows:

1. To help the teacher to become a more 'pupil-centred' teacher, adopting a low-key supportive role rather than an authoritative one.
2. To help the teacher to understand and handle a variety of classroom techniques aimed at developing specific language skills.
3. To remind the teacher of the skills all good teachers should have, regardless of whether they call themselves 'traditional' or 'pupil-centred'.

Once these objectives had been identified, it was necessary to decide what kinds of evidence should be gathered to determine whether they had been achieved. This involved interviewing key figures in the Curriculum Design and Development Centre of the Ministry of Education, including the Director of the Division of Languages, Social Studies and Religion; the Director of the Research Division; and the Director of the Technology Division (who was also the former Commissioner for the Department of Examinations). The results of these discussions can be found in Alderson and Wall 1989:A–8 to A–13. In summary, they involved the use of questionnaires, document and materials analysis, classroom observation, and individual and group interviews.

The next step was to find out whether the hoped-for features did in fact appear in the classroom. The final step was to determine what role, if any, the new examination played in encouraging or discouraging their appearance.

## What kind of impact could be expected?

The new examination was originally meant to assess all four language skills: reading and writing via a pen-and-paper examination at the end of Year 11, and listening and speaking through continuous assessment during Years 9, 10 and 11. It was believed that if all four skills counted towards the final result then teachers and students would pay them equal attention. These plans were short-lived, however: the continuous assessment programme was abandoned in 1989, for political as well as logistical reasons, and with it went all hopes of assessing listening and speaking.

The textbook series and the examination would now be pulling in different directions: the textbook would be encouraging the teaching of all the skills, but the examination would be assessing only reading and writing. This introduced the risk of 'negative washback': a restraining or distorting influence on what was taught and how. Teachers might not take all of the content and methodology goals seriously, and other activities, such as classroom assessment, might also be affected negatively. We saw in Table 2.2 what negative washback might look like in general terms. Table 6.1 shows what might occur in this particular situation in Sri Lanka.

**Table 6.1 Forms that negative washback might take in Sri Lanka**

| Type of washback | What would this look like in the classroom? |
|---|---|
| Content of teaching | Teachers might not teach listening and speaking because these skills were not assessed. |
| | Even when teaching reading and writing teachers might neglect certain text types or activities that did not appear in the early exams. |
| | Teachers might abandon the use of the textbook, and begin to use other materials more obviously related to the exam. |
| Methods of teaching | Teachers might neglect some aspects of the textbook's approach if they felt that these were not useful for examination preparation. |
| Assessing students | Teachers might write tests which reflected the content of past examination papers rather than the content of the textbook. They might adapt questions, or simply 'lift' them, from past papers or publications designed to prepare students for the exam. |
| | Teachers might adopt the marking criteria used by the examination and ignore advice in the textbook which went against this way of marking. |

In short, it was possible that teachers and students would place more value on the skills and activities assessed in the examination and less value on those that were not tested.

We saw in Chapter 3 that there were many claims about the impact of examinations in language education, but few were supported by empirical findings and even fewer by classroom observations. It was decided at the beginning of the Evaluation Project that the principal means of gathering data would be through observation. This would be achieved by means of a baseline study and a two-year observation programme. These were discussed in Chapter 2 but a brief summary of the results is given below in order to provide a point of comparison for the results of the group interviews, the main focus of this study.

# Results of the Baseline Study and the two-year observation programme

## Results of the Baseline Study

The Baseline Study was carried out in May 1988, seven months before the new examination was supposed to be implemented for the first time. The purpose of the study was to find out what and how teachers were teaching before they knew anything about the new examination and before it could have any impact on their teaching. The data was gathered during observations and interviews in 14 schools, and interviews in these schools and four additional ones.

The analysis showed that teachers were teaching the content of the *English Every Day* textbooks, but the way they presented the material and got students to practise bore little resemblance to the approach set out in *EED*. Their lessons were very formal and students spent a great deal of time either listening to the teacher or practising language form, rather than trying to use the language with their classmates. The teachers claimed that they had changed their approach to teaching when they began working with the new materials but the observers felt that many of them did not understand what they were meant to be teaching. Over half did not achieve the objectives they were supposed to. The examination was obviously not having any impact on their teaching since they did not know what it would look like. What was more interesting, however, was that the textbook also seemed to have little impact, apart from providing the content for the lessons.

## Results of the two-year observation programme

The observation programme was broader and deeper than the Baseline Study, consisting of six rounds of observations with up to 64 observations per round. Each observation included a short interview with the teacher, and all the information was recorded in a detailed observation schedule (see Appendix 3 for a copy of this schedule). The main findings are summarized in Tables 6.2 – 6.4, under the headings 'Content of teaching', 'Methods of teaching' and 'Assessing the students'.

The findings in Table 6.2 corresponded closely to the 'possible negative outcomes' presented in Table 6.1. Most teachers claimed that the examination affected their choice of content, and it was clear that they paid more attention to the written skills than to the oral skills throughout the year. They set aside their textbooks in the third term and depended heavily on commercial examination preparation material. What was not clear, however, was why so many teachers claimed to have covered the textbook thoroughly in their ordinary teaching. If this was true, then why did they give so much attention to reading and writing and so little to listening and speaking?

There was also some resemblance between the findings in Table 6.3 and the 'possible negative outcomes' in that most teachers were not following the *EED* approach to teaching. There were many 'teacher-centred' lessons all year round, with little of the student interaction that the textbook recommended. It was not clear why the teachers did not ask students to practise reading strategies and to work together when they were writing, since these were activities that the textbook promoted and which the examination was supposed to be reinforcing. Was the examination really having impact if it was not encouraging teachers to present exercises which involved the use of strategies, discussion approaches to writing, and so on?

## Table 6.2 Analysis of observations – impact on the content of teaching

| Type of impact | What did this look like in the classroom? |
| --- | --- |
| Content of teaching | The academic year was divided into two different periods: two terms of 'ordinary teaching' and one term of 'examination preparation'. |
| | Most teachers claimed that the examination was influencing the content of their lessons during both their ordinary teaching and the examination preparation period. |
| | **Ordinary teaching:** |
| | Most teachers claimed to follow the textbook, and to work their way carefully through all the exercises. |
| | Teachers tended to emphasize reading over the other skills, with writing generally in second place and speaking in third. Classes which were meant to focus on speaking often involved other skills more than speaking. There seemed to be very little teaching of listening. |
| | Teachers did not change the content of the textbook, but they did add comprehension questions. |
| | If teachers were using non-textbook materials, they often chose them because they were useful for the examination. |
| | **Examination preparation:** |
| | Most teachers finished or abandoned their textbooks and began intensive work with past papers and commercial publications to prepare their students for the exam. (Note, however, that 40% of the teachers claimed to be doing some form of examination practice in the first term, and 55% claimed this in the second term.) |
| | Teachers emphasized reading and writing. Listening and speaking virtually disappeared. |

## Table 6.3 Analysis of observations – impact on the methods of teaching

| Type of impact | What did this look like in the classroom? |
| --- | --- |
| Methods of teaching | Most teachers claimed that the examination influenced the methodology of their lessons, although when they spoke of methodology they often confused it with content. |
| | The lessons themselves were generally very teacher-centred, with few of the methodological innovations encouraged by EED. |
| | The methods used during the third term were 'exam-like' (Shohamy 1993), with much test-taking practice and routine correction and little discussion of the problems that students were having. |
| | Many teachers did not seem to understand the EED teaching approach or the principles of communicative language teaching. Many had not prepared their lessons adequately, and less than half were considered to have achieved the objectives they started out with. |

**Table 6.4 Analysis of observations – impact on classroom assessment**

| Type of impact | What did this look like in the classroom? |
|---|---|
| Assessing the students | Most teachers claimed that the examination influenced how they designed classroom tests. Fewer reported an influence on the way they did their marking. |
| | Analysis of classroom tests suggested that the examinaton was having a strong impact on classroom test design. |
| | There was very little testing of listening and speaking at classroom- or school-level. |

It was difficult to gain insight into classroom assessment from the observations alone, since the observers did not see many lessons where the teachers were conducting tests or giving feedback. However, they were able to collect copies of tests from many of the teachers and these were combined with tests from teachers in other parts of the country and analysed in a separate study (see Alderson and Wall 1992:195-200, and Wall 1994: 112-114). This study suggested that the examination was indeed having an impact on classroom assessment, mainly in the emphasis given to reading and writing as opposed to straight language form, and in the abundant use of certain testing techniques associated with the new examination (short-answer questions, true/false, matching, application forms, cloze, c-tests and grammar transformation). It was not possible to investigate the influence of the examination on the way that teachers marked their tests, however, since the tests that were collected were question papers only and did not contain student responses or guidelines for marking.

A separate survey was carried out at a seminar for teacher-advisers from 15 educational districts in November 1990. The survey revealed that only one of the 15 districts was testing listening on their mid-year examinations, and no district was assessing speaking. The advisers claimed that there was too little time in the Year 11 timetable to assess the oral skills since teachers had to prepare their students for the O level examination, and this tested only reading and writing.

There were many similarities between the findings of the observations and the 'possible negative outcomes' listed in Table 6.1. It was not clear, however, whether the examination had actually caused certain results to occur or whether these were the consequence of other factors not yet investigated. Many teachers claimed that the examination had influenced the content of their teaching, but was this really the reason there was so little listening and speaking? The teachers also claimed that the examination had influenced their methodology, but there were at least two questions that needed attention: the first was what they had understood by the term 'methodology' and the second was why the reading and writing activities which the textbook encouraged and which the examination was supposed to be reinforcing had very rarely been observed in their teaching. Similar points could be raised in a discussion of classroom testing. If, for example, teachers were making use of certain item-types was this because of the examination or could there be other factors influencing their decisions?

The observations were of value in that they revealed many areas where examination impact might be occurring. However, they did not establish a causal link between the examination and the type of teaching that was being observed. In the words of Messick:

> it is problematic to claim evidence of test washback if a logical or evidential link cannot be forged between the teaching or learning outcomes and the test properties thought to influence them. (1996:247)

It was therefore necessary to gather other types of information before definitive claims could be made about the impact of the examination. This was the rationale for conducting group interviews with teachers.

# Results of the group interviews

As reported in Chapter 5, ten group interviews were conducted in different areas of Sri Lanka. A total of 64 teachers participated in the interviews.

# What the teachers said about the new examination

## Awareness of the examination

The interviews were held at the end of 1991, three years after the first administration of the new examination. By this time most of the teachers were familiar with or gave the impression of being familiar with the contents of the examination. About 80% of them had seen a copy of at least one of the papers, and about a third of them had served as examiners. Nearly all were able to describe the item- and task-types accurately, and many were able to remember the year in which certain passages or questions had appeared. Those who had served as examiners were familiar with the rating scales and the problems that students had experienced in the years in which they had done their marking.

About half of the teachers were asked to give their predictions of what might appear on the 1991 examination. Most felt that familiarity with Book 11 was important for the examination, but many felt that earlier books were also important: 48% (ten teachers) said that Book 10 was important, 33% (seven) mentioned Book 9, and 19% (four) mentioned Book 8.

Some teachers were not worried about finishing Book 11 because they 'knew' it was not important for the examination, and one said that the Director of English in her province had instructed teachers not to cover more than half the book for the same reason. (It is interesting that teachers and officials claimed to 'know' these things, as examination security was taken very seriously in the country and members of the examination development team would not have passed on this kind of information.)

A few teachers made predictions about the way that reading would be tested in the next examination. They talked in terms of topics and text-types rather than reading skills or item-types. Several predicted that there would be 'seen passages' from the Finding Out sections of *EED* and several others predicted that there would be role plays or dialogues. When asked why they expected role plays or dialogues, the teachers replied that these types of things had not appeared on previous examinations. They did not see a contradiction in presenting speaking material in an examination which tested reading and writing. They saw role plays and dialogues as texts like any other and did not consider whether people would do this type of reading in 'the real world'.

Teachers also made predictions about writing. These were expressed in terms of text-types: there would be a form to fill in, a job application letter, other sorts of letters, a report, or an essay. One teacher predicted that the theme of the essay would be 'Pollution' or 'Endangered Species': these were *EED* Finding Out (reading) topics which had not appeared on previous exams.

There were also predictions about grammar. A few teachers thought that there would be a c-test (which they called 'partial production'), and one teacher predicted that a listening passage from the textbook might be given as a cloze text. They did not predict what structures would be tested.

The examination design team had decided to vary the content and the format of the examination paper every year so that teachers would try to cover all of the *EED* and not just the material that had appeared in previous exams. This strategy worked well with a handful of teachers, but others were quite confident about what was likely to appear.

There was less awareness of the criteria used for marking writing. The teachers who had served as examiners (about a third of them) would have been familiar with how the writing tasks were marked. Others indicated that they had received copies of the rating scales from friends or through one of the official examination preparation booklets. Not all of the teachers were familiar with the materials. Those who had received past papers through informal channels (friends or relatives), or had seen them in commercial examination preparation publications would not necessarily have seen the rating scales and would not have been able to use them when marking their own students.

## Attitudes towards the examination

Two thirds of the teachers talked about their attitude towards the new examination, and 90% of these were positive. Over a quarter liked the examination because it tested 'practical language'. Others liked it because students had to produce language in order to get good results (in contrast to the old examination which was mainly multiple-choice questions); it matched the content of *EED*; instructions were given in English (they were given in three languages in the old exam); and it forced both students and teachers to improve their English.

A few teachers expressed negative feelings: the subject matter was mundane and boring (compared to the literary passages which had been given many years earlier to students who were studying in English-medium); it was too easy (this from a literature teacher who had taken over a language class when another teacher left the school); it put a 'restrictive frame' on teaching (what in the literature is called 'narrowing the curriculum'); it gave too much importance to grammar (this forced students to seek help in 'tutories' [private language-teaching operations], and it made students dismissive of what was being taught in their schools).

About a quarter of the teachers who expressed an opinion said that they wanted the exam to test listening and speaking. Most thought that this would encourage teachers to devote more time to the oral skills. However, two teachers said that it would be fairer to test listening and speaking since some students were strong in these skills but poor in reading and writing.

To summarize these two sections, most teachers were aware of the contents and format of the new examination, and many were ready to give predictions about the 1991 paper. Fewer were familiar with the criteria for marking writing. Almost all of the teachers had a positive attitude towards the examination, although about a quarter of them stated that they would like listening and speaking to be tested as well as reading and writing.

It is with this background in mind that we proceed to an analysis of what the teachers said about their ordinary teaching and the examination preparation period, to see if the examination influenced teaching in the ways that were intended or expected.

## What the teachers said about their ordinary teaching

We saw earlier ('Results of the two-year observation programme') that Year 11 was divided into two fairly distinct phases: 'ordinary teaching' and examination preparation. The observations had shown that teachers concentrated on different types of things during each of these phases, so it seemed reasonable to treat the phases separately during the interviews. The teachers provided a great deal of information about their coverage of *EED*, the attention they paid to each of the four skill areas and grammar, the methods they used for teaching, the way they assessed their own students' learning, and their attitude towards their teaching.

## Coverage of *EED* during ordinary teaching

The teachers were asked to describe their coverage of *EED* to see whether they were paying attention to all of the material or whether they were leaving anything out because of the examination. They were asked to say which book they had started the academic year with, how much of this book and other books they had covered, and why they had made the decisions they had made.

Two thirds of the Year 11 teachers specified which book they had started the academic year with. More than a third had started with Book 10 rather than with Book 11. Most of these said that they had to finish one or two units from Book 10, but at least two had had to start the book from the very beginning. Several teachers were unable to say why their students had not completed Book 10 the previous year, but others gave explanations such as the following: the students were too low-level to finish the book in the allotted time, students had missed many classes because of bad weather (the monsoon), English classes could not meet regularly because of extra-curricular activities, and the schools were still trying to get back to a regular schedule after forced closures in 1989.

About a third of these teachers had tried to cover all of the material in Book 10 before starting Book 11. One teacher gave his reasons for going through Book 10 so thoroughly:

> T 53: I have completed the Year 10 book and then started the Year 11. I understood the value of teaching them because as far as this paper is concerned most of the questions are based on the Year 10 book. Filling in applications and applying for a job and all that kind of thing. Most of the cases appeared in the Year 10 book, and...I thought it was more important to teach the complete Year 10 book and then start Year 11. (Welimada 44)

(Note: 'T 53' refers to Teacher 53. 'Welimada 44' means that this teacher's utterance was the 44th in the transcript of the interview in Welimada.)

Quite a few teachers believed that Book 10 was the most important for the examination. Teachers who chose to cover all of it needed several weeks to complete each unit. This delayed their entry into Book 11 by a month or sometimes longer: in fact, two teachers were unable to begin Book 11 until Term 3. Several teachers gave extra lessons outside normal school hours to either get through Book 10 more quickly or to try to catch up in Book 11.

About two thirds of the teachers began the year with Book 11. Several decided to do this even though their students had not finished earlier books in the series: in at least three cases the students had not finished either Book 9 or

Book 10, and in at least one case they had not done any work in either because they had not had a teacher. Their Year 11 teacher explained:

> T 38: ... they haven't got the primary knowledge of that. There were no teachers at the Year 9 and 10 classes. There was no English teachers. When I went to this school then I started to teach from Year 11...(Ratnapura 116)

Another teacher, who taught in an area where there were many political disturbances, explained why she had chosen to start with Book 11 rather than with earlier material:

> T 44: I did not go back. I was struggling with the Year 11 book. I didn't want to take them ... because it will be the same plight. If I had used the Year 10 book it would have been the same thing, so I would have to go to Grade 8. And then come back to Year 6 and start from there. And that I can't do. And we've got a time structure, and within that we've got to finish all these things. (Trincomalee 238-240)

Several teachers who had taught the same students in Years 10 and 11 decided to give extra lessons the year before so that they would finish Book 10 before the start of Year 11. These included teachers from 'good schools' as well as from ordinary schools.

Half the teachers had attempted to cover the Year 11 book thoroughly, even if it meant giving extra lessons after school or during the school vacations. The teachers were not asked why they had decided to be so thorough, but several volunteered that it was good preparation for the examination. Comments like the following were not uncommon:

> T 57: If they do the exercises from Years 8, 9, 10 and 11, I am sure that the child will be able get through without any difficulties. (Wellawatte 630)

One Year 11 teacher had not been able to use any of the *EED* books as he had only been assigned to his group in mid-October, about a fortnight before the interview and only a few weeks before the examination. The class had not had a teacher since the beginning of the year. This teacher had chosen to go straight into examination preparation and was using model papers as his sole material.

All five of the Year 10 teachers had worked in Book 10 for some part of the year; however, two of them had worked in Book 7 as well, to help their students with language they had not yet mastered. One of these had begun the year with Book 7 and moved on to Book 10 at the beginning of Term 2; the other had begun the year with Book 10, found that his students could not cope, and started giving extra lessons every week using Book 7. This teacher knew that the students had not done the work in the earlier books, but he did not know why. The students were pleased to be able to work in the lower-level textbook:

> T 63: They like the lessons now. They have interest in those lessons because they can do something. They participate. Now when we go to Year 10, they say 'Sir, we can't follow this text.' (Wennapuwa 141)

In summary, there were important differences between the starting and finishing points for the teachers in this sample. The textbook designers had assumed that all Year 11 classes would work in Book 11, but approximately 60% of the teachers had either begun Year 11 teaching Book 10 or had given extra lessons so that their students could begin with Book 11. Teachers seemed to have covered Book 10 thoroughly because they believed it was important for the exam. Only about 40% of the teachers were able to complete the Year 11 book by the time they started examination preparation, and about 20% were still working in the first half of the book.

## Attention to skills areas during ordinary teaching

### *Reading*

Most of the Year 11 teachers talked about their teaching of reading during the ordinary school year. Just over three quarters of these made statements which suggested that the exam was having an impact on their teaching.

The clearest impact was on the amount of attention that teachers paid to reading as opposed to the other skills. Nearly three-quarters of the teachers tried to cover all of the Finding Out passages and many said that this was because of the examination. A number felt that the passages in the book might appear on the examination paper, while some felt that the students might need to use the facts in these passages to write essays for the examination. Most teachers presented the passages and questions just as they appeared in the textbook; however, a few said that they added extra questions, either of their own design or from commercial publications designed to supplement the *EED* series.

Some teachers said that they skipped some of the Finding Out passages: they knew that reading was important for the examination but they felt the passages were too difficult for their students. This was either because the students were weak or because the passages contained 'alien' subject matter. (Some of the teachers who attempted to cover all of the passages also felt they were difficult.)

Most of the Year 10 teachers said that the exam affected their teaching of reading. These teachers also commented on the difficulty of the passages: one said that it could take four or five periods to cover some passages adequately, and another said that he had given up trying since his students could not cope.

To sum up, the examination seemed to have an important influence on the amount of attention teachers devoted to reading and the types of materials they used in the classroom. It is important to note though that many teachers concentrated on the content of reading passages rather than on practising sub-skills or strategies.

These findings corresponded with the findings of the two-year observation programme.

## Writing

Nearly half of the Year 11 teachers talked about how they taught this skill. All but one of these stated or implied that writing was important because it was tested in the examination. About two thirds said they were covering all of the writing exercises in the textbook. Several were giving extra attention to the types of writing they expected to appear on the examination, including application forms and essays.

Only one of the Year 10 teachers mentioned writing. She said that she did not give extra attention to this skill when teaching but that it was a priority when she was planning her testing.

Some teachers did not talk about their teaching of writing but they claimed in other parts of the interview that they were covering their textbooks thoroughly. This means that more than half the Year 11 teachers and 40% of the Year 10 teachers were covering all of the writing exercises. We cannot be certain, however, that all of those who were covering the book thoroughly were doing this because of the exam.

The examination seemed to be having a fairly strong influence on the teaching of writing notwithstanding, and this corresponds well with the results of the observations.

## Listening

Roughly 40% of the 57 Year 11 teachers talked about their teaching of listening, and about 60% of these seemed to be influenced by the fact that listening was not assessed on the examination. Nearly half stated that they skipped some or all of the listening exercises: some gave the examination as their sole reason (one said that listening was 'a waste of time' since it was not tested, and another mentioned receiving instructions from an in-service adviser to ignore the skill for the same reason), and several others mentioned a combination of the examination and difficult classroom conditions (noise, too many students, students who would not listen). Several said they used the listening passages to practise other skills such as reading or writing, or that they only handled listening exercises if the question-type accompanying the passage resembled an item-type that might appear in the examination.

A few teachers said that they tried to cover all of the listening exercises, but one said that she did not devote much time to these exercises and another stated that she wanted to be familiar with the passages because they sometimes appeared as cloze passages in the examination.

Two of the Year 10 teachers talked about listening, and both mentioned that they used listening passages as texts for reading comprehension.

About 40% of the teachers did not talk about listening but indicated in other parts of the interview that they were trying to cover the textbook thoroughly. This meant that there was reportedly more listening activity taking place in the classroom than had been witnessed in the observations. Although it is possible that the observers were not present on the days that listening was being practised it is also possible that some of the teachers were attaching different meanings to the idea of 'teaching listening'. At least one of the teachers who said he taught listening was not using the approach advocated by *EED* (his method consisted of reading a passage aloud and asking his students to repeat after him), and there may have been others like him. The Coordinator of the Regional English Support Centre claimed that many teachers had troubles teaching this skill:

> T 21: When it comes to listening I think there is a technique of teaching that. Now when we had some seminars for the newly-appointed teachers … most of the teachers they didn't know how to teach listening in the classroom. Actually didn't know what it was. Then we had to give that teaching technique. That's how I came to know later why they tend to ignore this skill. (Nuwara Eliya 651)

However, he also felt that some teachers ignored listening because it was not tested in the examination:

> T 21: … some of them they tend to ignore the two skills. Listening and speaking. They concentrate more on reading and writing because it is tested. In that way, the test paper has an influence on teaching, because the teachers they always try to teach only what is tested. Because, as all of them say, we are a highly exam-oriented nation and we also try to tow that line. (Nuwara Eliya 653)

In summary, the examination seemed to be having an impact on the teaching of listening in that a number of teachers omitted or played down the skill and others used listening material to practise skills which were in the examination. However, the examination was not the only factor in operation: some teachers felt that it was hard to teach listening because of classroom conditions and others may not have known how to teach it. The observations had indicated that listening received less attention than the other skills but it was not clear what the cause was. The group interviews complemented the observations in illuminating the situation.

## *Speaking*

About 60% of the Year 11 teachers made comments about teaching speaking. About 60% of these had indicated in other parts of the interview that the examination was affecting their teaching, but most of them seemed to be teaching speaking in spite of its not being tested. Several teachers explained that the students had to have 'that talent' or that communication was the aim of *EED*. However, it was not always clear what they meant by 'speaking': two teachers worked on dialogues because they believed that they might appear as reading passages on the next exam, and another claimed that speaking was a reading skill because students had to be able to speak to answer reading questions. Several spoke about recycling speaking materials to practise other skills: dialogues could be used as cloze passages, picture description exercises could be used for writing practice, etc.

A third of the teachers who talked about speaking had not indicated elsewhere that they were influenced by the examination. Most of these said they were covering most of the speaking exercises, although some mentioned that it took them a lot of time (up to three or four periods for some role plays).

About a fifth of the Year 11 teachers did not talk about speaking in particular but they must have been paying some attention to this skill since they said they were covering the textbook thoroughly.

In all then about three quarters of the Year 11 teachers claimed to or could be assumed to be spending time on speaking, even though it was not tested in the examination.

Three of the five Year 10 teachers mentioned speaking and all of them seemed to be affected by the examination. One stated that he could not devote as much time to this skill as to the others, one ignored it all together, and one believed that it should receive less priority in classroom testing.

Several of the teachers who neglected speaking talked of the difficulties of trying to teach it, including overcrowded classrooms and the inability or reluctance of students to practise on their own. One teacher talked about how group work inevitably became individual work, as less proficient students left it up to their stronger classmates to do all the talking. Another reported that he never used pair work and group work because it was too difficult to do so in large classes. He had, however, used these techniques in earlier years, when they were required to do so by continuous assessment.

The picture that emerged from the interviews was different from the one that emerged from the observations. Many teachers either claimed to be teaching speaking or might be assumed to be doing so because they were working their way through the textbooks systematically. This is in contrast to the observations, where speaking was observed in only 17% of the lessons (see Chapter 2 for details). There may be explanations for these discrepancies. It should be remembered that *EED* Book 11 paid less attention to speaking than to reading and writing. The teachers may also have been using the term 'speaking' for activities where there was really not much oral practice. There were examples of this in the discussions of listening, so it might also have been possible for speaking.

### *Grammar*

A third of the Year 11 teachers talked about their teaching of grammar, and about 90% of these mentioned the impact of the examination. All but one said they paid special attention to grammar, and about half of them brought in extra materials. These were either exercises from earlier books in the *EED* series or from special books designed for practising grammar. Several felt that students needed grammar in order to do writing and that *EED* either did not give enough practice or was not systematic enough in its approach.

Another 40% did not say anything about grammar but mentioned that they were trying to cover the textbook thoroughly. This meant that they would be paying attention to grammar as well as to other skills.

The interviews suggested that more attention was being paid to grammar than was visible in the observations, where language form was the focus of only 10% of the lessons (see Chapter 2 for details). There were few grammar exercises in the textbooks though, so even if teachers were covering all of them they would not be using up very much teaching time. The fact that teachers believed grammar was important for writing and brought in extra materials was clearly an impact of the examination.

## Methodology during ordinary teaching

About 60% of the Year 11 teachers made at least one comment about the methods they used during their ordinary teaching. About a third of these spoke in general terms, either to say that they were trying to follow 'the method' (the ideas for teaching set out in *EED*) or that they were trying to be more active or to employ new ideas to motivate their students. Others may have wished to follow 'the method' but many did not seem to be able to do so, either because of local circumstances or because they did not understand what they were supposed to be doing.

Only a few teachers talked about teaching reading in ways that resembled the *EED*: one talked about getting students to use strategies of the sort encouraged by the textbook (skimming, getting the gist, guessing the meaning of words in context), another talked about the pre-reading support she gave to students, and another spoke of getting the students to skim and scan. Others taught in ways that the textbook designers would have discouraged: reading the Finding Out passages aloud, asking students to read them aloud, or explaining all the details. Several teachers talked about how long it took to get through the passages because their students were either too weak or were not motivated. One who worked with low-level students expressed this point particularly forcefully:

> T 2: I feel sorry for them and I make them read something. Yes. Loud reading. Though I ask them to read silently, they can do nothing. In that case you have to do something ... Two or three lines, like that. And give some questions on that three or four lines. Then the period is over. (Asgiriya 203, 205)

It was clear that this teacher was having problems because of her students' language level. However, other teachers showed that they might not understand the ideas that *EED* was trying to promote, even if they were able to repeat the metalanguage of the communicative approach.

This long quotation is from a teacher who used the jargon with confidence but who seemed to be confusing the notions of reading and listening, and was not interested in the idea of 'selective' reading:

> T 64: First of all I give them the pre-questions. I just introduce them to the passage by asking general questions about the passage. Now say if it's about science, or space, or about pets, I'll ask them about what pets? General questions that will lead them to the passage. Then I will read it once. Just once and the children won't look at the book. Then I will ask them to read. Not read. Just glance over it. And now that they are familiar with it, I will read it again. Only twice. First I will read it when they have closed their books, and I'll have them to glance it. And then I will read once again when they have opened their books. And then, depending on the level ... Because first of all I focus my questioning on the bright ones ... I'll ask questions for some specific information given in the text. Those I would categorize as 'post-questions'. Sometimes I may not be able to follow the exact guidance given in the Teacher's Guide. But I try my own techniques. But the aim I feel is to give them the opportunity to grasp some information from the passage. Find out something from the book. Even though it's simple. Simple objective questions. (Wennapuwa 247)

A number of teachers said they needed to use the students' first language in order to explain the content of certain texts, both in Finding Out lessons and for the poems. In some cases though it was not worth the effort to try to cover the material:

> T 43: Sometimes I'm not doing the poems. Because we have to explain each and every word. In mother tongue ... And even then they can't answer the questions. (Trincomalee 372,375)

There were only a few comments about the teaching of writing, which were not very illuminating, and a handful about the teaching of listening. These were also concerned with the need to use the mother tongue or to explain the passages to the students. One teacher felt particularly discouraged:

T 2: Oh, listening. That's also a failure, I feel. I'll have to explain it in Sinhala before doing listening practice ... Everything. New words and everything. I'll have to explain it in Sinhala, so I thought it's a failure also, with my children. (Asgiriya 72, 74)

In this case and several others the teacher's method was determined by the students' perceived proficiency level. In at least one case though the teacher's method, which consisted of reading the passage aloud to his students, getting them to read it aloud to him and then 'discussing' the content, indicated that he probably did not understand the type of listening the *EED* was trying to promote.

Finally, about a dozen teachers talked about the way they handled speaking. Here most of the comments were about role play, and dealt with the difficulty of handling pair and group work in large classes or where students were not proficient enough, in their teachers' eyes, to work on their own. One teacher talked about using pair work, but he was referring to the type of activity where two students stand up and read their parts aloud in front of the other students, rather than to students working together but apart from others. Another teacher felt that she could not handle the role plays properly because of the way they had been dealt with in the tutories:

T 10: Sometimes I find that the role plays have been massacred. By these tutories. If there's an important part in the speech, everything has been written in Sinhala – the pronunciation, the meaning. Then I don't do that role play. The kids say (she speaks in Sinhala). I say 'Shall we do this?' and then I start getting the books ready. (She speaks again in Sinhala) – some of them have the cheek to tell me that.

DW: What are they saying?

T 10: 'We know that. We have done it, teacher. Can't we do something else?' (Colombo 94–96)

Instead of taking the students through the normal procedure for role play, she put them into groups and instructed them to do question-and-answer exercises with one another.

A few teachers also mentioned how they handled Learning Together exercises and Picture Descriptions. The techniques they used were teacher-centred, involving teacher questioning or work in the mother tongue. One teacher gave this explanation of why she did not ask her students to do group work:

T 1: Really because they can't do it alone. Even in pairs and groups they can't do them without the assistance of teachers. So to do that we have to speak to them in Sinhala. Then we are using too much of mother tongue. And even then it is not very fruitful ... Only few answer well, and they

write what they have to. And the others depend on the others. The brighter
ones ... Then it becomes individual work. The brightest do it. (Asgiriya
82–86)

It is important to remember that 60% of the Year 11 teachers spoke about
their methodology, and most of these chose to talk about problems they had
rather than their successes in implementing *EED* methods. It is possible that
other teachers did not have difficulties with the approach described in the
textbook. However, this would not change the general picture, which also
emerged from the observations, of a large number of teachers who were not
teaching in the way the textbook designers intended. The teachers gave a
number of reasons for choosing certain techniques but the examination was
not cited by many of them. It seemed to influence many teachers' decisions
about how much of the textbook to cover and which skills or exercises to
emphasize, but it had little impact on the methods they used in the
classroom.

## Classroom assessment during ordinary teaching

A third of the Year 11 teachers and four of the five Year 10 teachers talked
about the types of classroom tests they wrote during their ordinary teaching
period. Most talked about the tests they wrote in Year 11, and several also
talked about the tests they wrote for the lower years. Six talked only of the
tests they designed for the lower years.

Nearly all of these teachers were influenced in their test design by the
examination, not only during Years 11 and 10, but also during the lower years.

In Year 11 the teachers designed unit tests, monthly tests and term tests; in
the lower years they designed all of these plus fortnightly and mid-term tests.
About 60% of the teachers referred to the influence of the exam on the item-
types they chose, and they mentioned getting ideas or even specific passages
and items from past papers, commercial examination preparation publications,
the textbook, and the official examination preparation booklets (*'Guidelines'*,
and *'Suggestions'*). One teacher spoke of the similarity between the tests that
she and her colleagues designed and the O level examination:

> T 59: Almost the same, you know. When we set the test papers we try to
> set it on those O level lines. Get the children to be sort of familiar with
> those types of questions. (Wellawatte 602)

The teachers were not asked to specify the types of items they designed, so
it is not possible to say whether they gave the same importance to short-
answer questions, true/false items, matching, application forms etc. which was
discovered in the analysis of classroom tests described previously ('Results of
the two-year observation programme').

The teachers mentioned several other features which resembled the examination (the use of unseen passages, instructions in English, a focus on writing, authentic texts and the O level criteria for marking writing), but it cannot be assumed that the examination was having a strong impact in these areas as only one or two teachers mentioned each of them.

About half the teachers said they were influenced in their test design in Year 10, and about a third said they were influenced in Year 9. There was influence in the earlier years as well, even as early as Year 6 (the last year of primary school and one year before the students began working in *EED*). One teacher explained how she tried to be creative when teaching young pupils, using techniques such as story-telling, but how she had to take a different approach when testing:

> T 7: ... Anyway, when we start teaching we do what interests them. But when it comes to testing we resort to the pattern. The format of the paper. (Colombo 554)

A third of the teachers had served as O level examiners but only a couple mentioned using the O level criteria when marking writing.

Finally, only a few teachers talked about the testing of listening or speaking. This may have been because they were not asked specifically about the oral skills (most of the interview questions were open-ended) but many teachers talked about testing the written skills without being asked about them directly. The few teachers who spoke indicated that they did not test listening and speaking. Two mentioned that they gave equal attention to all skills when teaching, but gave priority to reading and writing when it came to testing. Another said that he no longer tested the oral skills now that it was not required by continuous assessment.

In summary, the examination seemed to be having a strong effect on classroom test design, mainly in the amount of attention teachers gave to the written skills compared to listening and speaking and in their choice of item types. Its influence was felt not only in Years 11 and 10, but as far down as Year 6.

## Summary of ordinary teaching

The analysis of the teachers' comments about their ordinary teaching indicates that the examination was having significant impact on the content of teaching, no noticeable impact on methodology, and clear impact on the way that teachers assessed their own students. Table 6.5 presents the main results emerging from the analysis.

It is now appropriate to turn to an analysis of the examination preparation period, to gain a further perspective on how the examination was affecting teaching.

## Table 6.5 Analysis of group interviews – impact on ordinary teaching

| Type of impact | What did this look like in the classroom? | Correspondence between observations and interviews? |
|---|---|---|
| Content of teaching | Reading – Strong impact. Much attention paid to Finding Out passages. Teachers used listening and speaking materials to practise reading. However, many did not understand what they were supposed to be teaching. | Yes |
| | Writing – Strong impact. Much attention paid to writing exercises. However, many were not familiar with criteria for marking writing. | Yes |
| | Listening – Fairly strong impact. At least a quarter of teachers skipped listening passages or passed over them quickly. Some used listening materials to practise reading. However, some teachers didn't do listening because of classroom conditions or lack of skill. | The interviews suggested that teachers were paying more attention to listening than the observations revealed, but their notion of 'listening' was not necessarily the same as the EED's. |
| | Speaking – Some impact but not as clear as for listening. Many teachers claimed that they were teaching this skill while others may have been teaching it as they said they were covering their textbooks thoroughly. Some teachers used speaking exercises to practise other skills. Some teachers didn't do speaking because of classroom conditions and low student ability. | The interviews suggested that teachers were paying more attention to speaking than the observations revealed, but, as with listening, their notion of 'speaking' may have been different from the EED's. |
| | Grammar – Some impact. Some teachers brought in supplementary material to compensate for lack of grammar in EED. | The interviews suggested that teachers were paying more attention to grammar than the observations revealed. |
| Methods of teaching | Little to no impact. A number of teachers said that they were following EED ways of teaching, but many seemed to be using traditional methods, perhaps because of low student ability or because they did not have a clear idea of what else to do. | Yes |
| Assessing the students | Strong impact. This could be seen in the types of skills tested and the types of items employed. Impact not only in Year 11 but in earlier years as well. | Yes |

## What the teachers said about examination preparation

We learned earlier that teachers tended to dedicate a large part of the third term of teaching to examination preparation. 50 Year 11 teachers were asked if they set aside time for this kind of activity, how much time they devoted to it, what their teaching looked like, and what kinds of problems they experienced, if any.

### *Amount of time devoted to examination preparation*

The teachers were asked when they began doing examination preparation and whether they did it during their normal lessons or outside regular school hours. Their starting times can be seen in Table 6.6.

The table shows that 15% of teachers began their examination preparation activity as early as May, about a third were doing some form of preparation by early September and nearly half were doing preparation by the beginning of October. Almost 90% of the teachers would have done a month or more of preparation by the time the examination was given in early December.

**Table 6.6 Times when teachers began their examination preparation teaching**

| Starting time | Number of teachers (n=50) | Percentage of teachers | Cumulative percentage of teachers |
|---|---|---|---|
| Beginning of Term 1 (January 1991) | 1 | 2% | 2% |
| Beginning of Term 2 (May) | 5 | 13% | 15% |
| Beginning of Term 3 (September) | 9 | 21% | 36% |
| Beginning of October | 3 | 8% | 44% |
| Middle of October | 5 | 13% | 57% |
| Beginning of November | 12 | 32% | 89% |
| Middle of November | 4 | 11% | 100% |

About three quarters of the teachers were doing preparation during their daily lessons, often alternating between the textbook and examination-practice material and sometimes giving extra lessons before or after school. The remainder were devoting their normal lessons to the textbook and doing their examination practice outside school. Some teachers conducted 'seminars' for the Year 11 students in their schools: these were large assemblies where students from all the Year 11 groups worked their way through practice material and were given the correct answers and some explanations by their teachers. One of the teachers mentioned that his school gave 'study leave' for a week before the examination: this was a period in which students could work independently if they wished to, or come back into the school for exam-specific tuition.

Nearly half the teachers gave extra lessons outside their regular working hours. The number and types of lessons are presented in Table 6.7.

### Table 6.7 Number and types of examination preparation lessons

| Number and type of extra lessons | Number of teachers (n=23) | Percentage of teachers |
|---|---|---|
| 5 days/week, 6.00-6.45 a.m. | 1 | 4% |
| 3 days/week, after school | 1 | 4% |
| 2 days/week, after school | 7 | 30% |
| 1 day/week, after school | 5 | 22% |
| unknown, but at least 1 day/week | 5 | 22% |
| special lessons given at irregular intervals | 2 | 8% |
| 'seminars' | 2 | 8% |

Several teachers mentioned that these lessons were very long: one gave a three-and-a-half-hour session one afternoon a week, and another mentioned that he had given four four-hour sessions during the school vacations and expected to give at least three more sessions before the exam.

None of the teachers was paid for the extra work they were doing. Several teachers mentioned that it was 'voluntary service' or their 'sacred duty' to help their students pass the examination. This was the case in other parts of the curriculum as well, and not only in English.

### Materials used during examination preparation

The teachers used a variety of material during the examination preparation period. The types of material and the numbers of teachers using them can be seen in Table 6.8.

**Table 6.8 Types of material used during the examination preparation period**

| Type of material | Number of teachers (n=50) | Percentage of teachers |
|---|---|---|
| Model papers (commercial publications containing exercises which are similar to those appearing on the examination) | 28 | 56% |
| Past papers (copies of examination papers from the first three administrations of the examination) | 17 | 34% |
| Publications produced by the Examinations Department, of which: | | |
| The *Guidelines* booklet | 8 | 16% |
| The *Suggestions* booklet | 2 | 6% |
| The *Pupil Support* booklet | 2 | 4% |
| The *Past Papers* booklet | 2 | 4% |
| Earlier books in the EED series | 5 | 10% |
| Teacher-made material (usually derived from model papers) | 4 | 8% |

Model papers were by far the most popular kind of material. Their popularity could be attributed to their convenience, as teachers did not need to search for passages or design practice activities. One teacher explained their appeal in this way:

> T 53: Specially exam-oriented. And after studying the lesson they have to answer those questions. When they answer those questions some sort of practice is given and understanding is taking place and some questions are clearer than the questions given in the book. The children they find it easy. I too find it easy. (Welimada 219)

A few teachers also mentioned that they respected the knowledge of those who produced these publications and they believed that they would give good guidance:

> T 3: Because I think if we are preparing a passage for the students sometimes there may be mistakes. But I think those who have written the books they are the master teachers of English. Bernard de Silva is a person who taught at the Royal College and now he is a retired English teacher, and I think he knows better than us. Through his experience he can write something. And Mr Dharmasena is a person who was a lecturer in the

> training college. Maharagama Training College. And Mr Somapali
> Wijetunga also lectures in the training college. So they themselves have
> returned … have introduced those books for us. So I think without
> preparation of our own things, better to introduce a passage from them.
> (Asgiriya 266)

It was also suggested that these 'master teachers' were involved in the
design of the exam, and would have 'insider knowledge' of what might be
tested in future. (This was not true.)

The problem with model papers was that many students could not afford
them. Some had their own copies, but in many schools, especially in the rural
areas, families could not afford to part with 50 or 60 rupees. Several schools
provided students with mimeographed (*roneo*) copies at fairly low prices, but
this was still too expensive for many families. This seriously affected the way
the examination practice sessions were conducted: teachers had to copy
passages and questions on to the blackboard and students copied them into
their exercise books before they tried to answer them. This was very time-
consuming (one teacher described how it could take up to two periods to copy
a full examination paper) and it also meant that students did not get the
opportunity to practise reading long passages. A few teachers dictated
passages and questions to save time, but this was risky as the students'
listening or writing ability might prevent them from reproducing the passage
correctly. Students had no opportunity to practise skimming or scanning if
they had copied from the board or taken dictation.

The second most popular type of material was 'past papers'. Some teachers
received these papers when they served as examination markers, but many
received copies from friends or relatives, who may have got hold of them from
official sources or through other informal channels. All of the comments made
above about students not having their own copies also apply here. A few
teachers arranged to make copies of past papers (at two to three rupees per
copy) and a few knew that the Department of Examinations had released a
booklet containing the 1988, 1989 and 1990 papers (15 rupees), but the most
common pattern was that students copied the material that their teachers wrote
on the blackboard.

The publications produced by the Examinations Department were much
less used than model papers or past papers. This may have been due to a
shortage of materials: only one copy of the *Guidelines* and the *Suggestions*
booklets was sent to each school when they were first printed and many copies
had gone missing as the years went by. A paper mill had been bombed during
the political troubles, and this made it difficult to produce more copies for a
long time. Finally, the method for ordering these materials was not always
clear: several teachers said that they had written off for copies but they had not
received them. Only two teachers mentioned using the *Pupil Support* booklet,

which was produced by the Department of Examinations in 1990 for seminars in areas where the 1989 results had been especially low.

Few teachers mentioned using earlier books in the *EED* series although it was commonly believed that these books were important for the examination. This was probably because students had to hand their books back to the school at the end of the year so that they could be passed on to the next cohort of students. When the earlier *EED* books were used it was generally for revising reading passages.

## Content of examination preparation lessons

The content of the examination preparation classes was always reading and writing. All of the teachers were able to provide their students with shorter passages, but some were unable to present longer passages for reasons already mentioned. All teachers were able to give practice with lower-level writing tasks, but some did not ask for more extended writing, especially essays, because they felt that their students could not cope with them. Several teachers had deliberately adopted a policy of practising lower-level questions, thinking that if their students could answer enough of these correctly they could accumulate a lot of marks across the exam paper.

## Methodology during examination preparation lessons

About a third of the teachers talked about the methodology they used during the examination preparation lessons. Nine teachers gave descriptions of how they dealt with reading, and these were very similar to what has been described before and what was observed during Round 6 of the observations. Once students answered the questions they checked whether they had got the correct answers. 'Checking' generally meant reading the answers written on the blackboard and correcting what was written in the exercise book. In some classrooms students exchanged exercise books with their classmates. A couple of teachers made a point of collecting the exercise books so that they could correct the students' corrections.

Several teachers mentioned that they discussed difficult questions with their students, but this did not occur very often during the observations.

I have already mentioned the risks involved when teachers dictated reading passages to their students. In at least one case the teacher read all the material aloud to his students and they gave their answers without writing down either the passage or the questions.

About 20% of the teachers talked about writing, and they all seemed to follow the same pattern: they wrote the question on the board, got the students to copy it into their exercise books, and then tried to stimulate the students' thinking by asking them questions about essential content. Most teachers tried to do this in English, but some said they had to use the mother tongue. The students wrote their compositions during the lesson (the teachers could then be sure they were doing their own work) and then they usually handed them in for correction.

The students had to listen to their teachers' instructions or explanations in English, but it is unlikely that they practised listening in any other way. The observations showed that they rarely had the opportunity to listen to one another and the only 'speaking' practice they got was answering the teachers' questions and reading out their compositions to the rest of the group.

## Problems during examination preparation

It was clear that teachers considered this period to be essential to their students' success in the examination, and they were willing to devote many extra hours to teaching and to marking the writing tasks that they set for them. This must have been difficult for many teachers but no one suggested that it would be better not to do it. If there were any complaints it concerned the role of examinations in Sri Lankan society, but these were balanced out by the favourable attitude that many teachers showed towards this particular examination and the syllabus behind it.

One issue which did annoy teachers was the role of tutories during the final year before the examination, and the way in which their own attempts to help their students could be undermined by the way that the tutory masters conducted their classes. Several teachers felt that the tutories were teaching the wrong things (e.g. incorrect pronunciations, incorrect grammar), using 'the wrong method' (word-for-word translations and other forms of spoon-feeding), and preventing their students from attending after-school classes at their own schools or from paying proper attention to the homework their teachers gave them. This topic will be dealt with in more detail in Chapter 10: 'Characteristics of the User System'.

## Summary of comments on examination preparation

The interviews revealed that teachers devoted a great deal of time and energy to examination preparation: some began this work as early as May and most were doing some sort of preparation by late October/early November (the time of the interviews). Some teachers devoted their regular class time to this preparation, but others spent extra time before or after school and/or at weekends. The examination had an enormous influence on the content of the lessons: the focus was always reading or writing, and the material was specially chosen to mimic the contents of the examination.

The methodology was mechanical, often with students copying examination questions from the board and attempting to answer them during the lesson. Some teachers claimed that they discussed difficult questions with their students, and others said that they tried to help their students to come up with ideas for writing, but there is not enough data in the descriptions to allow us to say whether this kind of teaching resembled the ideas in *EED*, and whether the examination was therefore reinforcing good practice. This seems unlikely, however, given what was learned during the observations.

## Summary of what was discovered about examination impact in the group interviews

The analysis has shown the following about the relationship between the examination and teaching three years after the introduction of the new examination:

- teachers seemed to be very familiar with the contents of the examination and the types of techniques that were used, either because they had served as examiners, received copies of the examination from friends or relatives, or consulted commercial publications containing model questions;
- teachers were able to describe the contents of the examination accurately and many were willing to make predictions about the content of the 1991 exam;
- the teachers who had served as examiners were familiar with the criteria for marking writing, but others were less familiar with these than they were with the design of the exam;
- almost all of the teachers who expressed an opinion about the new English exam looked on it favourably, mainly because the content was 'practical', matching the kinds of things students would have to do in the real world in Sri Lanka;
- a number of the teachers said that they wanted listening and speaking to be tested, either to force students to work on the development of these skills or to provide a fairer assessment of students who were better at these skills than at reading or writing;
- the examination had a great deal of impact on the teaching of reading and writing during ordinary teaching. The impact was mainly on the amount of coverage given to these skills and on the topics covered, rather than on the teaching of sub-skills or strategies;
- the examination had a fairly strong influence on the teaching of listening, causing some teachers to skip the listening exercises completely or to spend less time on listening than on the other skills;
- it was difficult to pin down the impact on the teaching of speaking: many

teachers claimed that they continued to teach it but did not test it;

- the examination had a strong impact on classroom test design, especially in the area of item-types for reading and task-types for writing. Few teachers mentioned rating scales, however, so it is not clear how many of them used the O level criteria for marking their own students' writing;

- the examination had a dramatic impact on the content of teaching during the examination preparation period, mainly on the emphasis placed on reading and writing and the neglect of listening and speaking;

- the examination also influenced the types of materials that teachers used during the examination preparation period. Most teachers used commercial publications containing model examination questions and past examination papers. Relatively few teachers used official examination preparation materials;

- the examination had little impact on the methodology that teachers used, either during ordinary teaching or the examination preparation period;

- the examination had a strong impact on the teaching that reportedly took place in tutories, and this had an effect on some students' attitudes towards their regular English classes.

The information that the teachers gave generally corresponded to the results of the two-year observation programme. The only area where the teachers gave information that differed from the observation findings was in the teaching of the oral skills. More teachers either claimed to be teaching these skills or could be assumed to be doing so (because they said they were covering the textbook thoroughly) than were seen to be doing so during the observations. This may have been because the textbook contained fewer opportunities for listening and speaking practice than for reading and writing: the teachers may well have been covering all of the oral exercises but still have been spending most of their time doing reading and writing. It is also possible that teachers were going through the oral exercises without giving their students the types of practice that the Teacher's Guides suggested, either because classroom conditions did not allow it or because they did not really understand how to teach the skills in question. There was evidence from the interviews that at least some of the teachers had difficulties teaching these skills.

The interviews were important not only because of the light they shed on the relationship between the examination and teaching but also because of what they revealed about other factors influencing teachers' classroom practices.

In the next five chapters I will analyse the interview data from different perspectives, using my revised version of the Henrichsen Hybrid Model of the Diffusion/Implementation Process as a guide. Chapter 7 will present what the teachers said about the English language teaching situation before the introduction of the new textbooks and the new examination (the 'Antecedents'), and Chapters 8–11 will present what they said about the characteristics of the new textbooks and examination, the educational context, and themselves and their students. These chapters will throw more light on the findings that were presented in this chapter. I will conclude by relating the findings to theories of examination impact and educational innovation as explored in Chapters 3 and 4.

# 7 Antecedents: what did teaching look like before 1985?

## Background

One of the factors that Henrichsen (1989) considered to be important in determining whether an educational innovation would be successful was what the situation on the ground looked like before the introduction of the innovation. It was necessary to gain a good understanding of the 'antecedents' of a situation before attempting to introduce educational change. The 'antecedents' included the traditional pedagogical practices, the characteristics of the intended user-system (features in the context which might affect the success of an innovation), the characteristics of the intended users of the innovation (usually the teachers and the learners), and the experiences of previous reformers (to learn why earlier attempts at innovation had either succeeded or failed.)

I explained in Chapter 5 that I was not familiar with the Henrichsen framework when I conducted the group interviews, so I did not ask direct questions about the user system that the examination was being introduced into, the users within that system or the experiences of previous reformers. I was aware, however, of the need to find out about pedagogical practices during the 'Old Syllabus era' (the period before the introduction of the new textbooks), to understand how much change had occurred as a result of the examination or of any part of the Ministry of Education's 'innovation package'. The Baseline Study had provided insights into the teaching taking place before the introduction of the new examination but it did not provide information about teaching before the introduction of *English Every Day*. An evaluation of examination impact would have to include information about conditions at the 'true start' of the reform, to serve as a point of comparison with those at 'the finish' (the conclusion of the observation study at the end of 1991). (See Figure 7.1 for a reminder of the key activities in the Evaluation Project, including the Baseline Study, the observation study and the group interviews.)

It was for this reason that I included questions about Old Syllabus teaching during the group interviews. The first three groups that I interviewed all gave me similar information, so I decided that there was little to be gained by asking

## Figure 7.1 Key activities in the Sri Lankan O level Evaluation Project

| Year | Key activities |
| --- | --- |
| 1988 | May – Baseline Study observations carried out by exam design team. |
| | July onwards – Analysis in Lancaster of Baseline Study data, official documents, interviews, questionnaires. |
| | October to December – First training course for Impact Study observers. |
| 1989 | January to March – Second training course for Impact Study observers. |
| | Autumn – Delivery of First Interim Report for Project. |
| | Throughout year – Analysis in Lancaster of 1988 examination results, questionnaires. |
| 1990 | January to March – Third training course for Impact Study observers. |
| | May – Baseline schools revisited by exam design team. |
| | – Round 1 of Impact Study observations. |
| | September – Round 2 of Impact Study. |
| | November – Round 3 of Impact Study. |
| | Autumn – Delivery of Second Interim Report for Project. |
| | Throughout year – Analysis in Lancaster of 1989 examination results, Impact Study data, classroom tests, questionnaires. |
| 1991 | January–March 1991 – Third training course for Impact Study observers. |
| | April/May – Round 4 of Impact Study. |
| | June – Delivery of Third Interim Report for Project. |
| | July/August – Round 5 of Impact Study. |
| | October/November – Round 6 of Impact Study. Group interviews with 64 teachers. (This data forms the core of this study.) |
| | Throughout year – Analysis in Lancaster of Impact Study data, questionnaires. In December, analysis of group interview data. |
| 1992 | January-March – Analysis in Lancaster of all outstanding data, including group interview data. |
| | May – Delivery of Fourth and Final Report to Ministry of Education, Overseas Development Administration and The British Council. |

the same questions to the groups remaining. I changed my mind, however, when I met the teachers from the north and the east of Sri Lanka, who were present at a training seminar in Anuradhapura. The observation team had not been able to enter these areas during the Evaluation Project due to political disturbances, so it was important to talk to these teachers about as many themes as possible, including their teaching in the years before the start of the reform.

There were some risks involved in asking teachers to describe their teaching in a previous era, the most obvious ones being that they would not be able to remember things clearly or that they might be reluctant to talk in front of their peers about what was now out-dated practice. It was necessary to try to fill in the gaps though and interviewing allowed the possibility of expanding and clarifying ideas if this were necessary. I present in this chapter what the teachers told me, with reflections on the value the questions and responses might have had if the information had been gathered during the planning stages of the English language reform rather than several years after its inception. The main areas covered will be 'The Old Syllabus Examination', 'Pedagogic Practices', and 'Antecedents' including 'Characteristics of the User System', 'Characteristics of the Users' and 'Experience of Previous Reformers'.

## The Old Syllabus examination

The first thing that teachers remembered about the Old Syllabus examination was that it tested grammar, reading and writing (see Appendix 1 for a copy of the 1987 version). Grammar was tested in a very traditional way, with separate sections of the paper devoted to different structures: verb forms, word order, prepositions, determiners etc. (Asgiriya 503). Students were asked to choose the best option out of several offered (multiple-choice) rather than to produce an answer of their own:

> T 45: It was entirely structure-based. All the grammar part was given a lot
> of importance. The children were able to follow that because it was very
> mechanical. They could be drilled in that way, so they could mark the
> questions easily, without understanding the passage. (Trincomalee 7)

Reading was also tested in a traditional way. Students were given two or three passages, each several paragraphs long, and they had to select the best option:

> T 44: ... You give a comprehension passage and they give a set of
> questions and then you have to read and answer. So that is reading.
> (Trincomalee 45)

There was a choice of topics in the writing section. Two teachers remembered (slightly inaccurately) that students wrote on either an 'emotive' topic or a 'scientific' one:

T 18: And we had a choice there. 'Emotive' is to do with emotional feeling. You think and write. With 'scientific' the topic is there for you so you should write facts.

DW: What did they choose – emotive or scientific?

T 14: Emotive.

T 18: Emotive.

(No one else offers an opinion.) (Nugegoda 33-37)

Teachers also remembered that the content of the exam was very predictable. The same pattern was followed year after year and teachers and students knew how to prepare for what was to come:

T 47: ... the pattern of the questions that they were framing was 'a' to 'k'. So all multiple-choice, different areas. For example, spelling, then prepositions, then the grammar, then linking ... all those things. So the children knew that the same type of questions would be repeated every year. The children were able to guess ... to prepare themselves beforehand ... (Trincomalee 28)

Several teachers claimed that students could memorize essays for the writing section of the examination:

T 44: And for the exam they get the very same topics. About the village. About the town. So they can be sure of what they will get these for the paper. And there is a wide range of choices there for you. So you learn about three essays – about your country, about your hobbies – and you by-heart all these things and then you go to the test hall and you see – 'My village' is not there, 'My country' is not there, but of the three that you have by-hearted one will be there. And the student is at an advantage and he can easily write about what he has memorised. (Trincomalee 68)

The exam focused on language form rather than on using the language for practical purposes. Some teachers felt it was more difficult than the new examination because it demanded a good knowledge of grammar. One argued that the standards were much higher when she was learning the language:

T 18: I was a student during that time. What I could say was that to get a D-pass in the earlier exam, the student had to be a very clever person. Clever in language. But now it's not the same. To get a D-pass or a C-pass the student need not be that smart in the language. (Nugegoda 5)

Others were scornful of the results and what they indicated about the students' true abilities. One teacher doubted the value of the 'Credit' grade (the second-highest grade):

T 32: This paper (the new O level exam) gives the practical knowledge. The old one they didn't get practical knowledge. The students who could not write their names passed. With Credits they passed. (Ratnapura 475) while another questioned the value of 'Distinction' (the highest grade):

> T 27: The new paper is a practical paper. Because those who have got Distinctions in earlier exams, some of them don't know how to fill in an application form, how to write a letter, how to convey a message ... (Nuwara Eliya 411)

Many teachers believed that students could get better marks than they deserved as a result of 'guess work' (Ratnapura 615) – choosing the best option in multiple-choice questions. Other terms they used were 'underlining' (Nuwara Eliya 416) and 'copying' (Nugegoda 24). One teacher talked about the 'shot in the dark' way in which students handled such questions (Wellawatte 203), while others claimed that 'without understanding the language even they could have done it' (Wellawatte 212). Some told stories of how students could use this technique to their own advantage:

> T 20: There was a system. If you marked even without teaching you tell the students 'Underline all the B's' And then they will get a pass. Without changing. Or A's. Continuously if the child underlines 'A' you can get some marks. (Nuwara Eliya 417)

Students could not get by with guessing on the writing section, but they could either memorize essays (Trincomalee 68) or gamble on getting a good result without attempting the writing:

> T 44: For writing they gave only 40. Whereas for the multiple-choice questions, 60 marks. So easily you could get a 'Credit'. 60 is a Credit. (Trincomalee 89)

There were confusing answers when the teachers were asked about the marking of writing. Teachers who had not been markers did not know how writing had been judged (Nugegoda 43) or were unable to separate their own beliefs about what was important from what was included in the official rating scale (Wellawatte 58-70).

The only other feature that the teachers commented on was that the instructions for the old examination had been given in three languages: Sinhala, Tamil and English. This would have helped students to understand what they had to do (Wellawatte 115), though some teachers complained that it made the examination easier (Trincomalee 56-57).

Only a few teachers mentioned that the old examination had not tested listening and speaking, perhaps because the new exam also ignored these areas.

To summarize, the teachers remembered that the old examination had tested grammar and the written skills, and that it had over-used one particular technique which they believed promoted guessing (multiple choice). A few teachers felt that the examination was difficult because it focused on grammar, but others believed that students could get good results by guessing the right answer or by memorizing passages to reproduce in the writing paper. Not all of the teachers were familiar with the criteria used to assess writing.

# Pedagogical practices

The interviews revealed that even in earlier times teachers divided the academic year into two different phases: 'ordinary teaching' and 'examination preparation'.

## Ordinary teaching

### Content

The teachers used a textbook called *An English Course for Grade Ten* (Sri Lankan Ministry of Education: 1976). This was the final book in a series produced by the Educational Publications Department, and it was in use from the middle of the 1970s up to the beginning of 1988. Teachers typically used the textbook from January to the end of October, when they switched to other materials to prepare their students for the O level examination (Wellawatte 88).

The textbook focused on grammar and reading comprehension, and to a lesser extent on writing. Grammar was presented on its own and in a very systematic way. Some teachers thought that this approach was boring (Nugegoda 11) but others thought that it was easier to follow than the approach adopted by *English Every Day* (see Mosback 1994:57-58 for an explanation of the 'cat's cradle' approach). One teacher explained the difference in this way:

> T 3: ... they have introduced grammar here, but they have introduced it from here and there. Not like that earlier book we had. An English Course for Year 7, Year 8, like that. [There] they have introduced the grammar in order. So it's very easy to teach them. The structure is there. First the simple present, then the present continuous, then the present perfect, like that. It introduced order. But in this book, in EED Year 6 there's something about the present tense. Then in Year 7, something again about the present tense. Then Year 8, something again about the present tense. It's not in order. So when we are going to teach the children it's very ... yes ... confusing ... (Asgiriya 128)

The textbook presented two reading passages in every unit, and each was accompanied by a number of comprehension questions. Some teachers remembered these as being multiple-choice questions (Nugegoda 57), while others said that they were of the 'short answer' variety (Wellawatte 125). Some teachers thought that the questions in the textbook were more difficult than those in the examination, as they required 'discussion' (undefined) rather than 'underlining'. (Wellawatte 125-126).

Some teachers only had enough time to work on one of the passages (Nugegoda 57), while others were able to work on both and bring in extra materials. These were likely to be 'unseen' passages, since students were required to read unfamiliar passages in the examination. (Nugegoda 82)

Some of the teachers ignored writing, especially if their students' language level was low. This happened most often in rural schools:

> T 45: Remote areas. The children are very poor in English. And the environment was also like that. So, how will we teach ...

> T 47: They don't discuss more on this essay writing.

> T 45: They can't grasp it.

> T 44: And they don't get help at home, because nobody speaks English at home and they are helpless to help their children.

> T 47: So they don't put weight on this essay writing. They only concentrate on the first part of the paper. (Trincomalee 78-84)

The section on writing was not heavily weighted. For some teachers it was not worth the effort to teach writing if their students could accumulate marks in other ways.

The situation was different in other contexts, as explained by this teacher from a more privileged school:

> T 47: In some schools students were allowed to write on their own. Because I had taught in a convent. The standard was all right, so we gave guidance to them. We guided them how to write an essay: the introduction, the body of the essay, then the conclusion. Everything we taught. We guided them how to write an essay.

> DW: Okay, so you were saying because your students were ...

> T 47: Because it was a nice good school ... (Trincomalee 75-77)

Several general points arose in the discussion of content. The first, and most relevant for this study, had to do with the importance of the examination in the lives of the students. Their goal was not learning to use the language but getting through the examination:

> T 14: English was limited to the classroom. They wouldn't take it out of the class. It was all examination-based. The children did the exercises to pass the exam. They didn't have any practical knowledge. (Nugegoda 86)

Some teachers regretted the exam focus, but others accepted it as a fact of life. Some felt that it was easier to teach in earlier times when they were able to predict what would appear in the examination and prepare their students 'properly'.

T 15: It is very difficult for teachers now ... we don't know what to teach and what will come. Sometimes the child says (she gives the Sinhala words) – 'Nothing of what you taught was in the paper.' Earlier we didn't have that problem. The teacher has taught spelling and the spelling items have come, so the child was satisfied. The child had confidence in the teacher. Now here the teacher has failed some. Now that problem is there. (Nugegoda 397)

The second point had to do with the practicality of the content: were the students learning anything that would help them in the real world? Several teachers felt that too much attention had been paid to language form and not enough to skills. This teacher felt that the oral skills had been ignored:

T 44: They knew nothing about speaking or listening. They only knew ... prepositions. They didn't know how to speak. And when they spoke they structured it in a grammatically correct order and they spoke, but it would be very artificial. (Trincomalee 33)

There were similar comments about the written skills:

T 47: ... in those days the children were not able to write a notice or they didn't know how to read an advertisement and answer the questions. Or they didn't know how to write an advertisement ... (Trincomalee 139)

Some teachers admitted that they themselves had not known how to do useful things in English. They were having to learn these things now, alongside the students they were teaching:

T 53: ... Filling forms, writing applications. Those things are very much useful. But when we were schooling, in those days, when we were studying English as a second language, we hadn't any opportunity of learning those things. That type of question was not given in the paper. ... Now having followed this new method I have learned how to apply and fill these forms and all that. That is what I personally feel. (Welimada 475)

The third point was that the Old Syllabus material was hard for students to understand. Some teachers felt that it was more difficult to teach than *EED*:

T 58: The material in the textbook was difficult. And the teacher had to do quite a lot of work with that book, rather than the present-day book. In the present-day book everything is given and we have only to recreate it and use our ways of expressing, to make the child understand and respond. But in the earlier book the teacher had to do quite a lot of work to make the child understand and for the child to give a response. (Wellawatte 107)

It is clear even from this brief description that the content of the Old Syllabus was quite different from that of *EED*. More attention was paid to grammar and the written skills, accuracy was more important than communication, and the content was not very practical. Some teachers felt that the content was difficult, especially when it came to writing essays. However, there seemed to be a clear connection between what was taught and what was tested on the examination, which provided teachers with a sense of direction and some security.

## Methodology

'Pattern practice' was the term used most frequently to describe classroom methodology in earlier times. One teacher who had been a student during the last years of the Old Syllabus described the teaching of English in this way:

> T 18: Of course this was my favourite subject, but even then I noticed that it was more like language practice. Later I learned it was the oral-aural method. It was called that and I still remember we had a set of sentences and we had to do reading aloud. Sometimes we did it by heart. We didn't read the book. Say we had 20 sentences – after the 15th sentence the last sentences were just said by heart. We were just doing sentences. We really didn't know what we were saying ... (Nugegoda 49)

Teachers also used the term 'grammar translation', not only for their teaching of structures but also for their teaching of reading (Trincomalee 42). Another term they used was 'English through mother tongue' (Trincomalee 62). This teacher described her routine for teaching reading, which gave the students no opportunity to take the initiative or to solve any problems on their own:

> DW: What would you do with that reading passage?
>
> T 17: (Long silence.) First I explained the lesson. I explained everything. Then I asked some questions based on the lesson. Then I asked the children to read silently.
>
> DW: Is this familiar to the rest of you? Did you follow the same method? [Some indicated that they did.] And after they read silently, then what did you do?
>
> T 17: Then they read it aloud. They answered the questions in the book ... Multiple-choice. (Nugegoda 58-61)

The transcript shows that this teacher was not the only one who did this kind of teaching. One teacher talked about doing something 'practical' when he was teaching reading, but what this amounted to was practising vocabulary:

> T 14: ... I used to take out all of the difficult words from the reading passage and put them on the board. If the children wanted the Sinhala translation I gave it to them. Then I got them to learn all those words for dictation. Then I used to get them to make sentences of their own with the words. To make it a little practical. So they were not using the word only in the context in the book. They used the word in their own sentences. (Nugegoda 88)

None of the teachers talked about their teaching of writing, perhaps because they spent less time on writing than on grammar and reading.

Finally, there were a few comments about the general role of the teacher. One view was that the teacher needed to work very hard 'to make the child understand' (Wellawatte 107). A similar view was that the teacher 'became a dominator in order to help the students who were very weak' (Nugegoda 140).

However, at least one teacher believed that the teachers' life was easy before the introduction of *EED*:

> T 45: Yes, Madam. Now the children have to get involved on their own. Otherwise they can't answer the questions. They can't memorize all the way and come and write the questions. Because they have to read and comprehend, and then only they can answer the questions. So for this type of learning the teachers must pay a lot more attention to teaching in a proper way. The teachers cannot simply be seated and go.
>
> DW: So in the old days the teachers just sat there and then they went?
>
> T 45: Yes, in those days the teachers could do some work. They could read and they could go home. (Trincomalee 166-168)

To sum up, the methodology that was used before the introduction of the new textbooks was teacher-centred, with an emphasis on pattern practice when the focus was language form. The teaching of reading was also very directed, with a lot of teacher explanation and few activities which encouraged students to work out meanings on their own. The teacher's role was to 'make the child understand' rather than to provide opportunities for experimentation or learning by making mistakes.

# Examination preparation

As mentioned earlier, teachers worked their way through the textbook from the beginning of the academic year to the end of October, when they began intensive examination preparation. During this period they used past examination papers, model question papers from other schools and model questions from books that were published commercially (Wellawatte 88 and 154). Teachers worked their way through these materials in a systematic manner:

> T 15: Actually in those day the teacher knew what to give for the exam. We knew thoroughly the format of the paper. We taught children – 'Now, this is what you have to do. You will get 10 for spelling'. We knew the format. So we asked them to work through those items. Now we are not thorough. We do not know what we are getting for the paper. (Nugegoda 73)

Students were sometimes allowed to work through papers on their own (Nugegoda 125), but most classes were run in a lock-step manner. Teachers often had to spend time writing questions on the blackboard because their students did not have copies of the materials.

Some teachers used the blackboard because they believed that students would not make any mistakes when copying (Wellawatte 163); others chose to dictate the questions, both to save time and to make their students more 'confident and independent' (Wellawatte 148). These teachers felt that writing on the board amounted to 'spoon-feeding'.

Some teachers prepared their students for the writing component of the examination by putting a topic on the board, along with a few headings to guide the students' thinking. Students wrote in class rather than at home. One teacher explained why she preferred in-class writing to homework:

> T 54: ... I don't allow them to take it away because they go to tuition classes and copy and come. They ask their tutors to write that and they copy and come. If we have the children write in schools they have to think and write. (Wellawatte 139)

Some teachers did not practise writing with their students, but allowed them to memorize essays:

> T 45: Yes, they get the essays from the magazines or from the papers or from the ... books. Published essay books, published by the other people. So the children used to get the books and memorize the essays and they write the examination and get a pass. That is why they don't know the real right language. (Trincomalee 67)

Examination preparation took place during regular class hours, in 'seminars', and after school. 'Seminars' were held for all of the students in the school who were going to take the examination.

> T 15: Now, in our school after October we gather all the classes and have seminars. In each subject. The teacher comes and gives lectures on the topic she was given. Myself, I was given Finding Out, or Letter Writing. But in those days someone would be given 'Determiners'. So she had to prepare a lesson on determiners, and she would have to give that lecture. All the Year 11 students would be there. She would give a lecture on determiners and they had to take down exercises and notes and things like that. (Nugegoda 109)

Students also received 'hints for the exam' (Nugegoda 115). The teachers did not give an explanation of what these 'hints' consisted of, but they were no doubt similar to the 'clues' and 'system' mentioned in other parts of the data (Wellawatte 179 and Nuwara Eliya 417).

Some teachers felt that the examination preparation period was 'mechanical', but others looked back on it in a more positive way. One young teacher recalled that when she was a student this was 'the most interesting time':

T 18: ... During this period the students and the teacher – it was a personal experience. Before going for the exam the teacher would say that we would get a C-pass or a D-pass. So we knew what was going to happen. (Nugegoda 102)

One of the older teachers also felt that exam preparation had been more enjoyable in former times. This was because the examination contained interesting material, unlike the utilitarian content it contained now:

T 61: ... It has no interesting passages, as we had in the Old Syllabus. Enrichment-wise I think it is less. The language is more bent on the communicative aspect of language and the paper is, in my opinion, rather monotonous than those old days that we had to teach. Because we had some books. Now extra books and passages to do in the Old Syllabus. I mean the Syllabus B ... (Wennapuwa 499)

To summarize, the function of the examination preparation period was to familiarize students with the requirements of the examination and to give them practice answering exam-like questions. The teachers turned to past papers and model papers for the content of their lessons. They had a clear idea of what to do since the examination followed the same pattern every year. Some teachers had to spend a great deal of time copying passages, tasks and items on to the blackboard if their students could not afford examination practice material.

It is quite clear that the kinds of activities taking place during the Old Syllabus era were very similar to the kinds that took place during the late 1980s and early 1990s, which were described in the previous chapter.

## Characteristics of the user system

Henrichsen (1989) argues that in order to judge the likelihood of an educational innovation 'taking hold' it is essential to analyse not only the pedagogic practices followed in the antecedent period but also the 'characteristics of the user system' – the context into which the innovation is to be introduced. Henrichsen presented the features that he thought were most important in his explanation of the Hybrid Model of the Diffusion/Implementation Process (see Chapter 4 for details). I explained in Chapter 5 that I modified the Henrichsen model during my investigation, in order to respond to the kinds of issues that arose in the discussions with these particular teachers. The characteristics that I chose to look at are shown in Figure 7.2 below.

**Figure 7.2 Characteristics of the user system**

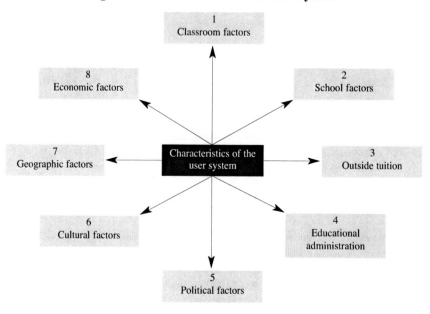

*Source*: (adapted from Henrichsen 1989)

## Classroom factors

The data did not contain information about classroom conditions under the Old Syllabus. There were, however, many comments about classroom conditions after the introduction of the new materials. (See Chapter 10.)

## School factors

Two main points emerged about schools during the Old Syllabus era. The first concerned the differences that existed between some rural schools and some schools in the cities, and how these might have affected the teaching that went on inside them. One of the teachers from the north of the country described some schools in 'remote areas' as being 'very difficult', with students who were very weak in English. These students could not 'grasp' essay writing, and their parents could not help them because they did not know English either. Teachers felt that it was useless to try to teach the students writing because it was beyond their abilities (Trincomalee 78-84). In contrast, a teacher from the east of the country described her own school, which was attached to a convent , as 'a nice good school'. Here she not only taught essay writing but also gave classes in religion in English medium (Trincomalee 15). Some of the students sat an O level examination in English as a First Language (Trincomalee 3).

The second point concerned the internal organization of schools, and whether students worked in mixed-ability groups or in sets corresponding to level. One school had at least nine sets for every year group (Wennapuwa 195). Teachers could do 'enrichment activities' with the higher-level students (singing in English, poetry, drama activities, supplementary reading), while teachers working with the lower levels had difficulties getting their students to do even the most elementary tasks.

## Outside tuition

The data did not contain much information about outside tuition during the Old Syllabus era. There were, however, many references to 'tutories' and their effect on classroom teaching under *EED* (see Chapter 10).

## Educational administration

The main message concerning the organization of education was that there seemed to be a dual system of schooling during the time the Old Syllabus was in operation. We have already seen that some students worked in English medium and would sit an examination in English as a mother tongue, while others learned English in school and worked towards a completely different examination.

The second message concerned the system of teacher training that existed during this era. It was interesting to realize that teachers may have had different understandings about how writing was marked in the old examination, and they might have passed these on to their students and colleagues. This raises the question of what the lines of communication were like within the education system. Were the teachers told the same thing about marking (or any other matter), and who, if anyone, was making sure that the messages were heeded?

## Political factors

There were no references to the political situation during the Old Syllabus era.

## Cultural factors

The main point emerging about culture concerned the role of English in society and the opportunities that were open to those who had enough language and those who did not. Those who had the language could aim high: there was a university examination in English (Wellawatte 18) and students who passed could pursue higher education. In the same country though there were people who could barely get by:

> T 20: In the past ... within the time of our parents they had to go in search of a person who knows English in order to get a paper or something read, no? Even to fill in a census form ... (Nuwara 576)

## Geographical factors

The only comments relating to geographical factors concerned 'remote' schools. We have already seen that proficiency of the students attending these schools was sometimes so low that their teachers did not think it worthwhile teaching them writing. It would be a mistake, however, to believe that there was a perfect correlation between geographical location and the quality of schools (Trincomalee 105-107).

## Economic factors

There were no direct references to economic factors in the user system, but the comments about remote schools and about parents who could not help their children with English were probably references to areas where there was also poverty (Trincomalee 78-84).

## Summary of characteristics of the user system

There was not much information available in the transcripts about the educational and broader contexts during the Old Syllabus era, but several points emerged which represented the types of information Henrichsen advocates collecting before making decisions about change. Perhaps the most important concerned the differences that existed between schools in the same country. On the one hand there were schools where the students' language was so good that they studied other subjects in English, while on the other there were schools where teachers ignored parts of the syllabus because they knew that their students could not handle them. It was not surprising, given the history of the country, that such differences existed. What was interesting was that the designers of the new textbooks seemed to have envisaged all students covering the same syllabus in the same period of time. The examination development team may have been acknowledging the differences when they considered a two-tiered examination (lower-proficiency students would sit a basic-level paper only and higher-proficiency students would sit an additional paper), but this idea was never implemented.

Both the observation study and the group interviews indicated that there were still important differences between the schools in 1991 (see Chapter 10 for more details).

## Characteristics of the users

Henrichsen (1989) also stresses the importance of analysing the characteristics of those who will be the principal users of educational innovations, to find out how their 'attitudes, values, norms, and abilities' (1989:80) will affect their reactions to the planned changes. Figure 7.3 shows the characteristics that I looked for when analysing the comments about the Old Syllabus era. Several of these characteristics (attitude to education, level of education, and attitude to seeking new ideas from the outside world) were used by Henrichsen in his

**Figure 7.3 Characteristics of the users**

*Source*: (adapted from Henrichsen 1989)

description of Japanese teachers and learning in the 1950s. Others emerged from the Sri Lankan data, but mainly from comments that teachers made about teaching with the new materials.

## Characteristics of the teachers

Unfortunately the transcripts contained little information about the teachers' attitudes towards new ideas, their levels of education and English, or details of their personal lives during the Old Syllabus era. This is not surprising, given that only four groups were asked about their teaching in earlier times, and no group was asked about these topics directly. The information that emerged concerned the teachers' attitudes towards teaching and the examination. We have seen in previous sections that the classrooms were quite teacher-centred and examination-oriented, and that many of their views about the examination were negative.

## Characteristics of the students

The teachers talked a little more about their students' attitudes and abilities, particularly about their attitudes towards English, teaching and the old examination. They felt that many students would not have seen English as a subject that was relevant to their lives, but examination preparation would have been a central part of their educational experience. The students would see the examination as language-focused rather than practical, and many (especially students from rural areas) would find the content very difficult.

## Experience of previous reformers

The final aspect that Henrichsen was interested in was the experience of previous reformers: had there been any attempts to introduce change into the education system in earlier days and if so what were the outcomes? If they were successful, what was this due to, and if they failed, what was it about their attempts that led to this failure?

The teachers referred to several attempts to innovate before the introduction of the new examination. The first attempt, naturally enough, was the introduction of the two new textbook series: *English for Me* in the primary schools, and *English Every Day* in the secondary schools. It might have been useful for the examination design team to have gathered more information about the teachers' reactions to these series before they began designing the new examination. This was not possible, however, since they had to make many decisions before the last books in the series were introduced into the classroom.

The next innovations were examinations which were introduced into the education system only shortly before the introduction of the new O level exam. The District English Language Improvement Centre (DELIC) examination was meant to determine whether candidates had enough English to allow them to become English teachers, and the National Certificate in English (NCE) was meant to be for adults who needed a higher qualification in the language. (It is interesting to note that in the first administration of the NCE about 15% of the 17,000 candidates were O level students or A level students. According to Pearson [1994:88], this was 'a striking comment on the public's generally low estimation of the status and worth of O and A level certification at that time ... '.)

Both of these exams were developed by the team that developed the new O level exam. In addition to serving the purposes mentioned above, they were also used as 'proving grounds' for ideas that were being considered for the O level: innovative item types, the testing of oral skills, rating scales for the marking of writing and speaking, training schemes for examiners, etc. Analyses of the NCE were carried out during the first two years of its existence (see Alderson, Wall and Clapham 1987 and Goonetillake, Samarasinghe, Senaratne and Sinhalage 1988) and the designers were able to use the findings to decide what could and could not be usefully transferred to the new examination. Unfortunately, however, the teachers only mentioned these examinations in passing: they did not give the details of their reactions to them.

The final innovation mentioned was continuous assessment. It has already been explained (Chapter 2) that continuous assessment was introduced across the curriculum in late 1986 and was withdrawn in early 1989. Despite the problems surrounding the programme some teachers felt that it had forced them to pay attention to the oral skills. One teacher said that it was too difficult to do pair and group work in his classes at present, because there were too many students, but he had managed to do it when continuous assessment was still in operation:

> DW: ... In the past when you have taught Years 9 and 10, did you do the pair and group work exercises then?
>
> T 40: That means, during the period of continuous assessment? Earlier, that we had to do ... when we had to do continuous assessment. During those days, I did that. Because the listening and speaking skills ... we had to test these. Listening and speaking abilities.
>
> DW: You had to test them?

T 40: During those periods I did that.

DW: You tested them? [Agrees.] And you also did pair and group work when you taught? [Agrees.] But as soon as continuous assessment disappeared you stopped ...

T 40: [Laughs.] Our main idea is to get these students through the examination. Especially in Year 11. In Year 11 I am not doing group and pair work. (Tangalle 136-140)

This teacher was willing to devote time to listening and speaking and certain techniques when an assessment programme required it of him, regardless of practical problems. The difficulties with this particular innovation were mainly the result of rushed implementation: teachers were not familiar with the underlying principles, they did not have enough training, the procedures for recording marks were not well worked out, etc. The teachers in these interviews did not give many reactions to the continuous assessment experience but it is this kind of information that would be useful to future innovators, to help them avoid the problems that eventually brought the programme down.

## Summary of antecedents

The purpose of this chapter has been to analyse the teaching situation and other factors in the educational context before the introduction of the new teaching materials and the new O level examination. I wanted to find out what the situation was like before the English language reform so that I could judge how much impact the new materials and examination had really had on the way teachers handled their classes. I used a modified version of the Henrichsen framework in my analysis to see not only how the exam had affected teaching, but whether there were other factors in the educational context which might have facilitated or hindered change.

What the analysis revealed about pedagogical practice was that there was a great deal of emphasis on grammar and some attention to reading and writing, but little, if any, attention to oral skills. The reading and writing work focused on accuracy rather than on the development of practical skills. The methodology was teacher-centred and depended on teacher explanation and translation, with little time set aside for student-to-student interaction. It would have been difficult for teachers to understand the new ideas about teaching in *English Every Day*, or to adopt them quickly. This may explain why the teaching observed during the 1988 Baseline Study was so unlike the suggestions in the new textbooks. The teachers said that they had adopted the 'new methods' but it is likely that they were either confusing the concepts of methodology and content or that the changes they believed they had made were minor in relation to the types of change that *EED* was encouraging.

Teachers worked out of their textbooks for ten or 11 months of the year, and switched to past papers, commercial papers and their own materials during an 'examination practice' period in the last few weeks of the year. Preparation for the exam was mechanical, involving a review of past papers or model papers question by question, unless there was a good reason (such as inability of the student to cope) for leaving out some of the questions. The preparation period was obviously a standard feature in the educational context. Teachers were used to using supplementary materials so the materials and exam design team or other materials writers could have taken advantage of this and produced more examination support materials, preferably with clear guidance so that the teachers could exploit them well.

The analysis also provided information about the old examination. It emphasized grammar and reading comprehension and followed a rigid pattern year after year. A good result did not necessarily mean that the student knew English: the contents may have been difficult but the techniques, according to the teachers, made it easy to answer the questions. The first few years of the new examination were bound to be difficult since it would shift the emphasis from language form to language skills, require students to produce answers rather than just select them, and make it difficult for students to reproduce work they had memorized.

The analysis produced limited but useful information on the characteristics of the user system, highlighting the differences between schools in different areas and how this could affect what was taught and learned; the differences between ability-sets in some schools and the frustration that this could cause teachers; and the difference between family and social backgrounds, which could have a great influence on students' achievement. The main question arising was how a new set of materials and a new examination could cater for such a diverse audience.

Even the limited information that emerged fills in some gaps that were present in the Baseline Study. Knowing how widespread and deeply ingrained the old style of teaching was can help us to understand why changes in behaviour might not have occurred early on in the reform. Understanding the differences between remote schools and town schools, weaker and stronger students, households with fewer and more privileges, etc. might help us to see why the changes that did occur took different forms in different circumstances.

It should be recalled at this point that the framework applied in this analysis was identified and developed subsequent to the gathering of data. The questions asked during the interviews were general questions, deriving from my analysis of earlier data rather than from theory. This meant that there were some areas of the framework which were not discussed in the interviews. Having more information about all of the topic areas would have been helpful not only for the project I was working on but also, presumably, for the designers who introduced the new textbook and the new examination in the first place. Such questioning needs to be carried out before an innovation is introduced rather than years afterwards – both so that there is less of a chance that memories will become distorted by the passing of time (or changing views of the world) and so that they can feed into the introduction of whatever the innovation might be. This is a justification for a more detailed baseline investigation, which looks not only at classroom teaching but also attempts to uncover what is in, and on, the minds of teachers, students and other important stakeholders in the innovation process.

# 8 Implementation factors: characteristics of the innovation: the textbook series

## Background

Henrichsen (1989) claims that the development of an effective strategy for introducing educational change depends not only on an analysis of the context into which an innovation is to be introduced (the 'antecedents', described in Chapter 7), but also on an understanding of the 'implementation factors' which are in operation once the innovation is in place. 'Implementation factors' are factors which can facilitate or hinder the success of the innovation. Henrichsen groups these factors into four general categories: those relating to the innovation itself (its originality, complexity, etc.), those relating to the user system (the classroom, the school and so on), those relating to the resource system (the management team and the management structure), and those relating to the interaction between factors in the previously mentioned categories ('inter-elemental factors').

My analysis of the group interview data included a search for any comments the teachers might have made about the presence or absence of these factors in their own context. The analysis uncovered many comments relating to the innovation itself and to the user system, but few relating to the resource system or to inter-elemental factors. The teachers said a great deal about two particular factors within the user system (the teachers and the students), and this led me to create a separate category of factors which I called 'Characteristics of the Users'.

Chapters 8–11 will be devoted to an analysis of the teachers' comments regarding characteristics of the innovation, the user system and the users. Each chapter will contain a discussion of the factors included in the relevant category, accompanied by quotations which either illustrate the factors that are being discussed or indicate problems in the way they are defined in the literature or in my attempt to employ them in the analysis of this particular innovation.

I begin with an analysis of what Henrichsen called 'the characteristics of the innovation', which Fullan (1991:68) refers to as 'characteristics of change' and Rogers (1995:208) refers to as 'attributes of the innovation'.

## Characteristics of the innovation

Henrichsen (1989) listed eleven characteristics which could make an innovation more or less acceptable to potential users: originality, complexity, explicitness, relative advantage, trialability, observability, status, practicality, flexibility, primacy and form. My analysis of the examination suggested that 'predictability' was also important. All of these characteristics are included in Figure 8.1 below.

It was clear from the beginning of my analysis that I would need to look at what the teachers had to say about the exam and how its features affected its chances of reinforcing the content and methodology of the textbook. However, it is important to remember that in the early years of the examination the *English Every Day* textbooks were still also quite new. The first book of the

**Figure 8.1 Characteristics of the innovation**

*Source*: (adapted from Henrichsen 1989)

series had only been introduced in the mid-1980s, and Book 11 had been in place less than a year when the examination was administered for the first time. The observations which were carried out in 1990 and 1991 had indicated that many teachers were not teaching in the way the textbook designers would have wanted. If teachers did not understand the textbooks or find them easy to work with then it would be difficult for a new examination to make things any better – no matter how favourably it was regarded. It therefore seemed necessary to analyse what the teachers said about the textbooks before looking at the exam: did they understand what the textbooks required of them and were they willing and able to comply with these demands? Only after analysing the comments about the textbooks would it be possible to understand whether the new examination had any potential to contribute to the move towards change.

What follows is an analysis of the characteristics of both innovations – the textbook series and the examination – based on the comments made by the teachers during the group interviews. I begin the analysis with a brief overview of the textbook series and then look at each of the components in the Henrichsen model in turn (this chapter). I then repeat the process, shifting the focus to the examination (Chapter 9). I conclude with my judgement about whether the two innovations were working together or whether they were pulling in different directions, and how this affected the possibility of examination impact on teaching.

## Characteristics of the *English Every Day* textbook series

The *English Every Day* (*EED*) series consisted of five textbooks (Books 7–11), which were written by a team of 12 Sri Lankan teachers and teacher advisers, and a British ELT consultant. The design team worked in the Curriculum Development Centre (CDC) of the Ministry of Education in Colombo. The textbooks were written after two years of consultation with teachers in many parts of the country. This consultation took the form of workshops, where, in the early days, teachers were shown how to use their old textbooks in more communicative ways, and, later on, were asked to give feedback on ideas which were being considered for the new series (Mosback 1994). The later workshops also served as training events, where teachers learned about the principles of communicative language teaching and discussed and practised the types of techniques that would be suitable for the new materials.

Many of the ideas that were dealt with in these workshops were published in a 90-page booklet called *Effective English Teaching* (*EET*) (Sri Lankan Ministry of Education: no date). Different sections of this booklet were then reprinted in the teachers' guides for the *EED* series.

The Year 7 teachers' guide was a key component in the series, as it presented many of the *EET* ideas on how to make classrooms more conducive to language learning and what the teacher's role should be in the learning process. It also presented procedures for teaching reading and writing in the early years of secondary school and a standard procedure for teaching listening.

The Year 8 guide repeated the ideas about the classroom and the teacher's role, and reproduced much of the remaining content from the *EET* booklet. It presented ideas for more advanced work in reading and writing, but it contained no information about listening.

The Year 9 guide was less ambitious, repeating only the core information about the classroom and the teacher's role and a few ideas about oral skills. The Year 10/11 guide presented only a brief 'Syllabus for the GCE O level' and teaching notes for some of the exercises.

The textbooks which are most relevant to this chapter are Books 10 and 11. The units in these books generally contained the following elements:

- a 'role play', which was a long dialogue illustrating new language points, following a story line introduced in Book 7
- 'Learning Together' exercises, which were simple communicative activities designed to encourage listening and speaking practice, and sometimes leading to writing
- 'Finding Out' passages, which provided practice in reading for a purpose and developing reading skills
- a poem, with questions about language and ideas, sometimes leading to a writing activity
- discussion exercises, based on reading or visual material
- a listening exercise, to give practice in understanding oral input the first time round.

(See Appendix 11 for a sample unit from Book 11.)

By the time the group interviews were held (late 1991) Book 10 had been in the schools for about four years, and Book 11 for about three years. The teachers made many comments about the textbooks as they discussed their way of teaching. These comments will be presented below, under headings that correspond to the components in Figure 8.1.

# Originality of *EED*

'Originality' refers to the origin of the innovation, and whether it is perceived as being appropriate for local circumstances. According to Pelz (1985, cited in

Henrichsen 1989:82) users may see an innovation as *custom-made* (invented locally for local needs), *modified* (patterned after an innovation invented elsewhere but adapted to fit local needs), or *ready-made* (copied from an innovation invented elsewhere with little change to fit local circumstances). The main problem with 'ready-made' innovations is that they may not be compatible with previously introduced ideas, or with the users' values, beliefs or needs. (Rogers 1995:224).

The *English Every Day* series contained features which were very different from those in the previous series: new topics for reading, including cross-curricular topics in the later books; a focus on language skills rather than language form; and an approach to grammar which was less direct and less intensive than that of the earlier series. There were many exercises for listening and speaking, and many activities which encouraged student-student interaction rather than the traditional pattern of teacher explanation. *EED* could have been perceived as a ready-made or modified innovation given that so many of its features were so novel and that the textbook consultant was not a Sri Lankan. However, there were no suggestions that the textbooks were an alien imposition. The teachers liked its relevance to everyday life, its focus on listening and speaking, and the possibilities it offered for more active student involvement. (See section on 'Relative advantage' for more details.)

However, the fact that the teachers expressed positive opinions does not necessarily mean that they understood the ideas underlying the series or that they were able to implement them in the way the textbook designers intended.

## Complexity of *EED*

Henrichsen claimed that the success of an innovation is inversely related to its 'complexity': the amount of new learning that it requires of its users and whether these demands are acceptable. Complexity is seen as a critical factor by other innovation specialists as well, amongst them Rogers (1995:242) and Fullan (1991:71).

There were two sets of users for the *EED* series: the teachers and the students. The teachers made many comments about the difficulty of the textbook series both for themselves and for their learners, and these will be examined in detail in the following two sections.

## Complexity of *EED* for teachers

There were three main areas of complexity for the teachers: two related to reading and one to oral skills.

   The area that was referred to most often was the difficulty of the 'Finding Out' passages: texts appearing in every unit which were supposed to give practice in various reading skills (skimming, scanning, etc.). The passages often dealt with unfamiliar topics, and students were supposed to use their skills to determine what the main ideas were, what information was relevant, what could be ignored, etc. Some teachers did not feel comfortable with the idea of presenting so much unfamiliar material. They did not see reading from a skills perspective but rather as an activity in which students collected facts that they would need for the examination, either when they were faced with 'seen passages' (Wellawatte 591, Colombo 548) or when they had to write essays (Colombo 42). They believed that the students needed to understand all of the details in the passages – not just how to find the information that was required in the questions – and they felt that it was their responsibility to explain what the students had not already understood. They believed that they had to become experts in the topics presented in the passages – otherwise they would not be able to explain everything or be able to answer their students' questions.

   Teachers reacted to this 'complexity' in different ways. Some were worried to start with but then became interested in learning things that they had not known before. This can be seen in an exchange between the head of a Regional English Support Centre and some of the teachers who used the centre:

> Head of centre: I used to conduct seminars. I used to introduce these books. And she [he points to Teacher 20] used to argue with me at the seminars. She used to say 'You are trying to ruin our children. What is this?' And I said, 'Now you go on teaching and you will see the results.'
>
> T 20: And actually we studied the books. The set...all the whole thing in *English Every Day*. We studied ...
>
> Unknown voice: And we learned something.
>
> T 20: ... teachers.
>
> T 28: And an English teacher can't be only an English specialist. She should be an all-rounder, no? Science, maths, home science, everything.
>
> T 20: Geography. Food. (Nuwara Eliya 434-440)

   Other teachers tried to acquire the background knowledge, but resented the fact that this was (in their eyes) necessary. This teacher felt it was wrong that the *EED* series taught 'subject matters' rather than English:

> T 32: ... And the other thing, some of these lessons cannot be done with them because they're all subject matters, no? Actually, not English, no? We can't teach them English. We have to teach them English, not subject

matters, no? They cannot be taught subject matters because they don't know English. First they must know English, no? (Ratnapura 175)

Another teacher did not see the point of presenting information that the students were not familiar with already:

T 3: ... There are some 'Finding Out' passages given in this book that is not relevant to Sri Lanka. There are some passages on Tbilisi and the panda and the lorikeet. I myself I don't know who is that lorikeet bird. And we can't explain that. The panda. I myself I don't know who is panda. What kind of animal is panda? And Tbilisi. Only when I go through that lesson I know where Tbilisi is. Otherwise I don't know. So I think it's better if they have introduced a country somewhere in Sri Lanka. It's better. And there are a lot of birds in Sri Lanka. Peacock and ostrich. The birds they can see in Sri Lanka. (Asgiriya 129)

These teachers believed that their students would be unable to deal with new content because they did not have enough language or because they did not have the background knowledge that they needed. They believed unfamiliar content was making reading difficult when it may have been the teachers' own attitudes towards reading. The teacher quoted above did not make a connection between her own way of gaining new knowledge ('Only when I go through that lesson I know where Tbilisi is') and the reading skills she could have been helping her students to develop.

There were some teachers who were unable to deal with this approach to reading. If they had no one to consult, or if they were too shy to ask for help, they simply omitted the Finding Out passages from their programme. One young teacher admitted that she skipped passages when she did not understand what they were saying. Her English was quite weak, and so she switched to her mother tongue to express her feelings in the interiew. The exam developer translated her main ideas, and wrote a summary of what she had said for the transcript:

Teacher 2 expresses her difficulty in introducing the meaning of difficult terms because she does not feel confident. The topics are too technical. She thought that she had to give all of the information to the students. She confessed to having omitted the lessons concerning the telephone and the computer because they were too difficult. She also mentioned a diagram/some diagrams showing the vocal chords. (Asgiriya 605)

Some of the passages that such teachers mentioned were in fact quite difficult (see, for example, the explanation of radio waves in Figure 8.2), but others were fairly simple. Some looked more difficult than they were because they were accompanied by diagrams or other visual means of presenting information (Asgiriya 69 and 71). Teachers who were not used to pie-charts, tables, etc. saw them as additional reading problems rather than as the aids to comprehension they were meant to be.

## Figure 8.2 A sample 'Finding Out' passage (*English Every Day*, Year 11)

**49**

| UNIT FIVE | FINDING OUT | RADIO BROADCASTS |

One of the many things space satellites are used for is to transmit radio broadcasts. The British Broadcasting Corporation (BBC) send out programmes in English for most of the day, but you need a special radio with "short" wave bands. Radio waves can be measured in metres—the length of the wave or "wavelength".

*wave length*

Even the shortest broadcasting short wave is 11 metres long from peak to peak. The longest can be 75 or 80 metres.

Another way of talking about radio waves is by their frequency—that is, how many thousand "peaks" travel out in one second. These are called Megahertz (MHz). Mega means "a thousand" and Hertz was the German scientist who discovered radio waves in the nineteenth century.

Clearly the longer the waves are, the fewer will pass in one second, so the MHz number will grow smaller as the metre figure increases.

Here is some information from the BBC magazine "London Calling." Scan through it to find the following information quickly. Sri Lankan time is 5 1/2 hours ahead of GMT.

1. What time of the day in Sri Lanka can you hear English lessons?
2. What metre bands can you hear them on?
3. What is the MHz frequency in the 25 metre band?
4. What should you do if the programme is too faint?
5. How should you adjust the aerial?
6. Is the time in France ahead of or behind Greenwich Mean Time?
7. Can you find two programmes that might be of more interest to teachers?
8. Which programmes might be based on drama?
9. Which programme might deal with English history?
10. To general English programmes for beginners are marked in a special way. Which do you think they are?

Bangladesh, Burma, India, Nepal, Pakistan and Sri Lanka

| DAY | PROGRAMME | DAY | PROGRAMME |
|---|---|---|---|
| Saturday | ONCE UPON A THRONE | Wednesday | 'OH WE GO |
| Sunday | CAN I HELP YOU? | Thursday | FOUNDATIONS |
| Monday | CHANGING SCENES | Friday | IMPROVISATIONS |
| Tuesday | TEACHING ALIVE | | |
| GMT | Metre bands SHORT WAVE | MHz SHORT WAVE | |
| 16.45 - 17.00 | 25, 41, 49 | 11.905, 7.155 & H.85 | |

**50**

| HOW TO FIND YOUR BBC ENGLISH BY RADIO PROGRAMME |

1. Discover the difference between local time in your own country and GMT. For example, if you live in France, in wintertime you are one hour ahead of GMT. So if it is 6.30 in the morning by your clock, it is 07.30 GMT — time for your English lesson (See 'When to Listen' section above).

2. Have a good look at your radio set. Find the SHORT WAVE band. It should be marked in Megahertz. Along it you may also find metres and little black oblongs which indicate the metre bands. The SHORT WAVE band may look like parts of this diagram below. We have illustrated the whole range which seems to find 6.15 Megahertz or only metres. The Megahertz which is in the 49 metre band and 15.39 MHz in the 19 metre band.

3. If you have an aerial on your set, raise it as high as possible. Then carefully move the tuning indicator to the appropriate place on the dial. Remember that metre readings increase from right to left and Megahertz increase from left to right. Some sets include only Megahertz or only metres. The arrows show where to find 6.15 Megahertz which is in the 49 metre band and 15.39 MHz in the 19 metre band.

4. Listen for a voice in English, speaking clearly. If you can hear it faintly, move your radio set around various points of the compass. Most of our signals to Europe originate from transmitters in Eastern England and as relayed from China or Berlin. Programmes for Asia are relayed from Singapore; for Latin America they are relayed from Ascension Island.

```
     6.15 MHz                    15.39 MHz:                         MHz
 5       6    7          8    9   10   12   15   15   15    5   20   22.5   25
 4                                                            16  11.3         11
75      60    49         40   31   30   25   19   20   19        15          Metres
        49    50                    20   19  19
        49 metre band               19 metre bar
                                    19 metre bar
```

The BBC has a wide variety of programmes, but Britain does not have the biggest world broadcasting service in English. The USA has far more hours of broadcasting. But can you guess the country with the most powerful English broadcasting service in the world? It is the USSR. Using the sets of information on the next page, answer these questions.

1. How many "Super-Transmitters" does the Soviet Union have?
2. How many "Super-Transmitter" sites does the U.S.A. have?
3. On how many continents does the U.S.A. have transmitters?
4. In how many countries does the U.S.S.R. have transmitters?
5. In how many African languages do the U.S.A. and U.S.S.R. broadcast?
6. For how many hours a day does Radio Moscow broadcast in English to the U.S.A.?
7. How many more languages does the U.S.S.R. broadcast than the U.S.?
8. North Carolina is a state of the U.S.A. What important radio equipment would you expect to find there?
9. Which of these two countries has a transmitter in Sri Lanka?
10. Write a paragraph of not more than fifty words comparing any three aspects of the U.S.A. and U.S.S.R. world programmes. Useful lining words might be "but", "whereas", "on the other hand", "while". Here is an example. While the U.S.A. has 160 transmitters, whereas the Soviet Union has nearly 300. While the U.S. broadcasts for 9 hours a day to China the U.S.S.R. broadcasts to them for 24, but in total number of hours of broadcasting the two countries are about the same.

The second area of complexity was how to deal with poems. The *EED* designers had decided to include poems 'in response to many teachers' expectations' (Mosback 1990:21). There were half a dozen poems in the Year 10 and Year 11 books, and these were accompanied by questions which encouraged the students to think about what they were reading, discuss their ideas with their classmates, and, occasionally, write their reactions. Some of the teachers who were graduates in English enjoyed working with the poems (e.g. Ratnapura 247, Nugegoda 247), but others either did not understand them:

> T 51: So far, I haven't missed any lessons. But when I explain poems sometimes I have some difficulties. Because I couldn't get the real hidden meaning sometimes. Then I had to refer to the dictionary also. But those students like those poems because they want something strange. But poems depend on the explanation of the teacher, I think. When I explain the poem, they like it very much. (Welimada 107)

or did not know how to deal with them in class:

> T 64: I told you, some listening activities and poems. Maybe that's been because I am not very competent in that. I have tried to avoid that because I am not very good at that rhyming business and all that. [Laughter.] I have tried as much as possible to avoid that. It is out of my sheer lack of confidence. (Wennapuwa 278)

The third area of complexity concerned methodology rather than content: did teachers understand how to teach the oral skills? This question was put by the head of the Regional English Support Centre mentioned earlier. He believed that some teachers were neglecting listening and speaking not because of the examination, but because they did not know how to teach them. Teaching listening was especially problematic:

> Head of centre: ... Now when we had some seminars for the newly-appointed teachers, most of the teachers they didn't know how to teach listening in the classroom. Actually didn't know what it was. Then we had to give that teaching technique. That's how I came to know later why they tend to ignore this skill. (Nuwara Eliya 651)

## Complexity of *EED* for students (as perceived by teachers)

The teachers also commented on what made *EED* difficult for their students. Two of the areas they mentioned matched areas they had found difficult themselves: the 'Finding Out' topics and the poems. However, they also identified a third area of difficulty, which was more general and which might have been at the root of the first two.

The 'Finding Out' topics that the teachers said their students found difficult included airport departure routines, foreign currency, travellers' cheques, general science, computers, police reports and courtroom procedures. Telephones also caused a problem in some of the more remote areas. More than one teacher talked about having to demonstrate how to use a telephone when their students were supposed to be learning how to take telephone messages:

> T 28: Now when I was giving these telephone messages I took them to the Post Office, showed them the real material, showed them how to dial. Then the telephone and the receiver, mouthpiece. Then I got them to speak from the Exchange to the Post Office because it was close to the school ... So they learned it, and after coming to class they mimed. One person dialling. One person taking the message and filling in the form. That is when the person is out. They fill in the form and convey the message to that person after he comes. (Nuwara Eliya 149)

This teacher supplied background information that the students really needed before they could tackle what they were supposed to be learning. In other cases though the teachers explained more than they needed to, believing, as was indicated in the previous section, that their students should be collecting facts for the examination. This excerpt is long, but it gives a good idea of the types of things that some teachers felt they should be teaching in their language lessons:

> T 47: For example, if you are teaching about the countries, you can't just confine yourself to Sri Lanka and just stop. You have to teach about the neighbouring countries.
>
> T 45: You have to bring the map and show the different countries.
>
> T 47: The world map and show where Sri Lanka is, where India is. You have to show the neighbouring countries. So that is extra work.
>
> T 45: Then only the children can acquire the names of the different countries, the neighbouring countries, and where the countries are.
>
> T 47: What are the industries ...
>
> T 44: How far is it from Sri Lanka ...
>
> T 45: What type of nations they are ...
>
> DW: So you're saying that ...
>
> T 45: It's sort of a motivation. Motivation and it helps the students to learn more. (Trincomalee 207-215)

We saw earlier that some teachers omitted certain passages if they themselves found the concepts difficult. Others skipped over material if they felt that it would be too hard for their students. Explaining such difficult material would be, in the words of one of the teachers, 'wasting time' (Wennapuwa 77).

The second area of complexity was the poems. Some teachers tried to cover these quickly, perhaps using the mother tongue to speed up the process (Welimada 107), while others postponed them until the end of the year because the students were 'not smart enough' to do them when they first appeared in the textbook (Nugegoda 245). Some teachers left them out altogether. One teacher offered this explanation for his decision:

> T 37: I feel that in some lesson units the contents are not familiar with my children, because we work in a remote area. Children can't understand some of those poems. I believe that those poems are not tally with their knowledge. So sometimes I used to skip them. And I had to choose certain parts. In the lesson units there are so many areas, no? So sometimes I used to skip. Not all. Like that. (Ratnapura 91)

It is not clear what this teacher meant by 'their knowledge' – whether it was language knowledge or background information – but some teachers felt that poems were more demanding simply because they were poems and not 'just a paragraph' (Wennapuwa 87).

Certain poems were felt to be particularly problematic. Amongst these were D H Lawrence's *The Snake* ('It's just like a snake, a very long poem' – Tangalle 391, Welimada 88 and others) and Shelley's *Ozymandias* (Ratnapura 93).

The third area of complexity was the general language level of *EED*. A number of teachers talked about how they had to modify the material or simplify the exercises (Ratnapura 118-125), spend many teaching periods on the same passage (Wennapuwa 225), use the mother tongue (Trincomalee 272), or simply rush through or skip lessons because their students could not understand the language. Even teachers who taught in prestigious schools had difficulties. One of these teachers explained why it had taken her so long to cover Book 11:

> T 36: Because I couldn't rush through. There are some lessons that you have to spend days and days. I mean, periods. More than three periods sometimes. Some structures. Even 'Finding Outs', though I alter them. Simplify them. Doing all that, sometimes I find that I come to a blank wall where I can't just penetrate. With the children. I hope you can understand what I feel. What I mean. And sometimes I have to re-do the lesson, in some other way. All kinds of things take your time, your energy, your imagination. So what I say is that I was able to finish it ... One reason was that I stayed back. The other reason was I spent time planning it. (Ratnapura 69)

To summarize, a considerable number of teachers felt that at least some of the *EED* material was too difficult for their students, and a few felt that it was also too difficult for themselves. These findings matched those of surveys carried out by Flavell and Randles, which indicated that teachers thought the *English Every Day* textbooks were difficult and that the 'Finding Out' sections were the most difficult of all (1994:69). Flavell and Randles report that poems were also problematic: one teacher wrote that 'complicated rhymes were far beyond the ability of students who came from homes where the parents did not even write the mother tongue'. (Ibid.)

It is important to note, however, that some of the teachers' complaints about difficult material may have had as much to do with their own lack of understanding of what they were supposed to be teaching as with the 'objective' difficulty of the passages.

## Explicitness of *EED*

'Explicitness' refers to two aspects of an innovation: how well thought out it is in terms of rationale, principles, aims, and so on; and how clear the explanations of these ideas are to the users (Henrichsen 1989:84).

Mosback explains that the textbook design team spent 18 months developing their thinking about how to put the *EED* series together (1994:58). Many of the ideas they used came from the 'communicative approach', which represented 'the latest thinking in the field' in the late 1970s and early 1980s. One of the attractions of this approach was that it emphasized the importance of a needs-based syllabus; another was 'that it would get teachers away from the rigid front-of-class stance that had become the norm in the system' (op. cit:53-54). Mosback points out though that the textbook team had to consider not only their own ideas about what was desirable but also educational traditions, a 'pupil development agenda', a moral and cultural agenda, the existence of a public examination, and the views of many teachers, teacher advisers and other educators. This meant that the finished series could only be 'communicatively-oriented' rather than 'communicatively-committed' (op. cit:56, 60). The fact that the ideas in the series came from so many sources may explain why there is little discussion of theories of language or language learning in the teachers' guides. In fact, most of the discussion concerns what Richards and Rodgers (1985) would call 'procedures': the arrangement of the classroom, organizing pair and group work, the role of the teacher, steps in handling dialogues, general points for handling 'Finding Out' passages, and so on.

A careful analysis of the Year 7 and Year 8 guides shows that they were not as explicit as teachers would need them to be if they were being exposed to the new ideas about teaching for the first time. Much information was given and many examples, but it is difficult to find the principles amongst all the detail. This is especially true in the explanations about reading in the Year 8 guide:

there are references to reading skills and different sorts of questions, and caveats about reading aloud and explaining everything to the students word for word, but there are no clear statements about getting the students to read silently or letting them work out meanings for themselves. There is no description of how to handle a complete lesson. The guidance in the Year 10/11 guide is also disappointing – little more than answers to the exercises in the textbook. There seems to be an assumption that teachers would already be familiar with the procedures introduced earlier in the series, but this required access to the Year 7 and Year 8 guides, which could not be taken for granted.

Returning to the interviews, we know that at least some teachers felt there was an *EED* approach to teaching. This was most evident when they discussed the teaching that took place in 'tutories' (institutions offering exam preparation tuition) as opposed to ordinary classrooms. The tutory teaching was 'not relevant to our teaching methods' (Trincomalee 661), the teachers followed 'a different methodology' (Trincomalee 662), they 'don't follow all the four skills' (Trincomalee 631) and 'all the meanings are given in Tamil' (Trincomalee 632). What is not clear, however, is where the teachers in the interviews got their ideas about *EED* from, since they make no mention of the teachers' guides.

There were other teachers though who mentioned the teachers' guides specifically. Several indicated that they followed the 'guidebook' carefully and implied that it was satisfactory.

> T 54: Read the guidebook. We study what we have to teach the children, and we set out to teach ... (Wellawatte 317; see also Welimada 157 and 163, and Asgiriya 562)

Other teachers were less impressed with the guides, for various reasons. One teacher felt that the objectives of the exercises were not clear:

> T 5: [Teachers should be] given the objective and how to handle each objective. I mean, they don't have to use the same method but then there should be guidance there. I think that's what teachers are looking for. They really don't know how to tackle each section of the book. (Asgiriya 576)

Another felt that the guides let her down when she had particular problems:

> T 36: You have to go through the lesson thoroughly, and then pick out the problematic areas. You have to study them and then take the guidebook. Sometimes I must say that the guidebook is not much of a help. But yet, you have to look at it and try to follow it. Failing that, you have to gather up your own techniques and then tackle the problem. That's how I did it. (Ratnapura 67)

Still another, who omitted 'Finding Out' lessons because she could not understand the content, thought that the guides should provide background information about the topic teachers were working on so that they could explain things to their students more easily (Asgiriya 566).

There were a few teachers, however, who felt that there was enough advice in the guides but that they could not follow them because of their own special circumstances. One teacher explained his situation in this way:

> T 64: Sometimes I may not be able to follow the exact guidance given in the Teacher's Guide. But I try my own techniques. But the aim I feel is to give them the opportunity to grasp some information from the passage. Find out something from the book. Even though it's simple. Simple objective questions. (Wennapuwa 247)

This teacher was working with low-level students and felt that they could not practise reading skills because they did not have enough basic proficiency.

One of the difficulties in determining whether the *EED* guidance was explicit enough was knowing whether the teachers had access to the teachers' guides in the first place. The observation study had revealed that 20% of the Year 11 teachers did not have access to the guide for their year and 40% did not have access to the guide for Year 7 (Alderson and Wall 1992). These figures are in line with Randles' survey, which indicated that only half the teachers had access to a Year 7 guide in 1989, and Flavell's study, which indicates that as many as 80% did not have access to the guide for the year they were teaching (Flavell and Randles 1994:70). However, even when the data indicates that teachers had the guides and read them, it is not always clear whether the problems that they were having were due to the quality of the guidance given or to a rejection of the guidance because of other factors in the context, such as their own beliefs or the low ability of their students.

## Relative advantage of *EED*

Rogers defines 'relative advantage' as 'the degree to which an innovation is perceived as being better than the idea it supersedes' (1995:12). I did not ask the teachers direct questions about the relative advantage of using *EED*, but I could infer from the opinions they gave about several of its features how they felt it compared with the earlier series or with the other materials that were available in 1991.

The major advantage that *EED* had over the earlier series was its relevance to everyday life. Many teachers commented on how the textbook prepared students for life outside the classroom. The topics made students 'knowledgeable' (Nugegoda 408), and the skills that it emphasized would help them in the future:

> T 28: ... But English I think they can pick up very easily, and especially the new books, no? They cater for everything. When they get out of class after O level they can apply for jobs. They know how to apply... (Nuwara Eliya 576)

Several teachers appreciated the attention given to speaking, a skill which had been neglected in the previous series:

> T 44: They knew only the contents and nothing more. Like speaking. They knew nothing about speaking. Listening. Only prepositions. They didn't know how to speak. And when they spoke they structured it in a grammatically correct order and they spoke, but it would be very artificial, when you went to pattern it in such a way and speak. Speaking should come naturally. Children were feeling very shy to speak at that stage. Nowadays they try to speak. Not so earlier. (Trincomalee 33)

One of the disadvantages of the *EED* was the difficulty of the 'Finding Out' passages, which was explained in the section on 'Complexity of *EED*'.

The other disadvantage of *EED* was its treatment of grammar. Several teachers felt that it did not include enough grammar or that it did not treat it in a systematic way. Two teachers mentioned that their students wanted more grammar because they felt that this was the best way to learn a language (Colombo 62, Wennapuwa 413), and two others talked about the importance of grammar for the writing section of the examination:

> T 64: ... I won't, say, completely rule out the possibility that this does not promote the child to do free writing, but it should be kept in mind that when free writing or composition is concerned that the child should have a fair knowledge of the structure. To design a grammatically correct structure. I have doubts whether this approach convincingly prepares the children for that kind of structural production. (Wennapuwa 606. See also Asgiriya 128.)

Several teachers said that they brought in supplementary grammar exercises to compensate for the lack of exercises in *EED*. (Colombo 58, Asgiriya 171.)

*EED* could also be compared with other teaching materials in the market place. There were two types of commercial publications available: those which helped teachers with their ordinary teaching and those which helped them with examination preparation. The first type was popular with teachers who wanted help teaching reading comprehension. We have already seen that the *EED* focus was supposed to be on skills development. There were only a few questions on some passages and the questions might be 'out of order' if the intention was to practice skimming or scanning rather than sentence by sentence comprehension. Some teachers had difficulty with this approach and bought special books which not only gave more questions but also ordered them in more conventional ways:

> T 1: ... Sometimes these questions are not understood by the children alone. They want our clarifications and all these things ... They're given in very simple English. They're going from the simplest to the most difficult. But not in this book. Sometimes the most difficult is coming the first. (Asgiriya 167)

The second type of publication was written specifically for examination preparation – e.g. *New G.C.E. (O.L.) Exam English Model Question Papers with Answers* (de Silva 1989). These books gave teachers ready-made material for practising reading and writing. Some teachers expressed faith in the ability of the authors to predict what would be on the examination:

> T 3: ... I think those who have written the books they are the master teachers of English. Bernard de Silva is a person who taught at the Royal College and now he is a retired English teacher, and I think he knows better than us. Through his experience he can write something. And Mr. Dharmasena is a person who was a lecturer in the training college. Maharagama Training College. And Mr. Somapali Wijetunga also lectures in the training college. So they themselves have returned ... have introduced those books for us. So I think without preparation of our own things, better to introduce a passage from their ... (Asgiriya 266)

The disadvantage of this material, however, was that it did not provide guidance for the teachers: no teaching notes and sometimes not even the correct answers.

To summarize, the main advantage that the *EED* series had over the previous series was its relevance to the everyday world, both in terms of the topics it dealt with and the skills that it tried to develop. Its main disadvantages were that some of its content was considered to be very difficult and its treatment of grammar was not systematic. These advantages and disadvantages did not affect whether teachers selected or rejected the *EED* series as they had no choice in the matter; however, it did affect the types of supplementary materials that they brought into the classroom.

The main disadvantages that the *EED* series had when compared with some of the other materials available on the market was that it did not contain the types of questions which teachers felt their students needed and it was not as obviously oriented towards the O level examination. Although many teachers praised the *EED* for dealing with so many topics and skills, they were happy to ignore it when it was time to concentrate on the examination.

## Trialability of *EED*

The term 'trialability' refers to whether potential users can try out an innovation on a limited basis before deciding to adopt it (Rogers 1995:16). The term is often used by marketing specialists, who give away 'trial size' containers of new products or urge readers to subscribe to serials or join book clubs for a 'trial period'. This concept was not relevant to the introduction of the *EED* series since it was introduced as the official national textbook series and all teachers were required to use it whether they approved of it or not. Consequently there were no comments about the trialability of the textbook during the group interviews and this lack of trialling may have led to some of the problems noted above.

## Observability of *EED*

According to Rogers, 'observability' is 'the degree to which the results of an innovation are visible to others' (1995:244). If potential users are able to see the benefits of using the innovation they will be more enthusiastic about adopting it. A number of teachers were positive about *EED* because it encouraged students to communicate and to perform tasks that were useful in everyday life (see section on 'Relative Advantage of *EED*'). This teacher was pleased because her students could speak with confidence

> T 47: ... Now they are able to speak a little. So by that we find that although they don't get the expected amount, they know how to rough out in their real life. (Trincomalee 34)

while another talked about the range of activities that her students were now capable of handling:

> T 28: ... But here what they have been doing in the classroom...filling in forms, biodata forms, messages, obituary notices coming from the newspapers and all. They're in touch with those areas. So because of that they can come to some standard in the paper, no? ... (Nuwara Eliya 406)

For some teachers observable success related more to examination results than to what students could do in the real world. Several teachers talked about how many of their students had passed the exam, or how many had received Credits or Distinctions (e.g. Wennapuwa 342).

Some teachers felt discouraged though because their students did not do as well as they wanted, either in the real world or in the examination:

> T 63: And very difficult to see the results. And at the end with so much of hard work if there are no results, you feel fed up. There are some questions that you can't find solutions. (Wennapuwa 189)

This teacher thought teachers should be allowed to choose their own textbooks:

> T 63: ... Teachers should be given freedom to choose their textbooks. Out of the Curriculum they can give ten textbooks and the teacher should be given the opportunity to select and pick the correct book for his students ... Even at (this college) we can use all the ten books. What we want is from where they are to bring them up to a certain standard. (Wennapuwa 717)

All of the other teachers who talked about what their students were capable of doing suggested that it was the exam that was driving their learning rather than the textbook. Teachers talked about how their students had improved in reading (Nuwara Eliya 422, 430 and 602), in writing (Tangalle 159), and in their general language use (Welimada 479, Ratnapura 483) as a result of the exam, and at least two felt that they themselves had improved because of the exam (Welimada 475 and 485). The observability of the exam will be discussed in Chapter 9.

In summary, teachers had quite a bit to say about the observability of *EED*, relating to success in the real world and to success in the examination. Some teachers were discouraged though, especially by examination failure. It is interesting that teachers using the same materials should have such different reactions: we shall see in Chapters 10 and 11 whether there were other factors besides the textbook that could account for such different outcomes.

## Status of *EED*

According to Henrichsen, 'status' refers to 'association with a higher social level which can impart legitimacy and attract attention to an innovation' (1989:85). An example of this would be the 'Keeping up with the Joneses Syndrome', in which consumers buy certain products to impress their neighbours. The products may in fact be useful but it is not their usefulness alone that makes them sell.

The notion of status is not relevant in the case of *EED* since schools were not given a choice of textbooks.

## Practicality of *EED*

'Practicality' refers to whether an innovation can be used in its original form, or whether local constraints prevent users from taking full advantage of it. Innovators need to consider whether the system that they wish to introduce their innovations into can respond adequately to the innovations' demands (Dow, Whitehead and Wright 1984, cited in Henrichsen 1989:85). If they are introducing a new textbook series they need to ask themselves several questions: whether teachers have enough time to cover all of the material, whether they have access to all of the resources that are needed and whether the costs involved are reasonable.

Most of the teachers' comments related to the amount of time needed to cover the textbook properly. A number of teachers mentioned that it was difficult, if not impossible, to deal with all of the material in a single year:

> T 20: Yes, in some schools that difficulty's there. Two schools that I went to, the difficulty is there. They have not completed the books. Year 7 ... frankly ... the others might agree with me ... but Year 7 I don't think any teacher completed the whole book because I tried my best to do that and I didn't. And even in Year 8 I had to do Year 7 work. And Year 9 I had to

do Year 7 work. Year 10 also ... (Nuwara Eliya 352, but see also Nuwara
Eliya 81 and Nugegoda 418)

Many teachers believed that they had to cover the books thoroughly
because of the examination. Book 10 was considered to be especially
important:

> T 30: Because all the writing and reading materials are in the test paper.
> You get all the writing – letter writing, invitations, and everything – you
> get it all in the Year 10 book. (Nuwara Eliya 36)

Some Year 11 teachers spent a lot of time (up to several months) finishing
off Book 10 before they proceeded to Book 11 (Colombo 14, Welimada 40).
This then made it difficult for them to complete Book 11. Some teachers felt
that it was Book 11 that needed to be dealt with thoroughly (Nuwara Eliya 88),
while others tried to cover what they thought was the most important material
in both books, even if this meant leaving out a lot of other material.

At least a quarter of the teachers reported giving extra lessons so that they
could finish the textbook. This figure included teachers from 'good schools'
(Ratnapura 48-50 and 69, Trincomalee 436) as well as teachers from average
schools (e.g. Welimada 66, 319 and 374, and Ratnapura 234). It was quite
common for teachers to give classes after the normal school day was over (e.g.
Colombo 21, Asgiriya 415-129, Ratnapura 232-244), and they also worked
during the weekends and holidays, and during school vacations (Trincomalee
305-308). One teacher was unable to teach after school because teachers of
other subjects had claimed this time for their own examination preparation
sessions, so he was forced to meet his students every morning, for an hour and
a half before the start of normal lessons:

> T 53: From 6.10 to 7.45. From the second term. Usually I don't get a
> chance for teaching after school because other teachers they take. So only
> five subjects can be taught during the week, and weekends nobody comes.
> So I have to. I was not given a day so I started in the morning.
>
> DW: So from the second term you've been teaching ...
>
> T 53: Actually speaking ... What I personally believe is without doing that
> I wouldn't be able to complete the text. The syllabus.
>
> DW: So do you teach every morning at 6.10?
>
> T 53: Yes. Unless there is a very special case.
>
> DW: And do all of the children come at 6.10?
>
> T 53: Yes. Otherwise I punish. [Laughter.] (Welimada 315-319)

There were a number of comments about individual units containing too
much material and particular activities requiring too much time. Some

teachers spent a lot of time on certain types of exercises – one teacher reported spending three to four periods on role plays (Nugegoda 238), others from three to five periods on 'Finding Outs' (Wennapuwa 67, 201-205 and 225), and others quite a lot of time on the poems (Asgiriya 110, Welimada 88).

If teachers felt they had to omit something, it would probably be listening (Asgiriya 100 and 103). One teacher revealed that she and other teachers in her area had been directed not to teach this skill:

> T 3: ... Now, in that seminar our madam asked us not to do listening passages because ...One reason is that there's no time to cover the book if we are going to do the listening passage. And the other thing is it doesn't come for the examination itself. So because of that I won't do that listening. I skip it. (Asgiriya 110)

However, teachers also reported leaving out role plays (Asgiriya 103), poems (Ratnapura 233, Trincomalee 370), and other material that they felt their students would not understand (Nugegoda 429). Some teachers tried to cover all of the skills in their teaching, but gave priority to reading and writing when they were doing their classroom testing (Trincomalee 266, 399 and 405).

It was often difficult to determine whether the problem that teachers were talking about was a problem of practicality – that the textbooks contained too much material or that the lessons were too long – or whether there were other problems in the environment that were preventing them from handling their material in the way that the textbook designers envisaged. The teachers mentioned several problems that made it difficult for them to proceed through the textbooks efficiently. These included problems inside the school and problems in the outside world.

There were at least two types of problems inside the school: classroom conditions and conflicts in the timetable. When teachers talked about problems outside the school they mentioned home environments which made it difficult for students to study, and weather and transportation problems that made it impossible for them to get to school or to stay for extra lessons. There were also references to political problems which sometimes forced schools to close or prevented the teachers from travelling to and from their workplaces (Trincomalee 352). All of these problems will be explored more fully in Chapter 10: Characteristics of the user system.

The teachers did not have much to say about resources. This may have been because the series was written to be self-contained: there were cassettes and videos to accompany the series but teachers did not need these aids in order to teach the basic syllabus. The biggest problem was that students had to hand in their books at the end of each year so that they could be passed on to the next year's students. This may have been why so many teachers were anxious to finish Book 10 before their students went on to Year 11, regardless of what this meant in terms of extra lessons. There was only one teacher who had found a way around this problem:

> T 20: No. Right throughout I had to do that. From the beginning itself. Because when I went into the detailed lesson, in Year 7 they had not done. Then in Year 8 they had to use the Year 7 book and the Year 8 book. When I taught them in Year 9 the Year 9 children had to bring in Year 7, 8, 9. Because there were books. They had the books and I told them not to give the English books back, to keep them with them until they finished their schooling. Because the Government gives free books. So I told them not to give the books back to the school. The English books to keep with them. And the children in Year 10 had the 7, 8, 9 books, along with the Year 10 book. So they had to do a little from Year 7, 8, 9 and 10. That is how I did.
> (Nuwara Eliya 337)

To summarize, there were a number of comments relating to the practicality of *EED*, most of which had to do with the time it took to cover the material properly. Many teachers gave extra lessons just to be able to get through the syllabus, while others felt it necessary to omit material (often listening material) so that they could cover what they thought was most important for the examination.

## Flexibility of *EED*

'Flexibility' refers to whether the innovation has to be used in a particular way or whether it can be adjusted or adapted to suit the local circumstances (Havelock 1969, cited in Henrichsen 1989:85). It is difficult to say whether this term is appropriate for *EED*. A number of teachers reported using the textbook in ways that were different from the designers' intentions, but they might have been revealing more about themselves or their contexts than about the textbook. If, for example, a teacher recycled a role play to give further practice in listening, did it mean that the material was flexible or just that the teachers knew how to make maximum use of it to reinforce the students' learning or increase their confidence (Ratnapura 549 and 557)? What did it mean if teachers 'mis-used' material, not practising the skill that was intended but practising another which appeared on the exam? The term 'flexible' carries a connotation of change for the better, but it is worth questioning whether all changes are equally useful and whether some are distortions that undermine the principles at the heart of the innovation.

## Primacy of *EED*

'Primacy' refers to the relative timing of an innovation: is it the first to occur in the context or does it follow a number of others? If it is the first innovation ever, or even the first of its kind, it might be welcomed as a fresh solution to old problems. However, there might be difficulties in implementation if it brings challenges the users have never faced before. If the innovation is the second or third in the context, its promoters might be able to learn from the experience of previous reformers. Potential users might not adopt it though, either because of loyalty to the first innovation or because of resistance as a result of the first experience.

The *English Every Day* series replaced a series which had been in place for more than a decade, so it could be seen as a new departure rather than just another attempt at change. It was introduced at the same time as a series called *English for Me*. The two series were directed at different audiences though (*English for Me* was for primary schools) and the introduction of one should not have had any effect on whether the other was accepted.

There were no comments in the data which related to this topic.

## Form of *EED*

According to Richards (1984), the form that a method takes is crucial to its survival: if a new approach to teaching is embodied in a textbook it is more likely to survive than if it remains in the form of a theory. This was certainly the case in Sri Lanka. The observations revealed that many teachers had not received training in the new methods, yet by 1991 every teacher who was interviewed had at least some idea of what the English language reform was all about. Some teachers may not have understood everything correctly and others may not have been able to cope with all the demands, but most teachers had some notion of what their teaching priorities were supposed to be just from using the textbook. The main problem though, as mentioned in several earlier sections, was that not everyone had access to the teachers' guides, and even when they did they were not always helpful.

## Summary of the characteristics of *EED*

The teachers who were interviewed were not asked direct questions about the characteristics of *EED*. Despite this, they made many comments about the textbook when they talked about their teaching, and these have provided insights into how they perceived the innovative features.

Originality – Although *EED* was very different from the previous textbook and contained many ideas that were new, the teachers seemed to see it as a custom-made innovation rather than a ready-made or modified one and they reacted favourably to most of what they saw.

Complexity for teachers – The teachers had difficulty understanding some of the content, especially the 'Finding Out' passages and the poems. They worried because they thought it was up them to explain the content to the students. They did not understand the notions of selective reading and of students trying to figure out meanings for themselves. Some teachers also found it difficult to teach listening, and some of them might have blamed their neglect of listening on the examination when in fact they did not know how to teach it.

Complexity for students – Teachers felt that the 'Finding Out' passages were difficult for their students, as were some of the poems. A few teachers commented that the general level of the textbooks was beyond their students' ability.

Explicitness – Some teachers felt that the *EED* teachers' guides were helpful, but it is difficult to know whether they really understood them or whether they could translate the ideas into practice. Others felt that they were less useful, either because they did not explain the objectives of the exercises, did not give help with particular problems, or did not give what the teachers believed was important background information.

Relative advantage – The main advantage of *EED* over the previous series was its relevance to everyday life in Sri Lanka. Its main disadvantage was the way it dealt with grammar, which was not always understood by the teachers. There were two main disadvantages to *EED* compared to commercial publications: the first was that it did not include as many questions as teachers would have liked for the reading comprehension sections (this indicated that the teachers might not have understood the function of the questions), and the second was that it was not as obviously oriented towards the examination.

Observability – Many teachers commented on what their students could do as a result of using *EED*, both in terms of surviving in the real world and in terms of examination success. Some felt discouraged, however, because no matter how hard their students worked they still met with failure. This led to the question of whether *EED* was the most suitable textbook for all students. It was clear that there were other factors involved in the problem and not just the nature of the textbook itself.

Practicality – The main problem with *EED* was that it was difficult to cover all of the material in a single year. Many teachers gave extra lessons in order to complete the syllabus, while others skipped over some parts of the textbook in order to concentrate on those that were more important for the examination. It was sometimes difficult to tell whether it was the practicality of the textbook that was the heart of the matter, or other problems, such as conditions in the classroom, the school or the wider environment.

Form – The fact that the new teaching approach was embodied in a textbook made it easier to spread the ideas about teaching. There were some problems, however, with the availability and quality of the teachers' guides.

The terms 'trialability', 'status' and 'primacy' did not seem to be relevant in the *EED* situation, and the term 'flexibility' did not seem suitable for the way the teachers used the *EED* material.

There was a positive side and a negative side to the introduction of *English Every Day*. Teachers welcomed the relevance and usefulness of its content, but they experienced difficulty when using it in the classroom. The biggest problem seemed to be that they did not always understand what they were supposed to be doing, especially when it came to teaching reading. The methods that they were using resembled methods that were used during the Old Syllabus. The teachers' guides to the series were partly to blame for this: the advice given in the earlier guides was not always suitable for the later textbooks and there was almost no advice in the guide for Books 10 and 11. This led many teachers to buy supplementary materials which matched their vision of what they should be doing and gave them a sense of security.

Chapter 9 will contain an analysis of the characteristics of the new examination, in an attempt to discover whether these were in harmony or in conflict with those of the textbook.

# 9 Implementation factors: characteristics of the innovation: the new examination

## Background

The New Syllabus O level Examination in English was meant to serve two main purposes: the first was to provide a valid, reliable and practical measure of students' achievement on the *English Every Day* syllabus; and the second was to provide a 'lever for change', to persuade teachers and students to take the *EED* course seriously (Pearson 1988:101). Other purposes included measuring the achievement of lower-ability students as well as those of higher ability, encouraging positive attitudes and successful classroom activities, evaluating the effectiveness of courses and teachers, and restoring public confidence in the examination (Alderson and Wall 1989:B3-6).

The examination team drafted the first set of test specifications in early 1986, but they had to change them several times due to other developments within the educational system. The most important development was the introduction of an across-the-curriculum continuous assessment programme, which was meant to measure abilities that were difficult to test in a pen-and-paper examination. The English examination would now consist of two parts: a formal paper at the end of Year 11, which would test the written skills; and a number of teacher-designed and marked classroom tasks, some of which would assess speaking and listening. The examination team devoted a great deal of time to preparing guidelines and sample activities for continuous assessment, but the programme suffered many practical and political problems and was scrapped after its first year. This put an end to the testing of listening and speaking. Two members of the examination team wrote of their disappointment at that time, regretting that 'this lever was taken from our grasp' (Nanayakkara and Webber 1994:100).

All that remained was the formal examination, which was meant to test reading and writing. There were still possibilities for innovation, however, using the experience that had been gained during earlier work on two other examinations (see section on 'Primacy of the examination' for details of the

DELIC and NCE exams). The team planned to use text-types and activity types like those in the textbooks, and to vary the topics and techniques every year so that teachers would not be able to predict what would appear on the exam and would not restrict their teaching to match their expectations.

The shape of the examination was finally decided in December 1987, and the examination team produced a 40-page booklet called *Guidelines for the Final Examination for O level English in December 1988 and After* (hereafter, *Guidelines*). A copy was sent to all secondary schools in May 1988, approximately six months before the intended first administration of the new examination. The booklet contained lists of the abilities and the text-types that might be tested on the examination, and included many sample activities to help teachers visualize the form the examination questions might take. There were 19 sample activities for reading and 22 for writing.

The examination would consist of two sections. The first would contain approximately eight low-level tasks, evenly divided between reading and writing, and would last 60 minutes. The second would contain eight higher-level tasks, also evenly divided between reading and writing, and would last 90 minutes. Some of the reading items would be of the 'recognition' type (multiple-choice, true-false, matching) but others would require student production. The writing tasks would be marked using task-specific rating scales. (A copy of the 1988 papers and rating scales can be seen in Appendix 2.)

The first administration was in late February 1989 (all examinations were administered three months late because of political disturbances), to about 197,000 candidates. The second administration was in late March 1990 to about 315,000 candidates, and the third was in early December 1990 (the traditional examination period) to about 350,000 candidates. The number of candidates grew each year because students who failed were allowed to repeat the exam the following year.

The examination team prepared and distributed a second booklet for teachers in 1989. This booklet was called *Suggestions and Guidance to Teachers Preparing Students for GCE O/L English New Syllabus* (hereafter, *Suggestions*). It was 56 pages long and contained 43 sets of instructions which had been extracted from the *EED* series and which teachers could use to help their students prepare for the second examination. (Many students had experienced problems in the first examination because the instructions were in English only, rather than in three languages as before.) The booklet also reprinted the abilities and text-types that might be examined in reading and writing, gave advice about designing examination preparation activities, reproduced samples of student writing from the first exam along with comments from the examiners, and reprinted the 1988 examination paper and rating scales.

Teachers were preparing for the fourth administration of the examination when the group interviews took place, in October and November 1991.

## Originality of the examination

It will be recalled that 'originality' refers to the origin of an innovation, and whether it is perceived as being appropriate for the context into which it is being introduced. It is important to comment not only on the origin of the innovation but also on how it compares to the entity (idea, programme, etc.) that it replaces.

None of the teachers commented on the origin of the innovation, so there is no reason to believe that they saw it as anything other than a natural development from the *EED* syllabus. In fact, several teachers expressed their appreciation of the close match between the examination and the textbooks, using phrases such as 'this paper is a success in checking aspects of studying, learning and teaching' (Welimada 407) and 'it's a happiness because what we have taught in the classroom is there for them to answer' (Nuwara Eliya 448). Some teachers would have preferred for the exam to test listening and speaking as well (see section on 'Relative advantage of the examination'), but no one suggested that the way it tested reading and writing was inappropriate for the context.

There were a number of comments about how the new examination differed from its predecessor. These could be divided into four main themes: content, techniques, instructions, and predictability.

Regarding content, quite a few teachers believed that the new examination was more relevant to everyday life than the old exam had been. Teachers remembered the old exam as testing mainly grammar, or grammar and reading, and one teacher mentioned that what was tested was 'very very technical' (Wennapuwa 575). It was claimed that the old exam tested nothing practical: students could get Credit passes even if they could not write their name (Ratnapura 475), or Distinctions even though they could not fill in an application, write a letter or convey a message (Nuwara Eliya 411). The new examination was very practical, testing skills like form-filling, writing telegrams, writing advertisements, etc. (Ratnapura 467).

The second set of comments concerned the techniques which were used in the examination. As discussed in Chapter 7, the items testing language and reading in the old examination were all multiple choice while the new exam included many short-answer items. Teachers felt that the former encouraged 'guesswork' while the latter required understanding and production. The writing tasks in the new exam were more authentic and less predictable than those in the old exam.

The third set of comments was about the fact that instructions for the new exam were given in English only, rather than in Sinhala, Tamil and English as before. The teachers were positive about this development, as it forced students to 'learn much' (Welimada 435) and to 'read the question and understand' (Wellawatte 222). One teacher admitted that she had been angry during the first year because the teachers had received no warning about the change, but she was satisfied now that she knew what to expect (Nuwara Eliya 426-428). (The problems that teachers faced because of inadequate communications will be discussed in Chapter 10, under 'Educational administration'.)

The fourth set of comments concerned the unpredictable nature of the new examination, compared to the previous one which had followed the same pattern every year. It was not clear whether teachers welcomed this feature. The new examination made the teachers' life more difficult because they did not know which areas to cover during the examination preparation period, and students got annoyed if their teachers did not predict the content of the examination accurately:

> T 15: ... So we don't know what to teach and what will come. Sometimes the child says (she gives the Sinhala words)–'Nothing of what you taught was in the paper.' Earlier we didn't have that problem. The teacher has taught spelling and the spelling items have come, so the child was satisfied. The child had confidence in the teacher. Now here the teacher has failed some. Now that problem is there. (Nugegoda 397)

Some teachers commented on the individual components of the new exam: students had to read quickly to get through everything (Nugegoda 153), they had to write more than before (Wellawatte 221) and they were given no choice about what to write on (Nugegoda 33-37). Several teachers mentioned that it was possible for students to reproduce memorized essays on the old examination (e.g. Trincomalee 38), whereas on the new exam this was less likely to happen (one teacher did admit, however, that her students memorized the short pieces of writing that the whole class constructed, so there was not necessarily a great deal of change in this area – Trincomalee 524). Several teachers felt that it would be better to test more grammar on the new exam, in ways that were 'more interesting' than the way it had been done before (Welimada 431).

To summarize, the teachers did not express any negative feelings about the origin of the examination, seeming to see it as complementary to the *EED* textbooks, about which they were generally positive. They mentioned several ways in which the new exam differed from the old exam. They saw most of these features (practical content, new techniques, instructions in English) as changes for the better, but one feature (the unpredictability of content) was perhaps less welcomed as it could lead to feelings of uncertainty amongst teachers and learners.

# Complexity of the examination

## Complexity of the examination for teachers

We saw earlier that a number of teachers found the content of the textbooks difficult, particularly the 'Finding Out' passages and the poems (see 'Complexity of *EED*'). There were few separate references to these features in the examination, perhaps because everyone understood that it was the fear of difficult passages appearing on the exam that drove teachers to invest so much time on them in the classroom. This is what the teacher in this long extract seemed to be saying:

> T 30: It (the exam) is a good influence. It makes the teacher active. Because the teacher has to prepare a lot. And also we have to plan. When we teach our lessons also we have to prepare. Without planning we can't go to the class. It makes the teacher think, because he has to prepare a lot of exercises and give them to them.
>
> DW: And that's the exam that makes you do that? Not the *English Every Day* textbook?
>
> T 30: Yes. Because all of the exercises are similar to the exercises in the exam paper also. Most of the exercises and the instructions and everything.
>
> DW: So you're thinking that this new exam is making teachers...
>
> T 30: Active. (Nuwara Eliya 383-589)

Another teacher expressed the same idea when she talked about having to be 'armed' when she walked into the classroom, because of the science passages that came in the exam (Nuwara Eliya 591).

However, two other teachers held the opposite point of view, saying that the examination was easier than the textbook because it did not require the understanding of 'subject matters':

> T 39: ... In the exam the questions are all skills, dealing with the practical knowledge of the students. And the questions deal with day-to-day life – writing a note, like that. But not the subject matters, I think. (Ratnapura 561. See also Ratnapura 559.)

There were only a few other comments about the complexity of the exam for teachers: relating to the teachers' need to improve their own language (Welimada 483, Wennapuwa 575) and to the kind of training that teachers needed if they wanted to write classroom tests that matched the examination (Trincomalee 572).

It was surprising that there were not more comments, especially since the examination was still quite new. One possible reason for this was that the teachers were unaware of the examination's real demands. Few teachers had received examination-related training. Many lacked access to the official support documents, and the commercial publications that they used provided only practice items and tasks, not marking schemes, rating scales or explanations.

## Complexity of the examination for students

About half the teachers commented on the complexity of the exam for their students. Most of these felt that the exam was quite difficult and that their students were having to work very hard in order to get the grades they desired. Only one teacher stated that the exam was too easy (Nugegoda 461), but she was new to Year 11 teaching and had not trained as an examiner or even seen a rating scale. Another said that the standard was not very high, but that the students still were unable to reach it:

> T 5: The standard is not high now, but still the children can't do. I don't know why. It is simple enough, the present O level paper. It couldn't be any easier. Paper 1 is for everyone to do, and I think they could attempt it. And I don't know how their performance is so weak. (Asgiriya 526)

The remaining teachers thought that the level was high, at least for the students they were working with. One teacher said that this type of examination was suitable for students who were growing up in an English-speaking environment, but not for students like her own, especially if they had to write out their answers rather than answering multiple-choice questions. Another teacher felt that there should be different examinations for students in different parts of the country (Ratnapura 617).

The teachers mentioned three specific areas of difficulty: the reading passages, the writing tasks and some techniques that were unfamiliar.

Some teachers believed that the reading passages near the end of the examination were either too long (Ratnapura 615) or too difficult (Ratnapura 294). Two teachers argued that students should be given a selection of passages to choose from:

> T 10: But there could also be an alternative for those unseen passages. Two passages if possible. Where the clever child wants to meet a challenge and he'll tackle the difficult one, while the average child tackles the one which is in his sphere of thinking. If that could be possible then there might not be that disparity in the question paper. I've felt it but I don't know if the time is right for me to tell it. (Colombo 191, and also Colombo 199)

Another teacher said that it was not the passages which caused problems, but the questions. She believed that the difficult questions at the end of the second paper had been included 'to avoid students getting a Distinction'

(Nuwara Eliya 402). This conclusion was in fact quite logical – one of the functions of the O level was to sort out which students were weakest and which were strongest – but teachers had trouble understanding or accepting that examinations should discriminate in this way.

Writing was also considered to be difficult by some of the teachers: there were comments about the problems that students had forming grammatically correct sentences (Trincomalee 502), deciding which conventions to use (Asgiriya 242), and writing reports (Nuwara Eliya 401). One teacher joked about how easy it was to be an examiner:

> T 3: ... Only the question paper is there. Not the answers because they have not answered. [Laughter.] So we can mark it very easily. All zero, zero, zero. (Asgiriya 522)

When it came to techniques, many teachers thought the new examination was superior to the old one because it required student production and not just recognition of the correct option. There was some concern, however, about techniques that were unfamiliar. One teacher commented that the jumbled sentence technique was difficult for her students because it did not appear in the textbook (Colombo 171). Another, who often omitted listening exercises because he was pressed for time, made a point of presenting the exercises if the technique looked useful for the exam:

> T 64: ... So I have not done all the listening exercises. I have given them what I feel is beneficial to them. Where you can use that same technique for some other purpose. For example, if they are supposed to fill a grid and that similar technique will appear in another situation. Say, when they take the exam. If I feel that that is going to benefit them then I will do that technique because at least by following that technique it will be beneficial to them. (Wennapuwa 233)

There was also some concern about the appropriacy of certain techniques for some learners. Some teachers had come to expect that there would be mainly recognition items on the lower-level paper. One teacher described how surprised her students were the year before, when there was a change in this pattern:

> T 55: It's very difficult for the children. So all these three years – not last year, before that – they will say, 'Of course we will get 75.' 'No, I think you'll get 60.' There were only one or two words that they had to underline. But last year really was an upset for the children. The first paper. As soon as they got the paper, the comprehension passage, they had to read, no? And they got upset. (Wellawatte 639)

What was interesting about these discussions of complexity was that teachers tended to speak about how difficult the exam was for their own students, rather than how difficult it was in relation to the textbook or some more 'objective' standard. It was therefore hard to see whether the exam was truly difficult, or whether the students' proficiency was too weak to achieve the standard expected.

This brings to mind at least two problems that must be faced in the examination development process: deciding what the general level of difficulty should be and determining just how difficult individual items really are. The examination team had found it difficult to decide on the appropriate level of difficulty. This was partly because of the political situation, which had forced a number of school closures during the 1980s and prevented teachers from covering all the material they were supposed to, and partly because of a resources and distribution problem, which had delayed the arrival of textbooks in many schools. The team had to decide between aiming the examination high, to match the difficulty level at the end of Book 11, and aiming it lower, to match the level in Year 10. This would help both the students who had not been able to attend classes regularly and those who had not had textbooks to work from. They opted for the second course of action, at least for the early years of the examination. This level was nevertheless still higher than most students could cope with. The team may not have realized how bad the situation was in many areas of the country. Alternatively, they may not have wanted to aim the exam as low as it needed to be to enable greater numbers to pass. This was because the exam had to serve several functions within the society, including 'restoring public confidence'. It could not be 'fair' to all students in all situations.

The second problem that the team had was determining how difficult their examination items were. Although they had pre-tested items (see Alderson and Wall 1989, and Nanayakkara and Webber 1994 for references to this process), they did not have the expertise to judge difficulty level independent of the ability level of the samples the items were tried out on. There is a danger of misjudging how difficult items are if they are tried out on a sample which is very able.

To summarize, a number of teachers thought that the new examination was complex for their students. Amongst the problems they mentioned were the general language level of the exam, and some aspects of reading and writing. Several teachers suggested that more choice be given in the exam: that there should be different papers for different parts of the country, and that students should be allowed to choose between different reading passages and writing tasks. Many of the teachers commented on their own students' difficulties rather than on some objective notion of difficulty. It is possible that it was not the level of the examination that made it so difficult for students to achieve the results they wanted, but rather problems in the educational context itself. (See Chapter 10 for an analysis of the User system.)

# Explicitness of the examination

We saw earlier that 'explicitness' refers both to how well an innovation is thought through in the beginning and how clearly explanations are transmitted to the users. The new O level examination was very well thought out in the beginning: the examination team had gone through intensive training in language testing and they had tried out many of their ideas while working on two earlier examinations (see section on 'Primacy of the examination', and Pearson 1994 and Nanayakkara and Webber 1994 for more details). When they decided on the form the examination would take they transmitted the information through various channels:

- the official information booklets which were sent to the schools
- training seminars which were conducted for teachers in various parts of the country, and for students in areas where exam performance was very low
- radio and television broadcasts by team members. (Wennapuwa 651)

The official information booklets were detailed and informative. The only obvious problem was that the list of skills at the beginning of the *Guidelines* booklet was presented in technical language (the language used by Munby [1978] in his work on syllabus design), and the meaning of some of the phrases (e.g. 'understanding the communicative function or value of sentences') was not clear to teachers who had not received special training.

The seminars for teachers were well organized and well delivered, but some of the ideas (e.g. 'scanning' and 'inferring meaning') were difficult for the teachers to understand and to put into practice. The seminars for students were also well planned, but many students were unable to cope with even the simplest language tasks, like writing their addresses or other personal details.

I did not hear any of the radio or television broadcasts so cannot comment on their quality or whether there were any problems.

The team had put a lot of thought into the best ways of disseminating information, but the problem as far as this analysis was concerned was trying to find out whether the teachers had ever received the information, much less read and understood it.

The teachers spoke about three aspects of the examination: the goals, the content, and the rating scales that were used for marking writing. The teachers who spoke about the goals were reasonably clear in their explanations, but it is not known whether they got their ideas from official sources or through their study of other materials (Wennapuwa 747 and onwards, Ratnapura 653-670).

Many teachers were able to discuss the content of the examination but, as was the case with the textbook series, it was not clear where they got their information from. It is likely to have been through informal channels though, given the large number who said that they used past papers and commercial publications and the relatively small number who mentioned the official material.

The situation is clearer in the case of rating scales for marking writing. Several teachers mentioned that they had learned about marking from the *Guidelines* booklet or from other information produced by the Curriculum Development Centre (Colombo 250, 258, 446 and 460), though none of them commented on the explicitness of the material. Several others had learned about marking through information sent by the schools that prepared tests for their cluster. It isn't clear where these schools got their information from and whether they understood it correctly. If we cannot tell where the information is coming from then we cannot make judgements about its explicitness.

Quite a few of the teachers had confused ideas about the exam, which suggested that they either had not seen information about certain aspects of it or had not understood what they had read. The most problematic areas were how broad the coverage of the textbook should be (did teachers have to work their way through all of Book 11 or was it enough to have covered Book 10 thoroughly?), the idea of using reading skills rather than just accumulating vocabulary and facts (see section on 'Explicitness of *EED*' for a discussion of this misunderstanding), and the idea of reading and writing for authentic purposes rather than for just getting marks on an exam. For example, several teachers talked about expecting a 'role play' or a 'dialogue' on the 1991 examination, even though the exam was devoted to reading and writing (Ratnapura 515, Welimada 244-248).

What emerged from the analysis was that many of the teachers did not know as much about the examination as they needed to know. However, it was not possible to say whether this was because the official publications were not as explicit as they needed to be or whether the teachers lacked access to these materials.

## Relative advantage of the examination

One way of identifying the relative advantage of the new examination was by comparing it with the old one. We have already discussed this comparison under 'Originality of the examination'. Teachers spoke positively of the new examination because it tested useful skills rather than just grammar (e.g. Ratnapura 467, Nugegoda 8), it used techniques which required student production and not just recognition (e.g. Wellawatte 21-215, Welimada 411), and its instructions were in English rather than in three languages (Welimada 435, Nuwara Eliya 422). Another feature which was mentioned but was not so whole-heartedly welcomed was the unpredictability of content.

One feature which has not been discussed was the effect of the examination on teaching. About a quarter of the teachers stated that the examination was having a positive effect on the teaching and learning that was taking place in their classrooms. Some teachers simply talked in general terms, while others mentioned specific features that would help students to develop in the outside world as well as in the classroom. One of these was the use of unseen passages, which some teachers felt was beneficial to students who had not yet developed the habit of reading (Wellawatte 182-187).

However, there were a few teachers who believed that the examination was having a negative influence on teaching and learning. One teacher thought that it was good for the students to have a target to aim for, but that the target this examination provided was very limited:

> T 1: ... when we are preparing them for the examination, we will limit them to a frame. Then they will not be able to write or express anything other than that frame. True or false. Replacing 'I' with 'he'. Restrictive. (Asgiriya 475)

Another teacher mentioned two different problems: the first was that the new exam sometimes included 'seen' passages, which gave teachers the idea that they should teach specific information rather than reading skills (Wennapuwa 753), and the second was that it paid too much attention to grammar and that this was undermining the 'communicative' approach that the *EED* was trying to promote (Wennapuwa 638).

It was not possible to compare the examination with any other in the school system, since the only alternative that was available was not yet known to many teachers (see comments on the 'optional paper' below). However, it was possible to make a comparison between the new exam and the teachers' 'ideal exam' by paying attention to the improvements that they suggested for the future. There were three main types of improvement: the testing of oral skills, the testing of grammar, and giving students more choice.

A number of teachers felt that the oral skills should be tested. Most of these thought that this would have a positive effect on the classroom, but some felt that it would also influence teaching in the tutories (Wennapuwa 696). The tutories did not offer speaking until after students finished their A levels and were beginning to prepare for university. If speaking were tested at O level then they would be pressured to teach speaking from much earlier on. The impact would be dramatic, at least for some segments of the population. (See Chapter 10, under 'Outside tuition'.)

Some teachers wanted the examination to test more grammar (Welimada 413 and Welimada 431, and Asgiriya 503). This did not mean going back to the traditional ways of testing (see Appendix 1 for an illustration of how grammar was tested in the old examination), but rather finding new techniques (the term 'tactics' is used below) which would give teachers new ideas about teaching and make learning more enjoyable for students:

> T 53: ... Some tactics must be used in the exam. So then the teacher should make it more interesting. So accordingly they will like it and they

have a clear picture about grammar. So then they will find it easy to construct sentences and all. So they may not make any mistakes. So we have to start from the very beginning. (Welimada 431)

Several teachers argued for more choice in the reading and writing sections (e.g. Wennapuwa 579-583), and one argued for having separate papers for different areas of the country (Ratnapura 617-620).

In fact, the Department of Examinations had introduced a set of ten 'optional papers' in 1990, though very few teachers knew about them in 1991. Students could choose the level they wished to be examined at, and sit this examination alongside the normal O level exam. One teacher who had heard of this development thought it was a good idea because it gave weaker students lower goals to aim for:

> T 64: ... I think giving birth to this optional English points out a serious drawback that has prevailed in our system. That's why it's picking up very fast. The optional English component. Because it gives them a proper banding. It's not a pass mark. Now here all are pushed towards running. Okay, run. Go first. Those who can ... (Wennapuwa 732)

What this teacher did not realize, however, was that no procedures were in place to validate the optional papers. The idea of differentiation may have been attractive but there was no way of establishing whether the papers were at the right levels and whether the levels were distinct and in the right relation to one another. (See Alderson and Wall 1992 for an analysis of the optional papers.)

To summarize, the new examination had a relative advantage over the old one in that it tested everyday language and tasks instead of just grammar, it contained techniques which teachers had confidence in, it used English instructions, and it had a good influence on the classroom. There were some suggestions for improvement, though, including expanding the exam to test listening and speaking, test grammar more overtly, and giving the students more choice regarding the level of paper they sat, the passages they read and the writing tasks they responded to.

## Trialability of the examination

There were no references to the trialability of the examination. This was to be expected, given that the exam was compulsory rather than optional: teachers did not have the opportunity to try it out for a brief period before deciding to switch over to it or stick with the old examination. It was also introduced 'in one go' rather than in stages, so it was not possible to evaluate any of the components before others were implemented. (See Mazuoliene 1996:25 for a description of the staged introduction of a school-leaving examination in Lithuania, and Appendix 15 for an illustration of how this was to be done.)

## Observability of the examination

It was explained under 'Observability of *EED*' that the more observable the results of an innovation are, the more likely it is to spread. There was no need to spread this examination, since all Year 11 students were required to sit it, but it would make for a more positive atmosphere if teachers could see that the exam was doing their students some good.

In fact, quite a few teachers thought that the exam was having a positive influence on the way their students were learning: they talked about its effects on their reading (Nuwara Eliya 422, 430 and 602), writing (Tangalle 159), and general language use (Welimada 479, Ratnapura 483). Several teachers stated that their own English had improved as a result of the exam's demands (Welimada 475 and 485, Nuwara Eliya 432 and 589).

The teachers had observed at least two further positive features. The first was that students who failed the exam the first time were more confident about re-sitting it than they would have been under the Old Syllabus (Nugegoda 147). The second was that some students who had finished their studies under the Old Syllabus wished they could have taken the new exam:

> T 28: Not only my children. The old students ... the previous students ...
> they resent not being able to sit this new exam. (Nuwara Eliya 409)

However, there were some teachers who had not observed positive changes: teachers whose students had little chance of passing (e.g. Wennapuwa 188-190) or whose students would blame them if they failed (Nugegoda 397). Some teachers were having to spend long hours preparing their students for this hurdle, with little likelihood that they would succeed in the end. It must be pointed out though that the exam was only one of the factors that was likely to cause discouragement amongst these teachers. Other factors will be discussed in Chapters 10 and 11: 'Characteristics of the user system', and 'Characteristics of the users'.

## Status of the examination

There were no references to the status that users might enjoy if they chose to use this innovation. This makes sense given that the exam was obligatory rather than a matter of choice.

## Flexibility of the examination

As was noted earlier, some teachers felt there should be more flexibility in the examination. There were recommendations that students from rural areas should be allowed to take a separate examination (Ratnapura 617), and that students should be able to choose which reading comprehension passages to tackle (Colombo 199) and which composition topics to respond to (Wennapuwa 579).

## Practicality of the examination

There were few comments about the practicality of the examination. The most significant had to do with the desirability of testing listening if only it were practical to do so (Nugegoda 463). The examination team had originally hoped to find a way of testing listening and speaking, and had tried out various techniques in the DELIC and NCE examinations (see next section for details). What proved workable in exams for a few thousand candidates did not transfer easily to an examination with several hundred thousand. The team then put their efforts into the continuous assessment programme but this was soon withdrawn, partly because it was not practical.

## Primacy of the examination

It has been mentioned in several sections that the O level examination benefited from work carried out on two other examinations in the system – the District English Language Improvement Centre (DELIC) examination, which served as a filter for a new teacher training programme, and the National Certificate in English (NCE), which catered for adults who needed a high-level qualification. The examination team was able to use these examinations to try out many new ideas before using them on the huge O level population. It was unlikely that the teachers in the interviews were aware of this connection. There were only two comments that referred to the NCE: one from a teacher who continued to teach her students listening because it was in the NCE (Nuwara Eliya 468), and one from a teacher who had not been an examiner for O level but felt she knew the system and criteria because she had marked for the NCE (Colombo 243). These comments indicated that there was harmony between the two examinations, which worked to the benefit of the new O level.

## Form of the examination

It was explained earlier that the form an innovation takes is crucial to its survival: an educational innovation which is accompanied by materials will spread more quickly than one which is not. There were many materials that teachers could refer to to learn about the examination, although there was a risk with some of them (the commercial publications) that the understanding they encouraged was only superficial.

We have already seen that the examination team put together two substantial documents to explain the goals and the format of the new examination. About a dozen teachers mentioned the *Guidelines* booklet and around a half a dozen mentioned the *Suggestions* booklet. They reported using the booklets to find out what was important for future exams (e.g. Ratnapura 79), for guidance in the design of classroom or school-wide tests, and to inform students of criteria for marking writing (e.g. Colombo 445-448).

The team had also produced two other documents: the *Pupil Support Booklet* and the *Teacher Support Booklet*. They used the *Pupil Support Booklet* in seminars in schools where student performance was very low. They sent the *Teacher Support Booklet* to all teachers after the 1989 examination, to explain the kinds of problems that students had experienced in the examination and the areas that they needed to improve upon. Only two teachers reported using the *Pupil Support Seminars* booklet (Wennapuwa 404, Tangalle 33) and no one mentioned the *Teacher Support Seminars* booklet.

The teachers talked much more about their use of past papers and commercial examination preparation materials. Nearly half reported using past papers, both to find out about the content of the first three examinations and to get ideas or take material verbatim for their classroom tests and examination preparation activities. Some teachers felt that if topics or item-types had appeared in previous examinations they might well appear again; others thought they should pay most attention to areas and techniques which had not appeared before:

> T 31: We have been checking on the past papers. I, of course, when I give a question I always read the past question papers and then what has not appeared in those we guess might come this year.

> T 28: We compare and contrast the past papers. [General laughter.] And if it has not appeared in the last year's paper, it might appear in this year's paper. (Nuwara Eliya 271-272)

The Department of Examinations had compiled a collection of past papers from the first three administrations of the exam, which it sold from its headquarters and at local festivals. Despite this, only two teachers mentioned getting their papers in this way; many said they received their copies from other teachers, or from relatives or friends (e.g. Wellawatte 279–296).

Many teachers turned to commercial publications ('model papers') to seek information about what might be in the exam or to find material for examination practice. Most of the teachers who used model papers used them in conjunction with past papers. Only rarely did teachers who used model papers use official publications as well (Colombo 452).

We have already discussed how the teachers used this material in the classroom (see Chapter 6). The biggest problem was that many students were unable to afford their own copies of the materials, so the teachers had to copy texts and questions on to the blackboard and the students had to copy from them into their exercise books. This was time-consuming and it was difficult to deal with long texts or exercises that required a great deal of space. Although the teachers were familiar with the form of the examination, the students did not get much exposure to as much of the material as would have been desirable.

It is important to note, however, that although the teachers were familiar with the form of the examination they may not have understood what was really required by the examination questions or how they should mark their students' performance. This was because it was only the official publications that gave explanations about what the examination was trying to assess. The collections of past papers and the commercial publications that were so popular with teachers gave exam questions only, with no lists of skills, no marking schemes, no rating scales, and no advice of any sort.

## Predictability of the examination

One of the operating principles behind the design of the new examination was that the topics and the techniques should be different every year, in order to encourage teachers to cover the entire syllabus rather than just the areas that they knew would be tested. This decision was a reaction to the practice in the previous examination, when there was always a section on prepositions, another on relative pronouns, another on word order, etc. and teachers could predict the topics of the composition questions.

Many of the teachers knew how the new exam was different from the old one, and some were willing to describe the types of items and activities that had appeared up to 1990, but they could not be sure about what would appear in 1991. Several teachers felt that if something had been tested before it was likely to be tested again (Welimada 270, Ratnapura 348, Asgiriya 232); others felt that areas which had been covered in the recent past would not be repeated for a while (Welimada 264 and 272, Asgiriya 233). Several said that they had been able to predict in the early years of the new exam, but that there had been a change in the 1990 exam (the third year the exam was given) and now they did not know what to expect (Wellawatte 536-541, 633 and 639). Others said that they had never been able to predict because all of the exams had been different (Tangalle 142-147).

The fact that teachers could not be certain of what would be tested in future did not stop them from making guesses. Some teachers talked about the topics they thought might appear, which included road safety (Nuwara Eliya 265-267, Nuwara Eliya 325), pollution or endangered animals (Colombo 52-54), telephone messages (Welimada 244 and 248-250), and travellers' cheques (Welimada 254-260). Others talked about the techniques they thought would appear and which they were making sure their students practised. These included jumbled sentences, true-false, cloze, C-tests, transformations, filling in the blanks, labelling diagrams, etc. (Asgiriya 228, 236 and 255; Welimada 254-260; Tangalle 142-147, amongst others).

Everyone knew that there would be reading comprehension passages, and a few teachers felt that these might come from the textbook (e.g. Nuwara Eliya 290-297). Others felt that there would be new passages but that they would be very similar to the ones in the textbook (Welimada 244, 248-250). This could be seen as positive since it gave students a better chance of answering correctly (Ratnapura 720), or it could be seen as negative, since it encouraged the memorization of passages rather than the practice of reading skills (Wennapuwa 753).

Teachers also knew that writing was important, and they gave practice in filling in application forms, writing messages responding to invitations, writing letters, and writing 'report type essays' (Ratnapura 420, Wennapuwa 332-336, Wellawatte 510-515, amongst others).

Only a few teachers spoke about the skills that students needed to master rather than about topics or item types. There were no references to the lists of skills printed in the *Guidelines* booklet.

To summarize, teachers devoted a lot of time and energy to 'question spotting' and to trying to predict the contents of the next examination. Some were confident that they could predict what would appear, while others worried because they could not predict and therefore could not focus their examination practice. The fact that they could not be certain meant that they needed to pay attention to many areas. This was in contrast to the Old Syllabus days, when the predictability of the examination led teachers to narrow the curriculum dramatically.

## Summary of the attributes of the examination

The teachers were not asked direct questions about the characteristics of the examination, but they made many references to it which can help to understand how they viewed it.

Originality – The teachers mentioned several differences between the new exam and the old one and they seemed to view most of these favourably. They liked the emphasis on everyday skills rather than grammar, the use of techniques which required production rather than just recognition, and the use of instructions in English only.

Complexity for teachers – There were few comments about the complexity of the exam for teachers. This was surprising given the number of comments about their difficulties with the *EED*. It is likely though that the teachers had the same worries about the exam as they did about the textbook, and that it was anxiety about what might appear on the exam that led teachers to work so hard on *EED*.

Complexity for students – There was a general feeling that the examination was complex for students. There were comments on the general level of language and about some aspects of reading and writing, and there was some feeling that more choice ought to appear on the paper. It was hard to tell whether the exam was really difficult or whether there were other problems that prevented students from performing as well as they should have.

Explicitness of the exam – There were several official publications to help teachers and students prepare for the examination, but it was difficult to know whether the teachers had consulted these booklets or had found them useful. Many teachers got their information from other sources (past papers, model papers), which contained practice items but no explanations of the principles of the exam, the skills that were being tested, how writing was assessed, etc.

Relative advantage – The advantages of the new examination over the earlier one were that it tested everyday English, it used techniques which required production and not just recognition of correct answers, and it had instructions in English. The main disadvantage of the new examination compared to an ideal exam was that it did not test the oral skills. A few teachers wanted it to test more grammar, and to provide students with more choice.

Observability – The most observable result of the examination was that it made students work harder and improve their skills. A few teachers felt that their own skills had improved as well.

Flexibility – Several teachers stated that there should be more choice in the exam.

Practicality – The biggest problem was that it was not possible to test listening and speaking. Some techniques had been tried out on the DELIC and NCE examinations but it was difficult to transfer these to an examination testing so many candidates. A number of teachers said that these skills should be tested to encourage more work on them in the classroom, but it was difficult to see how this could be managed.

Primacy – The O level had benefited from the development work carried out on the two earlier examinations. This had involved trying out new item-types, rating scales, and training procedures. There were only a couple of comments about the earlier exams but these were favourable, suggesting that the exams were working in harmony with one another.

Form – There were several official publications to help teachers and students prepare for the examination, and these, if studied carefully, would give a good idea of the thinking that had gone into its design. Teachers could also refer to past papers and 'model papers', but these only gave an idea of the surface features of the exam rather than information about principles, skills, rating scales, etc.

Predictability – The content of the exam was meant to be different every year, so that teachers would not confine their teaching to items they knew would appear in the exam. This did not prevent them from trying to guess what might appear. They studied past papers thoroughly and engaged in a great deal of 'question spotting'. The fact that they had different expectations probably meant that the teaching during the exam preparation period was more varied than it had been under the previous examination.

There were no comments relating to the trialability and status of the exam.

## What the analysis reveals about *EED* and the examination

The teachers seemed to have a positive opinion of *English Every Day*. It was very different from the textbook series that they had worked with earlier but they saw this as an advantage rather than as a drawback. They were particularly impressed with the focus on practical language and on activities that were relevant to life in Sri Lanka.

They did see some problems in the series though which made it hard for them to use it effectively. These included the amount of material that needed to be covered every year, the difficulty of the language in general, the difficulty of some of the 'Finding Out' passages and poems, and the unusual treatment of grammar. These problems may have been due to the shortage of teachers' guides or to a lack of explicitness in these guides. There were also problems in the context which made it hard for teachers to achieve what they wanted, such as gaps in the students' previous language training which prevented them from understanding the present material. The teachers sometimes had to spend more time than they wanted on difficult material, and some of them felt obliged to omit material that would not appear in the examination. They tried generally to cover the reading and writing exercises, but they did not always cover the listening or speaking exercises.

The teachers also seemed to have a positive opinion of the examination: they approved of the match between the exam and the teaching materials, its emphasis on everyday skills and not just grammar, the techniques which required production and not just recognition, and the fact that instructions were given in English. Not all of them were happy with the unpredictability of content. A number would have liked listening and speaking to be tested, some would have preferred more testing of grammar, and a few would have preferred for there to be more choice available to the students. The exam was considered difficult by many teachers, but it was not clear whether this was because it represented a high level in absolute terms or because the students' ability was lower than it should have been. There were also quite a few aspects of the exam which some teachers did not understand, particularly the skills focus in reading and the marking of writing, but it was not clear whether this was due to the difficulty of obtaining official support materials or to the lack of explicitness in these materials.

The examination and the textbook seemed to be pulling together in many respects, apart from the fact that the oral skills were not tested in the exam.

They were welcomed for the same reasons, but they also suffered from the same problems – mainly, that the teachers did not always understand what they were supposed to be doing. There was a need to revise the type of guidance given in the textbook – to give clearer explanations of the general approach, more organized explanations of how to teach particular skills, clearer examples of procedures to be followed (especially for reading and listening), etc. The examination guidance also needed some modifications – e.g. to get rid of the jargon in the lists of abilities and text-types – and some rationalization. It was essential to get copies of the teachers' guides and exam support booklets to all teachers, not just all schools.

What did the analysis say about the effect of the examination on teaching? Perhaps the most important information it offered was an explanation of why teachers spent so much time on reading. It was clear that they understood the importance of this skill for the examination, but they believed they needed to teach the content of individual passages rather than skills or strategies. This might have been natural in a society where the teacher traditionally explained everything to their students (see Chapter 11), but it is also possible that the examination itself, with its occasional use of 'seen passages', reinforced the notion that specific facts and specific vocabulary were important.

The interviews also provided some insights into why listening was given so little attention. If teachers felt swamped by the amount of material in the textbook, and even felt it necessary to give extra lessons to cover the syllabus, they might be tempted to drop elements which were not going to be important in the long run – i.e. materials not appearing in the examination. The fact that some teachers did not know how to teach listening made an even more powerful argument for dropping it.

There was some support for this idea in the comments of the teachers who favoured testing listening and speaking. They wanted these skills to be tested so that they would receive more attention in the classroom (and, according to some, in the tutories as well). These teachers must have felt that these skills were being neglected, despite other teachers' claims that they were going through the textbooks thoroughly.

Finally, the analysis shows that the examination was having an impact on teachers' attitudes. Many teachers felt that the exam represented a good goal for their students and several talked about how they themselves had benefited from its influence.

The purpose of Chapters 8 and 9 has been to analyse the characteristics of the new textbook series and the new examination, as they were understood by the teachers. The analysis has provided some insights into the type of impact that the examination was having on teaching and why it did not have all the impact that was expected. It is now necessary to analyse other factors in the environment to see what their contribution might have been to the teaching situation.

# 10 Implementation factors: characteristics of the user system

## Background

Henrichsen (1989) argues that innovators should analyse not only the characteristics of the innovation, but also those of the 'User System', the context that the innovation is being introduced into. This is important since 'various characteristics of the target society/organisation can be powerful determinants of success in diffusion/implementation' (1989:87). Henrichsen's views match those put forward by other innovation specialists, including Fullan, who discusses the role of local characteristics and external factors in the process of change (1991:68), and Kennedy, who discusses 'the hierarchy of interrelating subsystems in which an innovation has to operate' (1988:332). Kennedy presents these 'subsystems' in a diagram which is reproduced in Figure 4.5 of this book.

Henrichsen presents eleven characteristics which he believes should be analysed in detail: geographic location, centralization of power and administration, size of the adopting unit, communication structure, group orientation and tolerance of deviancy, openness, teacher factors, learner factors, capacities, educational philosophy, and examinations.

This categorization appealed to me initially, but I encountered difficulties with it during my first analysis of the data and decided to modify it in various ways.

The first difficulty, which appeared early on in the analysis, was that there was no place in the framework for some of the factors that were emerging from the data: for example, problems concerning classrooms, schools or outside tuition. These factors were clearly influencing the way that teachers and learners were behaving, and I believed that the framework should be adjusted to accommodate them. The political and economic situation also seemed to be affecting teaching and learning. Kennedy had included a political subsystem in his 1988 diagram, and Markee (1997) had suggested that economic factors might play an influential role in the success or failure of innovations. It therefore seemed reasonable to add these factors to those proposed by Henrichsen.

The second difficulty was that some of the factors in Henrichsen's framework seemed to be at the wrong level of generality. Both 'Group Orientation/Tolerance of Deviancy' and 'Openness' seemed to be characteristics of individuals rather than characteristics of a whole system; 'Capacities' seemed to make more sense as a characteristic of a classroom or a school rather than as a category on its own; and 'Communication Structure' seemed to be an aspect of 'Centralization of Power and Administration' rather than a category on its own.

The third difficulty was that there were many references to teacher and learner factors in my data, and these seemed to be of a different nature from those which referred to institutions, resources, or other parts of the educational context. Henrichsen had included a separate category for 'Characteristics of the Intended Users' when he discussed 'Antecedents', and it seemed logical to do the same when discussing 'Implementation Factors'. I decided to transfer all of the comments that concerned teachers and learners to a new set of implementation factors which I called 'Characteristics of the Users'. (See Chapter 11.)

The modified framework therefore contains eight components: classroom factors, school factors, outside tuition, educational administration, political factors, geographic factors, economic factors and cultural factors. These can be seen in Figure 10.1 below.

I will analyse each of these components in the sections that follow, to see how they might have affected the teaching that was taking place during the three years following the introduction of the new examination.

**Figure 10.1 Characteristics of the user system**

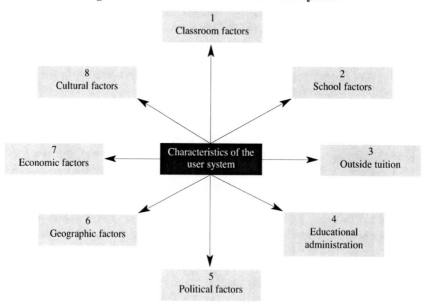

*Source*: (adapted from Henrichsen 1989)

# Classroom factors

The teachers who were interviewed mentioned a number of classroom factors which affected the way they conducted their lessons, and influenced whether they could react to the demands of the textbooks and examination as the designers would have wanted. These factors included the physical conditions they worked in, the level of the students they worked with and the way that they were grouped, the lack of materials, and the lack of time available to cover the syllabus and prepare students for the examination.

## Physical conditions

The physical conditions mentioned most frequently were overcrowding and noise. Overcrowding was very common: the observation study had shown that over half the teachers taught groups of 30 students or more, and several of the teachers in the interviews mentioned working with groups of 40 to 50 (e.g. Colombo 328-340, Nuwara Eliya 488, Tangalle 132). This discouraged some teachers from doing pair or group work (Tangalle 132), made it too time-consuming to test speaking (Trincomalee 266), and made it difficult to correct writing during the intensive examination preparation period (Colombo 328-340).

Noise was another serious problem. In addition to the usual sounds entering the schools from outside (street noises in urban areas and animal noises in the country) there was the noise from other classrooms or from other groups meeting in the same teaching area or 'hall'. Several teachers reported teaching in halls where six or seven classes were in session at the same time. They found it very difficult to do speaking lessons (Nuwara Eliya 639) or to give practice in listening (Asgiriya 69-72). One teacher described how she had to postpone lessons if it was too difficult to hear:

> T 10: I do everything but it all depends on the mood of the kids. If there is a lot of noise, I don't do the listening lesson then. I postpone it for a day when I can make it useful. I shift it. If there is a lot of noise or if it is raining and the environment in the school is terrible. The noise is so bad and I postpone the lesson and have it straight after school ... Then the school is quiet and the lesson is very profitable. (Colombo 88)

It was common for teachers to take their students outside, so they could hear the teacher's input and also hear one another:

> T 10: Because the noise is so great in the school. Sometimes I can hardly hear myself ... Grammar in Action, Working Together, Learning Together – it becomes a real chaos if you try it in a classroom. In a crowded classroom. So it depends on the time I take it. Even poetry. To get the kids to appreciate a poem – they must hear the rhythm, the tone,

the images the poet wants to emphasize. So for those things I and some of my colleagues take them out. (Colombo 92)

One of the places where teachers taught their students was 'under a shady tree' (Colombo 90).

The comments that the teachers made about their classroom conditions corresponded closely to my own observations, which I recorded in a chapter for the final project report (Alderson and Wall 1992). Excerpts from this chapter can be found in Appendix 12.

## Level of the students

Many teachers talked about the difficulties they had teaching students of low ability. Some teachers stated that their students had not had adequate training in their earlier years of schooling, and this made it difficult for them to understand the material in their textbooks. Others talked about how their students came from poor families where English was not spoken in the home:

> T 11: In my school most of the children are backward. They are not up to the standard. They come from very poor families. They have no English background, whatever it is. They seldom hear a word outside the school. Only within those 45 minutes they hear English in school. After that they never hear a word. And whatever they learn at school they forget when they go home because no one can help them with their work. They never do homework. When the teachers ask them to do homework they say we have no one to ask. So they don't do anything ... (Colombo 70)

These teachers reported that it took a long time to get through the *English Every Day* textbook: one teacher said that he spent four classroom periods on a passage on pets (Wennapuwa 67), while another said that it took four or five periods for her students to get through a lesson on telephones because 'they can't read' (Wennapuwa 201-205). Other teachers revealed that they had to simplify the material in some way (Colombo 130) or skip it entirely (Colombo 51-52, Wennapuwa 117).

The most common way of teaching students was in mixed ability groups. Several teachers mentioned how hard it was to give everyone the right amount of attention. One teacher talked about the problem of keeping 'the brighter ones' occupied (Colombo 64), but others were more concerned about what to do with the weaker students. One teacher explained her situation in these words:

> T 22: ... now they all think that I am teaching at the convent and I don't have any problems. We have a lot of problems now. In our classes there are about 50 children, and five are really good. They are equal to the teachers sometimes. But there's a crowd who are really weak. We have to tackle that crowd also, with the best crowd. So we have many many problems there. (Nuwara Eliya 488)

Another teacher wanted to use the interview she was participating in as a forum for discussing mixed ability teaching:

> T 18: Now, madam, I have a question. Of course it is not about this research on English teaching. Now, madam, when we have students – very good and very weak – what method should we follow for these very weak students? (Nugegoda 469)

Some of these teachers might have preferred teaching groups that were more homogeneous, but this mode of working also had its problems. One of the interviews was with a group of teachers who worked in the same school, where students were divided into ten different ability sets for English. There seemed to be tension at this school because the teachers who taught the higher-level groups were perceived to be having an easier time than those who taught lower-level groups. Those who worked with higher-level groups could use the 'normal methods which are taught at training college' (Wennapuwa 373) and could even ask their students to do extra reading and writing (Wennapuwa 282), while those who taught lower-level groups had to struggle just to get their students through the textbook that corresponded to their year. Two teachers had taken their students back to the Year 7 book to help them with basic material that they had not mastered in earlier years (Wennapuwa 119-139 and 193-199). These teachers used terms like 'wasting time with them', 'fighting in that H class', and 'dragging the horse to the water' to describe their efforts to teach students who they believed were not capable or not interested in learning (Wennapuwa 77, 787, and 791 respectively).

## Lack of materials

The next classroom-related problem concerned shortages of teaching materials. There were several aspects to this problem: the late arrival of *EED* in classrooms, the fact that students had to hand over textbooks at the end of the year, the inefficient distribution of official examination support material for teachers, and the lack of material that students could use to prepare for the examination.

The first problem had occurred in the mid-1980s, when the new textbook series was being introduced into schools. One teacher described what happened in her area:

> T 28: Because when these books were introduced they didn't come on time. Only when they were in Year 7 they got the Year 6. The Year 7 book when they went to Year 8. The 1988 paper we found it difficult to train the students on all the texts because the books came late and it was a new exam also. (Nuwara Eliya 340)

The problem seemed to have been sorted out by the time of the group interviews, but it had clearly affected teaching in the early years of the reform.

Several teachers mentioned another problem relating to the textbooks: that students had to hand their books back to the schools at the end of every school year. This was not so serious if they had managed to cover all the material before the end of the year, but it became problematic if they had not finished all of their lessons on time. It was also a problem if the students needed to revise something that they had studied in a previous year. One teacher talked about how he wanted his students to revise some material that they had studied a few years earlier, but this meant having to borrow books from the current Year 7 and Year 9 students (Welimada 184-191). Only one teacher had obtained a whole set of books for each of her students:

> T 20: But I made a point. I even collected some books, because we have enough books in the school which are thrown away. So I told my students never to give the *English Every Day* back to the school. Even if the teachers ask or the principals. And I went to the principal and told them that they must have the books because they need the English books. If they are to sit the GCE O level they should have *English Every Day* – Year 7, 8, 9 and 10. So I made a point for them to bind those books and my children all they kept ... (Nuwara Eliya 367).

When it came to teaching materials for the examination, several teachers said that they had not seen or did not have access to the official examination preparation documents (the *Guidelines* and *Suggestions* booklets discussed in Chapter 9). This problem first came to light during the observation study, and interviews which were conducted earlier in the evaluation project had revealed that the government printing press which produced the books had been destroyed during the troubles in the late 1980s. The press was back in operation by the time of these interviews, but there were still distribution problems which made it hard for teachers to obtain the books that they needed (Wellawatte 650 and 679, Ratnapura 267-269 and 278).

There was also a problem in that most students did not have their own copies of examination practice materials. Some teachers were able to provide their students with copies of past or model papers, either because they paid for them out of their own pockets (Colombo 24) or because the students were able to pay a very small fee (Asgiriya 371, Ratnapura 394). Many students could not afford even a minimal fee, and teachers felt they had to copy past or model papers, including whole reading passages, onto the blackboard and then wait for students to copy them into their exercise books (e.g. Colombo 301). The process of copying could take up most of a teaching period. Some teachers reported that they could not deal with long passages or complicated tasks in this way:

T 11: Sometimes I omit because there are long questions. The children find it difficult to write within a period even, so such questions I leave out. (Colombo 317)

The consequence of this decision was that some students would not get to practise some of the more demanding skills.

Some teachers dealt with the lack of materials by dictating examination questions to their students (Wennapuwa 443-446). They preferred this method of working because in addition to saving time it gave the students listening practice and made them 'confident and independent' (Wellawatte 148, Ratnapura 563). Other teachers felt that the practice was too risky, as their students would not be able to take the dictation correctly (Colombo 399).

## Insufficient time

We have already explored the problem of covering all of the *English Every Day* material in a single year (see 'Complexity of *EED*' in Chapter 8), and we have seen that at least a quarter of the teachers felt that they could not complete the syllabus without giving extra lessons. These problems were serious enough in Year 10 but they became even more serious in Year 11, when they also had to set time aside to do examination preparation.

At least a quarter of the teachers reported that they were giving extra lessons to help their students prepare for the examination. Some teachers had started their examination revision as early as May (e.g. Ratnapura 134 and 376), but nearly everyone had started by the time they were interviewed in late October or early November. Some of these teachers continued with *EED* in their regular lessons and did examination preparation in the afternoon (e.g. Nuwara Eliya 165-188), but others did examination preparation during their regular lessons and after normal school hours (Nugegoda 330-331). Most of the teachers who worked after school gave one extra session a week (e.g. Nugegoda 321); however, others taught two afternoons (Ratnapura 438, Nugegoda 313-315) or even three. One teacher had been doing examination revision during his regular lessons and three extra afternoons since September (Welimada 364-372).

## Summary of classroom factors

To summarize what has been said about classroom factors, it is clear that many teachers were facing great difficulties, which must have affected the amount and type of material they could work on in their classroom and the methods they were using. The most obvious problem was that their students were unable to cope with the demands of the textbook. This was most apparent in the lower sets when students were divided according to ability, but it was also a problem when there were groups of mixed ability. It was not clear whether this was due to the complexity of *English Every Day*, inadequate teaching in the past, or other problems, but many teachers felt that they needed to go through the materials in a very detailed way. This slowed down the whole process and put more pressure on what was already a tight schedule.

Some teachers also had to deal with over-crowded classrooms and excessive noise. If these teachers and their students could not hear one another then it was going to be difficult to carry out many types of activities (especially oral activities) at even the simplest level.

The fact that there were not enough materials also complicated matters, especially when it came to preparing for the examination. It was difficult for many classes to practise skills such as selective reading if the students had to copy passages word for word from the blackboard.

Given these circumstances it is not difficult to see why many teachers employed traditional methods of teaching, which were less disruptive to others and which required less energy and ingenuity.

# School factors

A number of important issues emerged when teachers discussed the schools they worked in. These included the differences between schools in Sri Lanka; the problem of teacher transfer, absenteeism and shortage; the role of the principal; and the tensions caused by conflicting demands within the curriculum.

## The differences between schools

The teachers did not mention this issue explicitly but it was clear that there were important differences between schools in Sri Lanka. Some of the factors that led to such differences were the location of schools, the relative wealth of the students' families, and the links that certain schools had with important people. The location of a school was very important: schools in towns or cities were likely to enjoy advantages that schools in rural areas could not, including exposure to English. Some teachers saw a close relationship between being in a town and having access to the language, which could help students to progress through the teaching materials more quickly:

> T 47: … So we are able to finish the syllabus because it's a town and most
> of the children there they know English. Some of them are weak but most
> of them are very good in their English. We don't have the difficulties that
> these (other) people have. We are able to finish the syllabus by September,
> having classes during the holidays. (Trincomalee 547)

Students in towns might also have access to better outside tuition (Colombo 468).

Another difference between schools was the relative wealth of the pupils' families. In some schools students could afford to pay for extra material (up to 15 rupees for cyclostyled copies of term tests or exam preparation materials, or 35–60 rupees for commercial materials), while in many the students were very poor and had to make do with copying from the blackboard. In some schools students could afford to go to tutories or have private tuition, while in others they could only stay after school to work with their own teachers. These teachers volunteered their time when they could; if they could not however, their students got no extra lessons.

A final difference concerned the connections schools had with powerful people. One of the schools represented was a 'national school', where teachers were under pressure to teach well:

> DW: Why is this school so special?
>
> T 64: Because this is a government school. It's a national school for the whole province. Not just the province. I mean district...
>
> T 63: This is a national school.
>
> T 64: It's a prominent place and there are politicians and administrators and very influential people having their hands in this. Not to disrupt but for the development of that. They have a very strong say in that. It has very strong connections outside.
>
> T 63: And if the children score poor marks, definitely their parents will ask what's the reason. Then they will come out 'Our teacher didn't finish the book'. So then they will blame the teachers for not finishing the books. And then they will complain and they will incur [sic] from our principal, and we are answerable to the principal.
>
> T 64: It might end up with the Minister. (National School – 480-485)

These teachers complained about the pressures they felt as a result of too much scrutiny. Others worried about being neglected. Some teachers from a different part of the country felt that the authorities were not aware of the true situation in the schools and therefore could not help them (Trincomalee 694-695).

It is important to mention all of these differences because the textbook and the examination teams were supposed to be catering for the whole country and not just for the more privileged schools.

## Teacher transfer, absenteeism and shortages

The second school factor to emerge from the interviews was a serious lack of continuity in teaching, mostly but not only in the rural or politically disturbed areas. Some teachers stayed with the same group of students as they moved from one year to the next (this was usually the case in schools which were considered to be 'better' schools – Colombo 10, Asgiriya 21, Nuwara Eliya 63, Welimada 63, Ratnapura 44-50), but about 20 of the teachers were teaching groups that they had not worked with before this school year. This was problematic for at least ten of the teachers, because they did not know how much material their students had covered in earlier years or why they had not covered more.

One of the reasons for this lack of continuity was teacher transfers: there was a great deal of disruption as teachers moved from one school to another. Most of the transfers took place at the beginning of the year, as explained by this teacher:

> T 21: ... Usually transfers are given in January or February. So the teachers who have applied for transfers, who are qualified for them, they just mark time. Because of that there's a backlog always ... (Nuwara Eliya 663)

However, teachers could also change schools at other times in the year. At least three of the teachers had arrived at their new school in May, which gave them only six months to get their Year 11 groups ready for the examination (Nuwara Eliya 41 and 53, Welimada 53). One of these teachers explained how many teachers his students had had in a single year, and what the consequences were likely to be:

> T 51: ... I think I'll be able to teach this whole group in another one year. But they can't face the O level examination now. Because the same thing has happened in their Year 10. One teacher was there and she couldn't complete the book. And she was transferred to another school. And another teacher came there. And in January that teacher started to do the Year 11 book. Not finish the Year 10 book. So far until I came, that teacher was able to finish Unit 3. But some cases I noticed in writing they can't write even a simple essay. One or two can. So I have to take the whole responsibility. But in another two or three or weeks I can't do all the things. That's the problem. I tried to do some extra classes but I wasn't able to get the time. Because there are some reasons in that school. So I understand they're in trouble to face the examinations. (Welimada 54)

Another teacher took over a new group very late in the year. His predecessor had been attending a training course since January, and had only been able to teach his groups two days a week. It was not until the end of October that the principal of the school realized that the Year 11 group needed more attention and asked this teacher to provide cover. The teacher explained his predicament:

> T 27: ... Now I can't do the syllabus. I can only do the model papers. But maybe two or three students will get through. That's the way that I can help ... (Nuwara Eliya 51)

There were several other reasons why teachers could not teach their classes. They might be summoned to Colombo to do extra work for the National Institute of Education (NIE) (Colombo 188, Nuwara Eliya 672), or to other areas to attend training seminars. The six teachers I interviewed in Anuradhapura had been directed to attend the week-long seminar where I met them, and they would have to give extra classes when they got home to make up for the classes they were missing (this was approximately one month before the examination). There was also the matter of official leave: every teacher was entitled to a certain number of leave days per year, in addition to official holidays and festivals, and if they did not take them they lost them.

The most serious problem, however, was that there simply were not enough teachers in some areas. One teacher from a rural area explained the situation in his school:

> T 27: ... In our school from Year 4 to Year 11 there are about 14 or 15 classes. So they have only five periods for a week, then it will be about 80 or 90 periods. So there are not enough teachers. We have only three teachers. One English teacher who is a trained teacher is working as vice-principal of the school. So sometimes we (the other two teachers) have to work all 40 periods. And earlier there was no English teacher. Sometimes even in Year 11 there are so many students who don't know their alphabet even. That's the real situation in the area. (Nuwara Eliya 524)

The shortage was particularly severe in the north and east. An in-service adviser explained that there were only 33 English teachers to cover the 85 schools in her area. Ten of these had been trained to teach; the others had only a Credit-Pass on their own O level examination (Trincomalee 285). The local educational authority was trying to recruit more teachers:

> T 45: ... Because of the dearth of English teachers now our Department is calling for applications from the retired officers (civil servants). Those who know English. And they are paying our hourly pay. So those retired officers they don't know the method of teaching so that tutory teaching and those retired officers teaching are the same. (Trincomalee 678)

The adviser was relieved that there would be more people to teach, but she was also anxious as she would now have to give basic training to people who had never given classes.

It is clear how this lack of continuity and the lack of teachers could affect the type of teaching that was taking place. Teachers who wished to teach in an innovative manner would find it difficult if they could not be sure that the proper foundations had been laid by their predecessors. The situation would be worse when outsiders were recruited to teach on a casual basis, as they were unlikely to understand why they should teach any differently from the way they had been taught before.

# Role of the principal

The third school-related factor to emerge was the importance of the principal in providing guidance and support to teachers who were trying to cope with an innovation. Teachers from three schools spoke positively about their principals: one had worked out a sensible system for assessing students and reporting back to parents (Trincomalee 545-553), one had instilled students and teachers with a feeling of pride in the school (Welimada 327-339), and one had attended official meetings and kept the teachers informed about developments such as the NIE 'pilot test' (Wellawatte 423-426. See also section on 'Educational administration'). These teachers seemed confident when they talked about their teaching and their ability to cope with the examination.

There were other comments, however, which indicated that the leadership in the schools was not always effective. We have already seen that one principal did not realize until very late in the year that students needed more attention if they were to succeed in the O level examination (Nuwara Eliya 51). We have also seen that some teachers did not know how much material their students had completed in previous classes or why previous teachers had made so little progress. This information should not have been difficult to obtain, so there must have been weaknesses in the way the principals organized communication within their schools.

# Conflicts within the curriculum

The final school-related problem involved the amount of time that was lost in many schools due to extra activities such as sports days, prize days, band practice, English Days, etc. At least 11 teachers said that they had had to give up class time because of these activities. One teacher said that it was a 'public secret', well known to everyone, that 'little work is done in classes' (Welimada 52). This teacher felt that it was reasonable to give students time for 'sports and other things', but others complained because these activities took time away from what was already a pressurized timetable. One teacher explained why she could not finish the syllabus unless she gave extra lessons during school vacations:

> T 36: Because the whole of the first term was taken up with sports. That's the usual way ... The first term is spent on sports. So we hardly get any time to meet all the girls in the class. And that's not fair. When half of them leave the class for some practice, that's not fair. So because of that we were doing something else. Not the actual work that we planned ...
> (Ratnapura 46)

## Summary of school factors

It was evident from this discussion that there were a number of differences between the schools in Sri Lanka, and that the teachers in less privileged schools needed support to compensate for the things their students lacked – among them material resources and exposure to English in the outside world. The role of the principal was critical, as this person not only formed a valuable link between the school and the outside world, but was also responsible for providing leadership and support within the school. Several of the problems discussed here needed to be dealt with by the principal and others at management level. These included improving working conditions, making sure that teachers did not waste time while waiting for transfers, improving record-keeping and internal communication, and making sure that extra activities did not obstruct teaching and learning.

## Outside tuition

A theme which appeared in almost all of the interviews was the importance of outside tuition. Many teachers talked about how their students attended classes after school (and occasionally even during the school day) in order to prepare for the examination. Some students were able to afford 'private tuition', which meant that they had their own tutor or studied with a small group of classmates; others attended 'tutories', where they studied in large groups. Some students studied several subjects but others could only afford to study one or two. Many students went without extra tuition because their families could not afford it. Some classroom teachers offered free lessons outside school hours, but this kind of help was not always available.

About a quarter of the teachers said that their students studied English outside the school. Some teachers did not know how many of their students did this, but others were able to estimate: in some classes 25% of the students attended tuition (e.g. Asgiriya 434-435), in quite a few 50-75% of the students did (e.g. Colombo 501, Asgiriya 427 and 455-463), and in one case 100% of the students attended classes elsewhere (Wennapuwa 527). A few of the teachers felt that their students benefited from the extra work they were doing (Colombo 468, Wennapuwa 527), but about half felt that the students were being misled by tutory masters who taught them the wrong content or used the 'wrong methodology' (Trincomalee 603, 624, 661 and 662). Teachers commented that tutories 'massacred role plays' (Colombo 64) or ignored listening and speaking altogether (Trincomalee 630-635), taught incorrect pronunciations (Colombo 503, Trincomalee 655), gave word-for-word translations of passages (Wennapuwa 548, Trincomalee 630-635), kept one lesson ahead of the teachers so that they appeared to be teaching something new (Trincomalee 630-635), and taught the *EED* units 'back to front' (Trincomalee 640-643).

Teachers felt that the bad practice in tutories affected their own teaching situations. If the tutories 'massacred' role plays, then they had to find other ways of presenting the material to salvage the situation (Colombo 101). If the tutories gave word-for-word translations then they were expected to do the same and the students respected them less if they did not conform (Wennapuwa 637). Some teachers felt that they could not give their students homework because they would either not complete it because they were in tutory sessions (Trincomalee 645, Colombo 486), or they would ask the tutory masters to complete it for them (Wellawatte 140). Worst of all, some teachers reported that their students played truant because they had outside tuition during the school day. I observed a class where only six out of 42 pupils were present. The rest were attending tuition classes in Mathematics or Science. When I described this situation in my next interview one of the teachers replied:

> T 8: We have that problem. During school hours they attend tuition. They have revision classes, or seminars. Even today I had about half the class absent because they seem to say that they do work in science and maths. What they do there is much profitable than what is done in school. [Laughter.] (Colombo 482)

Although many teachers were negative about the tutories, others felt that their students were benefiting from additional exposure to English. This exchange represents both points of view:

> T 47: Some children even go to tuition to those who are not English teachers. They don't know anything about English. Just because they speak English they go to them.

> T 45: In most of the schools in Killinochchi there are no English teachers. The children depend on the tutories. They will pass the examination and they will take Distinction too. (Trincomalee 663-664)

The first teacher, who was from a convent school in a town, believed that the tutories were undermining the work she was trying to do, while the second teacher, who was an in-service adviser in the north of the country, felt that students needed all the help and continuity they could get in situations where there were either no teachers or frequent disruptions in schooling.

The examination developer who attended most of the interviews admitted that the Ministry was aware of the problems in the tutories:

> The tuition problem is an issue which the Ministry is very aware of. I think that's why the programme like Extended School Hours and different other programmes were trying to be set up, to counter-act that ... (Colombo 611)

However, it seemed to her that a more powerful solution would be to 'educate the tutors'. If tutories were going to continue to play an important role in education, then perhaps the tutory masters should be given training in methodology so that they would not weaken the foundations in English that the classroom teachers had given the students already.

To summarize, there were three problems related to outside tuition. The most basic was that it was considered necessary in the first place: why did so many students, from the most privileged schools to the poorest, feel that they needed extra tuition? Was it because the syllabus was too ambitious, or because the students and their parents felt that the classroom teaching was not good enough to allow them to achieve their goals?

The second problem concerned the unfairness of a system which required students to pay extra for what they should have been receiving in the classroom. Many students seemed to think that they needed additional help, but wealthier students were able to get better quality help than poorer students – and some students were not able to get any help at all.

The third problem concerned the quality of the outside teaching and how this affected the lessons that the classroom teachers were giving. Some teachers felt that they had to adopt more conservative techniques because students were demanding the same kind of teaching that they were receiving in the tutories. This was obviously contrary to the approach that the textbook designers favoured.

## Educational administration

Several important points emerged concerning the administration of education at national and local levels. These related to the way in which the new examination had been introduced into schools, the amount of information that teachers received about the examination and where they got their information from (the communication structure of the educational system), the type of teacher training that was available, teacher shortages, and communication within the National Institute of Education and between this body and schools.

## Introduction of the new examination

Policy-makers had decided to introduce a new O level examination early in the 1980s but no official description was given to teachers until late 1987, only a year before the exam was to be administered for the first time. The description came in the form of a Ministry announcement, which was badly worded and which some teachers found confusing (Alderson and Wall 1989:N-24). The first clear description that teachers received was in the *Guidelines* booklet. This was sent to schools in May 1988, just six months before the exam was to be given for the first time. (See Chapter 9, under 'Explicitness of examination', for details.)

Several teachers were negative about the way the examination had been introduced. One teacher explained that they had barely had time to get used to the textbook before they were faced with the examination:

> T 28: Because when these books were introduced they didn't come on time. Only when they were in Year 7 they got the Year 6. The Year 7 book when they went to Year 8. The 1988 paper we found it difficult to train the students on all the texts because the books came late and it was a new exam also. (Nuwara Eliya 340)

Another explained that they had only received news about the examination a short time before it was to be introduced, which made it difficult to prepare their students properly (Nuwara Eliya 534). Although they were given information about the types of skills that would be tested and the new item- and task-types, they had not been notified that the instructions would be in English only, rather than in English, Sinhala and Tamil.

There were further complications in that teachers were having to cope with continuous assessment at the same time (Nuwara Eliya 347-351). This was a totally new concept which demanded a great deal of time and attention.

## Information about the examination

The second point to emerge about educational administration was that many teachers still did not have enough information about the examination, even though three years had passed since its first administration.

About a third of the teachers said that they had served as examiners: this would make them familiar with the content of the exam and how it was marked, including the rating scales for writing. The rest of the teachers had to get their information from other sources. Several had seen a copy of the first exam in one of the official support booklets, and one had bought a set of past papers that had just been published by the Department of Examinations; however, more than a dozen teachers had received their copies of past papers from friends or relatives and many had learned about the examination through commercial publications. These contained practice items but no marking schemes or rating scales, and there was no discussion of what was being tested or what teachers needed to know in order to prepare their students properly.

Why was it that so many teachers got their information from friends or family or through commercial publications rather than through the official booklets prepared by the examination development team? A copy of *Guidelines* and *Suggestions* had been sent to all of the secondary schools, but many teachers said they had not seen them (e.g. Wellawatte 443, 557 and 558; Ratnapura 271-273 and 275-278). This may have been due to distribution problems inside the schools (see section on 'Role of the principal') or because there were so many changes in teaching staff (see section on 'Teacher shortages'). Whatever the reason, some teachers were not as informed as they should have been and were therefore unlikely to be able to prepare their students properly. This was particularly evident when it came to informing the students about the criteria for marking writing (Wellawatte 648 and Wellawatte 673, Nugegoda 195).

## Teacher training opportunities

There were many problems in the training given to English language teachers. Some of these dated back to the late 1950s, when a change in language policy meant that English was to be taught as a second language in all schools rather than being the medium of education in a few privileged schools (Woolger 1994). The education system could not cope with the consequences of this decision: few people knew how to teach English to students who did not already speak it, nobody knew what standards should be aimed for in teaching, and there was little understanding of how to work with large mixed-ability classes or how to motivate learners from different age groups and social backgrounds. There was also a serious shortage of teachers, and many of those who were working lacked even basic teacher training qualifications. These problems continued throughout the 1960s and 1970s. The situation improved slightly with the introduction of the Old Syllabus textbook series and textbook-specific training, but this was not satisfactory in the long run. Teachers learned how to deal with specific problems but they were not equipped with the general skills they needed to face different types of challenges. Woolger described the situation in these words:

> teachers may learn how to 'borrow' some prescribed routines, and perhaps even some selected underlying theoretical principles (though commonly they do not or, if they do, only in a distorted way), but it is unlikely that they will learn how to take on the new professional roles (often unpredicted; largely unpredictable) which come with any curriculum reform, or make informed choices in the teaching according to the particular (and changing) circumstances they face. (1994:129)

The training process had to begin anew with the introduction of *English Every Day*. The textbook designers could deal with the concerns of the teachers in the beginning, but the training was then handed over to the in-service adviser network and there was no guarantee that the same messages were reaching all the teachers in the country. The situation became more complicated in the late 1980s, when many education tasks were devolved to the provincial councils. There was a plan to create Regional English Support Centres (RESCs) in all the provinces, where well-qualified trainers would conduct quality courses, but only a few of these had begun to function by the time of the group interviews.

Teachers in other areas had to count on whatever provision their local authorities could offer and some received no training. The examination developer explained the seriousness of the problem:

> I think that what has happened is that at the beginning the material writers themselves conducted the seminars. That was 1984. When the books were introduced. But that was finished. There was very intense training by the material writers, and they were happy with that and that has stopped. But these teachers have come up after that. ... It was the in-service training which had to continue with the same principles being given. The same thinking. It hasn't gone to the new teachers. It has stopped with that particular sort of in-service training. (Asgiriya 600)

The transcripts contained several references to teacher training: one concerning pre-service training and the rest concerning in-service training. The comment about pre-service training was negative, concerning staff shortages and the teaching of methods that did not work with students of low proficiency (Wennapuwa 373).

The comments about in-service training were mixed. Some teachers were quite positive (Welimada 105, Trincomalee 572), with one teacher remarking that she would teach her group 'the way we have been asked to do it' if she did not have to compensate for the bad teaching taking place in the tutories (Colombo 104). The problem was that there were significant differences between the training opportunities that were offered in different parts of the country. There was a RESC in Nuwara Eliya, which was headed by a well-respected adviser, and where teachers met frequently to discuss their problems (Nuwara Eliya 695-699). The adviser conducted seminars on the new examination (Nuwara Eliya 672) and visited schools to answer students' questions (Nuwara Eliya 674–676). The local education officers in the Vavuniyah and Killinochchi areas also provided strong direction (Trincomalee 281, 352). However, there was no training at all in other areas. The situation was summed up by the examination developer:

> In a way this is a deprived area. There are no in-service advisers here. No seminars have been held for quite some time. (Asgiriya 579)

One of the consequences of this was that some teachers did not understand what they were meant to be teaching:

> T 5: The teachers don't know the objectives of the exercises.

> Examination developer: Yes, that's what I think.

> T 5: Now, Learning Together, we don't know what the objective is. That's the problem ... If you are told what the objective is in seminars, I don't think this problem will come. (Asgiriya 559-561)

Other teachers had some access to in-service training but the things that they remembered about the sessions suggested that their trainers had concentrated more on the examination than on the objectives of the textbook. One trainer reportedly instructed teachers not to bother with teaching listening in Year 11 as it was not on the examination (Asgiriya 110). Another had told teachers not to cover more than the first half of the Year 11 textbook:

> T 45: (He) directed us to teach only four units in Year 11.
>
> DW: Why? Because he knew that it was only realistic?
>
> T 45: Yes, he knew that the Examination Department what they will do. So he directed us during the Year 11, to teach only four units. (Trincomalee 562-564).

It is unlikely that a teacher trainer would have had access to such information since security in both the Department of Examinations and the examination development team was very tight. What matters here though is that the trainer told teachers he had such information and they believed him.

One strong impression that emerged from the interviews was that teachers did not know very much about conditions in other schools and how other teachers managed their classrooms. It was only in the Nuwara Eliya and Anuradhapura interviews that the teachers seemed familiar with their colleagues' situations: in Nuwara Eliya this was because they were all members of the RESC and met regularly (Nuwara Eliya 695-699) and in Anuradhapura it was because several of the younger teachers had been pupils of the oldest teacher present (Trincomalee 113-115). Teachers in other places said that they had been happy to attend the group interviews because they had few opportunities to hear how other teachers were working.

## Teacher shortages

Another theme relating to educational administration was the shortage of teachers and the disruption caused by transfers. This was discussed in detail in an earlier section and will not be discussed here.

## The National Institute of Education

The National Institute of Education (NIE) was the division of the Ministry of Education which was responsible for curriculum development, teacher training and examination. Two points arose about the activities of the NIE: one concerning the communication between different sections within the institution and one concerning communication with the schools.

The first point concerned the communication between the curriculum design team and the examination development team. This topic arose during a discussion about whether teachers really understood the objectives of the textbook series and the examination. I had mentioned that the interviews were a way of finding out what teachers were thinking, and that the findings would be sent to the examination development team for their information and further action. One teacher thought that this was not sufficient:

> T 5: The material writers should also come in. Because they'll want to know. If the people who write examinations and the people who write the materials differ in their ideas, teachers will be lost. They would have meant something to be taught, but the exam writers are looking for something else. (Nuwara Eliya 597)

The examination developer who was present at the interviews tried to persuade this teacher that there was, in fact, adequate communication between the two teams, but no-one thought to ask the teacher why she had raised the point in the first place. Why did she feel that the teams might not be communicating? If teachers had this impression, they could become confused and disheartened and their work could suffer as a result.

The second point concerned communication between the NIE and the schools.

In one of the interviews it emerged that the NIE had designed a 'pilot test', which would be administered in schools a few weeks before the real exam. Several of the teachers had heard of the test, either from their principals or, in the case of one teacher, from her own child, who was a student in another school where the test was to be given. Other teachers were surprised to hear of its existence, and no one really understood its purpose. There was a general feeling that it was important, but no one had any details: even the examination developer was ignorant about its origin and why it was to be given. There seemed to be a problem in communication, but it was not obvious where the breakdown was: whether at higher levels in the communication chain (which would explain the examination developer's lack of awareness) or at lower levels – between the NIE and principals, or between the principals and the teachers (Wellawatte 403-426). There was also some confusion because the test had been postponed: this meant that the schools who knew about it and had planned their timetables around it now had to rearrange their teaching and figure out new ways to handle its administration (Nuwara Eliya 192–196).

## Summary of education administration characteristics

The main points emerging concerned communications, teacher shortages and teacher training. Communication difficulties were evident in the comments made about the introduction of the examination and the fact that so many teachers were still unaware of certain features even though the exam was in its fourth year of existence. There were also comments about the communication within the NIE, between the NIE and schools, and between teachers living in the same community.

The problems with teacher shortages were discussed earlier in this chapter and will not be repeated here.

There were many problems relating to teachers. The most serious was that many teachers had not received adequate training in their early years and may not have developed the skills they needed to cope with difficult and/or changing circumstances. There were also questions relating to the effectiveness of *EED* training: whether the initial training had reached enough people, whether it had been adequate, and whether teachers who had entered the system since the mid-1980s had received enough grounding in the basic principles and procedures. The transfer of some educational responsibilities to provincial governments made it difficult for the curriculum and examination teams to know whether there had been sufficient training and whether the right messages had been delivered to the teachers. There was an attempt to improve the situation by opening Regional English Support Centres, but there were only a few of these in operation at the time of the interviews. Until these centres were up and running many teachers would either go without training or receive training that was less than adequate.

## Political factors

The national political situation was very difficult in the 1980s and early 1990s. There were two major conflicts taking place, one in the north and east of the country, involving a struggle for a separate Tamil state, and one in the central and southern parts of the country, which involved more general social and political issues. The details of these conflicts are not of direct relevance here, but it is important to note that there was considerable violence and disruption throughout the time that the new textbooks and examination were being developed and introduced. This had serious effects on education, including many interruptions in schooling and long periods of school closure in 1988 and 1989, and delays in the first two administrations of the new examination (the 1988 examination was delayed by two months and the 1989 examination was delayed by four). The situation improved in 1989, when the conflict in the central and southern parts eased off, but there were still problems in the north and east at the time of the interviews.

It was no surprise that the teachers said little about the political situation. I had noticed during my visits to the country that people rarely discussed current affairs, even in private conversations. It was understandable that they would not discuss such matters in public, especially when they did not know one another and when the discussion was being recorded (see Chapter 5, regarding the disadvantages of group interviews). There were, nevertheless, a few brief references to how the conflicts had affected their teaching.

The first type of reference came from teachers in the central and southern parts of the country. One group of teachers recalled how difficult it had been to cope with the new examination when they were having to deal with a shortage of textbooks, the continuous assessment programme, and 'that difficulty' at the same time (Nuwara Eliya 347-350). Another teacher referred to 'The Troubles', which 'had affected them from Year 9' (Colombo 6). Some teachers were still suffering from the 'knock-on' effect of school closures: not being able to finish a textbook one year meant that it had to be carried over to the next year, and this in turn delayed the work in all future years.The other references to political problems came from the teachers from the north and the east, who were being interviewed at a training seminar in Anuradhapura. These teachers had had to travel to Anuradhapura because trainers from other parts of the country could not travel to them. They lived in areas where there was still frequent violence. This had three types of impact: there were severe shortages of teachers in some regions, there were still disruptions in the schools, and there were serious inconveniences in their own personal lives.

I have already discussed the shortage of teachers in certain parts of the country, but it is important to note how severe the shortage was in these areas. A teacher adviser from the north revealed how hard it was to recruit teachers:

> T 45: Yes, so if we had more trained English teachers then I could develop that area more. Even though it is a remote area. But unfortunately we couldn't get any English teachers. Teachers from town areas won't come because they have to undergo severe difficulties. So the teachers from that area only are serving the children.

> DW: Okay. Now, when you say that people won't come to your area, I think we all know why …

> T 45: Yes, even if they are posted to our area they will go to the Secretary or Ministry of Education or that high level and get the transfer and go to their own country. (Trincomalee 289-291)

'Their own country' means the area that the teachers came from originally. It was interesting, however, to learn of a surplus of English teachers in Jaffna, where some teachers were now helping out with other subjects. This suggests that the shortage of teachers in the adviser's area may have been due to geography just as much as to politics – i.e. teachers would rather stay in the cities than in the countryside (see comments on 'remote schools' in earlier sections).

The political situation was also having an effect on how quickly teachers reacted to the new ideas about teaching. One teacher felt that it would take a long time for teachers and students to 'come to grips with these books' and to start liking them. One of the reasons for this was that they had not had the necessary preparation to deal with the material, due to the political situation (Trincomalee 488-489). This teacher referred to 'the troubles there, on and off' and 'external elements interfering' (Trincomalee 232, 234). Another spoke of how 'this ethnic problem' could prevent teachers from getting through the syllabus (Trincomalee 352-354), and, in particular, how 'those troubles' forced the teachers to focus on the material that seemed most important for the examination:

> T 45: ... But this time we couldn't have that assessment test because of those troubles. So August was full of trouble. So in September also we couldn't start the school. So here is very complicated trouble. Even though our Director said 'Somehow or another you give them some important matters to teach the children. Not all.' So we selected the role-play and all the 'Finding Outs'. We do all the 'Finding Outs'. (Trincomalee 560)

The political situation also affected teachers personally. One teacher gave an account of the difficulties she experienced because there was too little reliable transportation and too many military roadblocks. She lived in Trincomalee and worked in a small village outside the town. Only a few buses travelled to and from the village, which meant that she had to leave her school before the end of the working day if she wanted to get home before dark. There were five checkpoints along her route, and passengers had to get out of the bus at every checkpoint. She explained how the previous week she had not been allowed to travel to the school:

> T 44: ... And again on Friday ... I went to the bus stand and got into the bus. It's just a few miles, I said. And when we went to the third mile post the bus was turned back. Because an incident took place and six were killed inside a van. An incident took place. And we couldn't proceed. We had to come back. I had all these programmes and I wanted to have a test for Year 10, and what happened? Then the next week I came here. No teacher there to continue my work. (Trincomalee 359)

The fact that the teacher had to leave school early meant that she was unable to teach all the classes she should have taught. She was also prevented from giving extra lessons after school to help her students to get through the syllabus and prepare for the examination. This was particularly unfortunate since there was no other English teacher who could take over this responsibility.

The only other references to political matters were at a more local level: the teachers at a national school talked about the influence of politicians and other powerful people in the way their school was run (National School 483-491), and another teacher talked about how the preparation he had received at training college had been affected by internal politics:

> T 63: At that time we didn't have lecturers. We didn't have enough lecturers there. And our principal at that time he didn't want to get down lecturers. He wanted to close the English section there. Because English people always made trouble there. But the English Unit is still going on. (Wennapuwa 779).

In summary, the political conflicts in Sri Lanka had serious effects on all aspects of life in the 1980s and early 1990s, including education. The frequent disruptions to schools made it harder for teachers to cope with the ELT changes. School closures set many teachers behind in their textbook coverage, and examinations had to be delayed during the first two years. There were still problems in the north and east at the time of the interviews, and these were having an impact on the numbers of teachers available to give classes, and the amount and type of material that could be covered in lessons.

## Geographic factors

There were a number of comments relating to the geography of the country. The most significant concerned the political problems in the north and east, which have just been discussed in the previous section. The other comments concerned the reluctance of most teachers to work in rural areas, the difficulties that rural students had with English and the *EED* textbook series, the lack of resources in rural areas and transportation difficulties.

We have already seen that there was a shortage of teachers in the north and east of the country, but teachers in other parts of the country were also reluctant to work outside the towns. One teacher explained the hardships that he and his students were facing:

> T 27: Though I am from Nuwara Eliya I am teaching in a very remote area, the most difficult area in this country. Today to come here I had to get up at 5.00 and I started out at 6.00 in the morning. So when you compare the same district ... the situation of the city schools and the remote areas ...all the students won't get the same chance. So in town the students are always with the language. Sometimes their parents speak English. In our areas even we forget our English because we don't have a chance to read a paper even ... (Nuwara Eliya 514)

Another teacher was so unhappy that she asked me to get her a transfer:

> T 44: Please get me a transfer to a town school. I'm getting wasted. I'm just ruined. I'm ruining myself there. (Trincomalee 463)

There was such a shortage of teachers that many students went without English for extended periods of time. Several teachers were working with groups that had gone without teachers at some point in the past (Welimada 49, Ratnapura 116, Trincomalee 409). One school could only offer classes to students in Years 6, 8 and 11; students in Year 7, 9 and 10 had to wait until they moved on to the next year (Trincomalee 409).

Students in rural areas lacked not only teachers but also exposure to English in their environment. One teacher described the problem in these words:

T 37: … the problem with my children is that they are very poor children. They have not any chance to even hear a word. I told them to switch on to the radio, the TV, like that. They do nothing. Due to that we teachers cannot deal with them within these 40 minute periods. In town areas … in Ratnapura … Somewhat … I feel that there is a difference. (Ratnapura 106)

Some students lacked familiarity with urban life, and with technology in particular. While some teachers felt that the textbook made students 'more knowledgeable' because it was 'Colombo-based' (Nugegoda 408), others described what they had to do to help their students understand modern life. I have already referred to the teachers who took their students to the Post Office or Telephone Exchange to learn about how telephones worked, so that they could better understand an *EED* dialogue on taking telephone messages (Asgiriya 553, Nuwara Eliya 149).

All of this meant that rural students were sometimes very far behind their urban counterparts. One teacher argued that rural students should be given a separate O level, so that they would not have to compete on the same terms as students in the town (Ratnapura 617).

The third type of comment relating to geography had to do with access to materials. Teachers who lived in Colombo could borrow books from The British Council (Colombo 557, Asgiriya 607), purchase books from bookshops (Colombo 566), and obtain examination preparation materials from the Examinations Department (Colombo 434-435). Teachers who worked in other cities could also get hold of commercial examination preparation books and newspapers that could be used for supplementary reading exercises (Nuwara Eliya 230-232). None of these materials were available in the rural regions.

The final problem relating to geography concerned transportation. Travelling by public transportation was quite difficult in the late 1980s and early 1990s. I have already spoken of the special difficulties in the North and East (Trincomalee 246, 277-279), but there were problems even where there was no longer any conflict. Some of the problems had to do with distance – e.g. one teacher said that her school did not give extra lessons in the afternoon because the students lived far away and they had to leave early to get home at a reasonable hour (Wellawatte 469-472). Other problems were the weather – e.g. one teacher spoke of how her students would not come to school when there was monsoon flooding (Nuwara Eliya 33).

# Economic factors

There were two types of comments regarding economic factors: those relating to the general situation in the country, and those relating to particular groups of students.

The general comments were about the pressure on students to succeed in their examinations in order to get by in the world:

> T 27: ... But being a Third World country the people's only stake is education. Somehow they have to get through their exams, and unless they get through the exams they won't get the jobs. Because of that they have to sit this paper ... (Nuwara Eliya 500)

Several teachers spoke about the competitiveness of the examination (Nuwara Eliya 502, Wennapuwa 497, Wennapuwa 598), and one commented on how passing the exam had become a means of 'social survival' (Wennapuwa 598). This teacher also spoke of how some students 'fail miserably', victims of the same social factors they were trying to escape from (Wennapuwa 739).

The comments about particular groups all came from teachers teaching students from poor families. These teachers talked about how their students were not exposed to English outside the classroom (e.g. Colombo 70, Ratnapura 106), how they were not encouraged to study by their families (Wennapuwa 154), how they could not afford books (Colombo 396 and 452), and how they could not pay for outside tuition (Ratnapura 762, Nugegoda 369).

# Cultural factors

There were few references to cultural aspects of the context, apart from references to the role of English in the society and its importance if students wished to get ahead in the world. These ideas will be explored more fully in Chapter 11, in sections on the teachers' and students' attitudes to English.

The only references to local culture were about festivals in rural areas, where the Department of Examinations was setting up stalls to sell booklets containing past examination papers (Colombo 432). Also mentioned was the fact that some parents of girls in single-sex schools preferred to send their daughters for private tuition rather than to tutories, so that they would not have to study with young men (Colombo 493-495). The latter comment is of interest because both young women and young men were following the *EED* storyline, where young women and men mixed freely, travelled widely, etc. It is not known whether such activities were seen as 'alien' by these Sri Lankan students.

# Summary of characteristics of the user system

The purpose of this chapter has been to analyse various factors in the educational context to see how they might have influenced the type of impact that the O level English examination was having on Year 11 classrooms.

The main ideas emerging were as follows:

Classroom factors – Many teachers had to work in overcrowded and noisy conditions, which made it difficult to teach listening and speaking or to use techniques which required discussion or other forms of interaction. Many lacked access to the teachers' guides for the *EED* series and the support documents for the examination, and were therefore not as aware as they should have been about the direction they should be following. The situation was more complicated when teachers were working with low-level students: it took a great deal of time to cover the material and teachers sometimes omitted certain exercises in order to cover others that they felt were most relevant to the examination.

School factors – There were major differences between schools in Sri Lanka, with some schools enjoying good reputations, good locations, good staffing etc. and others suffering because of difficult social conditions, lack of teachers and lack of access to resources. Conditions seemed to be worse in rural areas, and it was teachers in these areas who struggled most to complete the syllabus and prepare their students for the examination. Some problems that were shared by different sorts of schools included teacher transfers and absenteeism (which led to a great deal of lost teaching time), conflicts in the timetable (more lost teaching time) and poor communication within the school. The role of the principal was important in all schools: if the principal was weak the teachers might not be aware of developments in the education system or even of the situation in other parts of their own schools.

Outside tuition – Many students went to tutories to take extra classes in English and other subjects and to prepare for the O level examinations. Although some teachers were pleased that their students were getting extra help, others complained because the tutories taught badly. This had a negative impact on their own teaching because they had to undo the damage that the tutories had done and because they had to deal with students' demands for spoon-feeding.

Educational administration – Some teachers complained about the way the new examination had been introduced and the fact that they had not had time to prepare their students for many changes. The communication between the central administration and the teachers did not seem very effective because there were still teachers who did not know about certain features of the exam and who had not received news of new developments such as the NIE pilot test. The training situation was getting better in some areas, thanks to the establishment of regional in-service centres, but there were some areas with no in-service programme or where the advisers gave advice that was contrary to *EED*.

Political factors – The political situation was tense and recent conflicts had had a great impact on schooling. The most visible consequence in the central and southern areas was that some teachers were far behind in the textbook because of lengthy school closures a few years earlier. There were serious teacher shortages in the north and east, and problems with teacher training in various parts of the country. Retired civil servants were being recruited to teach English but this was likely to lead to new problems because they might not understand the philosophy and procedures of the new textbook.

Geographic factors – There were important differences between urban and rural schools, teachers were reluctant to work in rural areas, and there were difficulties gaining access to materials and teacher training. These factors led to fairly conservative examination-oriented teaching.

Economic factors – There was great pressure on students to pass examinations so that they could move on to higher education or get better employment. Many saw exam success as a means of social survival, and this clearly affected teaching and learning. There was a great deal of poverty in the country, especially in rural areas, and the fact that students could not afford supplementary materials meant that there was much ineffective teaching and much time wasted during the examination preparation period.

Cultural factors – The most important cultural factor was the role of English in society. Teachers and students were well aware of the importance of the language and this increased pressure to succeed in examinations.

The picture that emerged from this analysis was grim: poor teaching conditions in many schools, serious mismatches between student ability and the requirements of textbooks and the examination, shortages of materials, shortages of teachers, difficulties in communications, and inadequate teacher training – a host of educational and structural problems set against a background of political, geographic and economic difficulties. We saw in Chapter 7 that changes were needed to make English teaching more relevant to the needs of society, but the scope and nature of the changes proposed seemed very ambitious given the problems examined in this chapter. This does not mean that such changes should not have been considered, but rather that there needed to be more investment in training and other types of support to enable the innovations to survive in such difficult circumstances. We have seen that there was a training schedule for *EED* in the early days of the innovation, but this was not sustained in the years following the introduction of the textbooks. There were teachers' guides and examination support materials, but not all teachers had received them or knew what to do with them if they had them. There was a need for better communication between the centre and the teachers, and more effective training programmes in the regions. The Ministry was encouraging this through the establishment of the Regional English Support Centres (RESCs) and would be offering further support in the future through the new Regional English Language Testing Units (RELTUs), but facilities like these need to be present early on in the process of educational reform rather than being added later.

There were some educational problems stemming from the political and economic situation which would not be easy to solve. There were other problems, however, such as the mismatch between student abilities and curriculum expectations, where action could have been taken.

# 11 Implementation factors: characteristics of the users

## Background

It should be evident from Chapter 10: Characteristics of the user system, that there were many factors in the educational, political and economic systems which were affecting the amount and type of material that teachers could cover in their classrooms and whether they could use the 'pupil-centred' or 'communicative' methodology that was recommended by the *English Every Day* textbook series. Difficult working conditions, large class sizes, poor communication between central administration and the schools and sometimes within the schools, inadequate in-service support – all of these factors were bound to influence whether teachers understood and could implement the ideas that the textbook designers were attempting to transmit and that the examination was supposed to be reinforcing. However, an analysis of the context on its own is not sufficient to explain why an innovation meets with success or failure. It is also important to ask questions about the users of the innovation – in this case, the teachers and their students – to determine whether the *EED* and examination messages were compatible with their basic abilities, beliefs and values.

Henrichsen reminds us that it is the teachers who bear most of the burden for implementing educational innovations and that little change will occur unless they are both capable of and committed to using the innovation (1989:89-90). When Henrichsen discusses 'capability', he deals with aspects such as teachers' general level of education, the type of training they have received, and their proficiency in the language they are teaching (see also Beeby 1966, Maley 1984 and Dow, Whitehead and Wright 1984). Henrichsen does not elaborate on the notion of 'commitment', but it would be reasonable to assume that the degree of commitment that teachers felt towards an innovation would depend on the 'fit' between the new practice and their own attitudes towards education, classroom teaching, language teaching, and examinations. Commitment could also be influenced by the teachers' individual circumstances, in particular whether the innovation affects their private lives, and whether it matches or is in conflict with their personal interests and goals. All of these factors are presented in Figure 11.1 below. (See also Stern 1983:498 on the importance of 'presage variables', and

## Figure 11.1 Characteristics of the users

*Source*: (adapted from Henrichsen 1989)

Alderson and Hamp-Lyons 1996 and Watanabe 1996 on the influence of teacher variables on the form that examination washback will take in the classroom.)

This study focuses on the behaviour and reactions of teachers; however, it is important to remember that teachers will always be influenced by what they perceive their students' views to be. It was not possible during this project to elicit students' views directly; however, it was possible to analyse what the teachers had to say about their students and to find connections between these descriptions and the ways in which the teachers managed their teaching.

What follows is the information that teachers gave about themselves and other teachers, followed by what they said about their students. I discuss how these characteristics may have influenced the teachers in their selection of content and methodology, and whether their choices were in harmony or conflict with the goals of the *EED* materials and the examination.

# Characteristics of the teachers

## The teachers' attitudes towards education

Before analysing what the teachers had to say about education it is important to introduce several points relating to the history of education in Sri Lanka. The first concerns traditional styles of learning, the second, the purpose of education during the colonial period, and the third, the aspirations of post-Independence educators.

The origins of the Sri Lankan educational system can be traced back to the arrival of Buddhism on the island, during the third century B.C. (Punchihetti 1994:19). The system of education that prevailed at that time was known as the Pirivena system ('pirivena' is the Sinhala term for a school attached to a temple), and its main purpose was to train monks in Buddhist doctrine. The Tamil system of education can also be traced back many centuries, and according to Canagarajah (1993), the styles of teaching and learning associated with this tradition extended to the rest of the population. These were oriented toward the product of learning rather than the process (knowledge was to be 'preserved without corruption'), and were very teacher-centred (the guru was not only respected, but also revered). For Canagarajah, this approach did not favour the development of the students' critical faculties (1993:622-623).

The second theme concerns the purposes of education during the colonial period. Sri Lanka (then Ceylon) was colonized first by the Portuguese in 1505, then by the Dutch in 1658, and finally by the British, who occupied the coastal areas in 1796 and conquered the rest of the country by 1815. A number of missionary schools were set up during these colonizations, which provided education to the children of European families and to a limited number of Ceylonese families. These schools began opening their doors to more local families in the mid-19th century, as they took on the function of preparing local students for positions within the Civil Service (Punchihetti 1994:20). Canagarajah argues that the function of education under British colonial rule was to 'create a supportive lower administrative work force' (1993:602). He implies that this was also an attempt to reproduce the values of the dominant culture, with more emphasis on the instrumental value of education than was apparent under the traditional approaches.

Meanwhile, the majority of Ceylonese children attended state schools, many of which were in rural areas, and received their education in their mother tongue. Punchihetti writes of the great disparity in educational opportunities:

> Privileged upper class children, whose parents had money earned mostly through various employment avenues arising out of the fast-growing plantation industries under the British, received an English education, enabling them to enter government employment. Under-privileged rural children received education through their mother tongue (called 'Swabhasha' education), which got them nowhere in society. (1994:20)

This was the situation until just before Independence. There was a major educational reform in the mid-1940s, which provided free schooling for all children.

The third theme concerns the aspirations of post-Independence educators. There are two important points to make here. The first is that a number of policies were introduced by different governments to reduce the disparity between privileged and less privileged schools. The second is that the political and social situation was so difficult that the changes did not always reach the right people. Indeed, educators such as Kandiah (1979, cited in Canagarajah 1993) claim that some policies, such as the decision to teach English as a second language in all schools, from early primary school onwards, were so unrealistic that they actually left the people who were supposed to be benefiting from them worse off than before.

It is important to keep all three of these aspects (traditional styles of learning, instrumental motivation in learning, and aspirations to equality) in mind when analysing the teachers' comments about education.

The comments can be broken down into two categories: those concerning the concept or purpose of education, and those concerning the role of teachers. The comments about the concept or purpose of education were either quite vague ('He tries to inculcate in his child the value of education' [Wennapuwa 545] or 'They are interested in money, not education' [Wennapuwa 354]), or they were instrumentally-oriented, focusing on how students in less developed countries needed to get a good education in order to survive:

> T 2: ... But being a Third World country the people's only stake is education. Somehow they have to get through their exams, and unless they get through the exams they won't get the jobs. Because of that they have to sit this paper ... (Nuwara Eliya 500)

Two teachers referred to the 'competition' that was the driving force behind modern education, one talking about the struggle for 'social survival' (Wennapuwa 598) and the other talking about how students were trying to 'score marks as much as possible' (Wennapuwa 497) and therefore did not have time for, or interest in drama, music, and similar activities. The key to success in the competition was to do well in examinations, and this influenced the goals, attitudes and activities of both students and teachers. Many teachers reported that their main goal was to prepare students for examinations, or to help them to get the results they needed (see section on 'The Teachers' Goals' for examples). Their attitudes towards certain skills and activities were influenced by whether these appeared on the O level examination. This teacher was one of the many who concentrated on examination preparation during the last few weeks of the year:

> T 2: ... Our system of education is exam-driven. We have to get the
> students ready for the exam, so I am only doing the model papers. (Nuwara
> Eliya 49)

Only a few teachers stated that their teaching was not so exam-centred. One teacher said that she wanted to 'give them knowledge first, knowledge and then after that the examination' (Nuwara Eliya 136). A second believed that it was important for students to think, and not just play 'hide and seek' with multiple-choice questions on examination papers (Nuwara Eliya 420). It was more common, however, for teachers to equate education with success in examinations.

There were two general attitudes concerning the role of the teacher. The first, which seemed to be very common, was that the teacher was the source of all knowledge, and the second, which was also widely held, was that teachers should help their students as much as possible, even if it meant making personal sacrifices. The teachers did not express either of these views directly, but when they described how they handled their classes and how they offered extra lessons with no compensation it was clear that they were taking much of the responsibility for getting students through the examination on to their own shoulders. We have already seen numerous examples of how teachers believed that they needed to provide everything for their students: if, for example, there was a reading passage which described the parts of a computer many teachers felt they needed to find out everything about computers so that they could pass this information on to their students. The teachers who had managed to learn enough about such subjects were proud of their efforts, but others felt embarrassed that they could not cope (Nuwara Eliya 432-440, Asgiriya 539-540).

The second attitude was that teachers should do everything they could to help students to succeed. Many teachers gave extra classes outside normal teaching hours and spent long hours marking students' examination preparation exercises. Some teachers referred to this as 'honourable service' (Trincomalee 452-459) or 'sacred duty' (Colombo 818). None of them expected payment for the extra hours that they put in: their only reward was satisfaction if their students succeeded. This is illustrated by a teacher who presented her students' results as if they were her own:

> T 3: ... Now they have left the school, but I got the results. Out of 43, 35
> have passed, and I got 5 credits. (Asgiriya 26)

To summarize, a few of the teachers seemed to value the idea of 'education' in the abstract, but it was more common to see education as a competition with examinations as the key to success. The role of the teacher was to transmit knowledge to the students and to give whatever support was necessary to help them to pass their examinations.

## The teachers' attitudes towards classroom teaching

The comments about classroom teaching could be divided into two kinds: those that dealt with the 'what' of teaching and those that dealt with the 'how'. The 'what' issue was partially covered in the preceding section: many teachers felt, either consciously or unconsciously, that they were in the classroom to pass knowledge on to their students. There was some feeling that students needed to develop skills so that they could get by on their own (Ratnapura 659, Wennapuwa 745), but it was more common for teachers to believe that they needed to master all of the content (which involved not only studying the textbooks but also consulting other books and teachers), in order to be able to transmit it as if they were subject teachers (see Canagarajah's image of the guru with disciples at his feet in the previous section). This knowledge would be useful if the students came across passages on the same subject in the examination or if they were asked to write a composition about a similar topic (compare this with the 'product orientation' proposed by Canagarajah in the previous section).

When it came to the 'how' of teaching, attitudes were also mainly traditional. A couple of teachers said that teachers had to be more active now than in former times (Nuwara Eliya 583, Trincomalee 166-171) but the activity they were talking about was learning content knowledge. Two teachers who had recently completed their training talked about the teachers being 'coordinators' rather than 'dominators' (Nugegoda 140), but they did not give examples so it was not clear whether they knew how to bring this about in the classroom. Most of the references to new ways of teaching were accompanied by explanations of why such things were not possible: there was too much noise in the classroom (Colombo 92), it was too difficult for the students to work independently (Asgiriya 80), or it was not useful during examination preparation periods (Tangalle 140).

## The teachers' attitudes towards language teaching

Most of the teachers felt that it was important for students to learn 'practical' or 'everyday' language, so that they could function more effectively in contexts where English played an important role. One of the strong points of *English Every Day* was that it forced everyone to pay attention to the student's 'communicative needs':

> T 64: I think it's good because I look at it from the point of view of the changing world. Because I consider language to be dynamic. And it should not be the same, because as society changes it should also change. And what I feel is that language is a vehicle. A mode of communication. And I feel it's lifeless if you can't use language effectively for communication. It should be made use of. And I think the present context ... I won't say it's 100% effective, but ... It has laid good groundwork for that. (Wennapuwa 596)

There were, however, some teachers who favoured paying more attention to grammar, and teaching it more systematically. Their comments were surprising on the one hand, given the views that had been expressed about the role of grammar in the Old Syllabus and in the old examination (see Chapters 8 and 9), but they were understandable given the country's traditions of language teaching. Punchihetti refers to the attention that textbooks paid to grammar as far back as the 1950s (1994:23): the Old Syllabus textbook was not unique in this but just the last of several series emphasizing form over meaning. However, Canagarajah suggests that the preference for 'prescriptive, deductive, and formalistic methods' is not tied in with the materials in use at any one time but represents something much more deeply seated, at least in the Tamil community. He quotes Emeneau's belief that:

> Intellectual thoroughness and an urge toward ratiocination, intellection, and learned classification for their own sakes should surely be recognized as characteristic of the Hindu higher culture … They become grammarians, it would seem, for grammar's sake. (1981, cited in Canagarajah 1993:623)

He also refers to the methods used during the colonial period to teach European administrators the local languages: these were 'based on studying and memorizing learned grammatical treatises' (Ibid.).

Several of the teachers who expressed a desire to teach more grammar referred to this strength of tradition. One claimed that it was natural for teachers to teach in the way that they themselves had been taught:

> T 53: … That is how we were taught and we always think that the way we studied was correct. Whatever it is I feel it easy if I teach these grammar lessons well. And thereafter it is not necessary for me to worry much about teaching the other lessons, because they can understand it. (Welimada 354)

Another felt that the tradition was so strong that some teachers might not even understand new approaches to teaching, let alone be able to implement them:

> T 64: … the strains of the structural approach are still here … And there are people who still tread that path. It's very difficult to get away from it.
>
> DW: The structural approach in grammar teaching? [He agrees.] Language teaching?
>
> T 64: Yes, yes. It has made such an impact in the society. Especially the mature ones. They try to … they lobby for it. And this is being a novel approach. It's very difficult to get hold of a proper ground. It's easy if it's in an urban area, or as you said, with a higher … I won't say 'elite', but with people who are educated. But with the average level or those who are far away from the metropolis it is difficult to convince them about the effectiveness of this approach. So it will take time … (Wennapuwa 598-600)

This teacher was suggesting that there was a divide between more sophisticated teachers and those who were less 'in the know': the more sophisticated would adopt the innovation more easily (this corresponds to Rogers 1995 definition of 'early adopters') and the others (the 'laggards') would find it difficult. However, some of the teachers who spoke in favour of more grammar were amongst the most sophisticated, or at least the best trained and most effective. This teacher, for example, taught in one of the most prestigious schools in the country:

> T 7: ... I also have to bring many grammar exercises, because many children have this idea that grammar is the only way to acquire English. And we also feel that they should have a better knowledge of grammar in order to acquire language. So very often we have to give lessons on grammar. Purely on grammar. And then based on other exercises, on more interesting lessons, I also supplement other ways of acquiring grammar. Like stories, dialogues, and so on ... (Ratnapura 62)

There was a further reason why some teachers might have preferred a more overt focus on grammar, which concerned its true weighting on the examination. The teachers who had served as markers would certainly have noticed the importance given to structural control in the rating scales for writing. The same would have been true of the teachers who had studied the *Suggestions* booklet.

The second belief about language teaching was that it was important to improve the students' listening and speaking. Teachers who believed this were faced with a dilemma: the *English Every Day* series encouraged the teaching of oral skills but the examination tested only reading and writing. Several teachers were strong enough to resist the pressure of the exam, insisting that students 'must have that talent' (Colombo 80), that they should be able to 'speak out' (Colombo 590), and that speaking 'adds to the skill of the child' (Colombo 550). Others sympathized with these views but argued that it would be easier to motivate students if they were tested on this ability (Nuwara Eliya 484-487).

## The teachers' attitudes towards examinations

A number of teachers made comments about the functions of examinations within the education system, and the form that they should take.

Sri Lanka had had a national examination system for many years and no-one questioned the need for examinations at the end of compulsory schooling. The teachers seemed to agree that the main function of examinations was to measure the students' achievement. One expressed this idea in this way:

> T 53: ... the examination is the only way of understanding whether the learning and the teaching has taken place, so that sort of measurement

should be there. To check whether they have understood, whether they have studied, whether they have learnt, whether they have taught. In order to have an idea about those things. Some sort of evaluation must be there. Evaluation in the sense usually we have exams. (Welimada 403)

Several teachers talked about the importance of examinations within Sri Lankan education, both in the past (Nugegoda 125) and at present (Nuwara Eliya 49, Nuwara Eliya 647). These teachers used the terms 'exam-driven' and 'exam-oriented' to describe the whole system, while others used them to describe their own materials and teaching (Colombo 132, Welimada 219).

A few teachers spoke about the pressures they were under to get their students to succeed. One felt that the examination limited the work she could do with her students. It was good that they had a target to aim for, but it also limited what she could do in the classroom:

> T 1: ... The other [side of it] is, madam, when we are preparing them for the examination, we will limit themselves to a frame. Then they will not be able to write or express anything other than that frame. True or false. Replacing 'I' with 'he'. Restrictive. (Asgiriya 475)

Testing specialists use the term 'narrowing the curriculum' to describe this phenomenon (Madaus 1988:85). Another teacher spoke about how passing examinations had become the real aim of schooling:

> T 64: Yes. Our main aim is not to teach the language. We want to make them pass. To get a pass. And even their parents. And even the students. They don't want to speak English or anything. They want somehow just to get a pass. Get through the exam. (Wennapuwa 377)

Other teachers felt that examinations could have a positive effect on the curriculum. Some hoped for changes in the O level which would encourage students to study more grammar. No-one expressed a desire to return to the Old Syllabus way of testing grammar, which focused on discrete structure in isolated sentences, but a couple of teachers felt that students would study grammar more seriously if it were tested more overtly (Welimada 410-414, 415-417). One explained his thinking in this way:

> T 53: ... Then only the pupils are compelled to learn grammar because they know that they will get some or more questions based on that. And having that in their mind, you know, they have to study. It will make it something like compulsory. They're compelled to do it. (Welimada 415)

Other teachers wanted to see the testing of listening and speaking:

> T 18: Because from Year 4 they study English. They don't study, they learn. But they won't use. So using it is very important.
>
> DW: And you think that if they tested speaking ...

> T 18: Definitely they will improve. And they will try to speak English at school. Because they must. (Nugegoda 465-467)

There was a recognition, however, that using the examination to compel students to develop their oral skills would be unfair to schools without the resources to teach these skills effectively (Nuwara Eliya 479, Nuwara Eliya 623-635).

Opinion was divided about how difficult examinations should be. One side felt that they should act as filters, to ensure that only very good students got through to the next stage of education:

> T 4: Yes, otherwise unsuitable persons will be coming to the English field. That's my personal idea. If they are not sitting the four skills – that means, writing ability, speaking, listening, everything – they are unqualified persons. If they underline the correct word, fill in the blanks – with those questions unqualified persons come into the English field. (Tangalle 163)

Others thought that examination success should be within the reach of all students, not just higher-level ones. Several teachers commented that this exam, or parts of it, was too difficult for their own students. One way of lowering the difficulty level would be to give students more choices in reading:

> T 10: But there could also be an alternative for those unseen passages. Two passages if possible. Where the clever child wants to meet a challenge and he'll tackle the difficult one, while the average child tackles the one which is in his sphere of thinking. If that could be possible then there might not be that disparity in the question paper ... (Colombo 191)

Other teachers felt that there should be more choice in writing:

> T 60: ... That guided composition. They've only got one topic...So it has to be very specific. Only that topic. No choice. And you are restricted to write only that particular topic. So that if there are two or three choices, the student can select and write himself freely. That's what I think. That negative aspect. (Wennapuwa 579)

When the examination developer began to explain the types of problems that would occur if there were choices she was accused of only being interested in the markers:

> T 7: ... you only pose a problem for the marking examiner. I think we should go ahead and implement it because it would at least open the doors for the children who are interested to read more and also it wouldn't discourage the others very much because they'll have the option in the same paper. They wouldn't feel that they have something inferior ... (Colombo 199)

The final suggestion regarding choice concerned a choice of papers. One teacher spoke in favour of the 'optional papers' – an experimental set of papers which had been introduced alongside the O level when it was in its third year. Candidates who sat the O level were also entitled to sit one optional paper, at the level they thought was appropriate from a possible ten. The purpose of the papers was to give lower-level learners a chance to choose their own level and to receive some recognition of their ability, even if it was very low. Theoretically these papers were the answer to several problems within the system, but in reality they brought with them many new problems (see Alderson and Wall 1992:225-229 for details).

To summarize, many teachers acknowledged the importance of examinations in the education system and the effects that they had on their teaching. Some teachers focused on negative effects (when the exam replaced learning as the goal of education), but others believed that examinations had the potential for changing things for the better if they included the right elements and these were tested in the right way. The teachers were generally positive about this examination, although there were some differences of opinion regarding its difficulty level and some feeling that students should be given choices within the reading and writing components to play to their individual strengths.

## The teachers' attitudes towards English

There is much discussion in Sri Lankan essays and literature about the colonial heritage and the role and function of English within the society (e.g. Canagarajah 1993, Kandiah 1984), but the teachers made no comments about English itself and very few about English speakers. This might be because so many of them would have been educated in English (many were old enough to have gone through English-medium) or because they shared the same attitudes (all of them had chosen to teach the language so they were presumably positively disposed to it). There is also the possibility that they did not want to say anything about English speakers in front of me, an English speaker. The only indications of their feelings were when they spoke of families who did not speak the language at home. The descriptions they gave included phrases like 'very poor families' (Colombo 70), 'they don't get educated from their parents' (Nuwara Eliya 34), 'they are just from the fisher-folk' (Wennapuwa 97), and 'mostly their parents are farmers' (Trincomalee 520).

There were, however, many comments about the value of learning the language, mainly because of its importance in the world of employment. Several teachers mentioned making their students practise applying for jobs (Nuwara Eliya 57, Nuwara Eliya 160, Nuwara Eliya 392, Nuwara Eliya 392, Welimada 44) or that the students would need English in order to get a good job in future (Asgiriya 493, Nuwara Eliya 144).

## The teachers' attitudes towards new ideas (openness)

Henrichsen includes under 'Characteristics of the user system' a quality which he calls 'openness', which concerns whether the social system is open to new ideas. I felt that this quality was more relevant to individuals than to systems as a whole, and therefore moved it to 'Characteristics of the users'.

The introduction of *English Every Day* and the examination meant that teachers were on the receiving end of many new ideas. They were being asked to re-think their views of the function of English in society, the types of content that it would be most useful to study, the kinds of activities that were most likely to develop certain skills, etc. We have already seen that many teachers were positive about the new materials and the examination (see Chapters 8 and 9, under 'Relative advantage'), but they did not necessarily understand the implications for their own teaching. It must have been difficult for them to process so many new ideas at one time, especially when there was not enough guidance and feedback. The teachers needed more information and more practice, in the form of more explicit teachers' guides and more frequent teacher training. They especially needed help with how to implement the new ideas when there were so many constraints in the classroom.

## The teachers' levels of education

Little is known about the teachers' level of general education and their initial training, because most of them did not indicate when or where they had studied. A couple of the younger teachers used terminology which suggested that they were familiar with recent ideas in teaching (e.g. Nugegoda 140), so it is possible that they had participated in the pre-service training programmes which were being developed as part of the English language teaching reform (see Woolger 1994). Another young teacher stressed that whatever he knew he had learned on his own because there had been no English lecturers at his college (Wennapuwa 777-785). It is difficult to be specific about the other teachers in the sample.

We do know, however, that there were many teachers who had received no pre-service training. An in-service adviser from the north of the country said that of the 33 teachers who were working in her region, only ten had received initial training. The rest had received a Credit-Pass on their O level English paper and then gone straight into the classroom. There was a new regional initiative which invited retired civil servants to teach English, but there was concern that it might cause more problems than it solved:

> T 45: One more point. Because of the dearth of English teachers now our Department is calling for applications from the retired officers. Those who know English. And they are paying our hourly pay. So those retired officers they don't know the method of teaching so that tutory teaching and those retired officers teaching are the same.

T 47: That is definitely going to make the children go astray. (Trincomalee 678-679)

There were also problems with in-service education. The teachers in the interview were not asked whether they had attended in-service seminars, but we know from the observation programme that few teachers had had opportunities to update their skills. We have also seen that many of the seminars were exam-focused and teachers were sometimes given wrong information. There were, however, some examples of positive teacher training. One of the teachers paid tribute to the head of the training centre in which we were meeting and acknowledged the importance of talking regularly with other teachers:

T 22: And we have discussions like this all the time. Whenever we have a problem we come to him, and it really really helps. (Nuwara Eliya 698)

## The teachers' abilities

We saw in Figure 5.3 that there was a wide range of experience among the teachers who participated in the interviews. There were also differences in terms of their abilities to cope with the teaching. Perhaps the most important of these abilities was proficiency in the language and understanding the objectives behind different sorts of exercises and items in the textbook and the examination.

Most of the teachers spoke English fluently and were able to express their views on all the subjects that were covered. However, there were a handful of teachers who had problems following the discussions and expressing what they wanted to say. The fact that these teachers needed to switch to their mother tongue was sobering, given the level of proficiency that *English Every Day* demanded and the need for teachers to be able to think on their feet and react quickly when things were not going as planned in the classroom. One of the teachers felt that it was easier for 'older people', who were able 'to play with the language', to deal with unexpected problems (Colombo 602). She explained the kinds of things that teachers might have to face, and what might happen to less proficient teachers:

T 10: ... But they (teachers in tutories) misinterpret the whole thing, and then they make life a misery to the classroom teacher. Now you prepare things and you go in to have a nice lesson. But then you find children reacting because they have already heard about it in Sinhala, and they already know what is in the book ... When you know what is in store for you, you go prepared. With less experienced teachers ... You know, the teachers with limited language and methods, you find it very frustrating. (Colombo 604)

There was also a difference between teachers when it came to understanding the objectives of the exercises in *EED*. We have already seen (in the section on 'The teachers' attitudes towards classroom teaching') that some teachers did not understand the idea of helping students to help themselves, and that some teachers worried about whether they understood enough of the passages to pass on information to their students (e.g. Asgiriya 605). Some teachers were able to repeat some of the terminology that they had learned about teaching, but the way they described their own teaching raised the question of whether they really understood what they were supposed to be doing. This was apparent in the teaching of reading, when teachers either read aloud to their students or dictated reading texts to them. (Wennapuwa 427, 447 and 453.)

There were also problems in the teaching of listening. Quite a few teachers said that they did not give listening practice because it did not appear on the exam (e.g. Asgiriya 110); but others did not know how to teach it. This teacher, for example, used listening passages to practise other skills:

> T 37: Listening. I used to [this often means 'I usually' in Sri Lanka] read
> out the lesson. And then I ask them to read it and then we discuss it among
> the children. (Ratnapura 104)

The teachers did not give many examples of how they taught speaking. The observations had shown though that very few lessons contained activities which could be called 'communicative'. This may have been due to classroom conditions (see Chapter 10 for examples); but it is also possible that teachers who had received only a few days of training (or even no training) would not understand how to manage these activities successfully.

To sum up this section, there were significant differences in the teachers' proficiency in English and in their abilities to understand the objectives of the activities in the textbooks and the exam. Some teachers did not have the language they needed in order to teach *EED* effectively. Others had trouble with the notion that students needed to do their own learning, while others did not seem to understand which techniques were appropriate for developing different skills.

## The teachers' personal lives

The main information emerging here was that all teachers had to take the leave that they were entitled to each year, many teachers gave up their private time in order to give extra lessons to their students free of charge, and a few gave tuition classes for payment.

The comments about taking leave entitlement were important because they provide more insight into why teachers had so much trouble covering their syllabuses. Teachers were expected to teach 180 days a year, but from these 180 they could take up to 21 days 'casual leave', up to 20 days 'medical leave' and up to two hours a month 'short leave'. If they did not take their leave they lost it (Ministry of Education 1989). The head of a Regional English Support Centre explained that this was one of the reasons why so much class time was lost every year (Nuwara Eliya 663). A teacher adviser mentioned that some teachers were not able to finish the syllabus 'because of that delivery and all that' (maternity leave and other types of leave): this was particularly serious in her area because there were no teachers to do supply work when the official teachers were away (Trincomalee 357, Trincomalee 686). Another teacher talked about his predecessor, who had taken three days off every week to attend a training course (Nuwara Eliya 51). A further teacher talked about how if she took leave or had to be absent for other reasons (for example, to attend compulsory seminars) there was no one else to take her lessons. She explained her students' situation very simply: 'That will be their plight' (Trincomalee 359).

We do know however, that many teachers gave up their private time in order to help their students to get through the syllabus or to prepare for examinations (Table 6.7). Teachers stayed after school up to three times a week during most of the last term (September to December). A number of teachers spoke of giving lessons on weekends, holidays and during school vacations, and one teacher met his students every morning for an hour and a half before the normal school day started.

Only two teachers talked about giving private tuition for payment. One had to leave the interview he was participating in just a few minutes after it started (Nugegoda 107); the other said that she would not stay after school to teach her own students because they were all in private tuition in maths and sciences. She gave private tuition classes at home instead (Nugegoda 351).

## The teachers' economic situation

Sri Lankan teachers took home about 2000 rupees a month in 1991, the equivalent of 25 to 30 pounds sterling. This was probably enough money to cover their living expenses, but it would not have stretched far enough to provide for many comforts. One of the strongest images to emerge from the interviews was of a middle-aged male teacher being told by his students that their brothers, who were not well-educated, could afford to drive good cars while he, the teacher, had to travel on buses (Wennapuwa 534).

We know, however, that quite a few teachers were willing to spend their own money in order to provide materials for their students. One teacher talked about how when she had extra money she made photocopies of reading passages to distribute in her classes (Colombo 334). Others bought locally produced exam preparation material, which, at 35 to 70 rupees per item, was very expensive. Teachers who wished to buy a foreign book could expect to pay about 150 rupees. Only two teachers talked about making such purchases.

Some teachers tried to borrow books if they could not afford to buy them, but these were not always available (Colombo 556).

## The teachers' interests

Several teachers spoke of their outside interests. Some enjoyed poetry and other types of literature (Ratnapura 245-247, Nugegoda 245-247, Wennapuwa 282-288). These interests seemed to have some influence on their attitudes and on the way that they taught their classes – e.g. those who liked poetry made sure they included the poems from *EED* in their lessons, even if they had to postpone them until a time when their students could understand them better (Nugegoda 243).

Several teachers mentioned that aesthetic values were important (Wennapuwa 519-520) and one of them felt that the *EED* series and the examination were not as interesting as the Old Syllabus materials:

> T 61: ... It has no interesting passages, as we had in the Old Syllabus. Enrichment-wise I think it is less. The language is more bent on the communicative aspect of language and the paper is, in my opinion, rather monotonous ... (Wennapuwa 499)

This teacher was not able to do all of the 'enrichment activities' he wished to (drama, poetry and songs in English), but he managed, despite a very crowded timetable, to get his students to do reports on books they had borrowed from the library (Wennapuwa 282).

## The teachers' goals

About half of the teachers mentioned their goals in teaching, and about 80% of these were related to the examination. Many said that they were aiming to either prepare students for the examination, help them get Passes, or help them get Distinctions, and many of them stated that this was their main goal. While some teachers focused on specific aspects of language or specific skills, others wanted to prepare their students to face anything that might appear on the paper:

> T 41: My idea is to give them a knowledge of English so that they will be able to tackle any kind of question. If they know English – how to read and understand – then they will tackle any kind of question. Not a particular question. 'Now you will get this type' – I don't think this. You must be able to tackle any type of question. I have that in mind while I am teaching. I do it in such a way that they will be able to understand, to read, fill in a form – any task from essay to every day. (Tangalle 162)

Teachers who had mid- to higher-level groups and adequate resourcing were able to take their students through copies of past papers or model papers. Teachers who had lower-level students or little resourcing had to be less ambitious in their aims. One teacher who did not have the time to write long examination questions on the blackboard explained his strategy for helping his students to get more marks:

> T 2: ... somehow we have to train our students to get the marks. Their only concern is how to get through the exam, not about the knowledge. Because of that we have to do that kind of questions. Small ones. And somehow we have to train them to get the marks. (Nuwara Eliya 246)

He felt that if his students could gain a few points on many small questions then they would be able to get by.

Only a handful of teachers mentioned goals that were not related to the exam. These included helping the students to express themselves (Nuwara Eliya 106-112), helping them to become fluent (Nuwara Eliya 484-487), giving the students knowledge (Nuwara Eliya 136-146), and helping them to see that there was more to English than what appeared in the *EED* textbook (Welimada 211).

## Characteristics of the students

The original goal of the O level Evaluation Project was to investigate the effects of the new examination on teaching and learning, but the focus soon switched to teaching only. There were two reasons for this. The first was that the teachers were in the 'front line' when the new examination was introduced: it was not until they made decisions about how they would work in the classroom that anything could be said about how the examination might affect students. The second was that it was difficult to get at students' perceptions during the project as it was considered inappropriate to ask them questions about their lessons and about their learning experiences. The observation team had recorded their impressions of how students reacted to their lessons, but this was in the form of general statements about whether they seemed interested in the lesson or bored, rather than more detailed statements about why they reacted in the way they did. It was possible, however, to gain some 'second-hand' information about the students during the group interviews, by listening to their teachers' descriptions of their attitudes and abilities. This process did not offer evidence of what the students themselves were thinking, but it did produce a picture of what teachers believed they were thinking, which could contribute to an understanding of the teachers' reasons for teaching the way that they did.

## The students' attitudes towards education

The teachers made two types of comments about their students' attitudes towards education: the first had to do with the instrumental value of schooling for some students and the second with its irrelevance for others. The first type of comment was the most common: students went to school in order to secure a better future, and the key to this future was good results in the examination. Several teachers used the word 'competition' to describe the last few years of schooling:

> T 61: ... There's a competition. So everyone is trying to score marks as much as possible. So in that environment the students are bound by this competition. So they have to work for the exam. And we have to be competitive as teachers ... (Wennapuwa 497). (See also Nuwara Eliya 502, Welimada 315 and Wennapuwa 588.)

There were some students, however, who did not take part in the competition. These were students who were not interested in learning, who received no encouragement from home and who fell far behind their classmates. Several teachers believed there was a connection between family circumstances and what the students were able to aspire to or achieve in the future:

> T 60: The families ... You know that fisher-folk...they don't do homework or they don't come (to lessons). When we question them ... 'Yesterday Father came drunk' and other such (reasons). And then we find very difficult to teach such students because their mentality is out. 'Out' means very ... backward. (Wennapuwa 172)

These teachers tended to blame the parents for not encouraging their children, while educators such as Kandiah (1979) felt that there were broader social reasons. One was that the society could not deliver what it promised to its citizens: some students recognized early on that no matter how much effort they put into their studies they would not advance economically or socially. There were too many social factors working against them, including, ironically, the quality of their schooling.

Other students felt that they did not need any more education because they already had jobs waiting for them:

> T 11: ... Because they are leaving school as soon as they pass O level or only a few will continue their studies. So they think that English is not necessary for us. Some children think like that. Even without English we can do our jobs. That means very small jobs. Mechanics. Carpentry. Masons. They think they don't need English. And only very few in a class will work. So I find it very difficult to do the lesson. They are not interested in the other subjects either. (Colombo 70)

Others equated education, or at least the job of teaching, with low earnings, when what they wanted was material success:

> T 60: Yes. That's what they sometimes tell. 'Sir, you are travelling by bus. My brother does such-and-such a job and he has a motorbike. Or 'He has

a Lancer. He does such-and-such a job'. A Lancer is a good car. So they
are interested in money, not education … (Wennapuwa 354)

There were no comments about students being interested in education or
learning for its own sake, for developing thinking or for understanding what
the world had to offer. It is not surprising then that many teachers felt pressure
to get their students through the examination, or that they felt some stress
when students did not even have this much ambition.

## The students' attitudes towards classroom teaching

Most of the comments that the teachers made about their students' attitudes
towards classroom teaching related to language teaching as well. These will be
reported in the next section.

## The students' attitudes towards language teaching

The teachers made a number of comments about their students' attitudes
towards language teaching. Some of these comments related to the content
students felt they should be learning, but most related to the type of
methodology they preferred.

The comments about content were mainly about the importance of
grammar and the types of activities that students liked and disliked.

Several teachers said that their students were interested in learning
grammar. One teacher said that her students wanted to do more grammar
'because grammar is the only way to acquire language' (Colombo 62). Others
reported that their students wanted grammar for examination purposes, either
for the new O level (Wennapuwa 637) or for other important examinations
within the system (Ratnapura 348).

There were a number of comments about the types of activities that were
popular with students. Several teachers talked about how their students reacted
to visual material (Nuwara Eliya 125-128, Trincomalee 215 and 217,
Nugegoda 389), while others talked about their enthusiasm for role plays and
acting (Nugegoda 132 and 432, Colombo 588-590, Nuwara Eliya 114). Other
teachers reported that their students liked reading poems (Colombo 554,
Nuwara Eliya 344-346, Welimada 107-111) or writing about them (Nugegoda
243). One of the teachers said that his students liked poems because they
wanted something 'strange', meaning something different from the routine
(Welimada 107). Listening to or reading other types of literature was also
popular (Colombo 554, Wennapuwa 107, Wennapuwa 282-286). One teacher
explained how it was much more interesting for his students (and himself) to
work with literature than with the *EED* textbook:

> T 61: I like to enjoy the stories and the literature part. And also poems. And the boys also like. Apart from the book … Actually the passages are not so interesting as the passages we find in the stories like Oliver Twist and Around the World in 80 Days. Those passages which you can enjoy more than these passages in the textbook. (Wennapuwa 286)

Others felt that the textbook passages could be interesting. One teacher described how his students paid close attention when he read them something 'mysterious':

> T 50: … Take the Bermuda Triangle. That's one mysterious place we explained. So they like very much to listen and they understand what we say. And also when I give exercises they do properly, and almost all the answers are correct. They put more attention to hear those things because the lesson is very interesting. (Welimada 145)

Students also liked pop music, which they were able to listen to in the tutories but not in the classroom (Colombo 616).

The teachers also spoke about the content their students did not like. Several mentioned the Year 11 material on foreign travel – foreign exchange rates, travellers' cheques, airport departure times or maps of foreign cities. These topics could be very difficult, and sometimes boring, because they were so different from the things students thought about or had to deal with in their ordinary lives. One teacher explained how hard it was to discuss foreign travel in her lessons:

> T 18: … if you find at least one or two students who have travelled, gone abroad, they will be able to support you. But if the class is not at all interested in these topics … There are students who may not have heard the words 'exchange rates' or 'travellers' cheques' … (Nugegoda 423)

Another stated that he skipped over some of these topics because he felt that he would have to explain everything in the students' mother tongue (Welimada 82).

There were other topics which were not 'foreign' but which were still unfamiliar to the students. Several teachers mentioned the difficulties they had with a particular lesson on court hearings (Welimada 38 and 62, Nugegoda 434), and another said that her students were not interested in lessons about technical equipment such as telephones or computers. She explained their reaction in this way:

> T 2: They are not dealing with those instruments so they are difficult for the children as well as myself, because I don't know about computers. So I feel it difficult to do in the class. (Asgiriya 56)

What emerged from this comment and others like it was that some of the teachers who said that their students were not interested in certain topics were perhaps not that interested themselves. They may also have felt intimidated by the topics and by what they thought was their responsibility to explain them in detail (Welimada 38 and 62, Asgiriya 605). (See also Chapter 8: 'Complexity of *English Every Day*'.)

Two themes emerged when the teachers talked about their students' reaction to their methodology. The first concerned some students' preference for the type of teaching that took place in tutories, and the second concerned the need to convince students that they were successful so that they would want to continue to learn.

Several teachers said that their students preferred the type of teaching that went on in tutories to the kind that they experienced in the classroom (see, for example, Trincomalee 579 and 581). One reason for this was that the 'tutory masters' did the students' work for them: they finished the students' homework (Wellawatte 140), gave them answers to *EED* exercises before the classroom teachers dealt with them (Colombo 30), completed model papers for them (Colombo 606), and translated passages for them word for word (Colombo 98, Wennapuwa 535). The teachers then had to figure out how to deal with materials that the tutories had already covered, and how to convince students that they should be doing their own work rather than depending on the tutories to do it for them. One teacher explained the problem in these words:

> T 10: I take the material which is challenging to them. Because most of them have run through the text at tutories. With Sinhala pronunciations of English words. And some say that the tuition master finishes their language exercises for them. So much so that they haven't anything to do. They just attend tuition classes, fill their books with exercises which are already done for them. All the money spent on the books and on our fees – it's useless when they concentrate so much on tuition. (Colombo 30)

Some teachers complained that the tutories were giving students the wrong information (the wrong pronunciation – Colombo 616, the wrong vocabulary – Asgiriya 457, the wrong grammar – Asgiriya 461) and that they were using the 'wrong methods' (Trincomalee 603-605). The students were unable to see the problems though and complained when the teachers tried to make them do the work themselves.

> T 64: Then they have a negative impression about us. Because we don't give Sinhala translations. They have been exposed to that so much and so often they expect the same thing from us. (Wennapuwa 557)

One teacher was so annoyed by this that she asked why she should bother going to her lessons if the students were not going to appreciate her way of teaching (Trincomalee 673).

The second reason that some students preferred tutory teaching was that it was entertaining. One teacher talked about how her students learned pop songs in the tutories (Colombo 616), and how they enjoyed the 'actors':

> T 10: ... And there are some favourite actors who have tuition classes in
> our area. So these children they go most probably because of the actors ...
> (Colombo 503)

This comment was meant to be critical of the tutories, but the examination
developer saw it as an indication of what the teachers could be doing to win
back their students' interest:

> And the other thing I think is to do what people like ... To try to hold the
> class I think we have to make our teachers more creative. To create a
> challenge to the tutories so that we can hold them together ... (Colombo
> 617)

The second idea that emerged about methodology was that it was important
to make students feel successful so that they would want to continue learning.
One teacher explained how he was using the Year 7 book with his Year 10
students because this was the level they felt comfortable with.

> T 63: They like the lessons now. They have interest in those lessons
> because they can do something. They participate ... (Wennapuwa 141)

Another teacher explained how he used the same material over and over
again in order to convince his students that they could handle it. He would give
a listening lesson, for example, and would later use the same passage for
reading aloud, true-false questions, short answer questions, and as a gap-
filling exercise. This helped the students to feel a sense of achievement:

> T 60: When it goes on like that they can remember a little. Because when
> they get the correct answers they feel happy and then they have a little
> interest in learning some more. If all goes wrong 'I also can't do this'. Like
> that. So they get fed up. So that's why. That's why such techniques are
> used ... Even at that age group they like to get that right. (Wennapuwa
> 385)

These teachers appreciated how important it was for their students to feel
successful, as did others who advocated giving students more choice in the
examinations so that they would not become discouraged and give up
altogether (Colombo 196). However, most teachers would not be able to cover
all the ground they needed to if they went back to previous books or recycled
material several times before going on any further.

## The students' attitudes towards examinations

Many teachers reported that their students' main goal was to pass the
examination, and several commented on the students' motivation during the
examination preparation period. One teacher described how eager her students
were to practise the types of questions that might be in the exam (Colombo

287), while another explained that her students were more motivated than at any other time of the year:

> T 15: Each child tries his best – to do something. During the class teaching
> of course they just ignore – but here they try to do some sort of things.
> They like it. (Nugegoda 373)

Some teachers believed that students would practise speaking if they knew they would have to do a speaking test as part of the exam (Nugegoda 464-467, Wennapuwa 702-712). Such changes would affect not only the secondary schools, but also the primary schools and tutories, as the whole system would react to the students' exam-related demands.

A few teachers talked about the students' desire for predictability: they wanted to know what type of questions they would get (Wellawatte 638-639) and they were upset if their teachers were not able to prepare them for what was coming. Others talked about how students wanted questions at their own level of difficulty. One teacher talked about how students felt 'withered' when faced with questions that were too difficult (Colombo 196), while another said that students wanted choices that would not make them feel inferior (Colombo 196).

## The students' attitudes towards English

The teachers said little about their students' attitude towards English as a language, as opposed to their feelings about English as an examination subject. We know that some students came from homes where the family spoke English, and we can assume that these students would have understood not only the practical value of the language but also the prestige and power associated with it. It is important to stress the word 'assume', however, since the teachers did not discuss how these students used their English or were intending to use it in future.

The teachers gave more details when they talked about the students who did not intend to use English later (e.g. Colombo 70, Wennapuwa 348-350). These students were generally from poorer backgrounds, had little exposure to the language, and would probably be getting jobs where English would serve no purpose. Several teachers reported discussions in which the students or their parents stressed the importance of examination results over learning the language. This attitude had rubbed off on some of the teachers, one of whom admitted that even for him the students' marks were more important than their learning:

> T 63: … Our main aim is not to teach the language. We want to make them
> pass. To get a pass. And even their parents. And even the students. They
> don't want to speak English or anything. They want somehow just to get
> a pass. Get through the exam. (Wennapuwa 377)

## The students' attitudes towards new ideas (openness)

There were no references to the students' attitudes towards new ideas, other than comments about how bored some of them felt when faced with content they could not relate to.

## The students' level of education

There were also no references to the students' levels of education. There may have been no perceived need to discuss this feature because all of the students were in roughly the same age group and in either Year 10 or Year 11 of their schooling.

## The students' abilities

The teachers had more to say about their students' level of English proficiency than about their attitudes. This was logical given that most of them would have been working with their students for at least a year, and some of them would have been working with the same group of students for several years. About a third of the teachers reported that their students were either 'weak' or 'very weak' in English. They gave various reasons for this: lack of exposure to English in the environment, lack of encouragement at home, a shortage of teachers in the past, poor teaching in previous years, conflicts in the timetable at school, disruptions due to political disturbances, lack of ambition for the future. All of these factors are discussed in detail in other sections of this book.

Many teachers described their students' abilities in general terms, while others talked about particular areas that students found difficult. Ten teachers focused on basic language proficiency: grammar, vocabulary and spelling. One teacher had given his students a 60-word dictation and found that some had made up to 50 mistakes (Wennapuwa 165). Another reported that his Year 11 students could not recite the alphabet (Nuwara Eliya 524). Still another had begun the year by spending a month on grammar, because his students did not know any tenses (Welimada 40-43). Two teachers had decided to take their Year 10 students back to the Year 7 book, because they felt that they had missed out on the basics of language construction earlier in their education (Wennapuwa 157-163, Wennapuwa 193-199).

At least a quarter of the teachers felt that their students were weak in reading. They did not specify what it was that made reading difficult but it is likely that they were referring to poor grammar and vocabulary rather than to reading sub-skills. (The observations carried out in 1990 and 1991 indicated that few teachers offered students the opportunity to practise sub-skills such as skimming, scanning or guessing the meaning of words in context [Wall and Alderson 1993:53-54].) A number of teachers reported that they had to simplify the reading exercises in *EED* or leave them out altogether (e.g. Asgiriya 112, Nuwara Eliya 342, Ratnapura 115-120). Some teachers used simple listening comprehension passages for reading, since their students could not handle the texts they were supposed to be reading (e.g. Wennapuwa 116-121). One teacher said that she always asked her students to read aloud in her lessons: she would not ask them to read silently because they would not know how to do it (Wennapuwa 201-205).

The teachers said similar things about their students' writing ability. Several teachers claimed that their students could not spell properly (Colombo 310, Colombo 398-399, Wennapuwa 165), let alone write a composition. These teachers were not able to dictate practice questions during examination preparation, and had to spend valuable time copying everything out on the blackboard. Other teachers reported that they had to prepare their students carefully before they could ask them to write on their own (Asgiriya 220-222, Ratnapura 305). One teacher described how she helped her students to write a note accepting an invitation:

> T 34: ... First I write the invitation on the blackboard, and help them to read it. Otherwise they can't read it. Then I discuss with them. What should we write for this invitation? Now, we can go and inform him that we are coming. How do you start it? Then one by one I must tell them. First write the date. Then the date and everything first we discuss. And get them to read them after me. There I don't write on the blackboard. I orally do it.

> DW: You talk about it?

> T 34: Yes, talk about it. And then sentence by sentence I get them to say it after me. Then they must practise. Otherwise they can't write it.

She went on to say that after practising all of the sentences orally, the students would begin to write. She would still have to write some words on the board, however, to help them finish their letters. The product of all this effort was a message of three to four sentences (Ratnapura 305-313). It is important to remember that this was taking place in Year 11, after the students had been studying English for eight years.

Teachers also reported that their students had trouble speaking English (Asgiriya 80-85, Ratnapura 216-228). It could take teachers several lessons to get through a one-page 'role play' (extended dialogue) (Colombo 104 and 120, Nugegoda 236), and some teachers never used pair work or group work as it was just too difficult (Asgiriya 66, Tangalle 132). Similar problems occurred with listening. Two teachers reported that their students laughed at them if they tried to speak in English (Welimada 136-142, Trincomalee 272), but most teachers with weak students admitted that they did not attempt the listening exercises as there was not enough time and the listening skill would not be tested on the exam.

## The students' personal lives

About a quarter of the teachers made comments about their students' personal lives. Several were about whether students came from an 'English environment' (Wellawatte 544) or an 'English background' (Colombo 70) and whether they received encouragement from their parents in their studies.

When the teachers spoke about an 'English environment' or an 'English background' they were referring to whether English was spoken in the home. Although it was officially only a second language, it carried a great deal of weight socially and parents who knew the language tried to pass it on to their children. 'English environment' and 'English background' had other connotations as well: they represented a reasonable social standing, economic stability, and some measure of prestige. The parents were likely to have good jobs (government officers or doctors – Wennapuwa 170, teachers – Wennapuwa 438, computer specialists – Nuwara Eliya 129), and they might be able to buy their children extra materials, such as examination preparation publications (e.g. Wennapuwa 431-439), or send them to private tuition (Wennapuwa 156 and 171).

About a dozen teachers spoke about the problems students had if they did not come from this sort of environment. They were at a disadvantage because they only came in contact with English during their lessons at school. The teachers also made connections between the lack of the right 'environment' and poverty. About half of them said that their students were from poor families and/or remote areas of the countryside (Colombo 70, Nuwara Eliya 514, Ratnapura 106, Trincomalee 519-522, Trincomalee 80), and one of them used the term 'lower classes' (Wennapuwa 687). Several claimed that their students had no ambition (Colombo 70), received no education from their parents (Nuwara Eliya 34, Wennapuwa 154), or received no help with language because the parents did not know how to help (Trincomalee 80, Wennapuwa 172).

The most dramatic example of 'haves' versus 'have nots' appeared in a school where the students were divided according to ability, and where the students in the upper sets seemed to come from privileged backgrounds and those in lower sets from poorer backgrounds. A teacher from this school explained the situation as he saw it:

> T 60: That difference is mostly the family backgrounds also. Because as teachers we mostly meet the parents and find out how is their life at home also. Then some parents they say just teach them to get through even as S-Pass. But some say 'Sir, you must teach them so they work and then go to the Army or Navy or Police or some of the armed police in Italy, and in Italy they don't use English. So we'll just send them to Italy.' And there are such. Those children are from those families. Those who are in the A, B, C scholarship class are mostly families of government officers, doctors … (Wennapuwa 170).

Teachers who taught the upper sets were believed to have an easy life, while those who worked with the bottom sets saw their job as a constant struggle to force students to learn (Wennapuwa 61, Wennapuwa 783). The teachers seemed to accept this as the way of the world, which led the examination developer who was attending the interviews to question whether the practice of grouping students according to ability should be continued:

> You can see, it must be affecting the teachers also. Because you seem to think that children from one particular social background are in one group, and that's not good for the children also. (Wennapuwa 176)

What was not present in the data were references to students with even harder lives – for example, those in villages where most of the mothers had gone to the Middle East to work as servants, or students in the war-torn areas of the north and east. There was still enough evidence, however, to indicate that there were great differences between the home situations of the students across Sri Lanka and it would have been difficult for all teachers to deal with the national textbook and examination in the same way.

## The students' economic situation

The students' economic situation seemed to affect them in three ways: in their attitudes towards education, their access to outside tuition and their ability to buy supplementary materials for examination revision. All of these have been discussed at length in previous sections and the details will not be repeated here.

## The students' interests

One of the teachers stated that there was no standard way of teaching: she and her colleagues varied their methods 'according to our children's abilities, interests and their understanding of the second language' (Nugegoda 216). However, there is little information about the students' interests in the interviews. We have seen in previous sections ('Complexity of *English Every Day* for the students' in Chapter 8, and the section on 'Students' Attitudes towards language teaching' in this chapter) that some of the students found some lessons boring; what we do not know though is whether the students were truly not interested in the topics or whether they just did not like how they were dealt with in the classroom. Some of the textbook material was not very attractive, and if the teachers did not feel enthusiastic about a topic then this might have affected their students.

## The students' goals

The teachers made several comments about their students' long-term goals. We know that some wanted to go on to other schools (Nugegoda 349), some wanted to be teachers (Welimada 348), some would probably join the police or armed forces (Wennapuwa 170), and some already had 'small jobs' (carpentry, masonry) waiting for them (Colombo 70). We know that some of the students felt that they did not need English (Wennapuwa 97), but others who wanted to get ahead would need some command of the language, at least in specific domains (Asgiriya 493, Nuwara Eliya 500). The one thing that most students had in common was the need to pass the O level examinations, so this became their goal in their last year of schooling. The teachers were aware of this ambition and, as we have already seen elsewhere, they did their best to get their students through the syllabus and the teaching materials, and gave them many hours of extra tuition to prepare them for the exam.

## Summary of characteristics of the users

The teachers generally saw education as a struggle for social survival, and examination success as a key element in the survival process. They believed that their students' main goal was to succeed in the examination, and they saw it as their responsibility to help them to achieve this goal. Most teachers felt comfortable in a teacher-centred classroom and believed that their students did also. This style of teaching had deep roots in the country's culture, and it suited the students as they saw it as an efficient way of preparing for the examination.

Not enough teachers had received initial teacher training, and there were not enough resources to provide regular in-service training. Some teachers did not understand the ideas underlying the textbook and the exam, and some did not have the level of English that these innovations demanded. Many students also had very weak English, due to problems in both the school system and social system. Teachers expected more of students who came from 'an English environment', and felt pessimistic about the prospects of those who did not have this background. It was the teachers with weaker students who had the most problems, having to spend hours of free time going through essential materials, skipping over lessons which were too difficult, and finding ways of motivating the students when their recent history and their present problems were working against them.

The teachers were committed to their students, but they were not necessarily committed to the innovations. Their way of teaching seemed to be in conflict with the ideas underlying *EED* and, by extension, the examination. This might also have been a function of capability. It was clear that the teachers needed more guidance on how to teach their students and how to prepare them for the examination, especially in difficult circumstances. They needed opportunities to discuss their problems with advisers or with other teachers, to study good models and to receive constructive feedback. Many teachers seemed to be working on their own, so it was not surprising that they had problems understanding what they were supposed to be doing, given the complexity and other characteristics of the innovation, and the many complications of their working environment.

The purpose of Chapters 8–11 has been to analyse the implementation factors operating in Sri Lanka in the years just after the introduction of the examination. We have analysed the characteristics of the textbook and examination, the characteristics of the context the examination was supposed to fit into, and the characteristics of the teachers and students who were its prime users. It is now time to discuss how all these factors fit together and how they affected the impact that the examination could have on classroom teaching.

# 12 Discussion and future directions

## Background

The purpose of Chapters 7–11 was to analyse the antecedent conditions and the implementation factors in operation during an attempt to use examinations to support curriculum innovation in Sri Lanka. The purposes of this chapter are to explain how these factors worked together to produce the outcomes presented in Chapter 6 and to discuss the implications of this study for attempts to innovate in other educational contexts. I begin the chapter by summarizing what was learned in each phase (chapter) of this investigation and I then discuss what was learned about examination impact in this particular setting. I conclude with a discussion of the implications of this investigation for examination reform projects in the future.

## Summary of the investigation so far

The aims of this study were to investigate the impact of one particular examination in a specific educational setting, and to see whether it was possible to extract from this experience guidelines which could help educators in other settings to decide whether their plans to innovate through testing are realistic. The investigation required a critical review of the concept of examination impact as it has been presented in general education and in language education, and a survey of a number of important ideas in the literature of educational innovation.

The critical review of examination impact was presented in Chapter 3. Although much of the literature on impact was speculative rather than empirically supported, there were a number of ideas which were relevant to the new examination in Sri Lanka. It was important to remember the functions of this examination in society: it was not only there to encourage 'higher levels of competence and knowledge' (Eckstein and Noah 1993:11), but it was also a 'differentiating ritual' (Bernstein et al 1966) in that it was the prime means of 'allocating sparse places in higher education' (Eckstein and Noah 1993:12). There was a great deal of pressure on students to succeed, especially as Sri Lanka was a developing country where education was one of the few routes available for those who wished to improve their situation.

The review of the literature in general education indicated that examination impact could either be positive or negative. Popham (1987) argued in favour of using examinations to influence the curriculum in a positive way, while Madaus (1988) argued that such efforts could only lead to negative consequences. A number of educators joined the debate and produced studies which supported Madaus' way of thinking, either predicting or in some cases demonstrating, negative impact such as a narrowing of the curriculum (Smith 1991), test score pollution (Haladyna, Nolen and Haas 1991), unethical examination preparation practices (Mehrens and Kaminsky 1989), or effects on teachers' and learners' attitudes (Herman and Golan 1993). Some suggested guidelines for producing positive examination impact but there was more emphasis on (and evidence for) negative impact.

The treatment of impact in language education was superficial until the late 1980s, consisting mainly of assertions, predictions and accounts which were not accompanied by evidence. Useful empirical studies were produced by Westdorp (1982), who showed that the impact teachers believed examinations had was not really present ('the myth of washback'), and Shohamy (1993), who used a variety of research methods to identify the ways that different exams could affect teaching. Alderson and Wall (1993) called for a rigorous approach to research in this area, advocating tighter definitions, more diversified research techniques, and the use of insights from fields such as motivation studies and educational innovation. A number of new studies appeared in the mid-1990s which showed that examination impact was much more complicated than either Popham (1987) or Madaus (1988) had predicted.

The survey of key ideas in educational innovation was presented in Chapter 4. This was of special interest to me because my earlier work in Sri Lanka showed me that it was not only the features of the examination which affected the kind of impact that could occur, but also factors in the educational setting itself. I was most impressed with the ideas about the process of change: how complex it is, how long it takes for an innovation to prove itself either successful or unusable, and how much learning is required at every stage in the process. I was also impressed with the idea that every individual experiences change in a different way (Fullan 1991) and that it is difficult to understand from looking at individuals' surface behaviour what kinds of changes they are going through. I learned that it is easier for teachers to change the content of their teaching than to change their teaching style, and easier to change their style than their beliefs (Fullan 1991:42). I discovered a small but informative literature about innovation in language education, which led me to a framework developed by Henrichsen (1989) to analyse a language teaching innovation in Japan. I adopted this framework because it provided the most elegant compilation of ideas about the stages in the innovation process and the factors at work in every stage. After several modifications I applied it to interview data that I had collected at the end of my time in Sri Lanka, in the hope that it would help me to identify further factors and relationships between them and give me greater insight into the nature of examination impact.

I carried out two types of analysis during this study. The first, which is presented in Chapter 6, was an analysis of the impact that the new examination was having on teaching, three years after its introduction. This analysis looked at teachers' attitudes, the content of their teaching, their methodology and the way they assessed their own students. The second analysis, which is presented in Chapters 7–11, looked at the antecedent conditions of the English language reform programme, the characteristics of the innovation (the examination and the materials it was based on), the characteristics of the user system and the characteristics of the users. The focus throughout was on the teachers' views of their own situation, and many illustrations were given using their own words.

In Chapter 6 I reviewed the objectives of the *English Every Day* textbook in order to determine what the new examination was meant to be reinforcing, and I stated that since the examination could not test the oral skills, there was a risk that it would have a negative impact on teaching. I predicted that the following consequences might occur (from Table 6.1):

- Attitude – Teachers (and students) would place more value on the skills and activities that were assessed on the examination and less value on those that were not.
- Content of teaching – Teachers would not teach listening and speaking. When teaching reading and writing they would neglect certain text-types or activities that did not appear on the examination. They would abandon the use of the textbook and begin to use other materials which were more obviously related to the examination.
- Methodology – Teachers would neglect some aspects of the textbook's approach if they felt that these were not useful for examination preparation.
- Assessing students – Teachers would write tests which reflected the content of past examination papers. They would adapt questions or copy them directly from past papers or publications designed for examination preparation purposes. They would adopt the marking criteria used by the examination.

The analysis of the interviews showed the following:

- Attitude – The teachers placed a great deal of importance on the skills and activities that were tested in the examination. There was a recognition that listening and speaking were important but many teachers claimed that their aim in teaching was to help students through the examination and this meant paying more attention to the areas that were tested. A number of teachers wanted listening and speaking to be tested, and one of the main reasons for this was so that it would force students to work on the development of these skills.

- Content of teaching – The examination had considerable impact on the content of teaching, both during the 'ordinary teaching period' (roughly, the first two terms of the year) and the 'examination preparation period' (the third term, just before the examination). Teachers spent a lot of time on the reading and writing skills during ordinary teaching, taking care to cover as many of the textbook exercises as they could (even though they might not understand or give the students practice in specific sub-skills). A number of teachers claimed that they also tried to cover the textbook exercises for listening and speaking, but some admitted that they spent less time on these skills, both because they were difficult to deal with in the classroom and because they were not tested in the examination. There was no teaching of listening and speaking during the examination preparation period. During this time the teachers switched from using the textbook to using commercial examination preparation materials and past papers, and they concentrated on the skills that were tested in the examination.
- Methodology – The examination had little impact on the methodology that the teachers used, either during ordinary teaching or the examination preparation period. The teachers continued to use the teacher-centred lock-step approach that they had traditionally used rather than the student-centred activity-based teaching that *English Every Day* recommended.
- Assessing students – The examination had a strong impact on classroom test design, especially on the type of items and tasks that were used for testing reading and writing. The teachers did not discuss their criteria for marking, so it is not clear how many of them used the O level criteria, but the fact that few of them had served as examiners and that many of them did not have copies of the official examination support booklets suggests that they were unlikely to be familiar enough with the criteria to employ them in their own testing. Some teachers said they gave more priority to the written skills than to the oral ones in their testing. (Evidence gathered in other parts of the Evaluation Project indicated that few teachers, if any, tested listening and speaking in their classrooms.)

The results of this analysis generally matched the results of the two-year observation programme that was also carried out as part of the Evaluation Project. The major difference was that the teachers who were interviewed claimed to be teaching more listening and speaking than was recorded in the observations. A possible explanation for this was that the textbook devoted less time to oral skills than written ones. The teachers might have covered all the exercises for each skill but might still have been doing less oral work overall. However, a more likely explanation is that while they believed they were teaching listening and speaking they were doing it in ways that did not resemble the *EED* approach and would not have been recognized during the observation programme.

The teaching of reading and writing was also quite different from the textbook designers' intentions. Some teachers understood what the *EED* required and devised ways of developing these skills, but many others were experiencing the 'false clarity' (when teachers think that they have changed but when the changes have only been superficial) or the 'painful unclarity' (when they do not really understand what they are supposed to do) described by Goodlad et al (1970). It was necessary to look at factors beyond the examination to understand the situation more fully. This is where Henrichsen's ideas about analysing the antecedent conditions and the implementation factors operating in the context of the innovation took on importance, and it was to these analyses that I turned in Chapters 7–11.

In Chapter 7 I presented what the teachers remembered of their teaching situation before the introduction of the new textbook series and the new examination. The syllabus had been based on grammar rather than on language use, and was very examination-oriented. The methodology was teacher-centred and made use of pattern practice and mother tongue explanations. The last third of the year was devoted to examination preparation, and this followed the same pattern every year since the format of the examination never changed. The examination placed a heavy weighting on grammar and reading, and paid only minimal attention to writing. The level may have been quite high but many teachers believed that students could earn more marks than they deserved by 'guessing' and by presenting essays that were memorized earlier. Tutories played an important role in preparing students for examinations.

There were significant differences between schools, depending on whether they were in urban or rural areas and whether the students were exposed to English in their everyday environment. Students in some schools studied in English medium and prepared for examinations in English as a mother tongue, while students in other schools were so weak in the language that their teachers did not bother with teaching them writing. This was accepted because writing was not important for the examination. There was no listening and speaking in the examination, so these skills were ignored by many teachers.

It would have been difficult for teachers in this situation to understand the new textbooks and the examination which was meant to reflect and reinforce them. Introducing materials which played down grammar in favour of language skills and which encouraged teachers to let students work things out for themselves would have been confusing, if not alien. Teachers would have needed a lot of support, over time, to be able to understand the ideas underlying the materials and to be able to prepare their students for the examination. Some teachers attended training sessions when the textbooks were first introduced but these were generally not very detailed and were not followed up in many cases. The support they received to learn how to prepare students for the examination was also minimal, consisting mostly of written information (the *Guidelines* booklet) sent to schools shortly before the first administration. Few training sessions were held to help teachers to understand this material and generalize from it to create further materials for their own classrooms.

Chapters 8 and 9 explored the characteristics of the new textbook materials and the new examination. My justification for analysing the textbook was that it would not be reasonable to expect the examination to create positive impact if the textbook it was meant to support was not doing its job properly. I used Henrichsen's eleven characteristics in the analysis of the textbook and added a new one called 'predictability' for the examination.

It was clear from the interviews that the textbook was not having the effect that was intended. Teachers liked the fact that it was relevant to everyday life (relative advantage) and that students had more confidence and could do practical things after working with it (observability), but many of them did not understand the principles underlying the series (explicitness) and did not understand how to teach the skills or how to respond to the novel way of teaching grammar (complexity for teachers). They felt that they had to teach their students the details of every passage rather than help them to discover things for themselves. They bought commercial materials which helped them to cope with the content but did not help them to understand the *EED* methodology (form). They did not find it easy to switch to a supportive role rather than a directive one (this was predictable from the analysis of antecedent conditions), and they felt that classroom conditions and other problems in the context were working against them (this was discussed further in Chapter 10).

They were especially concerned that the language level of the textbooks was too high for their students, and that the readings were too hard to follow without a great deal of explanation (complexity for students). Although quite a few teachers claimed that they were covering all the skills during their ordinary teaching, they seemed to spend more time on reading and less time on skills which were not tested in the exam. (Table 12.1 presents a summary of the characteristics of *English Every Day* and whether they facilitated [worked in favour of] or inhibited [worked against] the goal of the innovators – to create less teacher-centred, more active and more skills-based teaching.)

The analysis of the examination produced a similar picture. Most teachers were pleased that the examination was different from its predecessor and that it matched the textbook (originality). They liked the fact that the content was relevant to everyday life, that students often had to write their answers instead of just recognizing the correct answer from a set of options, and that

**Table 12.1 Summary of the characteristics of *English Every Day***

| Characteristic | Manifestation | Facilitative or Inhibitive? |
|---|---|---|
| Originality | *EED* seen as very different from previous textbooks, but teachers liked relevance to Sri Lanka. | Facilitative |
| Complexity for teachers | Reading material considered difficult. Teachers do not understand how to teach reading. Teachers do not understand how to teach oral skills. | Inhibitive Inhibitive Inhibitive |
| Complexity for students (as perceived by teachers) | Reading material considered difficult. Required language level seen as too high. | Inhibitive Inhibitive |
| Explicitness | Teachers' Guides presented procedures rather than principles. Not enough guidance provided. | Inhibitive Inhibitive |
| Relative advantage | Teachers liked relevance to everyday life. Treatment of grammar not well explained. | Facilitative Inhibitive |
| Trialability | No comments. | – |
| Observability | Students had more confidence. Students learned to do practical things. | Facilitative Facilitative |
| Status | No comments. | – |
| Practicality | Too much material for time available, so teachers had to leave things out. | Inhibitive |
| Flexibility | No comments. | – |
| Primacy | No comments. | – |
| Form | Teachers learned about reform by using materials. Teachers' guides not always clear or available. | Facilitative Inhibitive |

the instructions were in English rather than the students' mother tongue (relative advantage). They thought that the examination had a good effect on teaching and that the students and they themselves learned something from preparing for it (observability), although a number would have preferred for listening and speaking to be tested so that students would take these skills more seriously. Some teachers used materials from the official examination support documents (form) and they said they were clear enough for their purposes (explicitness). (My own observations at training seminars suggested the contrary, however.) Although some of the teachers complained that the examination changed from year to year (predictability), it was useful that this happened because it prevented them from limiting their teaching to only certain features of the curriculum. Most of these factors facilitated a positive impact; however, this was countered by the fact that there was no testing of listening and speaking. This meant that teachers ignored these skills during the examination preparation period. Neither the contents of the exam nor its format could persuade them to adopt a more innovative methodology. There were also problems with the complexity of the material for both teachers and learners and with the presence of seen passages on earlier exams, which encouraged the learning of content rather than the development of skills.

In short, the examination had many positive features which made it an improvement over the previous exam; however, it was not powerful enough to do what the textbooks were failing to do – that is, to encourage teachers to pay equal attention to all skills, use student-centred techniques, and make full use of the other innovative ideas in the new textbook series. (See Table 12.2 for a summary of the characteristics of the examination.)

In Chapter 10 I examined what Henrichsen (1989) calls 'the characteristics of the user system': particular features of the context which could affect whether the goals of the innovators were met or frustrated. This analysis showed that there were many factors which made it difficult for teachers to adopt a new way of teaching. Perhaps the most obvious factors could be found in the classrooms and the schools. Many teachers found it difficult to teach in innovative ways when they were working in crowded and noisy classrooms, without the books or other materials that they needed. Many complained that there was too little time to cover the syllabus, although it was not clear whether the problem was one of time only or whether there were other factors complicating the picture: for example, that the materials might have been pitched at too high a level for the population in general ('complexity for students', discussed in Chapter 8), that the students did not have the level of knowledge that their teachers thought they should (because of poor teaching in the past), and that the teachers did not understand what the teaching goals should have been and attempted to exploit all the materials too thoroughly ('complexity for teachers' and 'explicitness', discussed in Chapter 8, or 'attitudes towards teaching', discussed in Chapter 11).

There were further factors at the school level which made it difficult for teachers to respond to the new textbooks and the examination. The shortage of teachers affected some schools very badly, and there were schools in which students might go for a year or more without English tuition. When they arrived in Year 10 or 11 they were far behind in their studies and the teachers who had to prepare them for their examination could do little to help them catch up to where they were supposed to be. There were additional problems in schools where the leadership was not strong and where there were poor internal and external communications. Many schools suffered because of the extra-curricular events which cut into the teaching timetable. There were also factors connected with outside tuition. Some teachers felt pressured to use

## Table 12.2 Summary of the characteristics of the new examination

| Characteristic | Manifestation | Facilitative or Inhibitive? |
|---|---|---|
| Originality | New exam seen as being different from previous exam (practical, better techniques etc.). | Facilitative |
| | New exam seen to match new materials. | Facilitative |
| Complexity for teachers | Some teachers felt that exam made them more active. | Facilitative and Inhibitive |
| Complexity of exam for students | Many teachers thought exam was difficult for the students | Facilitative and Inhibitive |
| Explicitness | Official materials were mostly explicit. | Facilitative |
| | Official materials had not reached teachers. | Inhibitive |
| Relative advantage | Teachers thought exam had a good effect on teaching. | Facilitative |
| | Presence of seen passages. | Inhibitive |
| | Exam didn't test oral skills. | Inhibitive |
| | Exam didn't seem to test much grammar. | ? |
| | Exam didn't offer choices. | ? |
| Trialability | No comments. | – |
| Observability | Teachers felt that students learned as a result of studying for the exam. | Facilitative |
| | Some teachers were frustrated because students would never pass. | Inhibitive |
| Status | No comments. | – |
| Flexibility | Exam wasn't flexible. | ? |
| Practicality | Exam was practical but did not test listening and speaking. | Inhibitive |
| Primacy | Exam benefited from work on NCE and DELIC exams and was in harmony with them. | Facilitative |
| Form | Official publications were clear for the most part. | Facilitative |
| | Commercial publications gave mock tests but no explanation. | Inhibitive |
| Predictability | Exam was not predictable. Teachers did not know what would appear next. | Facilitative |

certain techniques because they were used in tutories: their students thought these techniques were more effective and complained when their own teachers did not use them.

There were a number of problems relating to educational administration. These could be divided into two main categories: communication and teacher training. The communication problems included a lack of clarity in Ministry announcements about the exam, the late distribution of the examination support booklets, and continuing problems in the distribution of other material such as past papers. Many teachers got their information about the examination from commercial publications. These provided practice reading items and writing tasks, but they did not include explanations of what sub-skills were being tested and what the marking criteria were for writing. The main problem with teacher training was that there were not enough seminars to help teachers understand what was required of them when they worked with the textbooks or when they prepared students for the examination. Some teachers claimed that they had been given information which ran contrary to the spirit of *English Every Day*. Some of these problems were the consequence of administrative changes brought on after the transfer of educational responsibilities from the central ministry to the provinces. There were likely to be fewer problems when the Regional English Support Centres (RESCs)

**Table 12.3 Summary of the characteristics of the user system**

| Characteristic | Manifestation | Facilitative or Inhibitive? |
| --- | --- | --- |
| Classroom conditions | Overcrowding and noise. | Inhibitive |
| | Level of students. | Inhibitive |
| | Lack of materials. | Inhibitive |
| | Insufficient time. | Inhibitive |
| School factors | Differences between schools. | Inhibitive |
| | Teacher transfers, absences, shortages. | Inhibitive |
| | Role of the principal. | Facilitative and Inhibitive |
| | Conflicts within school curriculum. | Inhibitive |
| Outside tuition | Exam-centred, conservative methods. | Inhibitive |
| Educational administration | Manner of introducing new exam. | Inhibitive |
| | Channels of communication about exam. | Inhibitive |
| | Lack of teacher training, poor quality. | Inhibitive |
| | Poor communication between NIE and schools | Inhibitive |
| Political factors | School disruptions and closures. | Inhibitive |
| | Knock-on effects in teaching. | Inhibitive |
| | Restricted travel. | Inhibitive |
| Geographic factors | Reluctance of teachers to work in troubled areas or anywhere in countryside. | Inhibitive |
| | Lack of exposure to English in rural areas. | Inhibitive |
| Economic factors and scarcity of resources | Much poverty. | Inhibitive |
| | Lack of exposure to English in poorer areas. | Inhibitive |
| Cultural factors | Role of English in Sri Lanka. | Facilitative and Inhibitive |

and Regional English Language Testing Units (RELTUs) were up and running and once the pre-service institutions were in closer contact with the curriculum design and examination development teams, but these developments had not yet occurred at the time of this investigation.

It can be seen (Table 12.3) that most of these factors were inhibitive ones: they made it difficult for teachers to get access to information and to put ideas into action once they had the information. There were also political, geographic and economic factors in operation which would affect the success of the innovation. The cultural factor could be seen as both facilitative or inhibitive: facilitative in that some students would benefit from learning English and being able to use it to gain a better position in society, but inhibitive because many students knew that they would never be able to rise above their circumstances and the idea that English would help them was just an illusion. (See Table 12.3 for a summary of the characteristics of the user system.)

Chapter 11 presented the characteristics of the teachers and the teachers' views of the characteristics of their students. The most important issue here was whether the teachers had the capability and the commitment to implement the new teaching ideas in *English Every Day*. The biggest obstacle seemed to be lack of capability. Many teachers had the language knowledge needed to use the textbooks, but they did not seem to understand the principles underlying them. They found it difficult to let go of the traditional role of teacher as transmitter of knowledge, and to understand that they were supposed to be helping their students to develop skills rather than aiding them in attempts to learn specific information. This may have been the result of too little teacher training or of training which emphasized examination success rather than the process of learning. Some teachers did not have enough confidence in their own abilities, and this would have made it difficult for them to pass confidence on to their students.

It is also possible that some teachers were not committed to change since the new ideas about teaching were so different to those they were familiar with. It is difficult to be certain about this though since few teachers had opportunities (in the form of training seminars) to think deeply about the new approach or to discuss it with other teachers. They were committed to helping their students as much as possible, as evidenced by the amount of time they devoted to giving them extra lessons and the fact that they paid for materials out of their own pockets; however, they did not seem to have a clear idea of what the textbook designers wanted or the implications of this for their teaching. (See Table 12.4 for characteristics of the teachers.)

Chapter 11 also presented the characteristics of the students, as seen through the eyes of the teachers. The main points arising from this discussion were that most students wanted to pass the examination since it was their key to social survival, but many of them did not have the ability to do so. This was because of the poor or irregular teaching they had received in the past or

## Table 12.4 Summary of the characteristics of the users — teachers

| Characteristic | Manifestation | Facilitative or Inhibitive? |
|---|---|---|
| Attitude to education | Traditional views of education: transmission, memorization, product orientation. | Inhibitive |
| | Purpose of education — social survival. | Facilitative |
| | Traditional view of teacher: guru, holder of knowledge. | Inhibitive |
| | Teachers do all they can to help students. | Facilitative/Inhibitive |
| Attitude to classroom teaching | Traditional views of methodology. | Inhibitive |
| Attitude to English teaching | Good to teach everyday English. | Facilitative |
| | Important to teach grammar more systematically. | Inhibitive |
| | Important to improve students' listening and speaking. | Facilitative |
| Attitude to exams | Exams are key to survival. | Inhibitive |
| | Exams should cater for weaker students as well as stronger. | ? |
| Attitude to English | Teachers positively disposed to English. | Facilitative |
| | Importance of English for getting good job. | Facilitative |
| Attitude to new ideas | Teachers possibly open to new ideas, but not enough training. | ? |
| Levels of education | Lack of pre-service training. | Inhibitive |
| | Lack of in-service training and/or training which misses the point. | Inhibitive |
| Abilities | Many Year 11 teachers had strong English. | Facilitative |
| | Some Year 11 teachers had very weak English. | Inhibitive |
| | Lack of understanding of objectives of *EED*. | Inhibitive |
| | Lack of ability to teach listening, speaking. | Inhibitive |
| Personal life | Teachers had to take leave time. | Inhibitive |
| | Teachers gave up free time. | Facilitative |
| Economic situation | Many teachers could not afford extra books. | Inhibitive |
| | Some teachers bought them regardless of poor pay. | Facilitative |
| Interests | Some teachers enjoyed poetry, literature. | Facilitative |
| Goals | Teachers' main goal = preparing for the exam. | Inhibitive |

because they lacked exposure to English or encouragement in their family environment. *English Every Day* was supposed to be a practical course, but many students found it difficult because the language level was too high or because it presented topics that were beyond their immediate experience.

## Table 12.5 Summary of the characteristics of the users—students

| Characteristic | Manifestation | Facilitative or Inhibitive? |
|---|---|---|
| Attitude to education | Education as means of survival. | Inhibitive |
| | Some students alienated and did not take part in the 'competition'. | Inhibitive |
| Attitude to classroom teaching | See 'Attitude to English teaching'. | – |
| Attitude to English teaching | Importance of grammar. | Inhibitive? |
| | Students liked visuals, role plays, acting, poems, mysterious things, pop music. | Facilitative |
| | Students did not like topics they could not relate to. | Inhibitive |
| | Some students preferred tutory teaching methods—teacher-centred, spoon-feeding | Inhibitive |
| Attitude to exams | Students wanted to concentrate on what is on the exam. | Inhibitive |
| | Students wanted material at own level of difficulty. | ? |
| Attitude to English | Some students recognized importance of English in society. | Facilitative |
| | Some students only needed English to pass the exam, not get good results. | Inhibitive |
| Attitude to new ideas | No comments. | – |
| Levels of education | All at same level. | – |
| Abilities | Many students very weak because of problems in past—lack of exposure to English, lack of encouragement, shortage of teachers, poor teaching, etc. | Inhibitive |
| Personal life | Some students had 'English environment'. | Facilitative |
| | Many students lacked exposure to English or encouragement to use English at home. | Inhibitive |
| Economic situation | Many students could not afford outside tuition. | Inhibitive |
| | Many students could not afford supplementary materials. | Inhibitive |
| Interests | Some students did not like topics they could not relate to. | Inhibitive |
| Goals | Most students aimed to get good examination results to get ahead in life. | Inhibitive |

Some students preferred the methods of teaching that were used in tutories since these were more obviously examination-oriented, and they pressured their classroom teachers to teach in the same way. Other students were too poor to be able to afford outside tuition or even supplementary materials, and this, combined with other difficulties, prevented them from feeling successful or from feeling confident about their ability to succeed in examinations or in the world outside the classroom.

There is no data which can confirm whether the teachers' impressions of their students were correct or otherwise. What matters, however, is what the teachers believed the case to be, since their perceptions would contribute as much to the way they chose to do their teaching as to the 'objective reality' of the situation. (See Table 12.5)

# Further components of the Henrichsen framework

There are three more sections in the Henrichsen framework which must be discussed before drawing conclusions about the impact of the new O level examination in Sri Lanka: two sets of implementation factors operating during the diffusion/implementation process (the 'Characteristics of the Resource System' and 'Inter-Elemental Factors') and the outcomes of the process (the 'Consequences'). (See Figure 12.1 for a reproduction of Henrichsen's framework.)

The 'Characteristics of the Resource System' relate to the individuals or units responsible for planning the innovation, organizing it, turning abstract ideas into materials, communicating with teachers and other key parties, directing the implementation, evaluating the results etc. Henrichsen argues that it is necessary to investigate the 'Capacity' of this system (the ability to 'retrieve and marshal resources', convey and store information, influence opinions), the 'Structure' (the 'division of labour and coordination of effort'), the 'Openness' (the willingness to help and listen and to be influenced by user needs and aspirations'), and the 'Harmony' between different bodies working within it (the 'ability to get along and work together') (1989:86, based on Havelock and Huberman 1978:241). Unfortunately there was not enough relevant data in the interviews to allow a full discussion of these factors. Some of the factors were touched on in Chapter 10, under 'Educational Administration', where we learned that some teachers were dissatisfied with the way the examination was introduced, that communication problems were still occurring, and that teacher training was inadequate, but it would have been useful to explore this area more fully, with direct questions about the teachers' perceptions of how the reform was being managed.

The Inter-Elemental Factors are very important to this investigation, since it is in this section of the model that recognition is given to the interaction

## Figure 12.1 The hybrid model of the diffusion/implementation process

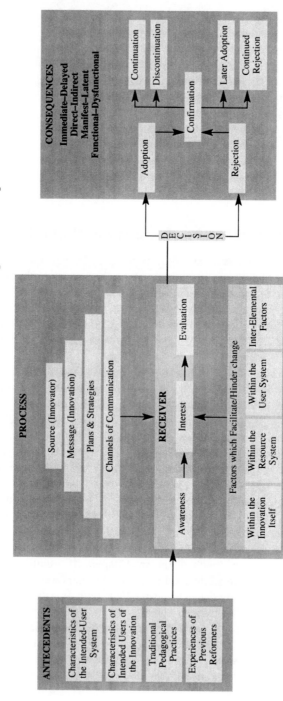

*Source:* Henrichsen (1989: 80). Reprinted from *Diffusion of Innovations in English Language Teaching: The ELEC Effort in Japan, 1956–1968* by L E Henrichsen. Copyright © 1989 by L E Henrichsen. Reproduced with permission of Greenwood Publishing Group, Inc., Westport, CT.

between all the previously analysed sections. (See also Smith's 1995 Propositions 5–15, relating to interactions between the components of change – presented in Appendix 6.) Henrichsen discusses five different sorts of inter-elemental factors: *Compatibility, Linkage, Reward, Proximity* and *Synergism*.

Under *Compatibility* Henrichsen focuses on two types of interaction: between the innovation and the intended user system, and between the resources system and the intended user system. He states that potential innovators should always try to determine whether the characteristics of one system will match the characteristics of the other, to avoid wasting time and resources if they are not compatible.

There are four areas that need to be investigated during an analysis of whether the innovation is compatible with the users:

1. Can the resource demands of the innovation be met by the structures and facilities of the user system?
2. Does the use envisaged for the innovation fit in with the policies and regulations of the user system?
3. Can the task demands of the innovation be met by the abilities and behaviour patterns of the individuals?
4. Are the benefits that can be expected of the innovation in line with the attitudes and values of the individuals?

In the case of Sri Lanka the answer to Question 1 was 'no'. If we define the innovation as the examination and the textbook series that it was based on then it must be recognized that the user system could not respond adequately to its demands. There was not enough information available about the exam or the textbooks, the distribution of textbooks and teacher's guides was poor, the distribution of official examination support material was inadequate, there was not enough teacher training, and there seemed to be, even in the better schools, too little time available to cover the content of the textbook. The lack of compatibility between resource demands and the ability of the user system to respond adequately was one of the major obstacles to a successful implementation of the innovation.

The answer to Question 2 was 'yes'. The use of the examination and the textbook series were definitely compatible with the policies and regulations of the country. There was no innovation in terms of function: the new examination took over the function of the Old Syllabus examination and *English Every Day* took over the function of the previous national textbook series. The innovation was not jarring in the sense of requiring new procedures or legislation, or new attitudes concerning, for example, whether it is the responsibility of the state or the school to say what is to be taught or tested.

The answer to Question 3 was 'no'. It is clear from the analysis of textbook and examination complexity, teacher and student ability, and the teacher training section of the discussion of Educational Administration that many teachers did not have the understanding that was needed of the principles underlying the innovation or the techniques that were needed to develop skills in the way that the original innovators intended. This was in spite of the care that the textbook design team took in the early days of the reform to meet with teachers, pilot materials with them, incorporate their views into revised versions of the materials, etc. The problem was that the intensive teacher training that took place in the early days of the reform did not continue, and there were not enough training opportunities to satisfy the needs of the constantly changing teaching population. This presented a major obstacle to successful implementation.

The answer to Question 4 was a qualified 'yes'. Most of the teachers approved of the content of the textbooks and of the examination, stating that they were practical and that they catered for the students' needs. Some of them would have preferred a more traditional presentation of grammar rather than the approach adopted by the textbook designers, but this did not dampen their enthusiasm for the rest of the content. However, the methodology recommended in the textbook was very different from the traditional way of teaching. The teachers did not complain about the approach or reject it, but they certainly needed more support to help them to understand it better – in the form of written material and teacher training courses. This leads us once again to the lack of compatibility between the characteristics of the innovation and the structures and facilities of the user system.

Henrichsen suggests that there are two ways of dealing with this incompatibility: 'adaptive implementation', which involves changing the innovation so that it can be assimilated more easily by the users, and 'programmed implementation', which involves changing the users so that they more easily accept the innovation (1989:92). Both of these courses of action were recommended in the Fourth and Final Report for the Evaluation Project: recommendations were made about re-writing the teacher's guides and adding additional explanatory material, and about providing specialized teacher training to help teachers cope with the demands of the examination (Alderson and Wall 1992).

When dealing with the compatibility between the resource system and the user system the major question seems to be whether the participants in each system are 'homophilous' or 'heterophilous' (similar or different) in their abilities, beliefs, attitudes, goals etc. (Rogers and Shoemaker 1971:14-15). As mentioned earlier it is not possible to comment on this type of compatibility because there was not enough information about the resource system in the interviews.

The second type of inter-elemental factor is *Linkage*, which refers to 'the number, variety, and mutuality of contacts between the Resource System and the User System' (Havelock 1969:20-21, cited in Henrichsen 1989:93). Such contacts can be made through professional teaching organizations, universities, journals, and other professional agencies. The teachers did not speak about these subjects; however, it was discovered in other phases of the Evaluation Project that the links were not very strong. The professional teaching organization was not operating in the late 1980s and early 1990s. The universities were not interested in English language teaching and not all of the pre-service teacher training institutions were familiar with the new materials or examination. There was some positive in-service work being done by the Regional English Support Centres, the newly formed Regional English Language Testing Units, and by the examination design team, but there were some problems with the teacher training offered by the local educational authorities (this is discussed in the section on 'Educational administration'). It was clear that these links needed to be strengthened and expanded.

The third inter-elemental factor is *Reward*, which refers to the need that teachers have for some form of positive reinforcement, to convince them that they are doing the right thing and that they should continue. This reward could take the form of a bonus or other tangible perk, recognition from colleagues, appreciation from students, or satisfaction at having helped others to achieve their goals. Some of the teachers in the sample may have felt satisfaction with the work that they had done, especially if their students received good results in the examination, but there were not many other rewards in the system. Life was harder for many teachers since the introduction of the new materials and the examination: it required more energy (they could not just 'be seated and go' [Trincomalee 166]), much of their own time (for after-school lessons to cover the syllabus and prepare for the examination), their own money (to buy supplementary materials because they found the textbooks wanting), and a tremendous amount of learning (to master the 'subject matters' that they felt they had to pass on to their students [Ratnapura 559 and 561]). Some felt that their students did not respect them because they did not teach properly or could not predict what was coming in the examination. It is not surprising that so many teachers seem to have 're-invented' the innovation to make it fit in with the type of teaching they were already familiar with, especially if there were so few professional development opportunities available to help them understand and teach 'the *EED* way'.

The fourth inter-elemental factor is *Proximity*: the 'nearness in time, place and context' of the resource system and the user system (Havelock 1969:20, cited in Henrichsen 1989:94). The idea here is that the more access potential users have to the resources that are required to make an innovation work, the more likely it is to be successful. The most obvious example of this in Sri Lanka was that the users who lived in or around cities generally had more access to training and materials than those who lived in rural areas. They could attend seminars at the Regional English Support Centres (RESCs) and could borrow materials from these centres or from the British Council in Colombo.

They also had access to English in the environment, through English newspapers and books and in offices, shops, restaurants etc. There were examples in the data of teachers who received little training because they lived and worked too far from the training centres (e.g. the teachers from the north and east of the country who had to travel to Anuradhapura for a training seminar since trainers from the centre could not travel to them), and teachers who felt that their own English was deteriorating since they had no English-speaking colleagues to practise with.

The final inter-elemental factor is *Synergism*, which Henrichsen claims is a function of:

> the number, variety, frequency and persistence of forces associated with the implementation of the innovation, as well as … the amount of cooperation and communication among them. (1989:186)

Synergism occurs when two or more forces combine and produce an impact which is greater than the sum of the impacts they would have had if they were acting separately. It is difficult to find examples of synergism in the Sri Lankan data because so many of the characteristics of the user system and the users themselves seemed to be working against the innovation rather than in favour of it. It is useful, however, to speculate on how some of these characteristics could have been combined with others to enhance the potential for successful impact. An interesting example came up during a discussion of the power of tutories: one teacher suggested that it would make sense to train the tutory masters how to teach in the *EED* way so that they would not undermine the efforts of the ordinary classroom teachers (Colombo 611). Another idea would be to make the most of the existence of an examination preparation period and to design special materials to be used during this time – materials explaining underlying principles and presenting creative ways of preparing that would increase general learning and not just focus on specific language or testing techniques. (This was one of the recommendations in the Fourth and Final Report for the Evaluation Project – Alderson and Wall 1992.)

The final component of Henrichsen's framework that will be considered here is the *Consequences* section, which deals with whether the innovation is adopted or rejected by potential users and whether this decision is confirmed or reversed with the passage of time. In the case of Sri Lanka the decision to adopt the innovation (the textbook and the examination) was not up to the individual; rather, the Ministry of Education made an 'authority decision' (Rogers and Shoemaker 1971:37-38, cited in Henrichsen 1989:94) which was imposed on all teachers, whether they were in favour of or against the innovation and whether they were ready for it or not. Henrichsen claims that this type of decision generally produces the quickest rate of diffusion and implementation, but it can also provoke negative reactions from the users and will not necessarily lead to fundamental or long-term changes in practice. We have seen that teachers generally spoke in favour of both the textbook and the examination; however, the attitudes they professed to have did not always translate into the kind of behaviour that was intended and did not necessarily indicate a change in their basic beliefs about teaching. The teachers accepted the content of the new materials but they did not adopt the recommended methodology. For Fullan this would count as superficial change only (1991:37). In Beretta's terms, most teachers had reached the 'Orientation' level of implementation, but few had progressed into the 'Routine' or 'Renewal' levels (1990). In Shohamy's terms the impact was 'instrumental' rather than 'conceptual' (1993).

## What this investigation has shown about examination impact in general

This study has confirmed the notion put forward by Alderson and Wall (1993) that examination impact is a complex phenomenon, which should not be seen as a natural or inevitable consequence of introducing a new examination into an educational setting. It should not be assumed that a 'good examination' will automatically produce positive effects on teaching or that a 'bad examination' will automatically produce negative ones. The design of the examination will always have some effect on the way that teachers react to it, but there are many other factors in the environment which help to determine what the true impact will be for any individual teacher. Amongst these factors are the antecedent conditions and the characteristics of the innovation itself, the resource system, the user system and the users. These factors will interact with one another and will change over time, so it would not be reasonable to predict the same impact for all examinations in all situations, or indeed even the impact in any one situation. The framework used here can only identify and help to describe variables that are important in any innovation equation. It cannot give these factors individual weightings or relate any factor or set of factors to a particular outcome.

What the framework can do, however, is allow us to make more informed judgements about the amount of risk that is involved in any new examination venture, and set us thinking about the characteristics an examination will need if it is to overcome problems in the user system or challenge long-held traditions or strongly-held beliefs amongst users. It may help us to see that examinations on their own will probably not cause profound changes in teachers' behaviour or in the way that they think about teaching and learning. Examinations have power but they also have limitations, and it is too much to expect them to succeed where the materials and methods that they are supposed to be reinforcing have not yet taken hold in the teaching community.

# Implications of this investigation for other examination reform projects

I have been involved in a number of other examination projects since finishing the work in Sri Lanka and I have been able to use insights from the Sri Lankan Evaluation Project when assessing the feasibility of examination projects in other countries, drawing up plans for new examination systems, training examination design teams and evaluating the success of their efforts. What follows is a list of the most important of these insights and others that would be useful in future projects.

1.  It is valuable to use a framework such as Henrichsen's when carrying out investigations into the feasibility of examination projects. It is especially important to analyse the antecedent conditions, in order to determine whether change is desirable and how much change should be attempted. This information can be used during the course of the project and at the conclusion, to decide whether change has occurred and whether it has been the right kind of change. (See Appendix 13 for guidelines to investigators carrying out a 'baseline study' for the St Petersburg Examination Reform Project [Wall 1995]. Although the headings used do not correspond directly to Henrichsen's headings, much of the information that the researchers were to gather is the same.)

2.  The revised version of the Henrichsen framework is suitable for future examination projects, both for baseline studies and for interim and final evaluations. I would make one further modification, however, moving the 'Education Administration' section from the 'Characteristics of the User System' component to the 'Capacity' and 'Structure' sections of the 'Characteristics of the Resource System' component. I would look very critically at the experience of previous reformers and the characteristics of the Resource System before deciding on the feasibility of a project.

3.  Although it is essential to talk to teachers, who are the implementers of any reform and whose opinions must be taken into account during the planning stages, it is equally important to consult representatives of all the stakeholders in any new project, including policy-makers, administrators, pre-service and in-service teacher trainers, and students. It is important to communicate directly with students rather than to rely on their teachers' views of what they think and feel.

4.  When consulting these parties, it is important to keep the groups small, to be able to ask many questions and go into depth in the discussion.

5.  It is advisable not to be too idealistic or ambitious when drawing up plans for examination reform. It is reasonable to expect teachers to change the content of their lessons, but it will be more difficult to get them to change their methodology or their beliefs about what is right and wrong in teaching. An important question to consider is what an examination would need to look like to encourage teachers to change their way of teaching – to get them to teach reading strategies, for example, or to employ other process-based means of teaching.

6.  It is important that the management team in any reform project include representatives of the key stakeholders, to facilitate better co-operation and communication amongst these parties and to ensure that the examination and associated procedures respect not only the traditional criteria for judging assessment systems (validity, reliability and practicality), but are also comprehensible to the teachers and students, acceptable to other relevant parties in the educational system (e.g. universities), fit in with the available training and development structures, etc. (In the Baltic States Year 12 Examination Reform Project, each national team included a ministry representative to handle political and budgetary issues, a university representative to co-ordinate the design work and ensure that the project would be seen as academically respectable, a teacher training representative to think about how changes could best be explained to teachers, and teachers from different types of secondary schools to make sure that the examination not only matched the curriculum but did not make excessive demands on classroom teachers.)

7.  It is important to draft examination specifications which can be scrutinized by representatives of all key stakeholders before they are adopted as the official examination blueprint. The specifications should be accompanied by sample examination items, tasks and marking criteria so that those who are charged with reviewing them will have a clear idea of what the demands will be on teachers and students. The specifications should also explain the purpose of the examination and the underlying constructs, and include a description of the intended test-takers, the envisaged levels, etc. (See Alderson, Clapham and Wall 1995:39 for a full checklist of features which should be included in an examination specification.) It will be easier for future users and evaluators if this information is included in a single document rather than appearing in parts of several different documents.

8.  It is essential to plan the examination support programme (materials and training events) at the same time as the test design so that issues such as complexity, explicitness, compatibility with beliefs, practicitness etc. are

    dealt with from the beginning, and adjustments can be made through 'adaptive implementation' and/or 'programmed implementation'.

9.   Thought must be given to the links that need to be established between the examination management and design teams (these may be the same team) and other stakeholders. These links can be represented in a 'communications web'. (See Appendix 14 for a communications web produced by the Estonian team involved in the Baltic States Year 12 Examination Reform Project.) Communications webs can be made more effective by specifying not only which organizations need to be contacted but also which individuals or groups within the organizations and for what purpose – e.g. to inform, to consult, to ask permission etc.

10.  It is important to pilot examinations before introducing them full-scale, both to test out the feasibility of the new ideas and procedures and to gather feedback from teachers and students. This is especially important when the components of the examination are very different from the examination which it replaces or when there is additional complexity in the structure of the examination. (See Alderson and Wall 1992:221 for a description of a new initiative in Sri Lanka to introduce the testing of the oral skills in a single region of the country before trying to introduce it throughout the country. See Appendix 15 for a timetable devised by the Lithuanian team in the Baltic States Year 12 Examination Reform Project, showing how new features in their examination would be phased in over the course of several years rather than all being introduced at the same time.)

11.  Evaluation should take place from the earliest stages of an examination reform project and at regular intervals, and it should cover not only the examination design and procedures but also the attitudes of teachers and students and the impact of the examination on teaching and learning. The results should be disseminated to key parties within the education system so that decisions can be made about the match between the examination and the curriculum, the appropriateness of the design and procedures, the adequacy of communications, the allocation of resources, the planning of further training, changes in overall or specific policy etc.

12.  Policy-makers and examination designers should not expect significant changes to occur immediately or in the manner they intend. They should be aware that examinations cannot cause positive change if the materials and practices they are based on have not been effective. They may, however, cause negative changes and the situation must be monitored continuously (see 11 above) to allow early intervention if problems occur.

# Significance of this investigation to other educational settings

The purposes of this investigation were to study the impact of a particular examination in a specific educational setting, and to see whether it was possible to generalize from this experience in order to help educators in other settings to decide whether their plans to innovate through testing are realistic. The analysis has shown not only the extent and nature of examination impact in Sri Lanka but also how many other factors need to be taken into account to explain why the impact took the form that it did and why it did not match the expectations of the examination designers. The Henrichsen framework has been useful in determining which factors facilitated and which inhibited the diffusion of this specific innovation. It cannot be used to make precise predictions of impact; however, it does allow educators to see where the pressure points are in any particular setting, which can alert them to the need to make adjustments either to that setting, the innovation, or their own plans for implementation.

The investigation has also shown that just as examinations have potential for changing teaching, so they also have limitations. While previous literature has suggested that a change in examinations is a necessary condition for change in the curriculum, this study has shown that it is not a sufficient one. Examinations cannot influence teachers to change their practices if they are not committed to the new ideas and if they do not have the skills that will enable them to experiment with, evaluate and make appropriate adjustments to new methods. It is also necessary for the right conditions to be in place in their classrooms, schools, local systems and higher levels of educational administration so that if teachers decide to open up to change they will be supported.

It is hoped that the ideas discussed in this book will provide general guidance for educators who wish to introduce change through examinations, and that the implications for examination development will prove particularly useful.

# Appendices

# APPENDIX 1:
## Old Syllabus Examination, 1987

සියලු ම හිමිකම් ඇවිරිණි]
முழுப் பதிப்புரிமையுடையது]
*All Rights Reserved*]

**04** E/I

№ 351853

ශ්‍රී ලංකා විභාග දෙපාර්තමේන්තුව/இலங்கைப் பரீட்சைத் திணைக்களம்/Department of Examinations, Sri Lanka

අධ්‍යයන පොදු සහතික පත්‍ර (සාමාන්‍ය පෙළ) විභාගය, දෙසැම්බර් 1987
கல்விப் பொதுத் தராதரப்பத்திர (சாதாரண தரப் பரீட்சை, டிசெம்பர் 1987
GENERAL CERTIFICATE OF EDUCATION (ORD. LEVEL) EXAMINATION, DECEMBER 1987

INTERNATIONAL LANGUAGE (SECOND LANGUAGE) — ENGLISH *One hour*
අන්තර් ජාතික භාෂාව (දෙවන බස) — ඉංග්‍රීසි පෑ එකයි
சருவதேச மொழி (இரண்டாம் மொழி) ஆங்கிலம் — ஒரு மணி

Index No./විභාග අංකය./கட்டெண் :..................................

*Answer all the questions on this paper itself.*
ප්‍රශ්න සියල්ලට ම පිළිතුරු සපයන්න. ඔබගේ පිළිතුරු මේ පත්‍රයේ ම ලියන්න.
எல்லா விஷுக்களுக்கும் விடை தருக. இவ்விஷுத்தாளிலேயே உமது விடைகளை எழுதுக.

### PAPER I / I වන පත්‍රය / விஷுத்தாள் I

**Candidates are advised to save time by reading the instructions in the medium they know best.**
තමන් ඉතාමත් හොඳින් දන්නා භාෂා මාධ්‍යයෙන් උපදෙස් කියවා කාලය ඉතිරි කර ගන්නා ලෙස අදාළ කරුවන්ට උපදෙස් දෙනු ලැබේ.
பரீட்சார்த்திகள் தமக்கு நன்கு தெரிந்த மொழியில் அறிவுறுத்தல்களை வாசிப்பதன்மூலம் நேரத்தைச் சிக்கனமாகக் கையாளும்படி ஆலோசனை வழங்கப்படுகின்றது.

**A**

Select the correct group of letters within the brackets and complete each of the parts of words in the following sentences.
වරහන් තුළ ඇති නිවැරදි අක්ෂර සමූහය තෝරා ගෙන, පහත දක්වෙන වාක්‍ය වල එක් එක් වචනය සම්පූර්ණ කරන්න.
அடைப்புக்குறிகளுக்குள் இடம்பெறும் எழுத்துத் தொகுதிகளில் சரியான தொகுதியைத் தெரிவு செய்து பின்வரும் வாக்கியங்களின் சொற்பகுதிகளை ஒவ்வொன்றையும் பூர்த்தி செய்க.

1. Ruwan waited anx..................ly (oius/ious/eous) for the postman.
2. I had to get an electri.................. (cian/tion/sion) to repair my cooker.
3. An interpret.............. (or/ar/er) must be good at languages.
4. Our neighbours are a quarrels .............. (om/ome/ume) family.
5. The illness of his son caused him great gr..............f (ee/ei/ie).

**B**

Underline the word or group of words in the brackets that is closest in meaning to the word in thick type in each of the following sentences.
පහත දක්වෙන එක් එක් වාක්‍යයෙහි තද කළ අකුරෙන් මුද්‍රිත වචනයට වඩාත් සමාන තේරුම දෙනා වචනය හෝ වචන සමූහය හෝ වරහන් තුළින් තෝරා, ඊය යටින් ඉරක් අදින්න.
பின்வரும் வாக்கியங்கள் ஒவ்வொன்றிலும் தடித்த எழுத்துக்களிலுள்ள சொல்லுடன் ரீங நெருங்கிய கருத்தொத்தமை வாய்ந்த சொல்லே அல்லது சொற்கூட்டத்தை, அடைப்புக்குறிகள் தரப்பட்டவற்றிலிருந்து தெரிவு செய்து அதன் மீழ்க் கோடிடுக.

6. Sita wonderingly **gazed** at the sunset. (looked/watched/stared).
7. We saw an **unusually** big elephant in the jungle. (uncommonly/wildly/wonderfully).
8. The stick **snapped** as he lifted it up. (broke/tore/fell).
9. "At the **outset**, we must draw up a plan" said the Chairman. (set out/going out/start).
10. Tissa was **exhausted** after the cross-country race. (finished/tired/honoured).

[ Turn over.

286

**C**

**Fill in the blanks with the most suitable words from the words given below :**

පහත දී ඇති වචනවලින් වඩාත්ම යුසු වචනය තෝරා හිස් තැන් පුරවන්න.

கீழே தரப்பட்டுள்ள சொற்களிலிருந்து மிகப் பொருத்தமான ஒரு சொல்லை உபயோகித்து வெற்றிடங்களை நிரப்புக.

*into, for, of, in, by, at, before, to, on.*

(11).......... the morning (12)............ the time we leave home (13)............ school the buses are very crowded and it is very difficult to get (14)........... a bus or get out (15)........... a bus.

**D**

**Fill in the blanks with the most suitable word from the words given below. You may use a word more than once.**

පහත දී ඇති වචන අතුරින් වඩාත්ම ගැලපෙන වචනය තෝරා හිස්තැන් පුරවන්න. එක් වචනයක් එක් වරකට වඩා යෙදිය හැකිය.

கீழே தரப்பட்டுள்ள சொற்களிலிருந்து மிகப்பொருத்தமான ஒரு சொல்லை உபயோகித்து வெற்றிடங்களை நிரப்புக. ஒரு சொல் ஒரு தடவைக்கு மேலும் பயன்படுத்தப்படலாம்.

*out, in, off, up, on, at.*

On the day of the trip I got (16)............ at about 4.30 in the morning because we expected to start (17)............ at 6.00 a.m. When I reached the school many of the other pupils had already turned (18)............ At about 6 o'clock the bus arrived and our teacher asked us to get (19)............ and sit down. After that the teacher called (20)............ the names of the pupils who were going on the trip.

**E**

**Underline the correct word from those given in brackets.**

වරහන් තුළ දී ඇති වචන අතුරින් නිවැරදි වචනය යටින් ඉරක් අදින්න.

அடைப்புக்குறிகளுள்குள் தரப்பட்டுள்ள சரியான சொல்லுக்கு கீழே கோடிடுக.

(21) (As/When/But) there were not many buses on that route we would have had to wait long (22) (although/since/if) we wanted to go by bus. (23) (As/So/If) we decided to walk. (24) (Although/Because/Until) it was a 3 mile walk we did not feel tired (25) (if/when/because) by that time the sun had set and a cool wind was blowing.

**F**

**A group of words is given in thick type at the end of each sentence. Select the blank in which the group of words should come to make the sentence meaningful and write the number of the blank within the brackets at the end of each sentence.**

එක් එක් වාකූය අවසානයෙහි වචන සමූහයක් තද කළ අකුරෙන් මුදුණය කර ඇත. කේරුවක් ඇති වාකූයයක් තුළදැන අදුරු මේ වචන සමූහය යෙදිය යුතු හිස් තැන තෝරා එම නිස්තැනෙනි අංකය වාකූය අවිමයෙන් ඇති වරහන තුළ ලියන්න.

ஒவ்வொரு வாக்கியத்தின் இறுதியிலும் சொற்கூட்டம் ஒன்று தடித்த எழுத்தில் தரப்பட்டுள்ளது. கருத்தமைய வாக்கியமாக்குவதற்கு இச்சொற்கூட்டம் இடம்பெற வேண்டிய வெற்றிடம் எதுவெனத் தெரிவு செய்து அவ்வெற்றித்தித்தின் இலக்கத்தை ஒவ்வொரு வாக்கியத்தினதும் இறுதியிலுள்ள அடைப்புக்குள் எழுதுக.

**Example :** The teacher (1)............ asked the pupils (2)............... to see the Principal (3)........... who were late. (2)

26. Vegetables (1)............... fetch high prices (2) ............... when they are brought to Colombo (3)............ grown in the upcountry ( )

27. The doctor (1)............ assisted by only one nurse (2)............... attended to all the passengers (3) ............ who were injured in the accident. ( )

28. The goods (1)............... were found in a shop (2) ............... not far from the house (3)............ they were stolen from. ( )

29. The house (1)............ and land (2) ............... were all his wealth. that his father had left him. ( )

30. People (1) ............ had to travel either on foot (2) ............... or by bullock cart (3)............ who lived about 900 years ago. ( )

*Appendix 1*

---

**G**

**Underline the correct word or group of words from those given in brackets.**

වරහන් තුළ දී ඇති නිවැරදි වචනය හෝ වචන සමූහය හෝ තෝරා, ඒය යටින් ඉරක් අදින්න.

அடைப்புக்குறிகளுக்குள் தரப்பட்டுள்ளவற்றிலிருந்து சரியான சொல்லை அல்லது சொற்றொகுதியைத் தெரிவு செய்து அதன் கீழ்க் கோடிடுக.

The rains (31) (coming/has come/have come) at last (32) (ending/ended/end) the long drought. It (33) (rain/rained/raining) for about 3 hours continuously last night. The rivers (34) (rises/rose/are rising) rapidly and before long there (35) (will be/has been/had been) floods.

**H**

**Underline the correct word-ending from those given in brackets.**

වරහන් තුළ ඇති නිවැරදි අක්ෂරය-අක්ෂර සමූහය තෝරා, ඒය යටින් ඉරක් අදින්න.

அடைப்புக்குறிகளுக்குள் தரப்பட்டுள்ளவற்றிலிருந்து சரியான சொல் விகுதியைத் தெரிவு செய்து அதன் கீழ்க் கோடிடுக.

36. I couldn't listen to the sad (dest/ness/ly) part of his story.

37. The old man was throw (s/n/ing) out of the bus.

38. We all had an enjoy (ed/ing/able) time at the party.

39. The soldier was honoured for his courage (ous/ing/ed) act.

40. We were interest (ed/ing/s) to know why he left school so early.

**I**

**Put the words or groups of words given within brackets in the right order and complete each of the following sentences.**

වරහන් තුළ දී ඇති වචන හෝ වචන සමූහය හෝ නිවැරදි පිළිවෙලට යොදා මේ එක් එක් වාකයය සම්පූර්ණ කරන්න.

அடைப்புக்குறிகளுக்குள் இடம்பெறும் சொற்களை அல்லது சொற்களின் தொகுதியைச் சரியான ஒழுங்கில் வைத்துப் பின்வரும் வாக்கியங்கள் ஒவ்வொன்றையும் பூர்த்தி செய்க.

41. It ...................................................................................................
    (Mars/man/to/journey/will/is/that/by/1990/hoped)

42. If ...................................................................................................
    (film/he/enjoy/the/Imran/it/will/sees)

43. I ....................................................................................................
    (were/my/I/in/that/wished/village)

44. Why ..............................................................................................?
    (Galle/town/an/is/important)

45. The bus ..........................................................................................
    (away/Arun/moved/get/before/in/could)

**J**

**Fill in the blanks with the correct form of the word given in brackets.**

වරහන් තුළ දී ඇති වචනයෙහි නිවැරදි ආකාරය යොදාගෙන මේ තැන් පුරවන්න.

அடைப்புக்குறிகளுக்குள் தரப்பட்டிருக்கும் சொல்லின் சரியான வடிவத்தைக் கொண்டு வெற்றிடங்கள் நிரப்புக.

Leela was brought up by an uncle of (46)............... (she) after (47)............... (she) had lost both (48)............... (she) parents. Leela's parents died in a motor accident when the car in which (49)............... (they) were travelling crashed killing both of (50)............... (they) on the spot.

[ Turn over.

**K**

**Complete each of the following questions so as to get the answers given at the end of each of them.**

මේ එක් එක් ප්‍රශ්නය අගින් දී ඇති පිළිතුරු ලැබෙන සේ පහත දැක්වෙන ප්‍රශ්න සම්පූර්ණ කරන්න.

விருக்கள் ஒவ்வொன்றினதும் இறுதியில் தரப்பட்டிருக்கும் விடைகளைப் பெறும் வகையில் பின்வரும் விருக்கள் ஒவ்வொன்றையும் பூர்த்தி செய்க.

51. What ........................................................? Tilak wants to buy a bicycle.

52. Where ........................................................? She lives in a house close to the sea.

53. Whose........................................................? Kumar's paintings won the first prize.

54. Why ........................................................? The students were punished for their bad behaviour.

55. How ........................................................? His father visits him once a month.

**L**

**Fill in the blanks with the correct form of the verb given in brackets.**

වරහන් තුළ දී ඇති ක්‍රියා පදයේ නිවැරදි ආකාරය යොදා මේ එක් එක් හිස් තැන පුරවන්න.

அடைப்புக்குறிகளுக்குள் தரப்பட்டிருக்கும் வினைச் சொல்லின் சரியான வடிவத்தைக் கொண்டு வெற்றிடங்கள் ஒவ்வொன்றையும் நிரப்புக.

56. Where have they all...........................................................(go).

57. The bell has not yet been ...................................................................(ring).

58. She.........................................................(do) all the work in the house.

59. He will .........................................................(come) to the wedding if

60. he is .........................................................(invite).

289

සියලු ම හිමිකම් ඇවිරිණි|
(முழுப் பதிப்புரிமையுடையது|
**All Rights Reserved]**

**01 E/II**

478423

ශ්‍රී ලංකා විභාග දෙපාර්තමේන්තුව/இலங்கைப் பரீட்சைத் திணைக்களம்/**Department of Examinations, Sri Lanka**

අධ්‍යයන පොදු සහතික පත්‍ර (සාමාන්‍ය පෙළ) විභාගය, දෙසැම්බර් 1987
கல்விப் பொதுத் தராதரப்பத்திர (சாதாரணதரப்) பரீட்சை, டிசெம்பர் 1987
GENERAL CERTIFICATE OF EDUCATION (ORD. LEVEL) EXAMINATION, DECEMBER 1987
INTERNATIONAL LANGUAGE (SECOND LANGUAGE) — ENGLISH *Two hours*
අන්තර් ජාතික භාෂාව (දෙවන බස) — ඉංග්‍රීසි පැ දෙකයි
சர்வதேச மொழி (இரண்டாம் மொழி) — ஆங்கிலம் இரண்டு மணி

Index No./විභාග අංකය./கட்டெண : .................................

**PAPER II / II වන පත්‍රය/விருத்தாள் II**

අන්තිම ප්‍රශ්නය හැර අනෙකුත් සියලු ම ප්‍රශ්නවලට මෙම පත්‍රයේ ම පිළිතුරු සපයන්න.
கடைசி விருத் தவிர்ந்த ஏனைய விருக்கள் பாவந்துக்கும் இவ்விருத்தாளிலேயே விடைபெயுதுதல் வேண்டும்.
*All questions except the last one should be answered on this paper itself.*

**A**

**In each of the following questions underline the correct answer.**
පහත දක්වෙන එක් එක් ප්‍රශ්නයේ නිවැරදි පිළිතුරට යටින් ඉරක් අදින්න.
பின்வரும் விருக்கள் ஒவ்வொன்றிற்குமான சரியான விடையின் கீழ்க் கோடிடுக.

1. Nimal has always been the first in his class except last term when he had been ill for most of the term.
  According to the above sentence
  (a) Nimal has never been beaten in his studies by the other students in his class.
  (b) Last term he could not become the first in his class.
  (c) Students in Nimal's class are very week in their studies.

2. We were at the station by 10.15 a.m. about half an hour before the train was due to arrive.
  According to the above sentence
  (a) The train was due at 10.45. a.m.
  (b) The train arrived at 10.15 a.m.
  (c) The train was late by half an hour.

3. Rohitha is a son of Mr. Daniels.
  According to the above sentence
  (a) Mr. Daniels has only one son.
  (b) Mr. Daniels has more than one son.
  (c) Rohitha is Mr. Daniels's eldest son.

4. Cyril knows one Francis Perera who repairs TV sets.
  According to the above sentence
  (a) Cyril repairs TV sets.
  (b) Francis Perera is known to Cyril who repairs TV sets.
  (c) Francis Perera repairs TV sets.

5. The doctor told Mr. Silva's wife that she is not well enough to leave hospital.
  According to the above sentence
  (a) Mr. Silva is in hospital and he cannot leave hospital yet.
  (b) Mrs. Silva is in hospital and she cannot leave hospital yet.
  (c) Mr. Silva is in hospital and he has been discharged from hospital.

**B**

**Read the following passage and underline the correct answers to the questions at the end.**
පහත දක්වෙන ජේද්‍ය කියවා ඒ පිළිබඳව අසා ඇති ප්‍රශ්නවල නිවැරදි පිළිතුරට යටින් ඉරක් අදින්න.
பின்வரும் பத்தியை வாசித்து அதன் இறுதியில் தரப்பட்டுள்ள விளக்கங்களுக்கான சரியான விடை கனிவின் கீழ்க் கோடிடுக.

Hides and skins are the raw materials of the leather manufacturer or tanner. When man first used animal skins is not known. However, the numerous sewing needles in our museums show that skins were prepared and used long before textiles.

Any animal skin can be made into leather, but the skins chiefly used come from cattle, sheep, goats, pigs and horses. To a lesser extent the skins from dogs, deer, reptiles, marine animals, fish and birds are also used. Snakes, lizards, seals, whales and sharks all contribute to leather manufacture.

[ Turn over.

'Hide' is the trade word for the skins of the larger animals such as full-grown cattle and horses ; and 'skin' for the smaller animals, and immature large animals such as ponies and calves. Some skins are made into leather after the hair or wool has been removed ; but the skins of the fur-bearing animals and sometimes of sheep, lambs and ponies are processed, or 'dressed', with the hair or wool still in place.

Most cattle hides come from South America, the U.S.A. and from Australia with smaller quantities from East and West Africa, Central America and Sudan. Sheepskins come from Australia and New Zealand, and the best goat skins come from India, Pakistan, Ethiopia, Arabia and Nigeria.

There is usually a long interval between the flaying, or stripping of the skin from the animal and putting it into the tannery for processing. If the flayed skins were left wet, they would go bad, just like, meat ; they must therefore be preserved in some way. The commonest method is salting. This involves sprinkling the skins with salt on their inner side; or immersing the skins completely in strong salt solution for some hours, after which they are drained off and sprinkled with solid salt.

Another method of drying is to stretch the skins out on the ground, or on frames and to dry them in the sun, or even better in the shade. Beetles and other insects eat skins and must be kept away from them by the use of some chemical such as D.D.T. The dried skins are called 'crust' leather and are sent in this form to the tanneries for the very complicated process of tanning. After tanning, only the 'corium' or middle layer of the skin is left to provide leather as we know it.

6. **Leather can be made from the skins of**
   (a) any animal except fish and birds.
   (b) any kind of animal.
   (c) cattle, sheep, goats, pigs and horses only.

7. **The difference between a hide and a skin**
   (a) depends on the type of tanning process.
   (b) is largely a question of the size of the animal.
   (c) varies from country to country.

8. **Cattle hides come mainly from**
   (a) The Americas and Australia.
   (b) Africa.
   (c) the Sudan.

9. **Skins are usually preserved with salt after stripping**
   (a) to make them taste better.
   (b) to preserve their moisture.
   (c) because they cannot be tanned immediately.

10. **Which of the following statements is not correct.**
    (a) D.D.T. can keep beetles and insects away from the skins.
    (b) 'Hide' is the trade word for the skins of ponies and calves.
    (c) Textiles started to be made long after the use of skins.

C

In the following Interview, Wickrema is discussing old age with one of the authors of a report on the subject, Dr. George Wilson. Read it and underline the correct answers to the questions at the end.

ඔබ දක්වෙන සටහුනු සාකච්ඡාවෙදී විකුම, මහලු වයස ගැන වාර්තාවක් ලියූ ලේඛකයකු සමඟ මහලු වයස පිළිබඳව සාකච්ඡා කරයි. එය කියවා, අවා ඇති ප්‍රශ්නවල නිවැරදි පිළිතුරට යටින් ඉරක් අඳින්න.

கீழு தரப்படுள்ள பேட்டியில், விக்கிரம, முதுமைப் பருவம் பற்றிய அறிக்கை ஒன்றை எழுதிய களொர்த்தி றோர்த் விஸ்னைடன் முதுமம் பருவம் பற்றி ஆராய்கிறார். பேட்டைய வாசித்து அதன் இறுதியில் தரப்படுள்ள விருக்களுக்கான சரியான விஸைகளின் கீழ்க் கோடிடுக.

| Wickrema : | Dr. Wilson, can you tell me what you think your report on old people will achieve ? |
|---|---|
| Dr. Wilson : | We hope that it will help to change people's feelings about old age. The problem is that far too many of us believe that most old people are poor, sick, lonely and unhappy. As a result, we tend to find old people, as a group, unattractive. And this is very dangerous for our society. |
| Wickrema : | But surely we cannot escape the fact that many old people are lonely and many are sick. |
| Dr. Wilson : | No, we can't. But we must also remember that the proportion of such people is no greater among the 60 to 70 age group than among the 50 to 60 age group. |
| Wickrema : | In other words, there is no more mental illness, for example, among the 60's to 70's than among the 50's to 60's ? |
| Dr. Wilson : | Right. And why should there be ? Why should we expect people to suddenly change when they reach their 60th or 65th birthday any more than they did when they reached their 21st ? |
| Wickrema : | But one would expect there to be more physical illness among old people, surely ? |
| Dr. Wilson : | Why should one expect this ? After all, those people who reach the age of 65 or 70 are the strong among us. The weak die mainly in childhood, than in their 40's and 50's. Furthermore, by the time people reach 60 or 65, they have learnt how to look after themselves. |

**Wickrema :** Do you find that young people these days are not as concerned about their parents as their parents were about theirs ?

**Dr. Wilson :** We have found nothing that suggests that family feeling is either dying or dead. There do not appear to be large numbers of young people who are trying, for example, to have their dear old mother locked up in a mental hospital.

**Wickrema :** But don't many more parents live apart from their married children than used to be the case ?

**Dr. Wilson :** True, but this is because many more young families can afford to own their own homes these days than ever before. In other words, parents and their married children usually live in separate households because they prefer it that way, not because the children refuse to have mum and dad living with them.

**Wickrema :** Is this a good thing, do you think ?

**Dr. Wilson :** I think that it's an excellent arrangement. We all like to keep part of our lives private, even from those we love dearly. I certainly don't think that it's a sign of the increased loneliness of old age.

**Wickrema :** Are people's mental abilities affected by old age ?

**Dr. Wilson :** Certain changes do take place as we grow older, but this happens throughout life. These changes are very gradual, and happen at different times with different people. But, in general, if you know a person well in his middle age and have seen how he deals with events and problems, you will easily recognize him in old age.

**Wickrema :** So that someone who enjoys new experiences - travel, education, and so on - in his middle years will usually continue to do so into old age ?

**Dr. Wilson :** Exactly. We have carried out some very interesting experiments in which a group of people aged 60 to 70 and a group aged 30 to 40 had to learn the same things. For example, in one experiment they began learning a new language. In another, they learnt how to use three machines in order to make a piece of furniture. The first thing we discovered was that the young group tended to be quicker at learning than the old group. However, although the old group took longer to learn, eventually they performed as well as the young group. And when we tested the two groups several weeks later, there was again no difference between the two groups.

11. **Dr. Wilson's report on old age hopes to**
    (a) prove that old people are not poor, sick and lonely.
    (b) show that old people, as a group, are unattractive.
    (c) change people's feelings about old age.

12. **Why do many married people nowadays prefer to live apart from their parents ? Because**
    (a) they refuse to have their parents living with them.
    (b) they can afford to run their own homes.
    (c) the family feeling of young people is either dying or dead.

13. **According to Dr. Wilson**
    (a) the proportion of sick people among the 60 to 70 age group is not greater than those among the 50 to 60 age group.
    (b) there is more mental illness among the 60's to 70's.
    (c) it is not wrong to expect that there is more physical illness among old people.

14. **The experiment Dr. Wilson carried out showed that**
    (a) the young group worked better than the old group.
    (b) both the young and the old did equally well at the end.
    (c) the old group was quick to learn from the young group.

15. **Which of the following statements is correct?**
    (a) The loneliness of old people is mainly due to their grown-up children.
    (b) The changes in old age very often take place suddenly.
    (c) What one does in his middle age usually continues into his old age.

**D**

**Fill in the blanks with the most suitable word from those given in brackets.**
වරහන් ඇතුළත ඉතාම සුදුසු වචනය යොදා ඒ ඒ හිස්තැන් පුරවන්න.
அடைப்புக்குள் தரப்பட்டுள்ள சொற்களிலிருந்து மிகப் பொருத்தமான சொல்லை வைத்து வெற்றிடங்கள் நிரப்புக.

Mohan and his uncle were talking about crocodiles. Mohan wanted to know (16)..................... (whether/that/where) crocodiles always live in (17)..................... (Colombo/houses/water). His uncle said that (18).........................(you/he/they) live in water as (19).........................(long/well/high) as on land. He (20).........................(so/also/now) told him that crocodiles (21)......................... (can/will/may) see very clearly under (22)............................... (a/an/the) water even at night. (23) ...............................(She/Mohan/Uncle) asked him where they (24)...............................(lay/eat/ hide) their eggs. His uncle (25)...........................(asked/knew/replied) that the female crocodile lays eggs on land.

[ Turn over.

**E**

**Fill in the blanks with the correct form of the verb given in brackets.**
වරහන් තුළ දී ඇති ක්‍රියා පදයේ නිවැරදි අාකාරය යොදා බිස් තැන් පුරවන්න.
அடைப்புக்குறிக்குள் தரப்பட்டிருக்கும் வினைச்சொல்லின் சரியான வடிவத்தைக் கொண்டு வெற்றிடங்களை நிரப்புக.

26. Our dog does not bite people. It only .................... (bark).
27. The field has to .................... (plough) before the seeds
28. ...................................(sow).
29. Don't worry. I .......................... (bring) the book tomorrow, definitely.
30. I was late for school today as I ....................(wake) up later than I usually
31. ...................................(do).
32. The patient ....................... (take) to the operating theatre when I went to
33. ...........................(see) him.
34. You can see the women ........................... (walk) along the road
35. ........................... (carry) baskets of vegetables on their heads to
36. ...........................(sell) at the fair.
37. You seem to ........................... (get) fatter and fatter. You must not
38. ........................... (eat) too much.
39. Crowns ........................... (stud) with many valuable gems
40. ........................... (wear) by ancient kings.
41. If the key is not in the drawer somebody may ........................... (take) it.
42. I did not know that you ....................... (return) from abroad until your brother
43. ........................... (tell) me yesterday.
44. The repair work on the house ........................... (complete) soon. Now the walls
45. ........................... (colour-wash).

**F**

**Write on ONE of the following using about 200 words.**
පහත දක්වෙන ඒවායින් එකකට වචන 200 කින් පමණ පිළිතුරු සපයන්න.
ஒருக்குறைய 200 சொற்களில் பின்வருவனவற்றுள் ஒன்று பற்றி எழுதுக.

1. **Write an article to a Children's Magazine/Newspaper on "Save Plants that Save Us."**.
   You may include the following :
   (i) The uses of trees.
   (ii) Why trees are cut down.
   (iii) How various organisations, departments, radio and other media encourage tree planting and preservation.
   (iv) Your participation in the National Tree Planting Campaign, 1987.

2. **Write a letter to a pen friend describing some Sri Lankan customs and traditions.**
   You may include the following :
   (i) Sinhala and Tamil New Year customs.
   (ii) Customs relating to happy occasions like weddings, taking up residence in a new house, opening a new building etc.
   (iii) Customs observed by young people in relation to parents, elders and teachers.
   (iv) The importance of preserving traditional customs in modern times.

3. **In July this year the population of the world reached 5 billion. Write on "The Frightening Situation".**
   You may include the following :
   (i) The serious problems created.
   (ii) Possible solutions to control population growth.
   (iii) How scientists can help to solve these problems.
   (iv) Do you think there is hope for a wonderful world in the future ?

4. **Read the following story, taken from a class reader.**
   There was once a foolish king. He reigned over Kekille for several years. One day, he ordered a mason to build a wall round his palace. When it was complete, the king wanted to see how he had made it. When he inspected it, he found that the wall was crooked. So the king was very angry and condemned the mason to death.

   Write a dialogue starting with the conversation between the king and the poor mason and finishing with the king's orders regarding the fattest man.

# APPENDIX 2:
## New Syllabus Examination, 1988

1. GCE O/L ENGLISH (NEW SYLLABUS) - 1988 - QUESTION PAPER

GENERAL CERTIFICATE OF EDUCATION (ORDINARY LEVEL) EXAMINATION,

(NEW SYLLABUS), DECEMBER 1988

---

This paper contains two sheets.

---

INTERNATIONAL LANGUAGE (SECOND LANGUAGE) - ENGLISH : ONE HOUR

Index No: ........................

PAPER I

Answer all the questions on this paper itself.

TURN OVER

- 35 -

(1) Your English teacher asked you to write a few lines about your hobby. You wrote it out but tore it up by mistake. Here are the pieces. Put them in the correct order by writing the correct no. in each cage. The first one has been done for you. (Time: 5 minutes)

(a) I am going to tell you something about my hobby.  ☐ 1

(b) I read all the newspapers that I come across, even paper that has been used for wrapping provisions that we buy at the boutique.  ☐

(c) Then I paste them in a used monitor's exercise book.  ☐

(d) After reading I cut out the interesting news items, articles, children's essays and poems.  ☐

(e) It really is an interesting one.  ☐

(f) Finally I draw pictures alongside the pasted paper cutting to make it look nice.  ☐

(2) Read the following passage and the statements given below. Put a tick ( ) in the box against the correct statements and a cross (X) in the box against the incorrect ones. (Time: 5 minutes)

RHINOCEROS

The rhinoceros lives in Africa and Asia. It is a large, powerful animal with horns. The Indian variety has one horn; its thick skin is in folds. The black and the white rhinoceroses of Africa have two horns.

The rhinoceros eats leaves and grass. Rhinoceroses can be very dangerous. In spite of their size, they can charge at 40 kilometres an hour. They cannot see very well, and depend on their senses of smell and hearing.

| STATEMENTS | TRUE | FALSE |
|---|---|---|
| 1. They depend a lot on their senses of smell and hearing. | | |
| 2. Rhinoceroses are not dangerous animals. | | |
| 3. The colour of the Indian rhinoceros is black and white. | | |
| 4. The Indian rhinoceros has one horn. | | |
| 5. The rhinoceros lives only in Africa. | | |

*Appendix 2*

(3) You are Mr. Sivalingam. Your secretary handed you these messages. Read them and answer the following questions by writing YES or NO in the box provided. (Time: 10 minutes)

---

10.20 a.m.
Mr. Sunil Rajapakse called.
Please call him back before
12.30. T'phone 123456.

---

10.00 a.m.
John Perera called.
Your car is ready and he is
sending it over.

---

9.30 a.m.
Your wife called.
Lunch will be one hour late.

---

10.15 a.m.
Gulf Air Called.
Please call back 54321.

---

10.30 a.m.
Mr. Joe Mendis will come to
see you in your office at 5 p.m.

---

1. Was the first telephone call you received for the day from John Perera?

2. Do you have to go home for lunch?

3. Will you have to make any telephone calls in reply to any of these messages?

4. Can you leave the office at 4.45 p.m. today?

5. Is your car ready?

- 37 -

(4) You have been given some letters to be handed over to the people whose names are on  them. The Managing Director is Mr. Dias, his Secretary is Miss Ramachandran and the Telephone Operator is Mr. de Saram. Look at the envelopes given below. Write how many letters should go to each person, in the boxes provided alongside their names. ( Time: 10 minutes)

Mr. Dias
George Brown & Co.
Colombo 1.

Telephone Operator,
George Brown & Co.
Colombo 1.

The Secretary
George Brown &
Colombo 1.

The Managing Director,
George Brown & Co.
Colombo 1.

Miss Ramachandran
George Brown & Co.
Colombo 1.

Mr. Dias            [      ]

Miss Ramachandran   [      ]

Mr. de Saram        [      ]

*Appendix 2*

(5) After completing your secondary education you want to join the
District Sports Association. Fill in this application form giving
the necessary and relevant information. (Time: 5 minutes)

---

TO BE FILLED COMPLETELY AND CORRECTLY IN BLOCK CAPITAL LETTERS

Name: ...............................................................

Home Address: ......................................................

...........................................................

Age: ...............................................................

Class (in school): ................................................

Favourite Subjects: ...............................................

Name of Teacher in
charge of sports: .................................................

---

(6) Read the following passage. Now rewrite this passage - replacing
'I' with 'He'. (Time: 5 minutes)

---

I make clay pots because I like to create beautiful things for the
home. My pots are works of art. They aren't cheap, but they give
art collectors a lot of pleasure. I earn money by selling these.

---

........................................................................

........................................................................

........................................................................

........................................................................

........................................................................

........................................................................

........................................................................

........................................................................

- 39 -

(7) This is a part of a letter describing a friend. Read it. Now describe one of your own friends. Use the given passage to help you. Do not copy the example given below. Use 50-60 words. (Time: 10 minutes)

My friend's name is John de Silva. He is Sri Lankan. He is a student of Vijaya Maha Vidyalaya. His address is 32, Rani Mawatha, Seeduwa. John is tall and smart. He is a very nice boy.

..................................................................................

................................................................................

..............................................................................

..............................................................................

..............................................................................

..............................................................................

..............................................................................

..............................................................................

..............................................................................

..............................................................................

..............................................................................

..............................................................................

..............................................................................

..............................................................................

..............................................................................

..............................................................................

..............................................................................

..............................................................................

..............................................................................

..............................................................................

..............................................................................

..............................................................................

*Appendix 2*

(8)  You want to send a Money Order for Rs. 200/- to the Registrar of the University of Moratuwa. Fill in the form given below to get the Money Order. (Time: 10 minutes)

---

APPLICATION FOR INLAND ORDINARY MONEY ORDER

Amount Rs. .... Cts. ...

No. ....................
for official use only.

Rupees (in words) ..............................

Payable at .......................................

Name of Payee (with initials) ...................................

Name of Sender (with initials) ...................................

Address of Sender ...........................................

...............................................................

Date: ................        Signature: ................

---

The receipt of the Money Order and a self addressed envelope has to be sent to the University. Write your name and address in the correct place on this envelope.

- 41 -

GENERAL CERTIFICATE OF EDUCATION (ORDINARY LEVEL) EXAMINATION

(NEW SYLLABUS), DECEMBER 1988

This paper contains three sheets

INTERNATIONAL LANGUAGE (SECOND LANGUAGE) - ENGLISH : ONE HOUR

Index No: .....................

PAPER II

Answer all the questions on this paper itself

TURN OVER

(9)  Read the following summaries about 5 books. Now match the summaries with the title of the book. Write the number of the summary against the title. (Time: 10 minutes)

> 1. Good set of stories about different aspects of gang life, with stories by Joan Tate, Shelagh Delaney and Evan Hunter, and others.

> 2. An old parchment discloses a secret passage through a volcano to the centre of the earth. Axel and his Uncle Lidenbrock decide that this is too good an opportunity to miss - though a dangerous one.

> 3. Detective story with a difference. Barney is haunted by someone who is possibly still alive. His mother's family show no surprise and no one will explain what is happening.

> 4. Story of a wolf-dog's life and nature, set in the wilds of Canada. Part of the same story as the same author's White Fang, and like the other novel, is concerned with the ways in which upbringing can influence character.

> 5. Probably the most famous of all Victorian novels about school. Contains the notorious Flashman - perhaps the most loathsome bully in fiction.

a. 'The Haunting' by Margaret Mahy.

b. 'The Call of the Wild' by Jack London.

c. 'Tom Brown's School Days' by Thomas Hughes.

d. 'Gangs and Victims' by John Foster.

e. 'Journey to the Centre of the Earth' by Jules Verne.

(10)  Complete the following text by filling the second half of the word. (Time: 10 minutes)

> KEEPING PETS
>
> If you want to keep a dog, first decide what kind you want. Dogs like a l _____ of exer _____, so i _____ you li _____ in a small apartment o _____ in t _____ centre o _____ a la _____ town, i _____ is prob _____ better n _____ to cho _____ a pu _____ that i _____ likely t _____ grow in _____ a ve _____ large d _____. You c _____ usually te _____ how la _____ a pu _____ is go _____ to gr _____ by t _____ size of its paws. So choose a dog that is going to be the right size for your home.

_ 43 _

(11) Read the following paragraph. Now show whether the following
statements are true or false by placing a tick in the relevant cage.
(Time: 10 minutes)

### HOW LONG CAN MAN GO WITHOUT FOOD?

Most of us feel upset if we skip just one meal, and if we tried
to go without food for 12 hours we would really be uncomfortable.
But there are some people who seem able to 'fast' for very long
periods.

Various records are claimed for long fasts, but in most cases
there is no medical proof and so the records are doubtful. One
South African woman claimed that she lived for 102 days on
nothing but water and soda water.

There are great differences among living things in their ability
to survive without food. For example, a tick which lives on
animals, may survive a whole year without food. Warm blooded
animals use up their stores of food in the body more quickly.

In fact, the smaller and more active the animal, the more quickly
it uses up its reserves. A small bird starves to death in about
five days, a dog in about twenty. In general, we can say that a
warm blooded creature will die when it has lost about half its
normal weight.

This matter of weight is important. Man and other creatures live
in a state of 'metabolic equilibrium', which means maintaining
the body weight once a certain point has been reached. This
regulation of body weight is done by thirst, hunger, and
appetite.

When your blood lacks nutritional materials, this registers in
the hunger centre of the brain and you feel 'hungry'. The body is
crying out for any kind of fuel (food). And it is our appetite
that sees to it that we choose a mixed diet, which is the kind
the body needs.

| STATEMENTS | TRUE | FALSE |
|---|---|---|
| 1. The brain makes you feel hungry. | | |
| 2. A warm blooded animal will die of starvation in ten days. | | |
| 3. Body weight is controlled by the food we take. | | |
| 4. There is a direct relationship between the size of the animal and the speed with which the reserve food is used up. | | |
| 5. There are many proven records which show that people can fast for very long periods. | | |

— 44 —

(12) Write a letter to one of the two people given below giving similar information about yourself using about 100 words. (Time: 15 minutes)

Jean Dubois
23, Rue St. Michelle                                   Age: 1o years
Rouen,
France.

Interests  -  to know about other countries
           -  stamp collecting and music

Miss Alice Gaborone                                    Age: 15 years
22, Village Lane,
Francistown,
Botswana.

Interests  -  flower making,
           -  collecting stamps, picture post cards

..........................................................................
..........................................................................
..........................................................................
..........................................................................
..........................................................................
..........................................................................
..........................................................................
..........................................................................
..........................................................................
..........................................................................
..........................................................................
..........................................................................
..........................................................................
..........................................................................
..........................................................................
..........................................................................
..........................................................................
..........................................................................

(13)  This is a plan for a trip you made during your last school
vacation. Using this information write a description about your trip
for your school magazine. Use about 125 words. (Time: 15 minutes)

| Day | Place | Accommodation | Activities |
|-----|-------|---------------|------------|
| 1 | Hikkaduwa | A friend's house near the sea. | Picnic on the beach. Swimming. Collecting sea shells. |
| 2 | Tissamaharama | Pligrims' Rest | Visit the Tissa Temple. Offer flowers. |
| 3 | Kataragama | Pilgrims' Rest | Bathe in the river. Visit the 'Devala'. Give alms to poor people. |
| 4 | Return | | |

Start this way :

During the last school vacation I went ...........................

...................................................................

...................................................................

...................................................................

...................................................................

...................................................................

...................................................................

...................................................................

...................................................................

...................................................................

...................................................................

...................................................................

...................................................................

...................................................................

...................................................................

...................................................................

...................................................................

*Appendix 2*

(14) Read the following text which has some words missing in it. Then complete the text by writing the appropriate word in the blank. The words are given at the bottom of the text in alphabetical order. (Time: 15 minutes)

WHY DOES THE BODY NEED WATER?

About o0 per cent of the human body is water. If you could squeeze out a human being like squeezing out a dish cloth , you would obtain about 11 gallons of water. This water, which is not _____ ordinary water because of the _____ it contains, is necessary to _____ life of the body. _____ a gallon of it is _____ the blood vessels and is _____ circulating by the heart. This _____ water bathes all the cells _____ the body in a constant _____. The water also acts as a _____ of heat through the body.

_____ if you take in no water _____ a day, you consume _____ a quart of water _____ the solid foods you eat. _____ when you eat fruit, vegetables, bread, _____ meat, you are getting water _____ they are from 30 to 90 _____ water. In addition, the average person _____ in about two quarts of _____ as fluids.

In the course of a single day, about ten quarts of water pass back and forth inside the body between the various organs. For example, when you chew something and swallow it, you suck some saliva from the salivary glands and swallow it.

| | | | |
|---|---|---|---|
| about | during | like | substances |
| about | even | of | takes |
| and | from | percent | the |
| because | in | so | vital |
| conductor | kept | stream | water |

306

(15) This is an article on weather. The paragraphs are not in order.
Read them and number them from 1-o in the correct order. The
first one has been done for you. (Time: 15 minutes)

What is the weather anyway? It is simply what the air or
atmosphere is like at any time. No matter whether the air
is cold, cool, warm, hot, calm, breezy, windy, dry,
moist, or wet - that's weather.  [ 1 ]

Weather may be any combination of different amounts
of heat, moisture, and motion in the air. And it changes
from hour to hour, day to day, season to season, and
even from year to year.  [   ]

Humidity, the amount of water vapour in the air, combined
with the temperature, causes many weather conditions.
Clouds are a kind of weather condition, and they are
formed when water vapour condenses high above the ground.  [   ]

The most important 'cause' of weather is the heating and
cooling of the air. Heat causes the winds as well as the
different ways in which water vapour appears in the
atmosphere.  [   ]

The daily changes are caused by storms and fair weather
moving over the earth. The seasonal changes are due to
the turning of the earth around the sun. Why weather
changes from year to year is still not known, however.  [   ]

When the cloud droplets grow larger and become too heavy
to be held up by the air currents, they fall to the
ground and we have the weather known as rain. If the
rain droplets fall through a layer of air which is below
freezing, the droplets freeze and fall as hail or snow.  [   ]

*Appendix 2*

(16) Your class is hoping to collect some food, clothes and toys to be distributed to the patients in the children's wards in the local hospital.

As organiser of this event write a short report to be presented at a meeting of the Social Service Association of your school. Use about 250 words. (Time: 30 minutes)

You may include these facts or other ideas of your own:-

- the date and time of distribution
- details of what you hope to collect
- how you hope to collect these items
- storing and transporting what is collected
- distribution

........................................................................
........................................................................
........................................................................
........................................................................
........................................................................
........................................................................
........................................................................
........................................................................
........................................................................
........................................................................
........................................................................
........................................................................
........................................................................
........................................................................
........................................................................
........................................................................
........................................................................
........................................................................
........................................................................
........................................................................
........................................................................
........................................................................

_ 51 _

2. PROFICIENCY BANDINGS FOR MARKING WRITING

GCE O/L ENGLISH (NEW SYLLABUS) 1988

- 52 -

QUESTION NO. 5

| BAND NUMBER | CRITERIA |
|---|---|
| (5) | - Completes form giving all relevant information<br>- Writes legibly using block capitals and correct spelling |
| (4) | - Completes form giving all relevant information<br>- Writes legibly using block capitals |
| (3) | - Completes form giving most of the relevant information<br>- Writes legibly not using block capitals |
| (2) | - Some relevant information is given<br>- Writes legibly not using block capitals |
| (1) | - Almost no information is given<br>- If information is given it is irrelevant and/or illegible |
| NA | Produces no writing at all. |
| QC | The question is copied. |

QUESTION NO. 6

| BAND NUMBER | CRITERIA |
|---|---|
| (5) | - Writes in the third person singular using the present tense<br>- No errors in structure, vocabulary or spelling<br>- All relevant information is included |
| (4) | - Writes in the third person singular using the present tense<br>- A few errors in structure, vocabulary or spelling<br>- All relevant information is included |
| (3) | - Writes in the third person singular using the present tense<br>- Some errors in structure, vocabulary and spelling<br>- Some relevant information is included |
| (2) | - Writes in the third person singular using the present tense.<br>- Many errors in structure, vocabulary and spelling<br>- Most information is irrelevant |
| (1) | - Is unable to write in the third person singular using present tense |
| NA | Produces no writing at all. |
| QC | The question is copied. |

- 53 -

QUESTION NO. 7

| NUMBER | CRITERIA |

(5)     - Describes a friend using appropriate language
      - Supplies relevant information
      - Uses correct language, spelling and appropriate
       vocabulary

(4)     - Describes a friend using appropriate language
      - Supplies most of the relevant information
      - Uses correct language, spelling and appropriate
       vocabulary with a very few mistakes

(3)     - Describes a friend
      - Supplies some relevant information .
      - Some errors in language and spelling and
       vocabulary not appropriate

(2)     - Describes a friend
      - Supplies hardly any relevant information
      - Many errors in structure, spelling and vocabulary.

(1)     - Does not describe a friend
      - No relevant information

NA       Produces no writing at all.
QC       The question is copied.

QUESTION NO. 8

In using the writing proficiency bandings in marking this item ignore name of payee.

| BAND NUMBER | CRITERIA |

(5)     - Supplies all relevant information
      - Uses correct vocabulary and spelling with
       almost no errors

(4)     - Supplies almost all relevant information
      - Shows weakness in vocabulary and spelling

(3)     - Supplies part of the information and it is
       relevant
      - Makes some errors in vocabulary and spelling

(2)     - Most information supplied is irrelevant
      - Makes many errors in vocabulary and spelling

(1)     - Almost no information given
      - Given information is irrelevant or writing
       illegible

NA       Produces no writing at all.
QC       The question is copied.

- 54 -

QUESTION NO. 12

| BAND NUMBER | CRITERIA |
|---|---|

(5)
- Writes a letter to one of the two people named
- Language used is effective
- All relevant information is given
- Uses the correct format
- Almost no errors in structure, vocabulary and spelling.

(4)
- Writes a letter to one of the two people named
- Language used is mostly effective
- All relevant information is given
- Uses the correct format
- A few mistakes in structure, vocabulary and spelling.

(3)
- Writes a letter to one of the two people named
- Language used is not very effective
- All relevant information is not given
- Some errors in format
- Some mistakes in structure, vocabulary and spelling.

(2)
- Writes a letter to a friend
- Does not use effective language
- Almost no relevant information is given
- Many errors in format
- Many mistakes in structure, vocabulary and spelling.

(1)
- Does not write a letter giving information
- Totally irrelevant information is given
- Writing is illegible

NA      Produces no writing at all.
QC      The question is copied.

- 55 -

QUESTION NO. 13

BAND NUMBER            CRITERIA

(5)
- Writes effectively describing the sequence of events given
- Uses appropriate language
- Uses the past tense with almost no errors in structure, vocabulary and spelling
- All information is included and is relevant
- Organises facts in sequential order

(4)
- Writes describing the sequence of events
- Uses appropriate language
- Uses the past tense with a few mistakes in structure, vocabulary and spelling
- All information is included and is relevant
- Organises facts in sequential order.

(3)
- Writes describing the sequence of events
- Language used is not very appropriate
- Uses the past tense, with some mistakes in structure, vocabulary and spelling
- All information is not included
- Some attempt is made to organise facts in sequential order.

(2)
- Some attempt is made at describing the sequence of events
- Does not use the past tense OR if the past tense is used many mistakes in grammar, vocabulary and spelling
- Almost no information is included
- No attempt is made at organising facts

(1)
- Does not write describing the sequence of events
- Totally irrelevant information is given
- Writing is illegible

NA          Produces no writing at all.
QC          The question is copied.

*Appendix 2*

QUESTION NO. 16

In using the writing proficiency bandings in marking this item, do not take format into account.

BAND NUMBER                    CRITERIA

(5)          - Writes a report very effectively using
               appropriate language
             - All information presented is relevant
             - Organises facts systematically
             - Almost no errors in structure, vocabulary and
               spelling

(4)          - Writes a report rather effectively using
               appropriate language
             - Almost all information presented is relevant
             - Organises facts systematically
             - A few errors in structure, vocabulary and
               spelling.

(3)          - Writes a report but not very effectively
             - Some facts presented are not relevant
             - Some attempt is made to organise facts
             - Some errors in structure, vocabulary and
               spelling.

(2)          - Attempts to write a report, but with many errors
               in structure, vocabulary and spelling
             - Does not organise facts
             - Almost all facts are irrelevant

(1)          - Cannot write a report
             - writing is illegible
             - Totally irrelevant

NA             Produces no language at all.
QC             The question is copied.

# APPENDIX 3:
## Observation schedule, Sri Lankan O level Evaluation Project – Impact Study, Round 6

SRI LANKAN O-LEVEL EVALUATION PROJECT:

IMPACT STUDY

ROUND 6 OBSERVATION/INTERVIEW SCHEDULE

SECTION 1: DETAILS OF SETTING

1. Date of the observation ...........................

2. Name of school .....................................

   Province ................. Division ...................

   District ................. Town/Village...............

3. Name of teacher .....................................

4a. Did you observe this teacher in Round 4?

   (Please tick one.)                    Yes ........ .
                                         No .........

4b. Was the teacher teaching the same group or a different
    group?

                                         Same .....

                                         Different ......

5. If you are not able to observe the same teacher as in
   Round 5, please indicate why. (Please tick one.)

       Original teacher has retired        ...........

       Original teacher has transferred
       to another school                   ...........

       Original teacher no longer
       teaches Year 11 classes             ...........

       This is the first time I have
       visited this school                 ............

       Some other reason:                  ...........
          (Please indicate below.)

315

- 2 -

## SECTION 2:  PRE-OBSERVATION INTERVIEW

## DETAILS OF THE GROUP YOU ARE GOING TO OBSERVE

**OBSERVER:**  Please request a Year 11 class if possible.  Ask the teacher these questions <u>before</u> you observe the class.

6.  What year is the group you are observing?
    (Please tick one.)

    Year 10  .........
    Year 11  .........

☐ *10*

7.  How have pupils been assigned to this group?
    (Please tick one.)

    Random assignment to this class  ...........

    Assigned to this class because
    of <u>overall</u> academic ability  ...........

    Assigned to this class because
    of particular ability in <u>English</u>  ..........

    Other  (Please specify.)  ...................

☐ *11*

8.  If pupils have been assigned to this group on the basis
    of their overall ability, how does <u>the teacher</u> describe
    their ability?

    High  ..........
    Average  ..........
    Low  ..........

☐ *12*

9.  If pupils have been assigned to this group on the basis
    of their English ability, how does <u>the teacher</u> describe
    their ability?

    High  ..........
    Average  ...........
    Low  ...........

☐ *13*

10.  How many pupils are enrolled in this class?  ........

☐☐ *14 15*

11.  How many pupils are attending the class today?  .......

☐☐ *16 17*

- 3 -

## DETAILS OF THE LESSON YOU ARE GOING TO OBSERVE

**OBSERVER:** Please ask the teacher these questions <u>before</u> you observe the lesson.

L

12. Will you be using EED in your lesson today?
    (Please tick one.)

    Yes ..........
    No ..........  [18]

13. If yes: .

    Which book will you be using?  ..............  [14 20]

    Which unit will you be using?  ..............  [21]

    Which exercise will you be  ..............
    working on?  [22 23]

    What page is it on?  ..............

14. If no:  What material will you be using?

    a.  Teacher-designed material.  ..............  [24]

        Describe the material:

        ..............................
        ..............................  [25 26]
        ..............................

    b.  The 'Guidelines' book  ..............  [27]

        Which page?  ..............  [28 29 30 31]

    c.  The 'Suggestions' book  ..............  [32]

        Which page?  ..............  [33 34 35 36]

    d.  The 'Pupil Support' book  ..............  [37]

        Which page?  ..............  [38 39 40 41]

    e.  Past examination papers  ..............  [42]

        Which year?  ..............  [43 44]

        Which question?  ..........  [45 46 47 48]

- 4 -

f.  Commercially-published materials  ..............  ☐
    49

    Which publication?

    ...................................  ☐☐
                                         50 51
    Describe the material:

    ...................................  ☐☐
    ...................................  52 53
    ...................................

15. Which of these descriptions best fits the teaching
    you are planning to do today?

        'Ordinary classroom teaching'  ..............  ☐
                                                       54
        'Exam preparation'  ................

16. What are your objectives for today's lesson?

    ...................................  ☐☐
    ...................................  55 56
    ...................................
    ...................................
    ...................................

17. What skill/s will you be focussing on?

    ...................................  ☐☐
    ...................................  57 58
    ...................................

## SECTION THREE:  OBSERVATION SCHEDULE

**OBSERVER:**  Please answer the following questions **after you
have taken a seat down the side of the class.**.

18. If the teacher is basing the lesson on EED,
    are any instructions given in the TG for
    the exercise he/she intends to use?                ☐
                                                       59
                                    Yes .......
                                    No .......

  b.  If so, what page are they on?    ...........

- 5 -

c. If there are no instructions in the TG,
   are there any instructions in the PT
   for this exercise?
   
   Yes ........
   No ........

**60**

## DESCRIPTION OF THE LESSON

**OBSERVER:** Please answer Questions 19 - 26 <u>during</u> the lesson.

19. DETAILED DESCRIPTION

   Please give a detailed description of the lesson as you are observing
   it.  Follow the model which is given to you in your instruction pack
   in Round 3, and give an indication of <u>the timing of each section</u>

   (Please use the reverse side of this sheet as well.)

**61**

**62**

**63 64**

**65 66**

- 6 -

(Please continue with description of the class.)

- 7 -

## 20. TEXT TYPES (for reading activities only

Please place a tick by the text types that you have observed in today's lesson:

_____  1. Accounts of events or experiences - e.g. diary entries, newspaper articles

_____  2. Addresses

_____  3. Advertisements

_____  4. Announcements - e.g. change of address

_____  5. 'Blurbs' - a short text used for publicity purposes. e.g a summary of a book printed on the back cover, a quote from a critic printed in an advert for a film

_____  6. Catalogues

_____  7. Contents pages or indices

_____  8. Forms - e.g. application for a passport. application to join a club

_____  9. Informative academic or semi-academic text - e.g. excerpts from encyclopedia, textbooks, first aid books

_____  10. Instructions

_____  11. Letters - formal or official

_____  12. Letters - informal

_____  13. Literary prose - e.g. folk tales, short stories

_____  14. Maps

_____  15. Menus

67 68

69 70

71 72

# Appendix 3

____ 16. Messages

____ 17. Non-linear text – e.g. graphs, bar charts, timetables, histograms

____ 18. Notes – key words representing fuller ideas

____ 19. Passages containing argumentive or persuasive writing

____ 20. Passages containing descriptions – of people, places, things

____ 21. Poems

____ 22. Postcards

____ 23. Posters

____ 24. Price lists – tariffs

____ 25. Public notices

____ 26. Questionnaires

____ 27. Recipes

____ 28. Reports – e.g. to a committee, to a superior

____ 29. Rules

____ 30. Single sentences, for grammatical exercises

____ 31. Single sentences, to match with pictures or symbols

____ 32. Telegrams

____ 33. Other:  Please describe below.

- 9 -

## 21. READING ACTIVITIES:
### WHAT DID THE STUDENTS DO?

Please place a tick by the reading activities that have taken place in today's lesson.

_____ 1. Arranging paragraphs in the correct order to form a coherent text

_____ 2. Arranging sentences in the correct order to form a coherent paragraph

_____ 3. Gap-filling (also known as 'cloze')

_____ 4. Identifying parts of a diagram

_____ 5. Interpreting graphically-displayed information - pie-charts, bar charts

_____ 6. Matching texts - e.g. matching summaries with titles of books, short articles with headlines

_____ 7. Matching text with visuals - e.g. matching warning with road symbols, matching captions with pictures

_____ 8. Multiple-choice questions: directly stated info (scanning)

_____ 9. Multiple-choice questions: indirectly stated information e.g. inference, problem-solving, interpretation

_____ 10. Skimming to get the main idea of a text

_____ 11. Transferring information from a passage to a chart, table or other visual form

_____ 12. True/false or yes/no questions: directly stated information (scanning)

_____ 13. True/false or yes/no questions: indirectly stated information e.g. inference, problem-solving, interpretation

_____ 14. Word-completion: filling in the second half of words

_____ 15. Writing long answers - directly stated information (scanning)

_____ 16. Writing long answers - indirectly stated information e.g. inference, problem-solving, interpretation

_____ 17. Writing short answers: directly stated information (scanning)

_____ 18. Writing short answers: indirectly stated information e.g. inference, problem-solving, interpretation

_____ 19. Other: Please describe below.

73 74

75 76

77 78

Appendix 3

22.    **WRITING ACTIVITIES:**
       **WHAT DID THE STUDENTS DO**

____  1.  Fill in forms or questionnaires

____  2.  Transfer information from a chart, table etc.
          into writing

____  3.  Write accounts of events or experiences - e.g.
          newspaper articles, diary entries

____  4.  Write an advertisement

____  5.  Write an announcement - e.g. change of address

____  6.  Write argumentative or persuasive texts

____  7.  Write a 'composition' on a given topic

____  8.  Write comments on literary extracts

____  9.  Write a description of a person, place, thing

____  10. Write a formal or official letter - e.g. applying for a job

____  11. Write an informal letter - e.g. writing to a pen friend

____  12. Write an invitation (or accepting or declining one)

____  13. Write instructions

____  14. Write a message - from a telephone conversation, to leave
          on a friend's door

____  15. Write notes - key words that represent full ideas
          e.g. notes from a textbook chapter

____  16. Write a postcard

____  17. Write a poster or public notice

____  18. Write a recipe

____  19. Write a report of an event or series of events

____  20. Write rules

____  21. Write a summary

____  22. Write a talk to be presented orally

____  23. Write a telegram

____  24. Other: Please describe below.

ROW 2:

| 1 | 2 |
|---|---|

| 3 | 4 |
|---|---|

| 5 | 6 |
|---|---|

- 11 -

### 23. LANGUAGE EXERCISES: GRAMMAR/VOCAB/COHESION

____ 1. Fill in blanks with the correct grammatical form

____ 2. Grammatical transformation, single sentences
  e.g. changing 'I' to 'he'
  changing past to future
  changing affirmative to negative

____ 3. Grammatical transformation, full text

____ 4. Guess the meaning of unknown words

____ 5. Cohesion exercises - to understand how parts of a text are connected   e.g. using connectors, pronouns

____ 6. Other: Please describe below.

### 24. OTHER EXAM-RELATED ACTIVITIES

____ 1. Teacher tells students that a certain text-type has been or will be on the exam

____ 2. Teacher tells students that a certain activity has been or will be on the exam

____ 3. Teacher tells students that a certain skill is important for the exam

____ 4. Teacher tells students that a certain set of instructions has been or will be on the exam.

____ 5. Teacher explains how writing has been or will be marked on the exam

____ 6. Teacher gives hints on 'examination skills' -
  e.g. students should time themselves
  they should attack all questions
  they should 'write something' for each writing task so that they will get at least a Band 1

____ 7. Teacher gets students to reflect on their own strengths and weakness vis-a-vis exam requirements

____ 8. Other: Please describe below.

- 12 -

## LISTENING/SPEAKING ACTIVITIES

25a. Did the students listen to any English in this lesson?

Yes ........

No ........

19

b. If yes, please describe what they listened to.

.......................................................

.......................................................

.......................................................

20 21   22 23

26a. Did the students speak any English in this lesson?

Yes ..........

No ..........

24

b. If yes, please describe the type of speaking they did.

.......................................................

.......................................................

.......................................................

25 26   27 28

- 13 -

# SECTION 4:   POST-OBSERVATION INTERVIEW

OBSERVER:  Ask the teacher to give you 30 minutes after the lesson and ask these questions.  Do not record your own thoughts here — there will be another place for these later in the form.

27.  Why did you choose this particular material to teach today?

........................................................

........................................................

........................................................

29 30 31 32 33 34

28.  If you were using material from an EED lesson, did you follow the guidelines provided in the TG or PT?

Yes .........
No .........
No guidelines provided .........

35

29a. If you did not follow the guidelines fully, could you please explain why you did not follow them?

(OBSERVERS:  Please probe here.  If the teacher says the guidelines were not suitable, find out why they were not suitable and why the teacher's own techniques were more suitable.)

........................................................

........................................................

........................................................

........................................................

........................................................

........................................................

36 37 38 39 40 41

29b. If there were no guidelines to follow, could you please explain why you taught the way you did?

........................................................

........................................................

........................................................

........................................................

........................................................

........................................................

........................................................

........................................................

42 43 44 45 46 47

- 14 -

## IMPACT OF THE EXAMINATION

30a. Has the new-style English O-Level influenced the way you
    chose the <u>content</u> of your Year 11 lessons - i.e. the topics
    you deal with, the material you use. For example, do you
    pay more attention to some parts of the text rather than
    others? Do you emphasise any particular text types.

Yes ........<br>
No ........<br>
I cannot tell ........

☐ 48

b. If yes, how?

   (OBSERVERS: Please probe. Do not be content with
   'I teach similar content.')

   ..........................................................
   ..........................................................
   ..........................................................
   ..........................................................
   ..........................................................

⊞⊞⊞⊞⊞ 49 50 51 52 53 54

c. If not, why not?

   ..........................................................
   ..........................................................
   ..........................................................

⊞⊞⊞⊞⊞ 55 56 57 58 59 60

d. If you cannot tell, why can't you?

   ..........................................................
   ..........................................................
   ..........................................................

⊞⊞⊞⊞⊞ 61 62 63 64 65 66

31a. Has it influenced the <u>methodology</u> that you use with your Year 11
    English classes - i.e. the techniques or activities that you use?
    For example, do you emphasise certain skills more than others?
    Has the exam affected the way you teach any of the skills?

   (OBSERVERS: Please probe here. Do not be content with
   'I use similar techniques'.)

Yes ........<br>
No ........<br>
I cannot tell ........

☐ 67

- 15 -

b. If yes, how?

.............................................................
.............................................................
.............................................................

68 69 10 11 12 73

c. If not, why not?

.............................................................
.............................................................
.............................................................

74 75 76 77 78 79

d. If you cannot tell, why can't you?

.............................................................
.............................................................
.............................................................

ROW 3:

1 2 3 4 5 6

32. Who prepares the following tests in your geographical area – you or the local education office? (Please tick the appropriate column.)

| | The teacher | The local education office | We do not give this kind of test |
|---|---|---|---|
| Monthly tests | | | |
| Term tests | | | |
| Mid-year tests | | | |
| End-of-year tests | | | |
| Other tests (Please specify.) | | | |

7
8
9
10
11

33a. If you prepare tests for your students, has the new-style O-Level exam influenced the way that you design the tests?

Yes ........
No ........
I cannot tell ........

12

329

- 16 -

b.  If yes, how?

(OBSERVERS:  Please probe.  Do not be content with 'I write
similar items'.  Find out what kind of items.)

.............................................................
.............................................................
.............................................................
.............................................................
.............................................................

```
┌──┬──┬──┬──┬──┬──┐
│  │  │  │  │  │  │
└──┴──┴──┴──┴──┴──┘
13  14  15  16  17  18
```

c.  If not, why not?

.............................................................
.............................................................
.............................................................

```
┌──┬──┬──┬──┬──┬──┐
│  │  │  │  │  │  │
└──┴──┴──┴──┴──┴──┘
19  20  21  22  23  24
```

d.  If you cannot tell, why can't you?

.............................................................
.............................................................
.............................................................

```
┌──┬──┬──┬──┬──┬──┐
│  │  │  │  │  │  │
└──┴──┴──┴──┴──┴──┘
25  26  27  28  29  30
```

- 17 -

**34a.** Has the new-style O-Level influenced the way <u>you mark your</u>
<u>students' tests</u>?

Yes ........
No ........
I cannot tell ........

31

**b.** If so, how?

(OBSERVERS: Please probe here. Teachers may say that they now
use 'criteria' or that they mark as the exam markers mark. If
they use this term, press them to tell you <u>which</u> criteria they
use.)

..................................................
..................................................
..................................................
..................................................
..................................................

32 33 34 35 36 37

**c.** If not, why not?

..................................................
..................................................
..................................................

38 39 40 41 42 43

**d.** If you cannot tell, why can't you?

..................................................
..................................................
..................................................

44 45 46 47 48 49

**35.** Have you seen a copy of the 1990 English O Level paper
(New Syllabus)?

Yes ........
No ........

50

**36.** If yes, how did you get access to it?

..................................................
..................................................

51 52

- 18 -

37. Have you seen a copy of the 1989 English O-Level paper (New Syllabus)?

Yes ........
No ........

53

38. If yes, how did you get access to it?

..................................................................
..................................................................
..................................................................

54 55

39. Do you have a copy or do you have access to a copy of the following publications? Have you used them in your teaching?

| | I have a copy | I have access to a copy | I have used this publica- tion in my teaching |
|---|---|---|---|
| a. TG - Year 7 | | | |
| b. TG - Year 8 | | | |
| c. TG - Year 9 | | | |
| d. TG - Yr 10/11 | | | |
| e. The 'Guidelines' book (1988) | | | |
| f. The 'Suggestions' book (1989) | | | |
| g. The 'Pupil Support' book (1990) | No | | |

56 57 58
59 60 61
62 63 64
65 66 67
68 69 70
71 72 73
74 75 76

40a. Have you attended any seminars to learn how to teach EED?

Yes ........
No ........

77

b. If yes, for how many days all together?

...................................................................

78 79

- 19 -

41a. Have you attended any seminars to learn about the new-style
O-Level English exam? (OBSERVERS: Please note that this
does not include examiner training.)

Yes ........
No ........

80

If so, for how many days all together?

..............................................................

ROW 4:

1  2

42. Have you been a marker for the new-style English exam?

| | | |
|---|---|---|
| 1988 | Yes ... | No... |
| 1989 | Yes .... | No... |
| 1990 | Yes .... | No.... |

5

- 20 -

43a. Do you have any comments to make about the EED textbook series?

Yes ........
No ........

☐
6

b. Put your comments here:

.................................................
.................................................
.................................................
.................................................
.................................................
.................................................
.................................................

⊞⊞⊞⊞
7  8  9  10 11  12

44a. Do you have any comments to make about the new-style O-Level English exam?

Yes .........
No .........

☐
13

b. Put your comments here.

.................................................
.................................................
.................................................
.................................................
.................................................
.................................................

⊞⊞⊞⊞⊞
14 15 16 17 18 19

45. What unit have you reached in the EED series?

Book .........
Unit .........

⊞⊞⊞
20 21 22 23

46a. Do you use any commercial publications in addition to EED?

Yes .........
No .........

☐
24

b. If yes, which ones do you use?

.................................................
.................................................
.................................................
.................................................
.................................................

⊞⊞⊞⊞⊞
25 26 27 28 29 3-

- 21 -

c. Why do you use them?

> (OBSERVERS:  Please probe.  If teachers says 'For further practice', please find out what kind of practice.)

.........................................................
.........................................................
.........................................................

31 32 33 34 35 36

47a. Are you doing anything special <u>this term</u>to prepare your students for the examination?

Yes ..,......
No ........

37

b. If yes, what sorts of things are you doing?

> (OBSERVERS:  Please probe here.  Do not be content with 'I give them model papers' or 'I practise similar questions'.)

.........................................................
.........................................................
.........................................................

38 39 40 41 42 43

c. How frequently do you do these things?

.........................................................
.........................................................
.........................................................

44 45

d. If you are not doing exam preparation yet, when will you start?

.........................................................
.........................................................
.........................................................

46 47

e. When you start, what sorts of things will you be doing

.........................................................
.........................................................
.........................................................
.........................................................
.........................................................

48 49 50 51 52 53

- 22 -

f. How frequently will you do these things?

......................................................
......................................................
......................................................
......................................................
......................................................

54 55

48. What kind of training did you receive to be an English language teacher - e.g. DELIC, PRINSETT, teacher training college.

......................................................
......................................................
......................................................

56 57

49. How many years have you been teaching English?

.......... years

58 59

## REQUEST FOR TEST PAPERS

50. Could you please lend me a copy of 2 or 3 of the tests that your students have taken since the beginning of this academic year. I will return them to you if you want them back.

Yes ___
No ___

60

OBSERVER: Please list here the papers the teacher gave you. Label them so that we know which school they came, and say who wrote the tests.

......................................................
......................................................
......................................................
......................................................
......................................................
......................................................

- 23 -

## REFLECTIONS

**OBSERVER:** Please fill in the remaining questions after you have returned home and have had some time to think about what you observed today.

51.  EVALUATION OF THE LESSON

   a.  In your view, was this an effective lesson?

$$\text{Yes} \dots\dots$$
$$\text{No} \dots\dots$$
$$\text{I cannot tell} \dots\dots$$

61

   b.  If yes, how?

   ..........................................................
   ..........................................................
   ..........................................................

62 63 64 65

66 67

   c.  If not, why not?

   ..........................................................
   ..........................................................
   ..........................................................

68 69 70 71

72 73

   d.  If you cannot tell, why can't you?

   ..........................................................
   ..........................................................
   ..........................................................

74 75 76 77

78 79

## IMPACT OF THE EED SERIES ON THIS LESSON

52.  If this lesson was supposed to be based on EED, which of the following statements best describes the lesson? (Please tick one.)

80

   ____  a.  The lesson matched the instruction in the TG or PT.

   ____  b.  The lesson basically matched the instructions in the TG or PT, but there were a few few insignificant changes.

   ____  c.  The lesson differed greatly from the instructions in the TG or PT.

- 24 -

    d. There were no instructions in the TG or PT, but the
lesson seemed in line with the 'EED way of teaching'
as described in earlier TGs.

    e. There were no instructions in the TG or PT. The lesson
did not seem in line with the EED way of teaching as
described in earlier TGs.

    f. There were no instructions in the TG or PT, and previous
TGs do not give guidance on this kind of activity.

53. If the teacher did not follow the instructions or 'the EED way of
teaching', how did the lesson differ from the way it should have
looked?

.........................................................
.........................................................
.........................................................
.........................................................
.........................................................
.........................................................

Row 5:

1  2

3  4

5  6

## IMPACT OF THE EXAMINATION ON THIS LESSON

54a. Did this lesson show the influence of the new-style English
O-Level examination?

Which of the following statements best describes the situation?

    (OBSERVERS: Please note that there is a new category here -
letter c.)

For lessons based on EED

7

    a. The exam may be having an impact on this lesson: The
teacher has followed EED guidance and this matches
what is seen in past exam papers or exam-support materials.

    b. The exam may be having an impact on this lesson: The
teacher did not follow EED guidance but changed the
activity so that it more closely matched what is seen
in past exam papers or exam-support materials.

- 25 -

_____ c. The exam may be having an impact on this lesson. The teacher did not follow EED guidance but the activity had some relation (even though slight) to the exam.

_____ d. The exam may not be having an impact on this class: The teacher followed EED guidance but this did not match what is seen in past exam papers or exam-support materials.

_____ e. The exam may not be having an impact on this class: The teacher did not follow EED guidance and the activity did not match what is seen in past exam papers or exam-support material.

For lessons not based on EED

_____ e. The exam may be having an impact on this class: The activity matched what is seen in past exam papers or exam-support materials.

_____ f. The exam may not be having an impact on this class: The activity did not match what is seen in past exam papers or exam-support materials.

54b. If you have comments to make about whether the teaching matched the exam or not, please enter them in this space:

```
.............................................................
.............................................................
.............................................................
.............................................................
.............................................................
.............................................................
.............................................................
.............................................................
```

8 9

- 26 -

## OBSERVER'S OPINION OF THE SITUATION

55. Please comment on each of the following statements by circling
either 'Yes', 'No'.  If you cannot tell, circle the '?'.

### Concerning the teaching

a.   The teacher seems to be qualified to teach Year 11 English          YES   NO   ?

b.   The teacher seems to understand 'the EED way of teaching',
as developed in earlier TGs                                         YES   NO   ?

c.   The teacher seems to be in command of communicative techniques      YES   NO   ?

d.   The teacher's own English is adequate to teach Year 11              YES   NO   ?

e.   The teacher seems to have prepared properly                         YES   NO   ?

f.   The teacher seems to have achieved the objectives he/she
set out with.                                                       YES   NO   ?

g.   Most of the pupils showed a positive attitude toward the
lesson.                                                             YES   NO   ?

h.   About half the pupils showed a positive attitude toward
the lesson.                                                         YES   NO   ?

i.   Only a few pupils showed a positive attitude toward the lesson.     YES   NO   ?

j.   Other - Please indicate below.

..........................................................
..........................................................
..........................................................

### Concerning the textbook

k.   There are enough copies of the textbook to go around               YES   NO   ?

l.   The content of this lesson is within the pupils'
realm of experience (i.e. not alien)                               YES   NO   **?**

m.   The content of this lesson is interesting to the pupils
(at least potentially).                                            YES   NO   ?

n.   The content of this lesson the right level of difficulty
for this group of pupils.                                          YES   NO   ?

– 27 –

o,   Other – Please indicate below.

..................................................................
..................................................................
..................................................................

Concerning the teaching/learning environment

p,   Classroom conditions are favourable to language learning.     YES   NO   ?
     If not, state why. (e.g. crowded, noisy, dark)

..................................................................
..................................................................
..................................................................

q,   Pupils' earlier English training seems to be adequate.        YES   NO   ?

r,   Other – Please indicate below.

..................................................................
..................................................................
..................................................................

## FINAL STATEMENT

56.  OBSERVER:  Do you have any other information to add which will help us
     to decide whether the new exam is having any impact on this class?

If you do, please write it below.

..................................................................
..................................................................
..................................................................
..................................................................
..................................................................
..................................................................

# APPENDIX 4:

## Summary of results from observations, Sri Lankan O level Evaluation Project – Impact Study, Rounds 1–6 (excluding Round 3*)

| | Round 1 | Round 2 | Round 4 | Round 5 | Round 6 |
|---|---|---|---|---|---|
| Dates | mid-May to mid-June 1990<br><br>1-2 months after 1989 exam<br>6-7 months before 1990 exam | 1 September to mid-October 1990<br><br>4-5 months after 1989 exam<br>2-3 months before 1990 exam | mid-March to 1 April 1991<br><br>3 months after 1990 exam<br>8 months before 1991 exam | mid-June to mid-July 1991<br><br>6 months after 1990 exam<br>6 months before 1991 exam | 21 October to mid-November 1991<br><br>4-6 weeks before 1991 exam |
| Number of schools visited | 49 (42 Year 11 classes) | 49 (42) | 39 (39) | 65 (64) | 42 (41) |
| % of teachers using *English Every Day* (*EED*) during observation | 81% | 67% | 90% (1/3 using Year 10 book, 2/3 using Year 11 book) | 75% (10% using Year 10 book, 90% using Year 11 book) | 36% (92% in Year 11 book) |
| Intended focus of *EED* lessons | Reading (R) - 38%<br>Speaking (S) - 26%<br>Writing (W) - 15%<br><br>but speaking lessons involved other skills more than speaking | R - 40%<br>W - 40%<br>S - 22%<br>L - 15%<br><br>but little free speaking actually taking place | R - 42%<br>W - 33%<br>S - 13%<br>L - 6%<br>G - 6% | R - 52%<br>W - 17%<br>S - 21%<br>L - 5%<br>G - 10% | R - 58%<br>W - 16%<br>S - 21%<br>L - 0 |
| Did teachers follow *EED* content? | 60% made no changes. 40% added comprehension questions. | 60% made no changes. 30% added comprehension questions. | 63% made no changes. The remainder added comprehension questions, tasks or explanations. | 50% made no changes. The remainder added comprehension questions. | 98% made no changes. |
| Did teachers follow *EED* methodology? | 25% did. The remaining classes were teacher-centred, lockstep, with detailed analyses of texts and much teacher questioning. Little interaction amongst students. | 25% did. The remaining classes - as in Round 1. | 25% did. The remaining classes were very teacher-centred although many teachers claimed to be following *EED*. | No. Very teacher-centred although 60% claimed to be following *EED*. | No. Very teacher-centred. |

| | | | | | |
|---|---|---|---|---|---|
| Evidence of exam influence on *EED* lessons | Little evidence of independent exam impact. Content of lessons resembled exam, but this is because *EED* matched the exam. | As in Round 1. | As in Round 1. | Some evidence. Focus on reading, plus 25% of those changing content said they were influenced by the exam. | Some evidence. 33% said they were doing examination practice in the lesson. |
| % of teachers using non-*EED* material during observation | 19% | 33% | 10% | 25% | 63% |
| Content of non-*EED* lessons | Similar to exam. R - 60% W - little S - little L - none | Similar to exam. R - 50% W - 40% | Similar to exam. Focus on R and W. | Similar to exam. R - 40% W - 40% G - 20% | Similar to exam. Half of teachers using commercial preparation materials. R - 63% W - 32% G - 11% |
| Methodology of non-*EED* lessons | Did not match *EED*. Exam preparation model - 50%. | Did not match *EED*. Exam preparation model - 67%. | Did not match *EED*. Exam preparation model - 75% | Most teachers following exam prep model. | Most teachers following exam prep model. |
| % of teachers claiming exam impact on non-*EED* classes | 50% | 50% | 75% | 100% | 100% |
| % of teachers claiming exam impact on the content of all their classes. | 86% | 95% | 94% | 92% | 97% |
| % of teachers claiming exam impact on the methodology of all their classes. | 81% but confusion throughout between 'content' and 'methodology' | 81% | 78% | 85% | 90% |
| % of teachers claiming exam impact on the tests they write for their students. | 86% but some teachers claim impact on listening and speaking tests | 97% | 100% | 96% | 97% |

*Appendix 4*

|  | Round 1 | Round 2 | Round 4 | Round 5 | Round 6 |
|---|---|---|---|---|---|
| % of teachers claiming exam impact on the way they mark their tests. | 50% | 63% | 75% | 66% | 72% |
| Have teachers seen exam? | 1988 exam - 85% 1989 exam - 57% (55% via friends, 35% via marking) | 1989 - 83% (70% via friends, 30% via marking) | 1989 - 86% 1990 - 70% (50% via friends, 30% via marking) | 1989 - 92% 1990 - 70% (50% via friends, 30% via marking) | 1989 - 98% 1990 - 93 (50% via friends, 30% via marking, 15% in commercial publications) |
| Have teachers got copies of Teacher's Guides? | – | – | Year 7 - 61% Year 8 - 58% Year 9 - 69% Year 10/11 - 81% | Year 7 - 58% Year 8 - 59% Year 9 - 67% Year 10/11 - 84% | Year 7 - 60% Year 8 - 60% Year 9 - 60% Year 10/11 - 88% |
| Have teachers seen copies of *Guidelines* booklet? (NB: This does not mean have access to a copy) | 75% | 83% | 53% | 49% | 50% |
| Have teachers seen copies of *Suggestions* booklets? | 33% | 55% | 47% | 47% | 50% |
| Have teachers seen copies of *Pupil Support* booklets? | – | – | 5% | 2% | 8% |
| Have teachers attended seminars on exam? | – | 67% | Less than 33%. | 37% | 26% |
| Do teachers use commercial publications? | – | – | 75% | 66% | 89% |
| Were teachers doing exam preparation during the period in which the observations were taking place? | – | – | 40% 50% of these doing sessions once a fortnight | 55% 80% of these doing sessions once a week | 98% 29% of these doing sessions every day. 23% doing sessions 2 to 3 times a week |

| | Round 1 | Round 2 | Round 4 | Round 5 | Round 6 |
|---|---|---|---|---|---|
| Observers' view of teachers' ability | Understand *EED* principles - 60% | Understand *EED* principles - 65% | Understand *EED* principles - 56% | Understand *EED* principles - 60% | Understand *EED* principles - 63% |
| | Understand communicative principles - 65% | Understand communicative principles - 60% | Understand communicative principles - 55% | Understand communicative principles - 66% | Understand communicative principles - 55% |
| | Gave sufficient practice - 65% | Adequate preparation - 80% | Adequate preparation - 53% | Adequate preparation - 61% | Gave sufficient practice |
| | | Gave sufficient practice - 60% | Achieved objectives - 49% | Achieved objectives - 50% | Adequate preparation - 67% |
| | | | | | Achieved objectives - 46% |
| Evidence of independent exam impact on lessons in general | Little evidence. | Little evidence. | Impact on content - evidence in 20% of lessons | Impact on content - evidence in 33% of lessons | Impact on content - evidence in 75% of lessons |
| | | | Impact on methodology - no evidence | Impact on methodology - no evidence | Impact on methodology - no evidence |

\* The results of Round 3 are not recorded here, due to problems during the data-collection period which prevented visits to a number of schools.

345

# APPENDIX 5:
## Generalizations summarizing research findings (Rogers 1995)*

### CHAPTER 5: THE INNOVATION-DECISION PROCESS

5-1    Earlier knowers of an innovation have more formal education than later knowers.

5-2    Earlier knowers of an innovation have higher socioeconomic status than late knowers.

5-3    Earlier knowers of an innovation have more exposure to mass media channels of communication than later knowers.

5-4    Earlier knowers of an innovation have more exposure to inter-personal channels than later knowers.

5-5    Earlier knowers of an innovation have more change agent contact than later knowers.

5-6    Earlier knowers of an innovation have more social participation than later knowers.

5-7    Earlier knowers of an innovation are more cosmopolite than later knowers.

5-8    At least some degree of re-invention occurs at the implementation stage for many innovations and for many adopters.

5-9    Later adopters are more likely to discontinue innovations than are earlier adopters.

5-10    Stages exist in the innovation-decision process.

5-11    Mass media channels are relatively more important at the knowledge stage and interpersonal channels are relatively more important at the persuasion stage in the innovation-decision process.

5-12    Cosmopolite channels are relatively more important at the knowledge stage, and localite channels are relatively more important at the persuasion stage in the innovation-decision process.

5-13    Mass media channels are relatively more important than interpersonal channels for earlier adopters than for later adopters.

5-14    Cosmopolite channels are relatively more important than localite channels for earlier adopters than for later adopters.

5-15    The rate of awareness-knowledge for an innovation is more rapid than its rate of adoption.

5-16    Earlier adopters have a shorter innovation-decision period than later adopters.

### CHAPTER 6: ATTRIBUTES OF INNOVATIONS AND THEIR RATE OF ADOPTION

6-1    The relative advantage of an innovation, as perceived by members of a social system, is positively related to its rate of adoption.

6-2    The compatibility of an innovation, as perceived by members of a social system, is positively related to its rate of adoption.

*Reprinted with the permission of The Free Press, a Division of Simon & Schuster Adult Publishing Group, from DIFFUSION OF INNOVATIONS, 4th Edition by Everett M. Rogers. Copyright ©1995 by Everett M. Rogers. Copyright ©1962, 1971, 1983 by The Free Press. All rights reserved.

6-3    The complexity of an innovation, as perceived by members of a social
       system, is negatively related to its rate of adoption.

6-4    The trialability of an innovation, as perceived by members of a social
       system, is positively related to its rate of adoption.

6-5    The observability of an innovation, as perceived by members of a social
       system, is positively related to its rate of adoption.

## CHAPTER 7: INNOVATIVENESS AND ADOPTER CATEGORIES

7-1    Adopter distributions follow a bell-shaped curve over time and approach
       normality.

7-2    Earlier adopters are not different from later adopters in age.

7-3    Earlier adopters have more years of formal education than later adopters.

7-4    Earlier adopters are more likely to be literate than are later adopters.

7-5    Earlier adopters have higher social status than later adopters.

7-6    Earlier adopters have a greater degree of upward social mobility than later
       adopters.

7-7    Earlier adopters have larger units (farms, schools, companies, and so on)
       than later adopters.

7-8    Earlier adopters have greater empathy than later adopters.

7-9    Earlier adopters may be less dogmatic than later adopters.

7-10   Earlier adopters have a  greater ability to deal with abstractions than do later
       adopters.

7-11   Earlier adopters have greater rationality than later adopters.

7-12   Earlier adopters have greater intelligence than later adopters.

7-13   Earlier adopters have a more favourable attitude toward change than later
       adopters.

7-14   Earlier adopters are better able to cope with uncertainty and risk than later
       adopters.

7-15   Earlier adopters have a more favourable attitude toward science than later
       adopters.

7-16   Earlier adopters are less fatalistic than later adopters.

7-17   Earlier adopters have higher aspirations (for formal education, occupations,
       and so on) than later adopters.

7-18   Earlier adopters have more social participation than later adopters.

7-19   Earlier adopters are more highly interconnected through interpersonal
       networks in their social system than later adopters.

7-20   Earlier adopters are more cosmopolite than later adopters.

7-21   Earlier adopters have more change agent contact than later adopters.

7-22   Earlier adopters have greater exposure to mass media communication
       channels than later adopters.

7-23   Earlier adopters have greater exposure to interpersonal communication
       channels than later adopters.

7-24   Earlier adopters seek information about innovations more actively than later
       adopters.

7-25    Earlier adopters have greater knowledge of innovations than later adopters.

7-26    Earlier adopters have a higher degree of opinion leadership than later adopters.

## CHAPTER 8: DIFFUSION NETWORKS

8-1    Interpersonal diffusion networks are mostly homophilous.

8-2    When interpersonal diffusion networks are heterophilous, followers seek opinion leaders of higher socioeconomic status.

8-3    When interpersonal diffusion networks are heterophilous, followers seek opinion leaders with more formal education.

8-4    When interpersonal diffusion networks are heterophilous, followers seek opinion leaders with a greater degree of mass media exposure.

8-5    When interpersonal diffusion networks are heterophilous, followers seek opinion leaders who are more cosmopolite.

8-6    When interpersonal diffusion networks are heterophilous, followers seek opinion leaders with greater change agent contact.

8-7    When interpersonal diffusion networks are heterophilous, followers seek opinion leaders who are more innovative.

8-8    Opinion leaders have greater exposure to mass media than their followers.

8-9    Opinion leaders are more cosmopolite than their followers.

8-10    Opinion leaders have greater change agent contact than their followers.

8-11    Opinion leaders have greater social participation than their followers.

8-12    Opinion leaders have higher socioeconomic status than their followers.

8-13`    Opinion leaders are more innovative than their followers.

8-14    When a social system's norms favour change, opinion leaders are more innovative, but when the norms do not favour change, opinion leaders are not especially innovative.

8-15    The network interconnectedness of an individual in a social system is positively related to the individual's innovativeness.

8-16    The information-exchange potential of communication network links is negatively related to their degree of (1) communication proximity, and (2) homophily.

8-17    Individuals tend to be linked to others who are close to them in physical distance and who are relatively homophilous in social characteristics.

8-18    An individual is more likely to adopt an innovation if more of the other individuals in his or her personal network have adopted previously.

## CHAPTER 9: THE CHANGE AGENT

9-1    Change agent success in securing the adoption of innovations by clients is positively related to the extent of change agent effort in contacting clients.

9-2    Change agent success in securing the adoption of innovations by clients is positively related to a client orientation, rather than to a change agency orientation.

9-3    Change agent success in securing the adoption of innovations by clients is positively related to the degree to which a diffusion program is compatible with clients' needs.

9-4     Change agent success in securing the adoption of innovations by clients is positively related to empathy with clients.

9-5     Change agent contact is positively related to higher social status among clients.

9-6     Change agent contact is positively related to greater social participation among clients.

9-7     Change agent contact is positively related to higher formal education among clients.

9-8     Change agent contact is positively related to cosmopoliteness among clients.

9-9     Change agent success in securing the adoption of innovations by clients is positively related to homophily with clients.

9-10    Change agent success in securing the adoption of innovations by clients is positively related to credibility in the clients' eyes.

9-11    Change agent success in securing the adoption of innovations by clients is positively related to the extent that he or she works through opinion leaders.

## CHAPTER 10: INNOVATION IN ORGANIZATIONS

10-1    Both the innovation and the organization usually change in the innovation process in organizations.

10-2    Larger organizations are more innovative.

10-3    A performance gap can trigger the innovation process.

10-4    The involvement of an innovation champion contributes to the success of an innovation in an organization.

## CHAPTER 11: CONSEQUENCES OF INNOVATIONS

11-1    The effects of an innovation usually cannot be managed to separate the desirable from the undesirable consequences.

11-2    The undesirable, indirect, and unanticipated consequences of an innovation usually go together, as do the desirable, direct, and anticipated consequences.

11-3    Change agents more easily anticipate the form and function of an innovation for their clients than its meaning.

11-4    The consequences of the diffusion of innovations usually widen the socioeconomic gap between the earlier and later adopting categories in a system.

11-5    The consequences of the diffusion of innovation usually widen the socioeconomic gap between the audience segments previously high and low in socioeconomic status.

11-6    A system's social structure partly determines the equality versus inequality of an innovation's consequences.

11-7    When special efforts are made by a diffusion agency, it is possible to narrow, or at least to maintain the size of, socioeconomic gaps in a social system.

# APPENDIX 6:

## Propositions concerning the success of projects (Smith 1991)

1. The success of a project is a function of the system's capacity for innovation. The more the roles, relationships and individual personalities of the system members and the administrative and professional structures of the education system are conducive to change, the greater are the project's chances of success.

2. The success of a project is a function of the originality of the innovation. The more like other projects it is, the more its expected outcomes exceed its unexpected outcomes, the more appropriate its match to the target problem and the shorter the time in which it can be completed, the greater are the chances of its success.

3. The success of a project is a function of the skills of the managerial team and the capacity of the management system to manage innovation. The more effectively the team can establish the structures to co-ordinate and direct innovation and the greater the managerial skills of those involved, the greater are the project's chances of success.

4. The success of a project is a function of the availability, in the amounts and at the time needed, of resources. The greater the availability of finance, personnel, materials and time, the greater the chances of the project's success.

5. The success of a project is a function of the compatibility of the environment with innovation. The less 'hostile' the environment, the greater the chances of the project's success.

6. The success of a project is a function of the harmony of the system and the innovation. The greater the willingness of the structures and members of the system to adopt to the innovation and the greater the consonance of the innovation with the target system, the greater the project's chances of success.

7. The success of a project is a function of the harmony between the target system and the management of the innovation. The greater the support by the target system for the management and the greater the involvement of the members of the target system in the management, the greater the project's chances of success.

8. The success of a project is a function of the harmony between the target system and the resources involved in carrying out the innovation. The greater the system's capacity to provide the necessary resources and the less the provision of resources (from whatever source) conflicts with the members and structures of the target system, the greater the project's chances of success.

9. The success of a project is a function of the influence of the environment on the target system. The more positive the influence of the environment towards change, the greater the project's chances of success.

10. The success of a project is a function of the way the innovation is managed. The greater the management's understanding of the innovation and the greater its skill in directing it, the greater the project's chances of success.

11. The success of a project is a function of the harmony between the innovation and the resources available. The more predictable the need for resources and the greater the flexibility in the availability of resources, the greater the project's chances of success.

12. The success of a project is a function of the influence of the environment on the innovation. The greater the support from the environment for the innovation, the greater the project's chances of success.

13. The success of a project is a function of the management of resources. The greater the management team's resource management skills and the more the resources available match their needs, the greater the project's chances of success.

14. The success of a project is a function of the environment on its management. The greater the support from the environment for the management, the greater the project's chances of success.

15. The success of a project is a function of the availability of resources in the environment. The more reliable the environment as a source of resources, the greater the chances of the project's success.

# APPENDIX 7:
## Interview guide for group interviews. October–November 1991

### 1. Background information
What is your name?
What school do you teach at?
How long have you been teaching?
Are you teaching Year 11 this year?
How long have you been teaching Year 11?

### 2.Teaching under the Old Syllabus
How did you teach your students before *EED*?
What materials did you use?
What techniques did you use?
Did you do anything special to prepare your students for the examination?
What materials did you use?
What techniques did you use?

Did you have any problems during this period?

### 3.The Old Syllabus examination
What do you remember about the Old Syllabus examination?
What was the reading comprehension part like?
What was the writing part like?
What was the grammar part like?
How was the marking done?
What did the markers look for in the writing?

What did you think about the Old Syllabus examination?
Did it influence your teaching in any way?

Did you have any problems during this period?

### 4.Teaching under *English Every Day (EED)*
How do you go about teaching under *EED*?
What materials do you use?
What techniques do you use?

Which book/chapter did you start the year off with?
How far have you got in the textbook?

If you did not start the year with the Year 11 book, what prevented you from doing so?

How long did it take before you could start in the Year 11 book?

Do you make it a point to cover all of the material?
If you leave out some of it, what do you leave out – and why?
If you bring in extra material, what material do you use – and why?

How do you teach reading?
How do you teach writing?
How do you teach listening?
How do you teach speaking?

Do you have access to the *English Every Day* Teacher's Guides?
Do you follow the suggestions for teaching?

Do you have any problems when teaching?

Do you write any tests for your classes or your school?
What kinds of tests?
How do you decide on the content?
How do you mark them?

Do you do anything special to prepare your students for the examination?
Do you have an examination preparation period?
When does/did you start it?
Do you do examination preparation during the normal timetable, or do you have sessions after school or at some other time?

What materials do you use?
• Official examination booklets
• Past papers
• Commercial publications

How do you use this material?
What techniques do you use?

Do you have any problems during this period?

## 5. The new examination

Is the new examination different from the Old Syllabus examination?
What differences are there?
Is the content any different?
Are the techniques any different?

How is reading tested?
How is writing tested?
How is the examination marked?
What do markers look for when they are marking writing?

Have you see the examination papers?
How did you get access to them?

*Appendix 7*

Have you seen the official examination support booklets?
How did you get access to them?
Have you used commercial publications?
Which ones?

Have you served as an examiner, and if so, for how many years?

What is your opinion of the new examination?
Do you think it affects your teaching?
If you do, in what ways does it affect it?

Do you think it affects your teaching in Year 10, Year 9 or earlier years?
If you do, in what ways does it affect it?

Can you predict what will appear on the examination this year?

# APPENDIX 8:

**Initial coding scheme** (based on Henrichsen's 1989 Hybrid Model of the Diffusion/Implementation Process, before analysis of group interviews)

## 1. OLD SYLLABUS

### 1.1 TEXTBOOK

| | |
|---|---|
| 1.1.1 | Content |
| 1.1.2 | Method |
| 1.1.3 | Attitude – teacher, student, whose? |
| 1.1.4 | Other |

### 1.2 ORDINARY TEACHING

| | |
|---|---|
| 1.2.1 | Content |
| 1.2.2 | Method |
| 1.2.3 | Attitude – teacher, student, whose? |
| 1.2.4 | Other |

### 1.3 EXAMINATION PAPER

| | |
|---|---|
| 1.3.1 | Content |
| 1.3.2 | Method |
| 1.3.3 | Marking |
| 1.3.4 | Attitude – teacher, student, whose? |
| 1.3.5 | Other |

### 1.4 EXAMINATION PREPARATION

| | |
|---|---|
| 1.4.1 | Content |
| 1.4.2 | Method |
| 1.4.3 | Marking |
| 1.4.4 | Attitude – teacher, student, whose? |
| 1.4.5 | Location – in-class, seminar, extra, tutorials, other |

### 1.5 PROBLEMS

| | |
|---|---|
| 1.5.1 | Textbook |
| 1.5.2 | Exam |
| 1.5.3 | Environment |
| 1.5.4 | Teacher |
| 1.5.5 | Student |
| 1.5.6 | Other |

## 2. NEW SYLLABUS

### 2.1 TEXTBOOK

| | |
|---|---|
| 2.1.1 | Content |
| 2.1.2 | Method |
| 2.1.3 | Attitude – teacher, student, whose? |
| 2.1.4 | Other |

## 2.2 ORDINARY TEACHING

| | |
|---|---|
| 2.2.1 | Content |
| 2.2.2 | Method |
| 2.2.3 | Attitude – teacher, student, whose? |
| 2.2.4 | Other |

## 2.3 EXAMINATION PAPER

| | |
|---|---|
| 2.3.1 | Content |
| 2.3.2 | Method |
| 2.3.3 | Marking |
| 2.3.4 | Attitude – teacher, student, whose? |
| 2.3.5 | Other |

## 2.4 EXAMINATION PREPARATION

| | |
|---|---|
| 2.4.1 | Content |
| 2.4.2 | Method |
| 2.4.3 | Marking |
| 2.4.4 | Attitude – teacher, student, whose? |
| 2.4.5 | Location – in-class, seminar, extra, tutorials, other |

## 2.5 PROBLEMS

| | |
|---|---|
| 2.5.1 | Textbook |
| 2.5.2 | Exam |
| 2.5.3 | Environment |
| 2.5.4 | Teacher |
| 2.5.5 | Student |
| 2.5.6 | Other |

# 3. INNOVATION

## 3.1 ANTECEDENTS

3.1.1 User system – exam paper, ordinary teaching, examination preparation, institution, education, administration, political, cultural, economics, geography

3.1.2 Users

3.1.2.1 Teachers – attitude to education, attitude to world, attitude to English, attitude to exam, educational level, economic status, home life, abilities, interests, beliefs, goals

3.1.2.2 Students – attitude to education, attitude to world, attitude to English, attitude to exam, educational level, economic status, home life, abilities, interests, beliefs, goals

3.1.3 Pedagogic practices

3.1.4 Previous reforms

3.2 IMPLEMENTATION

> 3.2.1 Innovation factors – originality, complexity, explicitness, relative advantage, trialability, observability, status, practicality, flexibility, primacy, form

> 3.2.2 Resource system – capacity, structure, openness, harmony

> 3.2.3 User system – geography, centralization, size, communication, orientation, openness, teacher factors, learner factors, capacities, educational philosophy, examinations

> 3.2.4 Inter-elemental – compatibility, linkage, reward, proximity, synergism

# 4. WASHBACK

4.1 PREDICTIONS

4.2 FACILITATING FACTORS

4.3 INHIBITING FACTORS

4.4 PARTICIPANT EFFECTS

4.5 PROCESS EFFECTS

4.6 PRODUCT EFFECTS

4.7 EXAM PREPARATION

4.8 OLD EXAM WASHBACK

4.9 OTHER

4.10 NEW PROCESSES

# APPENDIX 9:
## Sample of coded transcript

Q.S.R. NUD.IST Power version, revision 4.0.
Licensee: Dianne Wall.
PROJECT: PHDDISS, User Dianne
++++++++++++++++++++++++++++++++++++++++++++++++++++++++++++++++++++++++++
+++++++++++++++++++++
+++ ON-LINE DOCUMENT: NUWARA
+++ Document Header:
* DISCUSSION WITH TEACHERS, RESC Centre, Nuwara Eliya, 2 November
1991

+++ Retrieval for this document: 27 units out of 701, = 3.9%
++ Text units 149-175:

149   *Teacher 1: Now when I was giving these telephone messages I took them to
       the Post Office, showed them the real material, showed them how to dial,
       then the telephone and the receiver, mouthpiece. Then I got them to
       speak from the Exchange to the Post Office because it was close to the
       school. The Post Office as well as the Exchange. So they learned it,
       and after coming to class they mimed. One person dialling. One person
       taking the message and filling in the form. That is when the person is
       out. They fill in the form and convey the message to that person after
       he comes.
(2 2 2)      (2 5 3)       (3 2 1 16)    (3 2 5 10)    (3 2 5 11 1 9)
(12 1 1 16)   (12 1 1 20)    (12 3 10)     (12 3 20)     (12 4 1 9)
(12 4 1 20)   (13 2 2)      (20 4 6)

150   *DW: So you did this other activity in order to make the activities in
       the textbook seem more real. (Agrees.) Yes, that's a lovely idea.
       Okay, so we've established that in general it seems, with a few
       exceptions, you are covering the text … you are working in the
       textbook, you are pretty thoroughly covering it and even bringing in
       outside materials. You're omitting some things but you've given the reason why.
       But it doesn't sound like anybody is omitting anything because of the paper.
       You're not ignoring listening. You're not ignoring speaking. Is that right?
(2 2 1)      (3 2 5 4)     (3 2 5 11 2 12) (4 5)       (12 3 3)
(12 3 20)    (12 4 2 12)    (12 4 2 20)    (13 2 1)      (13 6 5)
(15 2 1)     (15 2 33)     (15 2 35)

151   *(Laughter.)
(2 2 1)      (3 2 5 4)     (3 2 5 11 2 12) (4 5)       (12 3 3)
(12 3 20)    (12 4 2 12)    (12 4 2 20)    (13 2 1)      (13 6 5)
(15 2 1)     (15 2 33)     (15 2 35)

152  *Teacher 2: In our school it's difficult to omit. The children tell
us 'Teacher, can you remember to do this?' They always remind us.
(2 2 1)      (3 2 5 4)      (3 2 5 11 2 12) (4 5)      (12 3 3)
(12 3 20)    (12 4 2 12)    (12 4 2 20)    (13 2 1)    (13 6 5)
(15 2 1)     (15 2 33)      (15 2 35)      (20 4 10)

153  *(Laughter)
(2 2 1)      (13 2 1)       (13 2 5 1)

154  *Teacher 3: What I feel is that the GCE O-Level paper is based on reading
and writing. So we have to do most things on reading and writing.
(2 2 1)      (2 3 1)        (2 5 3)        (3 2 1 13)   (3 2 5 10)
(4 5)        (12 3 10)      (12 3 20)      (13 2 1)     (13 3 1)
(13 3 20)    (13 6 5)       (15 2 1)       (15 2 33)    (20 4 4)

155  *DW: Now are you thinking about your particular case now, in the
circumstances you're in, where the children just haven't been able to
cover the material. So now you're concentrating on reading and writing.
You explained that you're going through past papers and model papers...
(2 2 1)      (2 3 1)        (2 5 3)        (3 2 1 13)   (3 2 5 10)
(4 5)        (12 3 10)      (12 3 20)      (13 2 1)     (13 3 1)
(13 3 20)    (13 6 5)       (15 2 1)       (15 2 33)

156  *Teacher 3: The other thing is this, that in the area where my school is
situated, it's a remote area. They need to get through the exam. We
have to give them the knowledge and we have to give them training for the
O-Level examination also. But we have to concentrate on that O-Level
examination. Because of that I am mostly concerned with reading and
writing.
(2 2 1)      (2 3 1)        (2 5 3)        (3 2 1 13)   (3 2 5 10)
(4 3)        (4 5)          (12 3 10)      (12 3 20)    (13 2 1)
(13 3 1)     (13 3 20)      (13 6 3)       (13 6 5)     (15 2 1)
(15 2 1 2)   (15 2 33)      (20 4 4)

157  *DW: What did you say about oral examinations? I didn't quite
understand. (DW has misunderstood – he said 'O-Level'.)
(2 2 1)      (2 3 1)        (4 3)          (4 5)        (13 2 1)
(13 3 1)     (13 3 20)      (13 6 3)       (13 6 5)     (15 2 1)
(15 2 1 2)

158  *Teacher 3: The GCE O-Level examination. We have to concentrate, in my
case, on reading and writing. All the paper is based on reading and
writing. Listening ... those things are also very important but those
things are not on the examination.
(2 2 1)      (2 3 1)        (4 3)          (4 5)        (13 2 1)
(13 3 1)     (13 3 20)      (13 6 3)       (13 6 5)     (15 2 1)
(15 2 1 2)   (20 4 4)

159   *DW: Okay, so in your case you're feeling the pressure to concentrate on the things you know will be on the paper. And that seems very understandable, given your circumstances. What about you, (Teacher 4)? You said that you started and that you had to cover all of the Year 10 book, and even now I think you're still working on the Year 10 book. Is that right?

(2 2 1)       (2 3 1)       (3 2 1 13)     (3 2 5 11 1 5) (3 2 5 11 1 12)
(4 5)         (12 4 1 5)    (12 4 1 12)    (12 4 1 20)    (12 4 1 22)
(13 2 1)      (13 3 1)      (13 3 20)      (13 6 5)       (15 2 1)
(15 2 34)     (20 4 5)

160   *Teacher 4: Now I'm doing application forms and all that. Paper cuttings and all that. I give the paper cuttings and I ask them to apply for those jobs. How to prepare the biodata and letters and all that. And they are doing some essay writing also because I want to help them to sit for the exam. That is my aim, in order to get passes for the exam.

(2 2 1)       (2 2 4 1)     (2 3 3)       (2 3 4 1)     (3 2 1 13)
(3 2 5 11 1 5) (3 2 5 11 1 12) (4 4)      (4 5)         (12 1 2 21)
(12 4 1 5)    (12 4 1 12)   (12 4 1 20)   (12 4 1 21)   (12 4 1 22)
(13 2 1)      (13 2 4 1)    (13 3 3)      (13 3 4 1)    (13 3 20)
(13 6 4)      (13 6 5)      (15 2 1)      (15 2 4 1)    (15 2 34)
(20 4 5)

161   *DW: So are you doing special exam practice now?

(2 2 1)       (2 2 4 1)     (2 3 3)       (2 3 4 1)     (4 4)
(4 5)         (12 1 2 21)   (12 4 1 21)   (12 4 1 22)   (13 2 1)
(13 2 4 1)    (13 3 3)      (13 3 4 1)    (13 3 20)     (13 6 4)
(13 6 5)      (15 2 1)      (15 2 4 1)

162   *Teacher 4: I gave them a test also. Last week I gave them a test. Rules on road safety and all that, and they did it.

(2 2 1)       (2 2 4 1)     (2 3 3)       (2 3 4 1)     (4 4)
(4 5)         (12 1 2 21)   (12 4 1 21)   (12 4 1 22)   (13 2 1)
(13 2 4 1)    (13 3 3)      (13 3 4 1)    (13 3 20)     (13 6 4)
(13 6 5)      (15 2 1)      (15 2 4 1)    (20 4 5)

163   *DW: Good. Good. Now, it seems that now in November, whether you have the exam in mind the rest of the year or not, in November there is something going on which is a little bit different from the rest of the year. Now in other parts of the country they call this the 'revision period'. Now I had heard about this before this year but I had never asked in a lot of detail about it. Can I just ask ... Do you all have revision periods in your school?

(2 4 1)       (4 5)         (13 4 1)      (13 6 5)      (15 4 1)

164   *??: (Some say yes and some say no.)

(2 4 1)       (4 5)         (13 4 1)      (13 6 5)      (15 4 1)

165   *DW: Okay, so Teacher 5, you're saying that in your school you don't have a special revision time during the school year but you do it after school.
(2 4 1)      (2 4 5 1)      (2 4 5 3)      (3 2 5 4)      (4 5)
(12 3 3)     (12 3 20)      (13 4 1)       (13 4 5 1)     (13 4 5 3)
(13 6 5)     (15 4 1)       (15 4 5 1)     (15 4 5 3)     (20 4 1)

166   *Teacher 5: Yes, after school I'm doing all the revision exercises.
(2 4 1)      (2 4 5 1)      (2 4 5 3)      (3 2 5 4)      (4 5)
(12 3 3)     (12 3 20)      (13 4 1)       (13 4 5 1)     (13 4 5 3)
(13 6 5)     (15 4 1)       (15 4 5 1)     (15 4 5 3)     (20 4 1)

167   *DW: And during the day?
(2 4 1)      (2 4 5 1)      (2 4 5 3)      (3 2 5 4)      (4 5)
(12 3 3)     (12 3 20)      (13 4 1)       (13 4 5 1)     (13 4 5 3)
(13 6 5)     (15 4 1)       (15 4 5 1)     (15 4 5 3)

168   *Teacher 5: During the day I concentrate on the textbook.
(2 4 1)      (2 4 5 1)      (2 4 5 3)      (3 2 5 4)      (4 5)
(12 3 3)     (12 3 20)      (13 4 1)       (13 4 5 1)     (13 4 5 3)
(13 6 5)     (15 4 1)       (15 4 5 1)     (15 4 5 3)     (20 4 1)

169   *DW: So you're still working on the ...
(2 4 1)      (2 4 5 1)      (2 4 5 3)      (3 2 5 4)      (4 5)
(12 3 3)     (12 3 20)      (13 4 1)       (13 4 5 1)     (13 4 5 3)
(13 6 5)     (15 4 1)       (15 4 5 1)     (15 4 5 3)

170   *Teacher 5: Now I am doing all revision exercises. Now in December we'll be having the examination and I've stopped all the teaching now and now I'm doing revision classes. After school also.
(2 4 1)      (2 4 5 1)      (2 4 5 3)      (3 2 5 4)      (4 5)
(12 3 3)     (12 3 20)      (13 4 1)       (13 4 5 1)     (13 4 5 3)
(13 6 5)     (15 4 1)       (15 4 5 1)     (15 4 5 3)     (20 4 1)

171   *DW: So did you finish the Year 11 book?
(2 2 1)      (2 4 1)        (3 2 5 4)      (4 5)          (12 3 3)
(12 3 20)    (13 2 1)       (13 4 1)       (13 6 5)       (15 2 1)
(15 2 33)    (15 4 1)

172   *Teacher 5: Yes. No, Year 11 only 4 units.
(2 2 1)      (2 4 1)        (3 2 5 4)      (4 5)          (12 3 3)
(12 3 20)    (13 2 1)       (13 4 1)       (13 6 5)       (15 2 1)
(15 2 33)    (15 4 1)       (20 4 1)

173   *DW: So you finished 4 units, then ...
(2 2 1)      (2 4 1)        (3 2 5 4)      (4 5)          (12 3 3)
(12 3 20)    (13 2 1)       (13 4 1)       (13 6 5)       (15 2 1)
(15 2 33)    (15 4 1)

174   *Teacher 5: Then I do all the Finding Outs as unseen passages. I'm
      giving the Year 11 book, all the passages, I'm giving them as unseen
      passages. I prepare all the questions and I give them out. I take all
      the picture descriptions from Year 11 and all the applications, like that.

(2 2 1)      (2 4 1)      (3 2 5 4)      (4 5)        (12 3 3)
(12 3 20)    (13 2 1)     (13 4 1)       (13 6 5)     (15 2 1)
(15 2 33)    (15 4 1)     (20 4 1)

175   *DW: When did you finish your normal work? In the Year 11 book? Was it
      last month? Or last week?

(2 2 1)      (2 4 1)      (3 2 5 4)      (4 5)        (12 3 3)
(12 3 20)    (13 2 1)     (13 4 1)       (13 6 5)     (15 2 1)
(15 2 33)    (15 4 1)

# APPENDIX 10:
## Revised coding scheme

Q.S.R. NUD.IST Power version, revision 4.0.
Licensee: Dianne Wall.

PROJECT: PHDDISS, User Dianne

| | |
|---|---|
| (11) | /Antecedents (revised) |
| (11 1) | /Antecedents (revised)/res syst? |
| (11 2) | /Antecedents (revised)/User system |
| (11 2 1) | /Antecedents (revised)/User system/classroom |
| (11 2 3) | /Antecedents (revised)/User system/school |
| (11 2 4) | /Antecedents (revised)/User system/tutories |
| (11 2 5) | /Antecedents (revised)/User system/ed phil |
| (11 2 6) | /Antecedents (revised)/User system/ed org |
| (11 2 7) | /Antecedents (revised)/User system/political |
| (11 2 8) | /Antecedents (revised)/User system/cultural |
| (11 2 9) | /Antecedents (revised)/User system/economics |
| (11 2 10) | /Antecedents (revised)/User system/geography |
| (11 3) | /Antecedents (revised)/Users |
| (11 3 1) | /Antecedents (revised)/Users/teacher |
| (11 3 1 1) | /Antecedents (revised)/Users/teacher/att ed |
| (11 3 1 2) | /Antecedents (revised)/Users/teacher/att world |
| (11 3 1 3) | /Antecedents (revised)/Users/teacher/att Eng |
| (11 3 1 4) | /Antecedents (revised)/Users/teacher/att teaching |
| (11 3 1 5) | /Antecedents (revised)/Users/teacher/att exam |
| (11 3 1 6) | /Antecedents (revised)/Users/teacher/ed level |
| (11 3 1 7) | /Antecedents (revised)/Users/teacher/econ status |
| (11 3 1 8) | /Antecedents (revised)/Users/teacher/homelife |
| (11 3 1 9) | /Antecedents (revised)/Users/teacher/abilities |
| (11 3 1 10) | /Antecedents (revised)/Users/teacher/interests |
| (11 3 1 11) | /Antecedents (revised)/Users/teacher/beliefs |
| (11 3 1 12) | /Antecedents (revised)/Users/teacher/goals |
| (11 3 2) | /Antecedents (revised)/Users/learners |
| (11 3 2 1) | /Antecedents (revised)/Users/learners/att ed |
| (11 3 2 2) | /Antecedents (revised)/Users/learners/att world |
| (11 3 2 3) | /Antecedents (revised)/Users/learners/att Eng |
| (11 3 2 4) | /Antecedents (revised)/Users/learners/att teaching |
| (11 3 2 5) | /Antecedents (revised)/Users/learners/att exam |
| (11 3 2 6) | /Antecedents (revised)/Users/learners/ed level |
| (11 3 2 7) | /Antecedents (revised)/Users/learners/econ status |
| (11 3 2 8) | /Antecedents (revised)/Users/learners/homelife |
| (11 3 2 9) | /Antecedents (revised)/Users/learners/abilities |
| (11 3 2 10) | /Antecedents (revised)/Users/learners/interests |
| (11 3 2 11) | /Antecedents (revised)/Users/learners/beliefs |
| (11 3 2 12) | /Antecedents (revised)/Users/learners/goals |

| | |
|---|---|
| (11 4) | /Antecedents (revised)/Ped practices |
| (11 4 1) | /Antecedents (revised)/Ped practices/textbook |
| (11 4 1 1) | /Antecedents (revised)/Ped practices/textbook/content |
| (11 4 1 2) | /Antecedents (revised)/Ped practices/textbook/method |
| (11 4 1 3) | /Antecedents (revised)/Ped practices/textbook/attitude |
| (11 4 1 3 1) | /Antecedents (revised)/<br>Ped practices/textbook/attitude/Teacher |
| (11 4 1 3 2) | /Antecedents (revised)/<br>Ped practices/textbook/attitude/Students |
| (11 4 1 3 3 | /Antecedents (revised)/<br>Ped practices/textbook/attitude/Whose? |
| (11 4 1 4) | /Antecedents (revised)/Ped practices/textbook/other |
| (11 4 1 20) | /Antecedents (revised)/Ped practices/textbook/collect |
| (11 4 2) | /Antecedents (revised)/Ped practices/ord teaching |
| (11 4 2 1) | /Antecedents (revised)/<br>Ped practices/ord teaching/content |
| (11 4 2 2) | /Antecedents (revised)/Ped practices/ord teaching/method |
| (11 4 2 3) | /Antecedents (revised)/<br>Ped practices/ord teaching/marking |
| (11 4 2 4) | /Antecedents (revised)/<br>Ped practices/ord teaching/attitude |
| (11 4 2 4 1) | /Antecedents (revised)/<br>Ped practices/ord teaching/attitude/Teacher |
| (11 4 2 4 2) | /Antecedents (revised)/<br>Ped practices/ord teaching/attitude/Students |
| (11 4 2 4 3) | /Antecedents (revised)/<br>Ped practices/ord teaching/attitude/Whose? |
| (11 4 2 5) | /Antecedents (revised)/Ped practices/ord teaching/other |
| (11 4 3) | /Antecedents (revised)/Ped practices/exam paper |
| (11 4 3 1) | /Antecedents (revised)/Ped practices/exam paper/content |
| (11 4 3 2) | /Antecedents (revised)/Ped practices/exam paper/method |
| (11 4 3 3 | /Antecedents (revised)/Ped practices/exam paper/marking |
| (11 4 3 4) | /Antecedents (revised)/Ped practices/exam paper/attitude |
| (11 4 3 4 1) | /Antecedents (revised)/<br>Ped practices/exam paper/attitude/Teacher |
| (11 4 3 4 2) | /Antecedents (revised)/<br>Ped practices/exam paper/attitude/Students |
| (11 4 3 4 3) | /Antecedents (revised)/<br>Ped practices/exam paper/attitude/Whose? |
| (11 4 3 5) | /Antecedents (revised)/Ped practices/exam paper/other |
| (11 4 4) | /Antecedents (revised)/Ped practices/exam prep |
| (11 4 4 1 | /Antecedents (revised)/Ped practices/exam prep/Content |
| (11 4 4 2 | /Antecedents (revised)/Ped practices/exam prep/methods |
| (11 4 4 3) | /Antecedents (revised)/Ped practices/exam prep/marking |
| (11 4 4 4) | /Antecedents (revised)/Ped practices/exam prep/attitudes |
| (11 4 4 4 1) | /Antecedents (revised)/<br>Ped practices/exam prep/attitudes/teacher |
| (11 4 4 4 2) | /Antecedents (revised)/<br>Ped practices/exam prep/attitudes/students |

| | |
|---|---|
| (11 4 4 4 3) | /Antecedents (revised)/<br>Ped practices/exam prep/attitudes/whose |
| (11 4 4 5) | /Antecedents (revised)/Ped practices/exam prep/location |
| (11 4 4 5 1) | /Antecedents (revised)/<br>Ped practices/exam prep/location/in-class |
| (11 4 4 5 2) | /Antecedents (revised)/<br>Ped practices/exam prep/location/seminar |
| (11 4 4 5 3) | /Antecedents (revised)/<br>Ped practices/exam prep/location/extra |
| (11 4 4 5 4) | /Antecedents (revised)/<br>Ped practices/exam prep/location/tutories |
| (11 4 4 6) | /Antecedents (revised)/Ped practices/exam prep/other |
| (11 5) | /Antecedents (revised)/pre reforms |

# APPENDIX 11:
## Sample unit from *English Every Day*, Year 11

---

**UNIT ONE** · **ROLE PLAY** · **PADMINI BOOKS A TICKET**

Padmini has been invited to represent Sri Lanka at an International Conference on Hospital Nursing in London. On the way, she wants to visit Moscow, where an old school friend, Nalini, is studying to be a doctor. Here she is at the Travel Agent's.

Clerk : Good morning. Can I help you?

Padmini : Yes. I want to go to London, with a day or two in Moscow on the way.

Clerk : Fine. We can arrange that for you. Have you brought your passport?

Padmini : Yes. Here it is

Clerk : Thank you. You will need visas. Please fill in these forms for the British High Commission and the Soviet Embassy.

(Padmini fills in the forms)

Padmini : Here you are. I hope I've filled them in correctly.

Clerk : Let me see....m-m-m-m-...yes, they are all in order. I'll telephone you when we are ready to make out the ticket. I've got your number here on this form.

Padmini : Thank you. Will you be able to arrange some travellers cheques for me, too?

Clerk : Certainly. We can issue them for you when you call for your ticket. If there's anything else you want, just give me a call.

Padmini : Thank you. Goodbye.

3

### EXAMPLE DIALOGUE

C : Have you got ...?
R : No ...
C : Then, can I have ...?
C : Yes. We can do that.
C : Fine. How much will that be?
R : That will be ... a night. ... altogether.
Your room number is ... Here's your key.
C : Thank you.
R : You're welcome. The porter will take your bags.

**UNIT ONE    LEARNING TOGETHER    TRAVELLED? LUCKY YOU!**

Pair work (as pre-writing activity)

| QUESTION | MARIE | SALIYA | KUMARAN | NIHARA |
|---|---|---|---|---|
| Where/travel to? | Japan | Russia | Spain | Pakistan |
| Who (m)/stay with? | Nakoya | Natasha | Pedro | Fareena |
| Which language/speak | Japanese | Russian | Spanish | Urdu |
| What/like most? | cherry blossom | food | the bull fighting | the mountains |
| When/return | June 1st | Sept 17th | Dec 23rd | March 2nd |

1. A : Where did ... travel to?
   B : He/She ....
2. A : Who did ... stay with?
   B : ...
3. A : Which language did ...?
   B : ...
4. A : What did ... like most?
   B : ...
5. A : When did ... return?
   B : ...

### WRITING

Marie travelled to Japan and stayed with her pen-friend Nakoya whose first language is Japanese. She liked the cherry blossoms most. She returned on June 1st.

1. Now write about one or two of the others.
2. Write a dialogue between Nihara and Marie or Saliya and Kumaran about their travels using the chart above.
3. Interview your pair partner about a holiday trip he or she has made and write about his or her holiday.

---

2

**UNIT ONE    LEARNING TOGETHER    A ROOM, PLEASE**

Choose five cue cards and write them out in your exercise book. Decide which hotel you want to be in. Use the dialogue both as a customer and as hotel receptionist with pupils around you.

**TOURIST CARDS**

**1A** A single room with bath for three nights

**1B** A single room with shower for four nights

**2A** A double room with shower for two nights

**2B** A double room with bath for two nights

**3A** A single room with bath for two nights

**3B** A single room with shower for two nights

**4A** A double room with shower for three nights

**4B** A double room with bath for three nights

**HOTEL LISTS OF CHARGES (RATES)**

**HOTEL ORCHID**

| Type of Room | Price Rs. per night |
|---|---|
| 1 Single with shower | 800/- |
| 2 Single with bath | 850/- |
| 3 Double with shower | 950/- |
| 4 Double with bath | 1,000/- |

**HOTEL STARFISH**

| Type of Room | Price Rs. per night |
|---|---|
| 1 Single with shower | 200/- |
| 2 Single with bath | 300/- |
| 3 Double with shower | 400/- |
| 4 Double with bath | 500/- |

*Note: In International English a 'Hotel' is always a place where guests can sleep for the night as in a Rest House or Guest House.

## 4

### UNIT ONE    FINDING OUT    TRAVELLERS CHEQUES

When Padmini was booking her ticket, she asked for some travellers cheques as well. These cheques are issued by private finance companies, banks or travel agencies. They are not official government documents, but will be changed for cash by most banks in the world. They may be issued in a variety of different currencies, but the most common have a face value in American dollars or UK pounds (sterling). Travellers cheques have two advantages over cash. Firstly, they can be cashed freely for the money of any country you happen to be in. Secondly, if you lose them, or someone steals them from you, the issuing company will, under certain conditions replace them immediately with new ones. Here is a travellers cheque. They are usually issued in values of 5, 10, 20, 50 or 100 dollars or pounds.

And here is an extract from the regulations which deal with the replacement of lost or stolen travellers cheques.

#### TRAVELLERS CHEQUE ASSOCIATES LTD. (TCA LTD)

PURCHASE AGREEMENT — CONDITIONS D'ACHAT — KAUFSBEDINGUNGEN

CONDITIONS DE VENTE EN LANGUE FRANÇAISE REMISE PAR LE VENDEUR

VERTRAGSBEDINGUNGEN IN DEUTSCHER SPRACHE ANFORDERN VOM VERKÄUFER AUSGEHÄNDIGT

IMPORTANT: Read this Agreement carefully. By signing, signing, or countersigning these 'TCA LTD Travellers Cheques' you agree to these conditions:

- These Travellers Cheques HAS NOT BE EN TAKEN On countersign
- to government action.
- REFER TO LTD will, through its appointed servicing agent,
- American Express Company (America), its attendance, advices,
- and Representatives, replace or refund the amount should an any
- lost or stolen Travellers Cheque only if you follow all of the
- requirements below:

AFTER LOSS:
- You IMMEDIATELY NOTIFY America of the loss or theft of the Travellers Cheque.
- You REPORT all facts of the loss in due to America and also to the police if America asks you to.
- You INFORM America of the serial number of the lost or stolen Travellers Cheque and the place and date of its purchase.
- You GIVE America all reasonable information and help.
- OFFER acceptable proof of your identity.

NO STOP PAYMENT: Neither TCA LTD nor America can stop payment on or refuse to pay any Travellers Cheque.

SIGN YOUR 'TCA LTD TRAVELLERS CHEQUES' IMMEDIATELY UPON PURCHASE . . . In the Upper Left Corner

Registered Office: 194 Fennel Street, Brighton BN2 2LH, England.    Incorporated in England under Company Registration No. 1321555.

---

## 5

(a) Which company issued the cheque?

(b) Can the cheque be used in all countries of the world?

(c) There are several numbers on the cheque. Which is the cheque number?

(d) How much is this cheque worth in rupees at the current rate? Use one of the tables in the next activity if necessary.

(e) What do you think the name of the TCA Chairman is?

(f) Find three things you must NOT do before cashing a travellers cheque.

(g) Find one thing you MUST do as soon as you buy a travellers cheque.

### UNIT ONE    LEARNING TOGETHER    EXCHANGE RATES

What is one American dollar worth? How many Sri Lankan rupees do you get for one pound sterling? We can't answer these questions exactly without checking the Exchange Rate for the day. The value of money changes from day to day—sometimes very sharply, but usually by only a fraction. These two tables show the international exchange rates for two different weeks early in 1986. First use the tables to find out which countries use the following currencies. See which pair can write them all down first. Then your teacher will give you another set.

#### Foreign Exchange

| Country/Region | Value of US $1 nov |
| --- | --- |
| Australia $ | 1.48 |
| Bangladesh Taka | 31.51 |
| Brunei | 2.13 |
| Burma Kyat | 8.07 |
| Canada $ | 1.44 |
| Egyptian £ | 0.85 |
| Eire Irish £ | 0.83 |
| Fiji $ | 1.15 |
| France French Franc | 7.35 |
| Germany (West) Deutsche Mark | 2.36 |
| Hong Kong H.K. $ | 7.80 |
| India Rupee | 12.50 |
| Indonesia | 1159.00 |
| Israel Shekels | 1.50 |
| Japan Yen | 211.17 |
| Kenya Shilling | 16.68 |
| Korea (South) Won | 920.44 |
| Lebanon £ | 19.63 |
| Malaya Ringgit | 2.13 |
| Malaysia | 2.55 |
| Nepal | 22.00 |
| Netherlands Guilder | 2.66 |
| New Zealand NZ $ | 1.99 |
| Pakistan Rupee | 16.29 |
| Papua New Guinea Kina | 1.04 |
| Philippines Peso | 18.42 |
| Singapore $ | 2.13 |
| South Africa Rand | 2.42 |
| Sri Lanka S.L. Rupee | 28.21 |
| Switzerland Swiss Franc | 2.37 |
| Taiwan T.N.F. Franc | 19.58 |
| Tanzania Shilling | 16.91 |
| Thailand | 26.36 |
| Uganda Shilling | 1403.22 |
| United Kingdom £ Sterling | 0.71 |

*Latest indicative middle rates quoted between banks on January 31 1986. Compiled by Standard Chartered Bank.*

**Standard & Chartered**

#### Foreign Exchange

| Country/Region | Value of US $1.51 nov |
| --- | --- |
| Australia $ | 1.13 |
| Bangladesh Taka | 29.13 |
| Brunei $ | 2.06 |
| Burma Kyat | 7.64 |
| Canada $ | 1.35 |
| Egyptian £ | 0.80 |
| Irish £ | 0.74 |
| Fiji $ | 1.07 |
| French Franc | 7.10 |
| Deutsche Mark | 2.32 |
| Hong Kong H.K. $ | 7.86 |
| India Rupee | 12.91 |
| Indonesia | 1089.00 |
| Israel | 12.01 |
| Japan Yen | 192.76 |
| Kenya Shilling | 15.38 |
| Korea (South) Won | 895.05 |
| Lebanon £ | 22.53 |
| France | 2.3 |
| Ringgit | 2.30 |
| Nepal | 19.81 |
| Netherlands Guilder | 2.62 |
| NZ $ | 1.78 |
| Pakistan Rupee | 15.25 |
| Kina | 0.96 |
| Philippine Peso | 18.42 |
| Singapore $ | 2.06 |
| S.L. Rupee | 25.11 |
| Swiss Franc | 2.04 |
| T.F.H. Franc | 18.04 |
| N.T.$ | 18.01 |
| Tanzania Shilling | 15.90 |
| Thailand | 25.50 |
| Uganda Shilling | 1417.24 |
| £ Sterling | 0.68 |

*Latest indicative middle rates quoted between banks on February 21 1986. Compiled by Standard Chartered Bank.*

**Standard & Chartered**

Was that great port Manthota, in Mannar, a commercial centre between the court of Rome and the court of Peking? Who knows? Only further research can tell. But it is true that Sri Lanka was well known for exporting elephants from this port. They were sent in specially made ships to fight for the armies of Alexander the Great, as far back as the third century B.C.

## UNIT ONE    READING AND WRITING    THE ROMAN EMPIRE

When the first Sri Lankan ambassadors went to Rome, the Roman Empire covered most of Europe, including Britain, the North African coast and parts of Asia. This empire lasted over five hundred years, longer than any other empire in history.

It lasted so long because the Roman army was so large and well organised, and its soldiers were loyal, brave and ready to make great sacrifices for their country. Life was often hard and dangerous for them in forts and camps in North Britain, Germany or Africa. Often they didn't see their homes and families for five or six years.

Most of the men in the army were foot soldiers. They marched in groups, or legions, of 5,000 men, and they had to carry everything with them—javelins, spears, helmet, shield, axe, bags of food and spare clothes and pots for cooking and eating.

Nevertheless, because of the fine straight roads the Romans built all over Europe, their armies could often march twenty-five or thirty miles a day for days together.

---

(a) Which countries use the— baht; won; rupiah; kyat; ringgit?

(b) How many countries use the dollar? Name them.

(c) How many countries use the pound (£)? Name them.

(d) On February 21st, how many Sri Lanka rupees went to one Deutsche mark? Work to one decimal place. 26.6 SL rupees to one US$. 2.3 DM. to one US$. (26.6 divided by 2.3 is....)

(e) Practise with your partner questions like, "What's the currency of... called? How many... to the... on (date)?

## UNIT ONE    FINDING OUT    THE ANCIENT ROMANS AND SRI LANKA

Padmini was lucky to get a trip to London. Sri Lankans though, have been travelling to Europe for at least three thousand years. We can say that the ancient Romans, for example, thought highly of Sri Lanka, from this account of a Roman general's visit around 2,000 years ago.

After enjoying the wonderful hospitality of the ruling Sinhala king, the Roman visitors left the shores of the island with the first Sri Lankan embassy to the west.

There were four Sinhalese ambassadors, and, as most Sri Lankan scholars agree, the head of the mission was a chieftain. The evidence for this comes from the records on Sri Lanka kept by the great Roman historian, Pliny the Elder. He states that the leader was called "Rachia".

The most interesting thing about the visit is the treatment the Sri Lankan ambassadors received in the Roman court. The Roman Emperor at that time, Claudius Caesar, welcomed them with the highest honour. Pliny, who was an eye witness to the visit, says, "The Sinhala Ambassador from the court of Anuradhapura sat on the right side of the Roman Emperor". Claudius Caesar. Captives from England were paraded in procession before the Emperor". They included Caredoc and Caractacus, two early kings of Britain. The very fact that the Ambassador was seated on the right side of the Emperor, tells us that Sri Lanka was important to the Roman Empire.

In the end, though, the Roman Empire became too large. There were not enough soldiers to guard such a huge area and the German, French and British tribesmen drove the Romans back. By 400 A.D. the Roman Empire came to an end.

1. Look at the map of the Roman Empire on the next page. With your group see how many countries you can write down that were part of the Empire. Use the modern names.

2. Imagine you were a Roman soldier. Write a letter home to your parents in Rome telling them about one or two days in your life and mentioning all the things you have to carry. Your legion might have beaten off an attack by tribesmen that day. Then, after a ten or twenty mile march, perhaps you had to set up a new camp, find wood for a fire and cook your evening meal of grain and dried fish.

UNIT ONE    LEARNING TOGETHER    COULD YOU TELL ME HOW TO GET TO ...?

When Padmini came to London for the International Nursing Conference, she stayed at the Royal Lancaster Hotel in Bayswater Road. Here is a map of Central London, showing the hotel. Underground railway stations (sometimes called tube stations) are marked by a circle with a horizontal line through it.

Use the map to ask your partner how to get from one place to another. Say whether nearby tube stations could be used, and how much walking might be necessary. Here is a sample dialogue. First establish your starting point, either as part of the dialogue, or pointing to it.

Excuse me. This is Kensington High Street isn't it?
Yes. That's right.
Could you tell me how to get to Marble Arch?
Yes, certainly. Walk up Kensington Church Street. When you get to Notting Hill Gate, turn right. Then go straight down Bayswater Road.
Is it far?
Yes. It's about two miles. You could take the tube from Notting Hill Gate.
Marble Arch is the third stop.
Thank you.

# Royal Lancaster Hotel

UNIT ONE    POEM    SEA FEVER

Nowadays we can fly to Moscow in eight or nine hours and to London in twelve or fourteen, but this has been possible only for the past thirty years or so. Before that, long distance travel between continents was by ship. Some people still prefer to travel by sea. They like to relax on a two or three-week sea journey. They enjoy the fresh air. They like to stop at interesting places on the way. They don't like the cramped seats and the possible dangers of flying. John Masefield, who wrote this famous poem over fifty years ago would not have liked modern air travel we can imagine.

I must go down to the seas again, to the lonely sea and the sky,
And all I ask is a tall ship and a star to steer her by,
And the wheel's kick and the wind's song and the white sail's shaking
And a grey mist on the sea's face and a grey dawn breaking.

10

I must down to the seas again, for the call of the running tide
Is a wild call and a clear call that may not be denied:
And all I ask is a windy day with the white clouds flying.
And the flung spray and the blown spume and the sea-gulls crying.

I must down to the seas again to the vagrant gipsy life,
To the gull's way and the whale's way where the wind's like a whetted knife;
And all I ask is a merry yarn from a laughing fellow-rover
And quiet sleep and a sweet dream when the long trick's over.

(a) The words 'spume' in verse 2 and 'trick' in verse 3 are special words used by sailors. Can you work out what they mean?

(b) Why do you think the poet made the lines so long, with so many long vowel sounds, 'o', 'ee', 'ay'?

(c) The sound 's' reminds us of the swish of the sea and the sighing of the wind. Can you find lines with many 's' sounds?

(d) Would you prefer air or sea travel? Write four short paragraphs giving the good points and the bad points of each form of travel. Work in pairs. Your teacher will help you with some ideas and sentence forms.

UNIT ONE    DISCUSSION    A TUNNEL FROM ENGLAND TO FRANCE

England is separated from France, her nearest neighbour, and the rest of Europe by 22 miles of water—the English Channel. The weather in the Channel is often rough. The journey from London to Paris can take six hours and more. Some days the ferry boats cannot even leave port.

11

The new tunnel under the Channel will be open night and day. High speed trains will carry cars and buses at 180 kilometres per hour. Charges made for the use of the tunnel will bring over $600 million in income. In the eight years it will take to build the tunnel, over 40,000 French and British workers will get employment. The journey between London and Paris will be cut to less than three hours. The English Channel, or La Manche (the sleeve) as the French call it, is one of the busiest waterways in the world. The tunnel will avoid the danger of dozens of ferry boats a day cutting across the main shipping routes.

Not everyone is in favour of the Channel Tunnel, though. The ferry boat owners and their workers will lose their living. They claim that in any case their service costs half as much as any tunnel. The tunnel entrances and railway yards and tracks will use up some of the best farming land in southern England. Many people will lose their houses, many of them historic and beautiful buildings, to make way for the construction work. Finally, there are still many people in England who do not want their country to be so closely connected to France. They say the Channel is valuable as a defence in time of war. During peace, it makes it easier to control smuggling and the illegal movement of drugs and undesirable people in and out of the country. In particular, they fear the spread of rabies, which Britain, as an island, has so far been able to control almost completely.

Write down in note form the main points for and against a channel tunnel between England and France. Do not write more than ten words for any one point.

UNIT ONE    DISCUSSION    WHAT'S HAPPENING HERE?

Study this picture and practise questions and answers about it with a partner.

371

Appendix 11

12

Here are some of the questions you might ask.

(a) About how many people are there in the picture?
(b) How many of them are men?
(c) How many of them are women?
(d) How old are they?
(e) What are they holding?
(f) Are they happy? sad? angry?
(g) What is (choose a person) wearing?
(h) What country are they in?
(i) Where do you think they might be standing?
(j) What do they want the government to do?
(k) Where might some of them live?

This picture is connected with the previous exercise. This should help you to answer some of the questions.

---

**UNIT ONE**          **LISTENING**          **DESCRIBING SOMEONE?**

Look at the pictures A, B and C. Listen carefully to the descriptions of three girls. Match the picture to the description. Make a list of the words which helped you to decide.

e.g. necklace, tall, short, etc.

Ⓐ          Ⓑ          Ⓒ

Mala          Lalitha          Shalini

372

# APPENDIX 12:
## Description of typical classrooms
## (Alderson and Wall 1992:87-88)

### 5.1.2 Classroom environment

It is customary for students to stay in their own classroom or part of a classroom all day long and for teachers of different subjects to come to them, rather than for the students to circulate to the History room or the Maths room or the English room. (The exception is for Science or Domestic Sciences classes, where students need special equipment to pursue their studies.) In general, schools do not establish a room or rooms for English, which would allow the teacher to have a quiet atmosphere so the students could hear oral input, set up resources for reading and writing, move furniture around for pair work etc.

There seem to be two basic types of classrooms: the separate or semi-separate, and the communal. Separate classrooms are found mainly in the larger, better-resourced schools. These are self-contained rooms, with a front and back wall (at least) that reach to the ceiling and block out some of the noise emanating from adjoining classrooms. The walls on the sides of the classroom may be built up to the ceiling and have windows in them, or one or both of them may be built up to about three feet high and then just stop. This design allows the air to circulate through the classroom, but also lets in some noise from other classrooms, the playing fields and the street. In these classrooms it is sometimes possible to find a cupboard which will contain materials for the group (this will appear only if there is some way to lock the classroom after school hours), and, occasionally, posters or students' work on the walls. The semi-separate classroom also has side walls but the front and back walls may only be a few feet high, which allows some privacy but not complete isolation from other classes. Both the separate and semi-separate classrooms will have a blackboard, usually fixed, often of poor quality. There will be a teachers' desk, sometimes on a platform. The furniture for the students may be individual desks or may be long narrow tables with individual chairs or benches that several students share. These desks and tables will invariably be arranged in rows, so that the students can face the teacher and the blackboard. Sometimes it is possible to move the furniture around, but other times the room will be too crowded to allow students to change their positions easily.

The communal classroom is most often seen in poorer schools, especially in the countryside. The school will consist of one or more long buildings, with no internal walls. Each of these buildings, or 'halls', will contain as many as 7 or 8 lessons taking place simultaneously. Each teacher will be standing or sitting in front of his/her own group of students, who will, as in the separate classrooms described above, be sitting in rows facing forwards. Since there is no physical separation between the classes there is no way of keeping the noise from one class from disturbing the others, and because the outside walls are probably not more than a few feet high there will be no way of keeping out noise from the playing fields and the street. The teachers will each have a very small blackboard, again of poor quality, which will probably be leaning on an easel-like support or on a chair rather than be fixed to a wall. If the blackboard is not fixed high on the wall it is often difficult for students in the back of the group to see what is written on the bottom of the board. It is rare to find storage cupboards in communal classrooms, and because there are very few walls it is unusual to find any student work or educational posters being displayed.

Some schools are not big enough to hold all of the students comfortably. Sometimes schools will build an extension off the back or the side of the main building, which will consist of wooden posts driven into the ground with a corrugated metal roof laid on top of the pillars. These extensions provide little shelter from the rains during the monsoon season, and sometimes the students have to leave their desks and go into the main building for shelter until the rains stop. Lessons which are taking place inside the main buildings often also suffer when the rains come, because the noise on the roofs prevents the students and teachers from hearing each other.

# APPENDIX 13:
## Recommendations for a baseline study – St Petersburg (Wall 1995:9-10)

### Specific focuses: a checklist

The areas that would need to be investigated are as follows:

Political/educational context: Division of responsibilities between Ministry, Mayor's Office and local schools; number of districts in St Petersburg region; organization of schooling in each district; number of schools offering English; number of schools offering Year 11 exam in English; number of students taking Year 11 English now and projections for the future

Social/economic context: Demand for English in the world outside school; views of employers, academics and students regarding the role of English and the adequacy of current teaching/testing provision

Current policy regarding foreign languages teaching, particularly English (with translations of extracts from important documents). It is especially important to understand where English stands in relation to other subjects, and whether developments in curriculum and assessment in English are in line with, ahead of or behind developments in other subject areas.

Curriculum: What laws and documents regulate English teaching, who decides on spirit and content of curriculum, relationship of the curriculum to the Year 11 examination, status of current curriculum, translation of current curriculum, plans for change in near future, description of mechanism for creating new guidelines.

Assessment: Responsibilities of Independent City Examinations Board, translation of ICEB reports on foreign languages, responsibilities of English panel, description and results of 1995 monitoring exercise, status of current Year 11 guidelines, translation of current guidelines, full description (and video if possible) of Year 11 examination, analysis of examination according to the framework in Appendix B, plans for change in near future, description of mechanism for creating new guidelines

Current language teaching situation: Teaching time available for English (specialized v non-specialized schools), availability and qualifications of teaching force, teaching approaches, methodology, textbooks and supplementary materials, general levels of proficiency amongst students, teachers' attitudes to strengths and weaknesses of present system. (N.B. This component should include classroom observations, interviews and tests as well as questionnaires.

Current language testing situation in schools (classroom testing): Purposes of assessment, timing of assessments, current practices, strengths and weaknesses of system as a whole, teachers' attitudes toward Year 11 exam and their views of how it affects their teaching and testing (N.B. This component should involve an analysis of classroom tests), students' attitudes toward Year 11 exam and university entrance exams

Current language testing situation in higher education: Comparison of entrance exams with Year 11 exams in English, enrolment in exam preparation courses, numbers of students taking entrance exams, numbers of students accepted or rejected from higher education and the part English language plays in this, attitudes of lecturers to entrance exams and to Year 11 exams, attitudes of students to entrance exams

Current teacher-training situation: What institutions provide teacher training in EFL, their curricula, numbers of teachers enrolled, expertise or courses in language testing, fate of graduates

Communication networks: Communication channels between Ministry, Mayor's Office, district education offices and teachers; the role of SPELTA; other teacher associations; the role of the British Council Resources Centre; educational press; availability of fax and e-mail

Educational resourcing: Equipment available in schools, including recording and playback equipment, photocopiers, computers, fax and e-mail

Relevant development in other parts of Russia and other parts of Europe: summary of relevant parts of World Bank report; summary of reactions to World Bank report; summary of work being done in Vologda by joint Dutch-Russian team to develop regional standards and measurement tools in several subjects including English and commentary on possibilities of future co-operation; summary of work done to date on IEA research project to determine levels of achievement in foreign languages and policy implications; information about school-leaving exams in other countries, to serve as a point of comparison for what could be developed in Russia.

## APPENDIX 14:
**Communications web. Year 12 Project – Estonia**
**(Lätt, Mere, Sass, Truus and Türk 1994:39)**

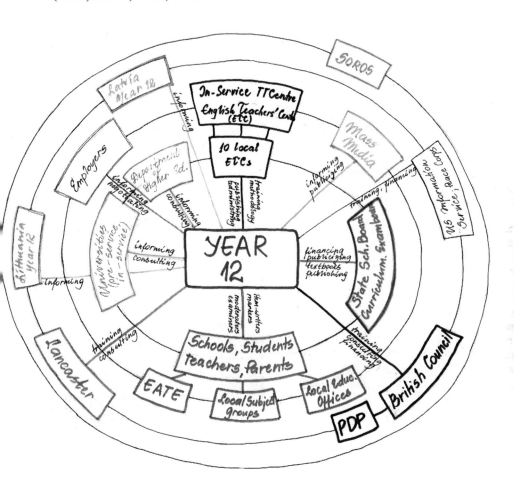

# APPENDIX 15:

Plans for phasing in a new examination. Year 12 Project – Lithuania (Berseniene, Jukneliene, Mazuoliene, Skapiene and Staneviciene 1994:29)

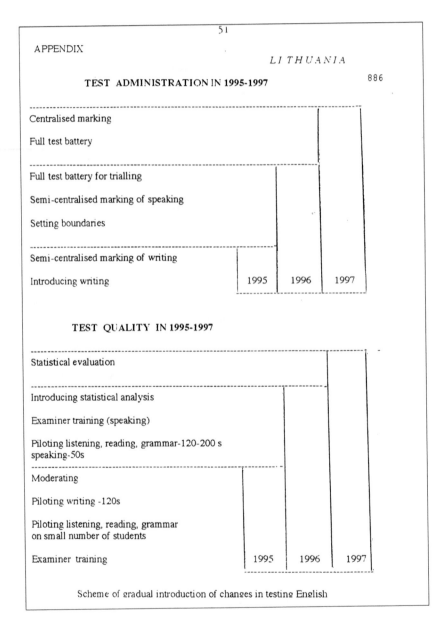

APPENDIX

*LITHUANIA*

886

## TEST ADMINISTRATION IN 1995-1997

Centralised marking

Full test battery

Full test battery for trialling

Semi-centralised marking of speaking

Setting boundaries

Semi-centralised marking of writing

Introducing writing

| 1995 | 1996 | 1997 |

## TEST QUALITY IN 1995-1997

Statistical evaluation

Introducing statistical analysis

Examiner training (speaking)

Piloting listening, reading, grammar-120-200 s
speaking-50s

Moderating

Piloting writing -120s

Piloting listening, reading, grammar
on small number of students

Examiner training

| 1995 | 1996 | 1997 |

Scheme of gradual introduction of changes in testing English

# References

Adams, R and Chen D (1981) *The process of educational innovation: An international perspective*, London: Kogan Page/UNESCO Press.

Agnew, J A (ed) (1980) *Innovation Research and Public Policy* 5, Syracuse: Syracuse University Press.

Aiken, L R (1982) Writing multiple-choice items to measure higher-order educational objectives, *Educational and Psychological Measurement* 42, 803–806.

Airasian, P (1988a) Measurement-Driven Instruction: A Closer Look, *Educational Measurement: Issues and Practice* (Winter), 6–11.

Airasian, P W (1988b) Symbolic Validation: The Case of State-Mandated, High-Stakes Testing, *Educational Evaluation and Policy Analysis* 10(4), 301–313.

Alderson, J C (1986) Innovations in Language Testing? In Portal, M (ed) *Innovations in Language Testing*, 93–105. Windsor: NFER/Nelson.

Alderson, J C and Banerjee, J (2001) Impact and washback research in language testing. In Elder, C, Brown, A, Grove, E, Hill, K, Iwashita, N, Lumley, T, McLoughlin, K and McNamara, T (ed) *Experimenting with uncertainty: Essays in honor of Alan Davies*, 150–161. Cambridge: Cambridge University Press.

Alderson, J C, Clapham, C and Wall, D (1995) *Language Test Construction and Evaluation*, Cambridge: Cambridge University Press.

Alderson, J C and Hamp-Lyons, L (1996) TOEFL Preparation Courses: A Study of Washback, *Language Testing* 13(3), 280–297.

Alderson, J C and Wall, D (1989) The Sri Lankan O level Evaluation Project: First Interim Report, Lancaster: Lancaster University.

Alderson, J C and Wall, D (1990) The Sri Lankan O level Evaluation Project: Second Interim Report, Lancaster: Lancaster University.

Alderson, J C and Wall, D (1991) The Sri Lankan O level Evaluation Project: Third Interim Report, Lancaster: Lancaster University.

Alderson, J C and Wall, D (1992) The Sri Lankan O level Evaluation Project: Fourth and Final Report, Lancaster: Lancaster University.

Alderson, J C and Wall, D (1993) Does Washback Exist? *Applied Linguistics* 14(2), 115–129.

Alderson, J C, Wall, D and Clapham C (1987) An Evaluation of the National Certificate in English, Lancaster, Institute for English Language Education, Lancaster University.

Allen, J P B and Davies, A (eds) (1977) *Testing and Experimental Methods*. Volume 4 in *The Edinburgh Course in Applied Linguistics*, London: Oxford University Press.

Anastasi, A (ed) (1966) *Testing Problems in Perspective*, Washington, D C: American Council on Education.

Andrews, S (2003) Washback and Curricular Innovation. In Cheng, L and Watanabe Y (eds) *Washback in Language Testing: Research Contexts and Methods*, Mahwah, New Jersey: Lawrence Erlbaum Associates.

Andrews, S, Fullilove, J and Wong, Y (2002) Targeting washback: A case study, *System* 30:207–223.

Bachman, L (1990) *Fundamental Considerations in Language Testing*, Oxford: Oxford University Press.

Bachman, L F and Palmer, A S (1996) *Language Testing in Practice*, Oxford: Oxford University Press.

Bailey, K (1994) Working for Washback: A Review of the Washback Concept in Language Testing. Unpublished manuscript.

Bailey, K (1996) Working for Washback: A Review of the Washback Concept in Language Testing, *Language Testing* 13(3), 257–279.

Bailey, K (1999) Washback in Language Testing, TOEFL Monograph Series MS-15. Princeton: Educational Testing Service.

Beeby, C E (1966) *The Quality of Education in Developing Countries*, Cambridge, Massachusetts: Harvard University Press.

Bennis, W G, Benne, K D, Chin, R and Corey, K E (eds) (1976) *The planning of change,* 3rd edition:22–45, New York: Holt, Rinehart and Winston.

Beretta, A (1990) Implementation of the Bangalore Project, *Applied Linguistics* 11 (4), 321–337.

Bernstein, B B, Elvin, H L and Peters, R S (1966) Rituals in Education. In *Philosophical Transactions of the Royal Society of London*, Series B, Volume 251, 429–436.

Berseniene, B, Jukneliene, L, Mazuoliene, Z, Skapiene, S and Staneviciene, V (1994) The Lithuanian Year 12 Project: Baseline Study. Unpublished Report.

Biggs, J B (1995) Assumptions underlying new approaches to educational assessment, *Curriculum Forum* 4 (2), 1–22.

Bowers, R (1980) War stories and romances: Interchanging experience in ELT. In Smyth, E (ed) *Projects in materials design*, ELT Documents Special, 71–81, London: The British Council.

Bowers, R (1983) Project planning and performance. In Brumfit, C J (ed) *Language teaching projects for the Third World*, ELT Documents Volume 116, 99–120, London: The British Council.

Broadfoot, P (1979) *Assessment, schools and society*, London: Methuen and Co Ltd.

Brumfit, C J (ed) (1983) *Language teaching projects for the Third World*, ELT Documents Volume 116, London: The British Council.

Buck, G (1988) Testing listening comprehension in Japanese university entrance examinations, *JALT Journal* 10 (1 and 2), 5–42.

Canagarajah, A S (1993) Critical Ethnography of a Sri Lankan Classroom: Ambiguities in Student Opposition to Reproduction through ESOL, *TESOL Quarterly* 27/4, 601–626.

Cannell, C F and Kahn, R L (1968) Interviewing. In Lindzey, G and Aronson, A (eds) *The Handbook of Social Psychology*, Volume 2, *Research Methods*. New York: Addison Wesley.

Carnoy, M and Levin, H (eds) *The limits of educational reform*, New York: McKay.

Chamberlain, D and Baumgardner, R J (eds) (1988) *ESP in the Classroom: Practice and Evaluation*, ELT Documents Volume 128, London: Modern English Publications.

Chapman, D W and Snyder, C W (2000) Can high-stakes national testing improve instruction: Re-examining conventional wisdom, *Journal of Educational Development* 20, 457–474.

Cheng, L (1997) How Does Washback Influence Teaching? Implications for Hong Kong, *Language and Education* 11(1), 38–54.

Cheng, L (1998) Impact of a public English examination change on students' perceptions and attitudes toward their English learning, *Studies in Educational Evaluation* 24, 279–301.

Cheng, L and Watanabe, Y (eds) (2003), *Washback in Language Testing: Research Contexts and Methods,* Mahwah, New Jersey: Lawrence Erlbaum Associates.

Chin, R and Benne, K D (1976) General strategies for effecting changes in human systems. In Bennis, W G, Benne, K D, Chin, R and Corey, K E (eds) *The planning of change,* 3rd edition, 22–45, New York: Holt, Rinehart and Winston.

Cicourel, A V (1964) *Method and Measurement in Sociology*, New York: The Free Press.

Clapham, C and Corson, D (eds) (1997) *Language Testing and Assessment*, Volume 7 of *The Kluwer Encyclopedia of Language and Education*, Dordrecht: Kluwer Academic Publishers.

Clark, J L D (1983) Language testing: Past and current status—directions for the future, *Modern Language Journal* 67(4), 431–432.

Coffey, A and Atkinson, P (1996) *Making Sense of Qualitative Data*, London: SAGE Publications Ltd.

Cohen, A D (1994) *Assessing Language Ability in the Classroom*, 2nd edition, Boston: Heinle and Heinle Publishers.

Cohen, L and Manion, L (1994) *Research Methods in Education*, 4th edition, London: Routledge.

Cooper, R L (1982a) A framework for the study of language spread. In Cooper, R L (ed) *Language spread: Studies in diffusion and social change*, 5–36, Bloomington: Indiana University Press and Washington, D C, Center for Applied Linguistics.

Cooper, R L (ed) (1982b) *Language spread: Studies in diffusion and social change*, Bloomington: Indiana University Press and Washington, D C, Center for Applied Linguistics.

Cooper, R L (1989) *Language Planning and Social Change*, Cambridge: Cambridge University Press.

Corbett, H D, Dawson, J and Firestone, W (1984) *School context and school change*, New York: Teachers College Press.

Corbett, H D and Wilson, B (1990) *Testing, reform and rebellion*, Norwood, New York: Ablex.

Council of Europe (2001) *Common European Framework of Reference for Languages: Learning, teaching, assessment,* Cambridge: Cambridge University Press.

Davies, A (ed) (1968) *Language Testing Symposium*, London: Oxford University Press.

Davies, A (1977) The Construction of Language Tests. In Allen, J P B and Davies, A (eds) *Testing and Experimental Methods*, Volume 4 in *The Edinburgh Course in Applied Linguistics*, 38–104, London: Oxford University Press.

Davies, A (1985) Follow My Leader: Is That What Language Tests Do? In Lee, Y P, Fok, A C Y, Lord, R and Low, G (eds) *New Directions in Language Testing*, 3–13, Oxford: Pergamon Press.

Davies, A (1990) *Principles of Language Testing*, Oxford: Basil Blackwell.

Davis, K A (1995) Qualitative Theory and Methods in Applied Linguistics Research, *TESOL Quarterly* 29(3), 427–453.

de Silva, B (1989) *New G.C.E. (O.L.) Exam English Model Question Papers with Answers*, Colombo: Royal College.

Denzin, N K (1978) *Sociological Methods: A Sourcebook*, 2nd edition, New York: McGraw-Hill.

Denzin, N K (1970) *The Research Act in Sociology: A Theoretical Introduction to Sociological Methods*, London: The Butterworth Group.

Dore, R P (1976) *The diploma disease*, London: Allen and Unwin.

Dore, R P (1997) Reflections on the diploma disease twenty years later, *Assessment in Education* 4, 189–206.

Dow, I I, Whitehead, R V and Wright R L (1984) *Curriculum Implementation: A Framework for Action*, Document ED 256 715, Alexandria, Virginia: ERIC Document Reproduction Service.

Ebel, R L (1966) The Social Consequences of Educational Testing. In Anastasi, A (ed) *Testing Problems in Perspective*, 18–28, Washington, D C: American Council on Education.

Eckstein, M A and Noah, H J (eds) (1992) *Examinations: Comparative and International Studies*, Oxford: Pergamon Press.

Eckstein, M A and Noah, H J (1993) *Secondary School Examinations: International Perspectives on Policies and Practice*, New Haven: Yale University Press.

Eggleston, J (1984) School Examinations—Some Sociological Issues. In Broadfoot, P (ed) *Selection, Certification and Control: Social Issues in Educational Assessment*, 17–34, London: The Falmer Press.

Eisemon, T O (1990) Examinations Policies to Strengthen Primary Schooling in African Countries, *International Journal of Educational Development* 10(1), 69–82.

Eisemon, T O, Patel, V and Abaji, J (1988) Read these instructions carefully: Examination reform and improving health education in Kenya, *International Journal of Educational Development* 8, 55–66.

Eisner, E W and Peshkin, A (eds) (1990) *Qualitative enquiry in education: The continuing debate*, New York: Teachers' College Press.

Emeneau, M B (1981) Indian and Linguistics, *Journal of the American Oriental Society* 75, 145–153.

Finocchiaro, M and Sako, S (1983) *Foreign Language Testing: A Practical Approach*, New York: Regents Publishing Co.

Firestone, W (1989) Using Reform: Conceptualizing District Initiative, *Educational Evaluation and Policy Analysis* 11(2), 151–164.

Flavell, R H (ed) (1994a) *ELT Policy and Its Impact: A Case Study. Review of English Language Teaching*, Volume 4, Number 1, London: Modern English Publications in association with The British Council.

Flavell, R H (1994b) Impact Research: The Diploma Course at the Department of English Education. In Flavell, R H (ed) (1994a) *ELT Policy and Its Impact: A Case Study. Review of English Language Teaching*, Volume 4, Number 1, 145–186, London: Modern English Publications in association with The British Council.

Flavell, R H and Randles, L (1994) The Impact of *English Every Day*. In Flavell, R H (ed) *ELT Policy and Its Impact: A Case Study. Review of English Language Teaching*, Volume 4, Number 1, 66–79, London: Modern English Publications in association with The British Council.

Forbes, D (1973) Selling English Short, *English Language Teaching Journal*, Number XXVII, 132–157.

Foster, P J (1992) Commentary, Chapter 9 in Eckstein, M A and Noah, H J (eds) *Examinations: Comparative and International Studies*, Oxford: Pergamon Press.

Frederiksen, N (1984) The Real Test Bias: Influences of Testing on Teaching and Learning, *American Psychologist* 39(3), 193–202.

Frederiksen, J R and Collins, A (1989) A Systems Approach to Educational Testing, *Educational Researcher* 18(9), 27–32.

Freeman, D (1989) Teacher training, development and decision-making: A model for teaching and related strategies for language and education, *TESOL Quarterly* 23/1, 27–45.

Fullan, M G with Steigelbauer, S (1991) *The New Meaning of Educational Change*, 2nd edition, London: Cassell Educational Limited.

Gipps, C V (1990) *Assessment: A Teacher's Guide to the Issues*, London: Hodder and Stoughton.

Gipps, C V (1994) *Beyond Testing: Towards a Theory of Educational Assessment*, London: The Falmer Press.

Goodlad, J I, Klein, M and associates (1970) *Behind the Classroom Door*, Worthington, Ohio: Charles A Jones.

Goonetillake, V, Samarasinghe, C, Senaratne, D and Sinhalage, S (1988) An Evaluation of the National Certificate in English, Sri Lanka 1987, Colombo: National Institute of Education.

Haas, N S, Haladyna, T M and Nolen, S B (1989) Standardized testing in Arizona: Interviews and written comments from teachers and administrators. Technical Report No 89–3, Phoenix, Arizona: Arizona State University West Campus.

Haladyna, T M, Nolen, S B and Haas, N. S. (1991) Raising Standardized Achievement Test Scores and the Origins of Test Score Pollution, *Educational Researcher* 20(5), 2–7.

Hall, G E and Loucks, S F (1977) A developmental model for determining whether the treatment is actually implemented, *American Educational Research Journal* 14/3, 263–276.

Halsey, A H et al (eds) (1961) *Education, Economy and Society*, New York: The Free Press of Glencoe.

Hamp-Lyons, L (1998) Ethical test preparation practice: The case of the TOEFL, *TESOL Quarterly* 32(2), 329–337.

Hargreaves, E (1997) The Diploma Disease in Egypt: learning, teaching and the monster of the secondary leaving certificate, *Assessment in Education: principles, policy and practice* 4(1), 161–176.

Havelock, R G (1969) *Planning for Innovation through Dissemination and Utilization of Knowledge*, Ann Arbor, Michigan: Center for Research on Utilization of Scientific Knowledge, Institute for Social Research, The University of Michigan.

Havelock, R G (1971) The utilization of educational research and development, *British Journal of Educational Technology* 2(2), 84–97.

Havelock, R G and Huberman, A M (1978) *The Theory and Reality of Innovation in Developing Countries*, New York: Praeger.

Heaton, J B (1988) *Writing English Language Tests*, New edition, Harlow: Longman.

Heaton, J B (1990) *Classroom Testing*, Harlow: Longman.

Henning, G (1987) *A Guide to Language Testing, Development, Evaluation, Research*, Cambridge, Massachusetts: Newbury House Publishers.

Henrichsen, L E (1989) *Diffusion of Innovations in English Language Teaching: The ELEC Effort in Japan, 1956–1968*, New York: Greenwood Press.

Herman, J L and Golan, S (1993) The effects of standardized testing on teaching and schools, *Educational Measurement: Issues and Practices* 12(4), 20–25.

Heyneman, S P and Ransom, A W (1990) Using Examinations and Testing to Improve Educational Quality, *Educational Policy* 4(3), 177–192.

Holliday, A (1992) Tissue rejection and informal orders in ELT projects: Collecting the right information, *Applied Linguistics* 13(4), 403–424.

Holliday, A and Cooke, T (1982) An ecological approach to ESP. In Waters, A (ed) *Issues in ESP. Lancaster Practical Papers in English Language Education* Volume 5, 124–143, Oxford: Pergamon Press.

Holmes, E (1911) *What Is and What Might Be*, London: Constable and Co.

House, E (1974) *The Politics of Educational Innovation*, Berkeley, California: McCutchan.

Huberman, M and Miles, M (1984) *Innovation Up Close*, New York: Plenum.

Hughes, A (1988a) Introducing a Needs-based Test of English Language Proficiency into an English-Medium University in Turkey. In Hughes, A (ed) *Testing English for University Study. ELT Documents* 127, 134–153, London: Modern English Publications.

Hughes, A (ed) (1988b) *Testing English for University Study. ELT Documents* 127, London: Modern English Publications.

Hughes, A (1989) *Testing for Language Teachers*, Cambridge: Cambridge University Press.

Hughes, A (1994) Backwash and TOEFL 2000. Unpublished manuscript, commissioned by Educational Testing Service.

Institute for English Language Education (1988) Research proposal for Sri Lankan O level Evaluation Project, Lancaster.

James, M (2000) Measured lives. The rise of assessment as the engine of change in English schools, *Curriculum Journal* 11, 343–364.

Kandiah, T (1979) Disinherited Englishes: The case of Lankan English, *Navasilu* 3, 75–89.

Kandiah, T (1984) 'Kaduva': Power and the English language weapon in Sri Lanka. In Collin-Thome, P and Halpe, A (eds) *Honouring E F C Ludowyk*, 117–154, Colombo: Tisara Prakasayo.

Kaplan, A (1964) *The conduct of inquiry: Methodology for behavioral science*, San Francisco: Chandler.

Kellaghan, T and Greaney, V (1992) *Using Examinations to Improve Education: A Study of Fourteen African Countries*, Washington, D C: The World Bank.

Kellaghan, T, Madaus, G F and Airasian, P W (1982) *The Effects of Standardized Testing*, London: Kluwer Nijhoff Publishing.

Kelle, U (ed) (1995) *Computer-aided qualitative data analysis: Theory, methods and practice*, London: Sage.

Kennedy, C (1982) Language Planning, *Language Teaching* 15(3), 264–284.

Kennedy, C (1987) Innovating for a change: Teacher development and innovation, *ELT Journal* 41/3, 163–170.

Kennedy, C (1988) Evaluation of the Management of Change in ELT Projects, *Applied Linguistics* 9(4), 329–342.

Kerlinger, F N (1973) *Foundations of Behavioral Research*, New York: Holt, Rinehart and Winston.

Khaniyah, T R (1990a) *Examinations as Instruments for Educational Change: Investigating the Washback Effect of the Nepalese English Exams*, unpublished PhD dissertation, Edinburgh: University of Edinburgh.

Khaniyah, T R (1990b) The Washback Effect of a Textbook-based Test, *Edinburgh Working Papers in Applied Linguistics* 1, 48–58.

Kirk, J and Miller, M L (1986) *Reliability and Validity in Qualitative Research*, Beverly Hills: Sage.

Kirkland, M C (1971) The Effect of Tests on Students and Schools, *Review of Educational Research* 41(4), 303–350.

Lam, H P (1993) *Washback—Can It Be Quantified?* Unpublished MA thesis, Leeds: University of Leeds.

Lambright, W H and Flynn, P (1980) The role of local bureaucracy-centered coalitions in technology transfer to the city. In Agnew, J A (ed) *Innovation Research and Public Policy* 5, 243–282, Syracuse: Syracuse University Press.

Larsen-Freeman, D and Long, M (1991) *An introduction to second language acquisition research*, London: Longman.

Lätt, V, Mere, K, Sass, E, Truus, K and Türk, Ü (1994) The Estonian Year 12 Project: Baseline Study. Unpublished report.

Lazaraton, A (1995) Qualitative Research in Applied Linguistics: A Progress Report, *TESOL Quarterly* 29(3), 455–472.

Lee, Y. P., Fok, A. C .Y., Lord, R. and Low, G (eds) *(1985) New Directions in Language Testing*, Oxford: Pergamon Press.

Levin, H (1976) Educational reform: Its meaning. In Carnoy, M and Levin H, (eds) *The limits of educational reform*, New York: McKay.

Lewin, K (1997) The Sea of Items Returns to China: backwash, selection and the diploma disease revisited, *Assessment in Education: principles, policy and practice* 4 (1), 137–160.

Li, X (1990) How Powerful Can a Language Test Be? *Journal of Multilingual and Multicultural Development* 11(5), 393–404.

Lin, N (1976) *Foundations of Social Research*, New York: McGraw-Hill

Lindzey, G and Aronson, A (eds.) (1968) *The Handbook of Social Psychology. Research Methods* 2, New York: Addison Wesley.

Little, A (1992) Commentary, Decontextualizing Assessment Policy: Does It Make Economic Sense? In Eckstein, M A and Noah, H J (eds) *Examinations: Comparative and International Studies*, 127–132, Oxford: Pergamon Press.

Littlejohn, A (1988) How to Fail Interviews. In Littlejohn, A and Melouk, M (eds) *Research Methods and Processes*, 67–75, Lancaster: Department of Linguistics and Modern English Language, Lancaster University.

Littlejohn, A and Melouk, M (eds) (1988) *Research Methods and Processes*, Lancaster: Department of Linguistics and Modern English Language, Lancaster University.

London, I D (1949) The role of the model in explanation, *Journal of Genetic Psychology*, 74, 165–176.

Madaus, G F (1988) The Influence of Testing on the Curriculum. In Tanner, L N (ed) *Critical Issues in Curriculum: Eighty-seventh Yearbook of the National Society for the Study of Education* 83–121, Chicago: NSSE, University of Chicago Press.

Madsen, H (1976) New Alternatives in EFL Exams or 'How to Avoid Selling English Short', *English Language Teaching Journal* 30(2), 135–144.

Madsen, H S (1983) *Techniques in Testing*, Oxford: Oxford University Press.

Maley, A (1984) Constraints-based Syllabuses. In Read, J A S (ed) *Trends in Language Syllabus Design* 68–90, Singapore: SEAMEO—Regional Language Centre.

Markee, N (1986a) The importance of sociopolitical factors to communicative course design, *ESP Journal* 5(1), 3–16.

Markee, N (1986b) Toward an appropriate technology model of communicative course design, *English for Specific Purposes* 5(2), 161–172.

Markee, N (1993) The diffusion of innovation in language teaching, *Annual Review of Applied Linguistics* 13, 229–243.

Markee, N (1997) *Managing curricular innovation*, Cambridge: Cambridge University Press.

Mason, J (1996) *Qualitative Researching*, London: SAGE Publications Ltd.

Mathews, J C (1985) *Examinations: A Commentary*, London: George Allen and Unwin.

Mazuoliene, Z (1996) The Year 12 Project in Lithuania (1995), *Language Testing Update* (19), 25–27.

Mehrens, W A and Kaminski, J (1989) Methods for Improving Standardized Test Scores: Fruitful, Fruitless, or Fraudulent? *Educational Measurement: Issues and Practice*, Spring 1989, 14–22.

Messick, S (1981) Evidence and ethics in the evaluation of tests, *Educational Researcher* 10 (9), 9–20.

Messick, S (1996) Validity and Washback in Language Testing, *Language Testing* 13(3), 241–256.

Miles, M B (1964a) Educational Innovation: The Nature of the Problem. In Miles, M B (ed) *Innovation in education* 1–48, New York: Teachers College Press.

Miles, M B (ed) (1964b) *Innovation in education* 1–48, New York: Teachers College Press.

Miles, M B and Huberman, A M (1994) *Qualitative Data Analysis* 2, London: SAGE Publications Ltd.

Min, H and Xiuwen, Y (2001) Educational Assessment in China: lessons from history and future prospects, *Assessment in Education* 8 (1), 5–10.

Morrow, K (1986) The Evaluation of Tests of Communicative Performance. In Portal, M (ed) *Innovations in Language Testing,* 1–13, Windsor: NFER/Nelson.

Mortimore, P, Sammons, P, Stolle, L, Lewis, D and Ecob, R (1988) *School matters: The junior years*, Somerset: Open Books.

Mosback, G P (1982) The Quality Improvement Programme for the Teaching of English in Schools in Sri Lanka, unpublished manuscript.

Mosback, G P (1990) National syllabus and textbook design on communicative principles, *ELT Journal* 44(1), 18–24.

Mosback, G (1994) Communicatively-oriented syllabus and textbook design for a national school system: *English Every Day*. In Flavell, R H (ed) *ELT Policy and Its Impact: A Case Study. Review of English Language Teaching*, Volume 4, Number 1, 50–66. London: Modern English Publications in association with The British Council.

Munby, J (1978) *Communicative syllabus design*, Cambridge: Cambridge University Press.

Nanayakkara, E and Webber, R (1994) Sri Lankan English O level: Practical Considerations. In Flavell, R H (ed) *ELT Policy and Its Impact: A Case Study. Review of English Language Teaching* 4(1), 94–102, London: Modern English Publications in association with The British Council.

Newstead, S E and Findlay, K (1997) Some problems with using examination performance as a measure of teaching ability, *Psychology Teaching Review* 6(1), 23–30.

Nicholls, A (1983) *Managing educational innovations*, London: George Allen and Unwin.

Nihalani, P, Tongue, R K and Hosali, P (1979) *Indian and British English*, Oxford: Oxford University Press.

Nolen, S B, Haladyna, T M and Haas, N S (1989) A survey of Arizona teachers and administrators on the uses and effects of state-mandated standardized achievement testing, Technical Report 89–2, Phoenix, Arizona: Arizona State University West Campus.

Norton Peirce, B (1992) Demystifying the TOEFL Reading Test, *TESOL Quarterly* 26(4), 665–689.

# References

Norton Peirce, B and Stein, P (1995) Why the 'Monkeys Passage' Bombed: Tests, Genres, and Teaching, Harvard Educational Review, Volume 65(1), 50–65.

Nunan, D, Berry, R and Berry, V (eds) (1995) *Bringing about change in language education*, Hong Kong: Department of Curriculum Studies, University of Hong Kong.

Patton, M Q (1987) *How to Use Qualitative Methods in Evaluation* 2, Newbury Park, California: SAGE Publications, Inc.

Pearson, I (1988) Tests as Levers for Change. In Chamberlain, D and Baumgardner, R (eds) *ESP in the Classroom: Practice and Evaluation*, ELT Documents 128, 98–107. London: Modern English Publications.

Pearson, I (1994) The National Certificate in English and its Role in Examination Reform. In Flavell, R H (ed) *ELT Policy and Its Impact: A Case Study. Review of English Language Teaching* 4(1), 84–93. London: Modern English Publications in association with The British Council.

Pelz, D C (1985) Innovation Complexity and the Sequence of Innovating Stages. *Knowledge: Creation, Diffusion and Utilization* 6(3), 261–291.

Phillipson, R (1992) *Linguistic imperialism*, Oxford: Oxford University Press.

Popham, J (1987) The Merits of Measurement-driven Instruction, *Phi Delta Kappan*, May 1987, 679–682.

Popham, W J (1991) Appropriateness of Teachers' Test Preparation Practices? *Educational Measurement: Issues and Practice* 10 (1), 12–15.

Popham, W J (1995) *Classroom Assessment: What Teachers Need to Know*, Boston: Allyn & Bacon.

Portal, M (ed) (1986) *Innovations in Language Testing*, Windsor: NFER/Nelson.

Punchihetti, S (1994) English in Sri Lanka: A Historical and Contemporary Perspective. In Flavell, R H (ed) *ELT Policy and Its Impact: A Case Study. Review of English Language Teaching* 4 (1), 19–27. London: Modern English Publications in association with The British Council.

Qi, L (2003) Has High-stakes Testing Produced the Intended Changes? In Cheng, L and Watanabe, Y (eds) *Washback in Language Testing: Research Contexts and Methods,* Mahwah, New Jersey: Lawrence Erlbaum Associates.

Qualitative Solutions and Research Pty Ltd (1996) *QSR NUD*IST: User Guide*, Victoria, Australia: LaTrobe University.

Raimes, A (1990) The TOEFL Test of Written English: Causes for Concern, *TESOL Quarterly* 24(3), 427–442.

Read, J A S (ed) (1984) *Trends in Language Syllabus Design*, Singapore: SEAMEO—Regional Language Centre.

Richards, J C (1984) The secret life of methods, *TESOL Quarterly* 18(1), 7–23.

Richards, J C (1985) *The Context of Language Teaching*, Cambridge: Cambridge University Press.

Richards, J C and Rodgers, T S (1985) *Approaches and Methods in Language Teaching*, Cambridge: Cambridge University Press.

Richards, J C, Tung, P and Ng, P (1992) The culture of English language teachers: A Hong Kong example, *RELC Journal* 23(1), 81–102.

Roach, J (1971) *Public Examinations in England 1850-1900*, Cambridge: Cambridge University Press.

Rogers, E M (1983) *The diffusion of innovations* 3, London: Macmillan.

Rogers, E M (1995) *The diffusion of innovations* 4, New York: Free Press.

Rogers, E M and F. Shoemaker (1971) *Communication of innovations: A cross-cultural approach* 2, New York: Free Press.

Rondinelli, D, Middleton, J and Verspoor, A M (1990) *Planning educational reforms in developing countries*, Durham: Duke University Press.


Saville, N and Hawkey, R (2003) The IELTS Impact Study: Investigating Washback on Teaching Materials. In Cheng, L and Watanabe, Y (eds) *Washback in Language Testing: Research Contexts and Methods*, Mahwah, New Jersey: Lawrence Erlbaum Associates.

Scopes, P (1994) Pulling It Together at the Beginning of the Decade: The British Council/ODA Contribution. In Flavell, R H (ed) *ELT Policy and Its Impact: A Case Study. Review of English Language Teaching* 4 (1), 28–30. London: Modern English Publications in association with The British Council.

Seidel, J and Kelle, U (1995) Different functions of coding in the analysis of textual data. In Kelle, U (ed) *Computer-aided qualitative data analysis: Theory, methods and practice* 52–61. London: Sage.

Shepard, L (1990) Inflated test score gains: Is the problem old norms or teaching to the test? Educational Measurement: Issues and Practice. Fall 1990, 15–22.

Shohamy, E (1992) Beyond proficiency testing: a diagnostic feedback testing model for assessing foreign language learning, *The Modern Language Journal* 76(4), 513–521.

Shohamy, E (1993) The Power of Tests: The Impact of Language Tests on Teaching and Learning, *NFLC Occasional Papers*, Washington, D C: The National Foreign Language Center.

Shohamy, E (1997) Testing methods, testing consequences: Are they ethical? Are they fair? Language Testing 14 (3), 340–349.

Shohamy, E (2001) *The power of tests: A critical perspective on the use of language tests*, New York: Longman.

Shohamy, E, Donitsa-Schmidt, S and Ferman I (1996) Test Impact Revisited: Washback Effect over Time, *Language Testing* 13(3), 298–317.

Smith, H W (1975) *Strategies of Social Research: The Methodological Imagination*, London: Prentice-Hall.

Smith, H J (1989) ELT project success and the management of innovation. Unpublished manuscript.

Smith, M L (1991) Put to the Test: The Effects of External Testing on Teachers, *Educational Researcher* 20(5), 8–11.

Smith, M L, Edelsky, C, Draper, K, Rottenberg, C and Cherland, M (1989) *The role of testing in elementary schools*, Los Angeles, California: Center for Research on Educational Standards and Student Tests, Graduate School of Education, UCLA.

Smyth, E (ed) (1980) *Projects in materials design*, ELT Documents Special. London: The British Council.

Snow, R, (1973) Theory Construction for Research on Teaching, in *Second Handbook of Research on Teaching: A Project of the American Educational Research Association*, Chicago: Rand McNally, 77–112.

Somerset, A (1988) Examinations as an Instrument to Improve Pedagogy. In Heyneman, S and Fagerlind, I (ed) *University Examinations and Standardized Testing: Principles, Experience, and Policy Options*, Technical Paper 78, 167–194, Washington, D C: World Bank.

Somerset, A (1997) Treating the Diploma Disease in Kenya: a modest counter-proposal, *Assessment in Education: principles, policy and practice* 4(1), 91–106.

Spolsky, B (1995a) *Measured Words: The development of objective language testing*, Oxford: Oxford University Press.

Spolsky, B (1995b) The examination-classroom backwash cycle: Some historical cases. In Nunan, D, Berry, R and Berry, V (eds) *Bringing about change in language education*, 55–66, Hong Kong: Department of Curriculum Studies, University of Hong Kong.

Sri Lankan Ministry of Education (no date) *Effective English Teaching*, Colombo: Curriculum Development Centre.

Sri Lankan Ministry of Education (1976) *An English Course for Grade Ten*, Colombo: Educational Publications Department.

Sri Lankan Ministry of Education (1985–1986) *English Every Day*, Year 7–11 Pupil's Books and Year 7–9 Teacher's Books, Colombo: Curriculum Development Centre.

Sri Lankan Ministry of Education (1987) *English Every Day*, Year 10–11 Teacher's Book, Colombo: National Institute of Education.

Sri Lankan Ministry of Education (1988) *Guidelines for the Final Examination for O level English in December 1988 and After*, Colombo: National Institute of Education.

Sri Lankan Ministry of Education (1989) *Suggestions and Guidance to Teachers Preparing Students for GCE O/L English, New Syllabus*, Colombo: National Institute of Education.

Stake, R (1995) *The Art of Case Study Research*, London: SAGE Publications Ltd.

Stiggins, R (2001) *Student-involved classroom assessment*, 3rd edition. NJ: Prentice Hall.

Stern, H H (1983) *Fundamental Concepts of Language Teaching*, Oxford: Oxford University Press.

Stobart, G and Gipps, C (1997) *Assessment: A teachers' guide to the issues* 3, London: Hodder and Stoughton.

Stoller, F L (1994) The diffusion of innovations in intensive ESL programs, *Applied Linguistics* 15/3, 300–327.

Swain, M (1985) Large-scale Communicative Testing: A Case Study. In Lee, Y P, Fok, A C Y, Lord, R and Low, G (eds) *(1985) New Directions in Language Testing*, 35–46, Oxford: Pergamon Press.

Swales, J (1980) The educational environment and its relevance to ESP programme design. In Smyth, E (ed) (1980) *Projects in materials design*, ELT Documents Special, 1–70, London: The British Council.

Swales, J (1989) Service English programme design and opportunity cost. In Johnson, R K (ed) *The Second Language Curriculum*, 79–90, Cambridge: Cambridge University Press.

Tanner, L N (ed) (1988) *Critical Issues in Curriculum: Eighty-seventh Yearbook of the National Society for the Study of Education*, Chicago: University of Chicago Press.

Tuckman, B W (1972) *Conducting Educational Research*, New York: Harcourt Brace Jovanovich.

Turner, R H (1961) Modes of social ascent through education: Sponsored and context mobility. In Halsey, A H et al (eds) *Education, Economy and Society*, New York: The Free Press of Glencoe.

van Ek, J A, Alexander, L G and Fitzpatrick, M A (1980) *Waystage English*, Oxford: Pergamon Press.

Vernon, P E (1956) *The Measurement of Abilities* 2, London: University of London Press.

Wall, D (1994) Measuring examination 'washback': The Sri Lankan Evaluation Project. In Flavell, R H (ed) *ELT Policy and Its Impact: A Case Study. Review of English Language Teaching* 4 (1), 103–122, London: Modern English Publications in association with The British Council.

Wall, D (1995) Report on a Consultancy Visit to St Petersburg, Lancaster.

Wall, D (1996) Introducing New Tests into Traditional Systems: Insights from General Education and from Innovation Theory, *Language Testing* 13(3), 334–354.

Wall, D (1997) Test Impact and Washback. In Clapham, C and Corson, D (eds) (1997) *Language Testing and Assessment* 7 of *The Kluwer Encyclopedia of Language and Education*, 291–302, Dordrecht: Kluwer Academic Publishers.

Wall, D (1999) The Impact of high-stakes examinations on classroom teaching: A case study using insights from testing and innovation theory. Unpublished PhD dissertation: Department of Linguistics and Modern English Language, Lancaster University.

Wall, D (2000) The impact of high-stakes testing on teaching and learning: Can this be predicted or controlled? *System* 28, 499–509.

Wall, D and Alderson, J C (1993) Examining Washback: The Sri Lankan Impact Study, *Language Testing* 10(1), 41–69.

Wall, D, Kalnberzina, V, Mazuoliene, Z and Truus K, (1996) The Baltic States Year 12 Examination Project, *Language Testing Update* 19, 15–27.

Watanabe, Y (1996) Does Grammar-Translation Come from the Entrance Examination? Preliminary Findings from Classroom-based Research, *Language Testing* 13(3), 319–333.

Watanabe, Y (2003) Methodology in Washback Studies. In Cheng, L and Watanabe Y (eds) *Washback in Language Testing: Research Contexts and Methods*, Mahwah, New Jersey: Lawrence Erlbaum Associates.

Waters, A (ed) (1982) *Issues in ESP. Lancaster Practical Papers in English Language Education* 5, Oxford: Pergamon Press.

Watts, M and Ebbutt, D (1987) More than the sum of the parts: Research methods in group interviewing, *British Educational Research Journal* 13/1, 25–34.

Webb, E J, Campbell, D T, Schwartz, R D and Sechrest, L (1965) *Unobtrusive Measures*, Chicago: Rand McNally.

Webber, C (1989) The Mandarin Mentality: Civil Service and University Admissions Testing in Europe and Asia. In Gifford, B R (ed) *Test Policy and the Politics of Opportunity Allocation: The Workplace and the Law* 47–48, Boston: Kluwer Academic Publishers.

Weir, C J (1990) *Communicative Language Testing*, Hemel Hempstead: Prentice Hall.

Weir, C J and Roberts, J (1994) *Evaluation in ELT*, Oxford: Blackwell Publishers.

Weitzman, E A and Miles, M B (1995) *Computer Programs for Qualitative Data Analysis*, Thousand Oaks: SAGE Publications.

Wesche, M (1987) Second Language Performance Testing: The Ontario Test of ESL as an Example, *Language Testing* 4(1), 28–47.

Wesdorp, H (1983) Backwash Effects of Multiple-Choice Language Tests: Myth or Reality? In van Weeren, J (ed) *Practice and Problems in Language Testing* 5, 85–104. Arnhem: CITO.

White, R (1993) Innovation in curriculum planning and program development, *Annual Review of Applied Linguistics* (13), 244–259.

Wijemanne, E L and de Silva, M A (1994) Pulling It Together at the Beginning of the Decade: The Imperatives of the Host Ministry. In Flavell, R H (ed)(1994) *ELT Policy and Its Impact: A Case Study. Review of English Language Teaching* 4(1), 31–36. London: Modern English Publications in association with The British Council.

Wiseman, S (1961) *Examinations and English Education*, Manchester: Manchester University Press.

Wolf, A (1997) Growth Stocks and Lemons: diplomas in the English market-place 1976–1996, *Assessment in Education: principles, policy and practice* 4(1), 33–50.

Woods, P (1988) Pulling out of a project: Twelve tips for project planners, *ELT Journal* 42(3), 196–201.

Woolger, D (1994) Through the 1980s: Trends and Issues. In Flavell, R H (ed)(1994) *ELT Policy and Its Impact: A Case Study. Review of English Language Teaching* 4(1), 126–136, London: Modern English Publications in association with The British Council.

Zeidner, M (1998) *Test Anxiety – The State of the Art*, New York: Plenum Press.

# Index

Lightning Source UK Ltd.
Milton Keynes UK
06 February 2010

149650UK00001B/66/P